Popular cu...

NE WEEK... N

c. 18?0–1918

MANCHESTER
UNIVERSITY PRESS

STUDIES IN
POPULAR
CULTURE

General editor: Professor Jeffrey Richards

Already published

Popular culture in London c. 1890–1918

The transformation of entertainment

ANDREW HORRALL

Manchester University Press

Manchester and New York

distributed exclusively in the USA by Palgrave

The right of Andrew Horrall to be identified as the author of this work
has been asserted by him in accordance with the Copyright, Designs
and Patents Act 1988.

Published by Manchester University Press
Oxford Road, Manchester M13 9NR, UK
and Room 400, 175 Fifth Avenue, New York, NY 10010, USA
http://www.manchesteruniversitypress.co.uk

Distributed exclusively in the USA by
Palgrave, 175 Fifth Avenue, New York,
NY 10010, USA

Distributed exclusively in Canada by
UBC Press, University of British Columbia, 2029 West Mall,
Vancouver, BC, Canada V6T 1Z2

British Library Cataloguing-in-Publication Data
A catalogue record for this book is available from the British Library

Library of Congress Cataloging-in-Publication Data applied for

ISBN   0 7190 5782 5   hardback
         0 7190 5783 3   paperback

First published 2001

10 09 08 07 06 05 04 03 02 01   10 9 8 7 6 5 4 3 2 1

Typeset by
D R Bungay Associates, Burghfield, Berks

Printed in Great Britain by
Biddles Ltd, Guildford and King's Lynn

STUDIES IN
POPULAR
CULTURE

There has in recent years been an explosion of interest in culture and cultural
studies. The impetus has come from two directions and out of two different
traditions. On the one hand, cultural history has grown out of social history to
become a distinct and identifiable school of historical investigation. On the other
hand, cultural studies has grown out of English literature and has concerned itself to
a large extent with contemporary issues. Nevertheless, there is a shared project, its
aim, to elucidate the meanings and values implicit and explicit in the art, literature,
learning, institutions and everyday behaviour within a given society. Both the cultural
historian and the cultural studies scholar seek to explore the ways in which a culture
is imagined, represented and received, how it interacts with social processes, how it
contributes to individual and collective identities and world views, to stability and
change, to social, political and economic activities and programmes. This series aims
to provide an arena for the cross-fertilisation of the discipline, so that the work of
the cultural historian can take advantage of the most useful and illuminating of the
theoretical developments and the cultural studies scholars can extend the purely
historical underpinnings of their investigations. The ultimate objective of the series is
to provide a range of books which will explain in a readable and accessible way
where we are now socially and culturally and how we got to where we are. This
should enable people to be better informed, promote an interdisciplinary approach
to cultural issues and encourage deeper thought about the issues, attitudes and
institutions of popular culture.

Jeffrey Richards

For
Mum and Dad

Contents

List of figures

All illustrations are reproduced by permission of the British Library

General editor's foreword

The mass-market leisure industries – music hall, organised sport, cigarette smoking, large-circulation newspapers and popular fiction – developed in the last decades of the nineteenth century. The necessary preconditions were all in place – a concentrated urban market, a mass working-class audience with rising wages and increased spare time, a viable transportation system, the widespread use of advertising and new technologies.

In his absorbing study of the entertainment industry in London between the years 1890 and 1918, Andrew Horrall draws on a wide range of contemporary newspapers and journals, memoirs and autobiographies, to present a panorama of popular culture in a pivotal period of modern British history – the end of the Victorian age, the Edwardian era and the Great War.

He explores the mechanics of promotion and publicity, the achievements of colourful and imaginative impresarios like Fred Karno and C. B. Cochran, the strong American influence represented by the likes of P. T. Barnum and Buffalo Bill Cody, and the emergence of celebrities such as Harry Lauder and George Robey. He explores the fascination with those new-fangled inventions: the bicycle, the motor car and the aeroplane, and with the stars of football, cricket, boxing, even baseball. Above all, he recreates the extraordinary symbiotic relationships of the music hall, transportation and sport – early films of big fights are shown as music hall novelties, stage melodramas are produced featuring real-life boxing champions like John L. Sullivan and Gentleman Jim Corbett, charity sports matches are staged by music hall artistes, and bicycles, motor cars and airships are featured in stage shows. Horrall concludes with an analysis of the influence of this rich mix on the culture of the trenches in the Great War. The whole adds up to a vivid recreation in fascinating detail of a lost world of entertainment.

Jeffrey Richards

Preface

This book began life as a Ph.D. thesis at the University of Cambridge on the topic of London popular culture before the First World War. While reading about the period I noticed that many of the same names appeared in histories of theatre and of sport. Pursuing these leads, I discovered an unexplored interaction between sport, music and theatre in the early days of professional entertainment. As the thesis took final shape I became increasingly aware that, because of this encompassing interaction, this study should be carried into the war years to assess the impact of London's popular culture. Therefore, the last chapter of this book illuminates the strong links between pre-war culture and the battle front.

I would like to acknowledge the staffs of the Cambridge University Library, British Library, Newspaper Library, Bruce Castle archives, Tower Hamlets archives, Lambeth archives and the Theatre Museum archives for their assistance when researching this book. I would also like to thank the trustees of the Elizabeth Davies fund and the Master and Fellows of Fitzwilliam College for their financial support during the course of my studies.

It is quite humbling for me to recall the amount of help and support on which I relied when completing this work.

My greatest intellectual and academic debt is to Alastair Reid whose encouragement, enthusiasm and erudite criticism guided this project from tentative research proposal to successful doctoral thesis. His insistence that research projects should have personal meaning greatly influenced and enriched the shape and scope of this work. Andrew Davies and Jay Winter's critical examination of my thesis was tempered with an encouragement to publish. Adrian Gregory provided valuable advice in the first stages of research. Jeffrey Richards and the editors at Manchester University Press have given a high degree of encouragement and support over the past two years. An older debt is owed to Karl Wegert and Michael Childs whose teaching at the undergraduate level stimulated an inchoate academic interest in history.

By tempering the solitariness of a demanding research project with discussion, companionship and laughter, the support of friends has been equally remarkable. Bruce Hurrell humbled me constantly with his insight, erudition, passions and immense kindnesses. Sue Robinson tempered these same qualities with laughter. Their friendship enriches me. Housemates at one-twenty-eight, especially Shaun, Chun-Wei, Kanwaldeep, Wylie, Michael, Luis and Gennady, alongside Darryl and Axel, made Cambridge fun as well as creative. Jody made me smile. More recently, colleagues at the National Archives of Canada have provided a nurturing professional home. Jennifer encouraged and supported me.

My family – Stanley and Ruth, Sean and Ellen, Caitlin and Dylan – have supported me in absence and presence over many years. This book would not have been possible without their ongoing financial, emotional, intellectual and personal support. Thank you deeply.

The largest, though lightest, debt is the one I owe my parents, Stanley and Sarah. Childhood in a house filled with stories made the past both immediate and palpable. The precocious curiosity they inspired in a young boy is now more structured and rigorous, though I hope it has matured without being spoiled by undue seriousness. Mum's death, just as I began to enjoy academic pursuits, has forever tempered these pleasures with the sadness of her loss. This book is dedicated to her memory and to the ongoing personal example I find in her scholarship.

Though my debts are manifest, all errors and omissions in the text are entirely my own.

Introduction

At the end of the nineteenth century London was the richest, largest and most important city in the world. Its growth over the preceding hundred years had been dramatic as the profits of Empire, industry and shipping had enriched London's banks and merchant houses and fuelled a building boom that had transformed the city. This material prosperity in turn attracted immigrants from throughout the country and the world. Popular culture, by which is meant those idioms and performances that were most appealing to the greatest number of Londoners, was not immune to these forces. From the middle of Victoria's reign to the First World War, entertainers had not truly succeeded until they had conquered London's music halls. The myriad performers who converged on London, brought 'foreign' influences, idioms and ideas with them. These new perspectives on popular culture were adapted before London, in her role as an imperial capital, broadcast performances around the world.

And yet histories of Britain in the two decades before the First World War have been surprisingly silent about popular culture. Writers have generally portrayed this as a climacteric era during which the Victorian idyll had been threatened by Continental tensions, Irish Home Rule, Labour, women's suffrage, and a swaggering, conceited Imperialism. In looking at popular culture, historians have generally seen that capital investment and social tensions transformed an authentic folk culture whose roots stretched back to mediaeval maying, the morris and charivari into a sanitised, morally acceptable professional industry voicing conservative nationalism, jingoism and a complacent acceptance of class distinctions.[1]

This evolution from music hall to 'variety entertainment' need only be briefly recounted. Music hall grew out of public-house singing evenings at which men and women had entertained their fellows from stages and table tops. Performers who pleased the assemblage were rewarded with free drinks, favours and the respect of the neighbours, while disappointed listeners just as readily hurled their drinks, dregs and worse at performers. During the day these performers worked alongside their audiences, so that to class-focused researchers none was professional and this was not an industry. Moreover, the bawdy songs and smutty jokes recounted in these proletarian halls had articulated an 'authentic' radical working-class critique of industrial society.[2]

Then, according to a familiar tale, in 1852 the Lambeth publican Charles Morton erected an auditorium alongside his Canterbury Arms pub. Seeking a salubrious name for this new venue, Morton christened it a 'music hall'. But in reality, Morton was one of many London pub landlords erecting such halls. Singing evenings changed little at first, for despite its novel dignity and separation from the pub's tap rooms, food and drink were dispensed liberally within the Canterbury. Moreover, Morton and his rival 'caterers', as these early hall proprietors were known, soon saw how profitable these houses were. Their business acumen improved steadily over the next four decades as tip-up seats replaced benches and tables, while drinking was restricted to enclosed bars, before being banned outright. As the entertainment was cleaned up, enterprising businessmen grouped music halls together in chains called syndicates. Syndicates then hired artistes to exclusive contracts, so that by the 1890s a 'turns' system had developed in London whereby performers played a ten- or twenty-minute set of songs or jokes at several different halls each night. Between turns artistes sped back and forth across the city.

Historians have lately acknowledged that a peculiar form of capitalism characterised professional music hall. We know now that successful caterers exercised 'judgement', a mixture of intuition and commercial calculation about which acts would 'go' in their halls. This essentially capitalist relationship was embodied in the Falstaffian caterers and chairmen, the legendary comperes who sat at the front of the halls to introduce performers, calm the house, and eject the unruly. Such men were believed to be magnanimous philanthropists because of their ostentatious liberality in buying drinks, generous donations to local benevolent societies, and, especially in smaller neighbourhood music halls, the large number of families whose livelihood depended on the work they offered.[3]

As we will see, a peculiar method of performance, rooted in the mid-nineteenth century, also survived all efforts at commercialising and sanitising music hall. As music hall was commercialised, and songs and skits were written and performed increasingly by professionals, the first few moments on stage were crucial for sizing up the audience, because artistes altered their acts subtly each evening, to emphasise what would 'go' in a particular town. Constant references to topical events created 'in-jokes' that rested on a mutually understood font of knowledge. Artistes, managers and the public called this basic ingredient of popular culture 'topicality' or 'up-to-dateness'. We can now listen as three artistes explain how they updated their turns constantly in order to grab and sustain the audience's attention. Firstly, Calvin Kaye recalled:

> Well, there are little devices you see. As it happened we had a little quip about the referendum which is topical. One topical quip is worth three belly laughs they say. Secondly, when beginning to play suddenly I had the pianist do that very loud note. You make a startled expression and everybody isn't sure whether it's meant or not and the visibility is aroused. Then another little strain, then another bang and after those two bangs the resistance is broken.[4]

Meanwhile, the Londoner George Chirgwin, who as the 'White Eyed Kaffir' was one of the most popular Edwardian minstrels, read the newspapers each morning in search of 'any sporting international event taking place' that he would then work 'up into a humorous parody and invariably set it to some popular or well-known melody and give it out the same evening'.[5] These sporting references were adopted equally readily by Datas, 'The Memory Man', who rehearsed a 'usual gamut of questions' that inevitably included sporting matches, for an act in which he provided the correct dates of the historic events suggested to him by the audience.[6] The result was that regular music-hall patrons like the milliner Frederick Willis, who attended the Camberwell Palace in the early twentieth century, expected performers to pepper their acts with local, topical references.[7] Professionals may have written the songs and skits, but they still relied on performers' intuition in order to make them 'go' in the halls.

Music hall was Britain's first entertainment industry, with professional managers, performers, writers and advertisers. As such it was a model for later ones. As we will see, professional football, boxing and early flying each adopted elements of music hall for purposes of publicity. In return, the halls drew close to these emerging industries as long as they provided fodder for up-to-date performances. Therefore, after briefly discussing the ancestors of topical performance, this book explores three broad elements of up-to-date culture. Firstly, music hall's incorporation of sensational developments in transportation technology. Secondly, the way the halls and professional sports interacted. Finally, the close relationship between London popular culture and the battle-fronts of the First World War will be investigated. These three elements of popular culture will be examined from the perspective of the topical techniques outlined by Kaye, Chirgwin and Datas. That is to say that this book is not a history of

London music hall, transportation or sport. Rather, it is a history of the way these three interacted in sensational and up-to-date ways.

Though the crazes described in each section were transmitted by techniques that had first been developed in the music halls, they were played out simultaneously in London's stages, sports pitches, public spaces, cinema screens and sitting rooms, reflecting the way that Londoners switched readily between these venues for their entertainment. This interplay between different sectors is central to understanding up-to-date culture: though at times such a perspective reads like a bewildering laundry list of people and events, for the most part it is not the individual performers who are important. Rather, it is more rewarding to see the pattern followed by up-to-date culture. Once a craze erupted, tyros, established artistes, playwrights and songwriters would incorporate it into their work. Up-to-date references to the craze could then be heard in music halls, stadiums and from ballad singers. Organ grinders and other street performers were compelled by their listeners to perform the latest music-hall hits. From the middle of the nineteenth century such street performers shared public spaces with professional music-hall artistes and, increasingly, with professional athletes and sportsmen. While professional performers appeared in the streets in order to attract patrons to music halls, these public performances gave even the poorest Londoners access to up-to-date culture.

This topical cross-over between industries created 'celebrities': individuals, not necessarily professional performers, who mastered sensations. Celebrity, by its very nature, was ephemeral. In dominating these sensations, performers appealed to aficionados of various types of popular culture. They drew these fans, however briefly, to patronise particular performance venues. This endowed some men and women with a personal fame that could be transported between industries. If one had accumulated a sufficiently high level of fame, one did not have to be an adept performer to please audiences. Therefore, in the years before the First World War, Londoners saw both athletes sing and act and artistes play sports. Audiences patronised these representations for as long as crazes lasted. Celebrity was difficult to grasp and hard to hold; those performers who could harness a coming craze survived, those who could not disappeared.

Up-to-dateness is therefore an important, yet unexplored, way of understanding music hall. With its extensive use of biographical, oral, musical and journalistic material, this book allows Londoners to describe the up-to-date culture they witnessed during a series of crazes between about 1890 and 1918. It is possible to find so many witnesses in part because increasing affluence over the course of the nineteenth century gave many Londoners the disposable incomes to spend on entertainment. Simultaneously, a series of labour acts reduced the length of the work week, giving many people the free time to attend professional entertainment. In addition, technological developments in photo-reproduction meant that books and magazines could be produced more cheaply than ever before. A corollary spread of education enlarged the potential audience for such works. This was, therefore, the age that saw the first appearance of the celebrity autobiography, the illustrated tabloid newspaper and the ordinary person's memoirs. Therefore, the sources on which this study relies most heavily reflect these changes in British society.

London's importance as a popular cultural centre and the impact of up-to-date music hall can be gauged in part by examining First World War popular culture. London music halls, West End variety theatres and sports pitches hosted recruiting rallies, and entertainments that ranged from blindly patriotic to absurd. At the same time 'trench culture', an up-to-date mixture of music hall and sport, helped men from opposite ends of the globe to communicate with one another and to survive emotionally and mentally in the horrific conditions of the front. In this way topical culture helped bridge the distance between the home front and the trenches. Historians have begun to look at trench culture, but because little research has been done on Edwardian popular culture the relationship between the battle-front and the home-front has not yet been explored.

London music hall changed between 1890 and 1918, becoming a broad and encompassing medium, though it remained rooted firmly in expressions and techniques that had been developed in mid-century. Up-to-dateness made metropolitan popular culture malleable, incorporative and difficult to control by middle-class managers. Londoners witnessed a frenetic popular culture which searched constantly for the next craze that would 'go' in the halls. This unending search broke down barriers between various industries and created a popular culture that, while rooted firmly in the past, was also identifiably modern.

Notes

1 Richard Price, *An Imperial War and the British Working-Class*, London, Routledge and Kegan Paul, 1972, *passim*.

2 Laurence Senelick, 'Politics as entertainment: Victorian music-hall songs', *Victorian Studies*, 19 (1975), pp. 149–80; Laurence Senelick, 'A brief life and times of the Victorian music hall', *Harvard Library Bulletin*, 19.4 (1971), pp. 375–391; and Gareth Stedman Jones, 'Working-class culture and working-class politics in

London, 1870–1900: Notes on the remaking of a working class', *Journal of Social History*, 7 (1974), pp. 460–509.

3 Jim Davis and Tracy C. Davis, '"The people of the people's theatre": the social demography of the Britannia Theatre (Hoxton)', *Theatre Survey*, 32.2 (1991), pp. 137–172, *passim*; see also Standish Meacham, *A Life Apart: The English Working-Class, 1890–1914*, London, Thames and Hudson, 1977, p. 55.

4 Calvin Kaye, Oral history interview transcript, Martha Vicinus collection, National Sound Archives, London, unnumbered pages.

5 George Chirgwin, *Chirgwin's Chirrup*, London, J. & J. Bennett, 1912, p. 63.

6 Datas, *Datas: The Memory Man, By Himself*, London, Wright and Brown, 1932, p. 162.

7 Frederick Willis, *London General*, London, Phoenix House, 1953, p. 24.

1

London

'London is before all things an incomparable background'.[1] So wrote the journalist Ford Madox Hueffer in 1911 about the grandeur, beauty and *élan* of the Edwardian metropolis. Indeed, in the early twentieth century it was easy to rely on superlatives when describing the city, because over the preceding hundred years London had been transformed physically and materially. Though the city's startling growth had been accompanied by dire misery, Edwardian London's wealthy public areas were beguiling. Merchant ships tramped up the Thames under grand bridges, to tie up at the world's busiest port. These docks abutted the world's wealthiest financial district and a city core which had been transformed over the course of the nineteenth century into a minor rival to Baron Hausmann's Paris by a construction boom unrivalled since the days of Wren and Hawksmoor.[2]

For the most part, this scenery had been constructed during the nineteenth century, at the start of which London had been a city of some 750,000 people, ringed by market towns. Though already the largest urban area in Britain, London was only first among relative equals in economic terms, with industrial Manchester and the midlands rivalling her prosperity. This had changed drastically by 1900 when London numbered 4.5 million inhabitants, making her five times larger than the next British city and, at fifteen miles across, the world's largest urban area.[3]

London also physically reflected her new wealth. The immense commerce of Empire was funnelled through her merchant houses and docks into which £5 million had been invested at the start of the nineteenth century. The city's port was linked to the rest of the country by railways. In 1834 the London and Brighton Railway was completed, setting off a frenzy that, over the next two decades, scored the city with tracks running in all directions. By 1852 London had become the national railway hub, and London time had been established as the national standard. Some of these new railways ended in great terminal stations, with their mammoth hotels, while smaller local lines enabled people to commute to work from outlying residential districts.

But trains were only one facet of a comprehensive revolution in London transportation. Omnibuses worked on London streets from 1832, trams first appeared in 1861 and the first underground railway opened in 1863. Because of this revolution in urban transport during the second half of the nineteenth century, 'garden suburbs' such as Brixton, Camberwell, Hampstead, Islington and Golders Green were erected. Such areas coupled residential tranquillity with easy access to the City.[4]

Another effect of this transportation infrastructure changed London irrevocably. By far the largest part of London's phenomenal population growth resulted from an influx of immigrants chasing the capital's high wages.[5] Initially, this was an internal migration as people from throughout the British Isles descended on the capital in search of work and wealth, bringing with them provincial ideas and interests. Alongside this, new ethnicities settled in London. Firstly, like all dock-side districts, the East End teemed with an itinerant international population of sailors, stevedores, casual labourers and petty criminals. Next, the failure of the potato crops in the 1840s touched off a wave of Irish immigration. Though well over 80 percent left Ireland for the United States, the second largest group settled in England, and especially London. There were over 180,000 Irish in the city by 1861, living mostly in Southwark and the East End.[6] In addition, smaller, permanent communities, especially of Italians and Germans, had established themselves by mid-century. In Londoners' imaginations, these men worked typically as street traders and musicians. Next, a wave of East European Jews, fleeing Tsarist pogroms, settled in the city at the end of the century. Though Jews were no longer officially discriminated against, these new immigrants, over half of whom settled in London, were Orthodox and therefore easily distinguishable as foreign. They settled originally in the East End and worked in artisanal crafts, but by the turn of the century this community numbered more than 50,000 and had begun expanding northward into such areas as Hackney and Tottenham.[7]

If not yet cosmopolitan, by 1914 London's population was far more ethnically diverse than it had been a century earlier. The cultural influence of these communities was evident from the fascinations for northen clog dancing, Irish comedians and Scottish singers on the music halls, and in a dynamic Yiddish-language popular theatre. Though popular culture borrowed liberally from these new ethnic communities, their presence bred fear in middle-class neighbourhoods. In the public imagination the East End came to be seen as an area of endemic crime and vice. Sailors were alcoholic men who had divorced themselves from society's moral constraints, the Irish were felt to be shiftless intemperate Catholics, while Russian Jews were either anarchists or nihilists. At mid-century, Londoners lived in fear of the East End.[8]

While many were wary about the poorest parts of the city, others were prompted into action. Throughout a good part of the nineteenth century, much of the city and many new immigrants lived in squalid, airless, crowded slums and rookeries. These districts, many of which were controlled by local gangs, lacked sanitary amenities, running water and access to parks and green spaces. This London was revealed to the public at mid-century in the writings of Charles Dickens, Henry Mayhew and others. Such revelations inspired the first generation of social reformers who worked through municipal bodies and with private charities such as the university settlements and the Fresh Air Fund to provide access to salubrious uplifting leisure and educational facilities. Meanwhile, London's municipal government evolved from a series of inde-pendent parish- and borough-based institutions, to the Metropolitan Board of Works in 1855 and the London County Council in 1888. Each successive body was more stridently interventionist in ameliorating living conditions, with the result that the worst slums had been cleared by the end of the century.[9]

Many of the worst features of poverty had been drastically improved by 1900 and Londoners' fear had begun to transform into concern and action to improve living conditions. As a result, numerous social investigators, most notably Charles Booth and Octavia Hill, revisited the poorest areas of London in the last decades of Victoria's reign, in order to discover whether conditions had ameliorated. Such investigations were now motivated by compassion and concern rather than by fear. As in any large city, poverty was endemic in London, but by the beginning of the twentieth century a broad, co-ordinated response had gone a long way to rectify the problem.[10]

Such squalid districts were balanced by leafy residential areas. These were developed during the nineteenth century because, unlike in typical industrial cities, a disproportionate number of Londoners were employed in the profes-sions, small artisanal workshops, or as white-collar clerks and office func-tionaries. In consequence the growing suburbs were inhabited by an ever-increasing middle class of Pooterish functionaries.[11] If not exactly affluent, the residents of these neighbourhoods had sufficient disposable incomes to spend on leisure. Therefore, by the end of the nineteenth century these districts had their own music halls and professional sports clubs, which for the most part belonged to either metropolitan or national syndicates and leagues. Thanks in part to the development of the Tonic Sol-Fa system for teaching music, many residents of these areas also played the latest songs avidly.[12]

The Victorian middle classes equated recreation with edification and social improvement.[13] Therefore, as a means of both providing themselves and poorer Londoners with venues for edifying leisure, a number of elaborate entertainment sites were constructed. Firstly, the Crystal Palace, which had originally been erected in Hyde Park to house the Great Exhibition of 1851, was moved south of the river to Sydenham two years later. Here patrons played in the extensive parks, heard concerts in the great hall, watched fireworks, ballooning and all manner of exhibitions. Then the Alexandra Palace was built atop a hill in North London in 1877. The 'Ally Pally', which housed the biggest pipe organ in Europe, and immense hot-houses and exhibition halls, was surrounded by an extensive park complete with lakes and a race course. In the East End, the People's Palace was opened in 1887 with a more strictly didactic function as an educational centre and concert venue for inhabitants of London's poorest boroughs.[14] The last of these amusement venues, West London's White City, was opened in 1908 to host the Olympics and, subsequently, a series of international exhibitions. These elaborate venues were complemented by smaller ones such as Earls Court and Olympia.

There is one final aspect of turn-of-the-century London that must be mentioned. In 1900 parts of the city reverberated with social prestige because the winter 'season', during which aristocratic families resided in their town houses, still existed. Members of this small community patronised West End Theatres, and from the 1890s the enormous, plush music halls in Leicester Square, the Strand and Piccadilly. These Londoners took their exercise at various exclusive establishments and by riding in Rotten Row.

As we will see, no matter the area of the metropolis, significant aspects of London's popular culture took place in public. This was helped in part because the nineteenth-century construction boom had transformed the city. Throughout London, new parks and squares had been created to complement ancient ones, while older buildings had been replaced with ones that reflected the Empire's grandeur. The most dynamic part of this physical regeneration dates from the burning of the Houses of Parliament in 1834. Westminster was rebuilt over nearly two decades in an exuberant Gothic style, chosen as the most innately 'English' architecture. Builders flanked Gothic buildings with equally ornate porticoed temples and Italianate palazzos. Such buildings were erected throughout the metropolis. For instance, as the new parliament was completed, the profits from the Great Exhibition were used to erect the Victoria and Albert Museum, the Royal Albert Hall and other cultural institutions on Exhibition Road, a broad avenue extending south from Hyde Park. The new century was marked by the opening of Tower Bridge in 1895 and the remodelling of Buckingham Palace eighteen years later.

The confident grandeur of these buildings ranged along equally impressive avenues. Many of these – such as The Strand, Regent Street and Oxford Streets – dated to earlier eras, while in addition to Exhibition Row, the 1860s saw Holborn Viaduct and the Embankment laid out, to be joined in the next decade by Northumberland Avenue. Finally, these impressive avenues were complemented as outdoor venues for popular culture by London's myriad parks. Many of these – such as Hyde Park and Regent's Park – predated the boom, but green space was maintained in new suburbs as they were developed. Such was the importance that Victorian social reformers placed on access to open spaces, that they regularly lobbied municipal bodies and private landlords to ensure that it would be maintained. Therefore, as a result of this interaction between public and private concern for the city's poor and the provision of rational recreation, by the early twentieth century Londoners had a panoply of parks, open spaces and exhibition grounds in which to spend their leisure hours.

This very brief description is meant to establish that at the beginning of the twentieth century London boasted a core that featured impressive buildings, broad avenues and public parks. Though poverty and overcrowding remained appalling in many districts, the worst rookeries had been replaced, thanks to a committed urban administration and middle-class charities. Instead of market towns, the city was now surrounded by ever-expanding middle-class residential districts. As we shall see, both public and private facets of popular culture existed in each district. These worked together, rather than against one another, in a way that was probably determined largely by economics. Inhabitants of poorer areas saw many more itinerant street performances for every time they visited a music hall or professional sports venue. The relationship was more balanced in wealthier areas, though even in the most socially exclusive parts of London it was not uncommon to encounter up-to-date culture.

Though access to up-to-date culture was spread across London, segments of the population, and women in particular, may have had more limited access to private entertainment. However, because sensations and public crazes were played simultaneously in music halls, sports arenas and various public spaces, very few Londoners were divorced completely from up-to-date popular culture. As we shall see, it is the importance of public spaces like parks, fields, streets and squares as venues for up-to-date culture that make Hueffer's description of the city resonate. London's physical, cultural and material transformation during the nineteenth century made the city a superb background setting before which to perform up-to-date culture.

Popular culture was equally expansive and confident during the forty years before the First World War . The most important source for this culture was not the new buildings which had been erected, but rather London's street markets, traders and performers. These were distinctly London expressions of popular culture. In the 1850s Henry Mayhew had noted many instances of music-hall songs being performed in the streets. The first volume of Charles Booth's exhaustive study of London, published in 1892, found that most East-Enders looked to local music halls for their leisure where clog-dancing, which often carried over on to the street, was especially admired.[15]

Costermongers were proletarian barrow traders whose name derived from the French costard apples which they traditionally sold. Clad in suits to which were sewn hundreds of pearl buttons in elaborate patterns, costers were idealised as the invariably optimistic, cheeky, quick-witted genesis of the modern cockney. Because their demeanour provided an engaging model for stage performers, coster idioms had begun to dominate the halls by March 1894 when *The Era* announced that they had taken 'the affections of the music-hall frequenter' away from swells and so the phrase 'Jack Jones "dunno where 'e are"', the title of one of the most popular coster songs, was heard 'on the cab rank, in the 'bus, tram or train, in society, (and) in every kind of drama'.[16] London omnibus passengers at this same time were regaled with a 'constant echo of the latest music-hall gag' as passing drivers saluted one another.[17] Though they were immensely popular, costers were quintessentially London characters, forcing Fred Mason to explain the slang included in his songs to provincial audiences who were not 'in the know' about the East End.[18]

The barrow traders who inspired the two most famous coster impersonators – Gus Elen, a genuine cockney from Seven Dials, and Albert Chevalier, the middle-class product of formal theatrical training – topped a street-trading hierarchy which had at its base the most destitute roving kerb-side sellers.[19] Thus the 'roaring trade' done by the busiest street dealers was a primitive form of social welfare that attracted distressed families and failed businessmen who hired their barrows daily from the fleets owned by small capitalists. No government agency applied means tests to prospective costers who worked arduously to survive. In whatever weather, traders obtained their produce at dawn wholesalers' markets and did not return home again until after storing their barrows and left-over stock in the evening.[20]

A mixture of compassion and competition informed people's views of barrow trading.[21] In 1886 the Hackney Board of Works recognised that forcing costers to move would 'prove disastrous' in economically depressed times.[22] However, the following year residents petitioned the same body to remove traders from the High Street where their markets 'ought to be nipped in the bud'.[23] Such governmental benevolence was mute five years later when the Hackney Board ejected stalls from Kingsland High Street, at the behest of local shopkeepers.[24] More compassion was shown by the ten thousand residents, worried about ballooning numbers on local poor relief, who signed a petition asking that barrow traders be permitted to remain outside a Holborn tube station in 1892.[25] Above all, costers were resilient: fifteen years later when the Christmas markets at Ludgate Hill and St Paul's Church Yard were forcibly evicted, sellers decamped to Holborn where their trade carried on seemingly unaffected.[26] Incidents such as these created a widespread belief in costers' stoic steadfastness that was distilled into one of the most popular music-hall songs, Chevalier's maudlin 'My old Dutch', a husband's lament as he and his wife were separated at the workhouse door after forty years' successful resistance to life's hardships and travail.[27]

Though street selling might be a weekday nuisance, brightly lit Saturday night markets – the ubiquitous sensuous festivals where jostling crowds haggled with costers, smelled foods frying and admired kerb-side performers – were enormously popular. Booth's researchers counted no less than 106 such markets in London, where the poor haggled with stall owners for the week's last gristly scraps of meat and limp vegetables.[28] In order not to lose out, shopkeepers erected barrows and naphtha lamps on the pavements outside their businesses in order to capture some of this custom.[29] Some residents attended local markets without such purposeful intent as penurious showmen and 'drawers' dressed as either gaudy mountebanks or clowns enticed people into the penny gaffs (the myriad small halls, pubs and rooms in which the most impecunious, proletarian forms of music hall took place, so called because they charged a penny for admission) and peep-shows that ringed the stalls, meaning that 'every suburban High Street on a Saturday night was a mixture of market and music-hall', resounding to the cries of provisioners hawking their wares.[30] Courting couples watched the shows while others stepped from music halls into a continuation of their night's entertainment, at which they could purchase pirated versions of the most popular up-to-date songs.[31]

Saturday night markets drew singers as well as music sellers who both capitalised on this geographical and cultural proximity to the halls. People sang for pennies on street pitches, performed 'cellar-flap' dances on the pavements outside public-houses, or sang for coins at pub doorways in what was called 'keyhole whispering'.[32] Music halls were aware of the talent on the streets. Fortunate people, like the popular artiste George Lashwood, who began his career performing music-hall songs in Kidderminster marketplace, eventually triumphed on the formal stage.[33] Similarly, a troupe of female street dancers from Walworth earned a trial at a small neighbourhood hall in 1906, from whence they were booked to the Camberwell Palace.[34] A similar progression from the streets to the stage was acknowledged by the popular performers Gus Elen, Jenny Hill, Leo Dryden, George Mozart, Harry Champion, Ada Reeve and George Chirgwin who each recalled that they had alternated between stage and street performances during the earliest days of their careers.[35] Even if such tales were as much myth as fact, they pointed to a public veneration of artistes' humble origins.

Given their own experiences, established artistes recognised that talented street performers might 'go' in the music halls. The frankest acknowledgement of such origins was that of Auguste van Biene, a Dutch actor and cellist, whose 'Broken melody' was a music-hall standard. After quitting the orchestra of the Rotterdam Opera House in 1867, van Biene sought his fortune in London. Unable to find an engagement, he played in the streets of the West End for a year until an amiable stranger offered him a job (Figure 1). The Samaritan was Sir Michael Costa, the proprietor of Covent Garden Opera House.[36] For the next forty years van Biene demonstrated his lasting humility and gratitude on the anniversary of this encounter by playing on West End streets to raise money for performers' charities.[37] As van Biene celebrated four decades of success in 1908, the popular soubrette Alice Lloyd arranged an audition with a theatrical agent for the young Polish refugee Mirzka Gynt whom she had heard keyhole-singing in Whitechapel.[38] After learning to read music, and commissioning songs, Gynt sailed with his father for an American tour before returning to England where he played a forty-eight-week music-hall engagement.[39]

Street entertainment reflected the many ways in which music hall was evolving beyond singing and comedy. Other street acts were more elaborate as horse-drawn carousels offering half-penny rides vied for attention throughout London with singers, pianola players, female impersonators, escapologists, acrobatic bears and amateur minstrels.[40] Londoners eagerly requested the most up-to-date tunes from itinerant street singers and so it is probable that musical

Cellist Auguste van Biene celebrates his humble beginnings by playing on the streets in 1908.

street acts included the up-to-date music-hall favourites which were also available as sheet music in the markets.[41] Because of this public demand, music publishers fought a continuous battle for practical copyright legislation that could combat the menace of street hawkers selling the latest songs. Increasingly severe copyright acts were passed in 1906, 1911 and 1914.[42]

The majority of those who relied on street entertaining for their livelihood were not likely to have had much to offer the music halls, because such singing was a sign of penury and desperation, not choice. Both Henry Mayhew and his Edwardian successors felt that street music was a widespread social welfare mechanism akin to barrow selling, because organ-grinding required little skill beyond shoulder muscles that were hardened sufficiently to turn a crank.[43] Nevertheless, this widespread phenomenon of street entertaining meant that the poorest Londoners had some awareness of and access to up-to-date popular culture.

This fluid interaction between street and stage made successful performers recognisable by crowds who insisted that they be entertained on the spot. J. W. Rowley was a popular singer in the 1880s most noted for performing somersaults on stage. He was inevitably greeted by the gallery with the eager command 'over Rowley' which he obeyed.[44] A public primed by Rowley's antics saw cartwheels introduced into the halls by Fannie Leslie in 1893. During that summer artistes were accosted regularly from the gallery with the familiar 'over'. While this occurred on stage, cartwheels were appropriated for the streets by the young urchins who turned them for pennies.[45] Meanwhile, Leslie was irate about the public's demand that other artistes perform her act on stage because she feared losing credit for having introduced it.[46] Ada Reeve, a renowned soubrette who was born in Whitechapel in 1874, first played the London halls during this craze and discovered how leaden the transmission of popular cultural sensations between the Imperial epicentre and colonial peripheries could be: during a 1906 stint at the Johannesburg Empire, the audience greeted her with 'over Ada!', a cry she had not heard for many years.[47]

Not content to turn cartwheels or watch aspiring novices at markets, audience members waited for their heroes on the streets after a show.[48] The most adept artistes knew how to exploit this atmosphere of intermingled public and stage performances. During such encounters the comedian Dan Leno, music hall's most universally beloved performer, teased his listeners with a store of absurd jokes, while handing out coins to the most destitute.[49] Harry Pleon's fans were not so easily satisfied when one night in 1900 they pursued him as he walked home along the Strand. The mob would only disperse at three in the morning after he had sung a topical Boer war song and recited some burlesque verses to them from his balcony.[50] That same summer the minstrel Eugene Stratton was compelled to give an impromptu show before holiday-makers on the Margate promenade.[51] Finally, while appearing in a 1913 Coliseum hospital charity gala George Robey, W. C. Fields, George Formby, Will Evans and Fred Emney, who were amongst the most successful comedians of the day, performed in full make-up for the assembled crowds on the pavements outside. Market-place experiences had also taught the quintet how to pass the hat amongst their listeners for donations afterwards.[52]

Sports were rooted equally firmly in London's streets, parks and waste-grounds where any kind of ball, even rolled-up sheets of newspaper, sufficed for a children's game of football. Given that play of this kind on the streets was forbidden by municipal authorities, serious matches were assisted by a 'policeman watcher' who warned of the of the local constable's impending arrival.[53] In many neighbourhoods, despite these prohibitions, particular streets, tenements and parks were represented by teams which competed in impromptu local leagues. At the end of the season the best players were lured to other clubs with offers of such things as cigarette cards.[54] The best players graduated to more formal competitions as schoolboys played football in city-wide leagues, while adults also met in formal competitions. Professional players were also seen in public. Because the Football Association forbade its clubs from training formally before the start of September, London parks were crowded with their unofficial late-summer practice sessions. Clubs encouraged their supporters to attend and contemporary writers felt that the crowds at these matches exerted their will on directors by vociferously cheering the players they wished to see included in the opening day line-up.[55] Astute directors did not disavow this spectator influence publicly, though Herbert Chapman, the legendary Arsenal manager, insisted that no team had ever been swayed by fans' appreciation of individual players.[56] Nevertheless, Tottenham and Woolwich stood out as venues for this interaction where one could see crowds 'some thousands strong and all these would be criticising, praising and condemning, hoping and despairing, but all of them yelling as they watch the first practice games of the season in which old and new players are weighed in balance and accepted or rejected for the League team as the case may be'.[57] Many of these matches took place in amateur football's North London locus at the Lea or Tottenham Marshes, part of the system of fields which stretch along both banks of the River Lea as it runs south-easterly into the Thames beside the East India Dock. They were originally a disagreeably pungent conduit for London's effluvia, but in 1890 the London County Council endorsed a popular subscription which raised the £80,000 to purchase the fields from their private landlords.[58] Once access had been granted the Marshes became the home to outdoor sports in North London, as 'on the marshes, from where the gasworks were to Bailey's Lane, there were football pitches, and there were two or three football leagues whose clubs played over there'.[59] Just like Saturday markets, this swathe of green pasture was a popular recreation ground with the least wealthy because 'at holiday times many thousands of the poorer classes from the east and north-east of London find their way there on the score of economy, and the easy means by which they can be reached'.[60] Therefore, many of the first, most prominent national football clubs in London, at Tottenham, Clapton, Millwall and West Ham were established either on or within fairly easy access of such public football grounds. South of the Thames, Woolwich Arsenal was nestled amidst the football pitches on Plumstead Common until 1913. Football teams and leagues could be found wherever there was a strip of land big enough to accommodate a pitch.

Just like artistes, footballers were also keenly aware of amateur players. Charlie Buchan, one of the most famous athletes of his day, was a Plumstead lad who grew up watching Arsenal. He perfected his ball skills in the High Street by passing and dribbling against the kerb with a tennis ball after which he played for a variety of local schools. On Saturdays he waited outside Arsenal's ground, where he followed the match by gauging the crowd's cheers, before dashing into the stadium as the gates were opened in advance of the final whistle. Once on the terraces Buchan noted the techniques used by the best players, hoping to incorporate them in his own games. Buchan's passion displayed itself in this manner until he signed with Arsenal in 1909, before transferring to Clapton the following May.[61]

This interaction between watching others and himself playing football continued unabated after Buchan had turned professional. He attended school matches on Plumstead Common before going north to Leyton for his Saturday afternoon game. One morning he saw a lad 'weaving his way past the defenders like an electric eel' and was enthralled by the ingenious feints the young player employed. Buchan used them successfully that afternoon and for many years to come.[62] Later on, aspirants also copied Buchan. While playing for Sunderland Buchan occasionally visited the pub owned by Raich Carter's father. The young Carter was impressed by this guest and practised football in the streets until 1934 when, to his immense pride, Arsenal, then Buchan's team, scouted him.[63] When eventually it was Sunderland who signed him, Carter's mind still recalled that he was joining the team for which he had watched his great hero play.[64] Jimmy Seed also spent hours watching Buchan play and then emulating his dribbling techniques with a small rubber ball in Sunderland's streets. After a trial in April 1914 Seed was signed to that club, before winning greater renown by managing Charlton Athletic for twenty-five years.[65]

Music also linked the public spaces to professional entertainment. Some of the lasting results of this continuous, broad interaction were noted in 1917 by Norman Douglas, who documented music-hall influences on London street songs such as;

> My young man is so lively,
> Takes me to the Wells every Friday,
> Wears brown boots on a Sunday,
> With half a dozen buttons on his coat.[66]

'Wells' in this rhyme refers to Sadler's Wells Theatre, Islington, then a music hall, and not to the city in Somerset. The songs by which local characters were memorialised were often carried by music-hall melodies.[67] Teachers were frequently guyed in these rhymes, as with Miss Cole from Tottenham whose authoritarian manner was most memorable;

> Old guvvy Cole is a merry old soul,
> She goes to church on Sunday,
> To pray to God to give her strength
> To cane the girls on Monday.[68]

Smarting palms and inflamed knuckles also inspired those Stratford students who immortalised Mr Heather before the First World War with the words

> Mr Heather's a jolly good man
> Tries to learn you all he can
> Reading, writing, 'rithmatic,
> Never forgets to give you the stick.[69]

Artistes did not only have to fear unofficial public appropriation of their material by children or pirates trading in the street markets as Chelsea football club updated 'I do like to be beside the seaside' with references to the team's most renowned players, for their official song in 1906.[70] The title to this number, Mark Sheridan's greatest hit, was also the caption to a 1910 celebratory cartoon in *Oriental Notes*, Clapton Orient's official programme.[71] In the same year *Hammers' Gazette*, West Ham United's official programme, recounted how a player spontaneously recalled one of the great music-hall stars of the 1860s on the pitch after missing a scoring opportunity. His words were set to 'the Great Vance's song, the original of which many of you have no doubt heard':

> Tho' I own half an acre at Barking,
> And am known pretty well on the spot,
> Since from daylight to sunset I'm shooting,
> I'm not yet a penalty shot.[72]

That a footballer had adapted these verses 'on the spot' seems apocryphal. It is more likely that the reporter made them up or that he heard them being sung over a long time by the team and spectators.

Because so few people recorded London street songs, latter-day investigators have struggled to recapture these orally transmitted, ethereal verses. Vast numbers of such songs existed, as at least one Edwardian investigator felt that every street game was accompanied by its own chant.[73] However, during the 1950s the Oxford researchers Iona and Peter Opie identified and uncovered a long-standing, vibrant children's culture which had incorporated and modified popular songs. Eventually the resulting rhymes had been seen merely as nonsense verses. The Opies illustrated their view by the resilience of the song 'Ta-ra-ra-boom-de-ay', which Lottie Collins had introduced at Westminster's Tivoli music hall in 1891. This *risqué* tune – every boom was accompanied by a can-can inspired kick of the leg – was an instant smash whose popularity was cemented when Collins sang it in the 1891 pantomime at the Grand Theatre, Islington. The song inspired many imitators. Collins enjoyed a long and prolific career, but in the public imagination she was linked inextricably to her first big success.[74] In Bow, the resounding rhythm of 'Ta-ra- ra-boom-de-ay' made it a favourite song for young girls as they skipped.[75] Once the song had entered the public consciousness, Lottie Collins' name remained in children's verses long after her popularity had ebbed.[76] For instance, the nineteenth-century children's rhyme

> When I was young and had no sense
> I bought a fiddle for eighteen pence.

became

> Lottie Collins, she had no sense,
> She bought a piano for eighteen pence,
> And all she played on it all day
> Was Ta-ra-ra-boom-de-ay.[77]

Over time the song was updated as

> Charlie Chaplin had no sense,
> He bought a fiddle for eighteen pence
> And all the tunes that he could play
> Was Ta-ra-ra-boom-de-ay.[78]

As we have seen, Saturday markets were ringed by peep shows and penny gaffs, and it is to the items presented in this equally influential aspect of public culture that we now turn. As a young child in the mid-nineteenth century George Sanger, who later became England's most popular circus promoter, pattered for his father's travelling twenty-six-seat peep show, which presented candle-lit, string-operated dioramas of sensational events like the Newport Chartists' capture, trial and sentencing, along with gory representations of sensational crimes. Especially popular amongst these was Maria Marten's 1828 death, immortalised as the 'murder in the red barn', at the hands of William Corder.[79] Sanger's show presented an up-to-date facet of the immense public fascination for this deed which had accounted for the concourse of between 7,000 and 20,000 people at Bury St Edmunds for Corder's execution.[80] Corder's body was then autopsied in front of

Cambridge undergraduates before his skin was tanned to make a cover for the published history of the crime that was exhibited, along with a section of his scalp, in the window of a Regent Street book seller.[81] Meanwhile, the red barn was splintered into souvenir toothpicks and one and a half million copies of a broadside were sold.[82] Twenty-three years later Henry Mayhew found itinerant London song chanters and street singers, some of whom had been lured into the profession by the profitability of Corder songs, still performing this broadside.[83] The red barn incident predated the first music halls; however, 'Ripper' songs appeared in 1888, and the Surrey music hall in Blackfriars subsequently included furniture and implements linked to crimes in its murder dramas, and only the reticence of the 'chief actor in a recent murder trial' prevented his accepting 'sensational offers' to tour the London halls in 1907.[84]

Despite this lingering fascination for the macabre, music hall most fully adopted a pathetic case concerning two men's supposed consanguinity. Arthur Orton was the virtually illiterate, fair-haired, obese Wapping butcher's child who, after running away to the South Seas at fifteen in 1849, became an Australian bush-ranger. He never met Roger Tichborne, the wan, raven-headed heir to a Catholic Hampshire baronetcy whose ship disappeared with all hands in 1855. Tichborne's widowed mother refused to accept her son's loss and placed advertisements constantly in colonial newspapers soliciting his whereabouts. An 1865 response from Sydney announced that someone fitting Roger's description, Orton(!), had surfaced in Queensland. After some preliminary correspondence, the elderly lady summoned him to her Paris apartments, where she, her solicitor, servants, Roger's brother officers and the family's neighbours swore they recognised a man who now topped twenty-four stones. Only the rest of the family were sceptical. Orton drew a £1000 annuity until he hubristically attempted to eject the Tichborne estate trustees in early 1871, three years after the dowager's death. The trustees won a sensational eleven-month civil trial, initiated by Arthur Orton to gain control of the family money. Two years later, after an equally public and protracted criminal trial, Orton was found guilty of fraud and sentenced to fourteen years' imprisonment.

Orton revelled in public attention throughout his trials and exploited every chance to defend his claim before enthralled listeners, many of whom believed that he was the victim of hidden class and religious chicanery.[85] The interaction between public and professional entertainment was visible during this time when an enormous Bermondsey bacon smoker entered the Canterbury's stalls to a chorus of 'speech, speech, speech' from eager gallery dwellers who thought they recognised 'the claimant'. Order was regained by the chairman only after he reminded the audience of the recent judicial fiat that had forbidden Orton from speaking in public. Nevertheless, the legally muted fat man was obliged to salute his audience with a bow.[86] Given such public fervour, artistes updated their acts with Tichborne gags throughout the controversy during which at least two comic songs, a pair of polkas, a galop and a schottische were published.[87] Leslie Ward drew Orton for *Vanity Fair*, which magazine sat on bookshelves alongside whole forests' worth of Tichborne *Almanacs, Gazettes, Times, Pictorial Souvenirs*, collections of suppressed case 'facts' and more sober records of court proceedings.[88] Crockery, children's toys and a wax model at Madame Tussaud's familiarised people with Orton's image and, despite the Lord Chamberlain's protests, Hoxton's Britannia Theatre staged a Christmas pantomime about the case called *The Claimant*.[89]

After Orton's condemnation his barrister was elected to parliament with a brief to investigate the case further, but his bill for a royal commission was defeated by 433 votes to 1. With its main actor incommunicado the 'Tichborne claim' had, seemingly, run out of steam. Orton confessed eventually, only to recant on his 1884 release from Pentonville prison. He was met at the gaol gates by a theatrical agent who attempted to resuscitate interest in Orton's story through public appearances, including Sanger's peep show and a stint as a sensational New York saloon barman.[90] He was then hired by the magician Charles Morrit 'who was especially clever in seizing hold of the topic of the day and presenting an illusion to suit it' for a sketch in which a man sitting on a chair suspended in mid-air vanished.[91] This feature at the Prince's Hall, Piccadilly, was eventually updated with the witness to a sensational murder who had fled rather than testify.[92] Prison, alcohol, waning popularity, competition from rival Tichborne claimants and failed business ventures broke Orton's spirit. He retreated to Leadenhall Market where he earned one pound per day sitting in a peep-show booth, before dying destitute in 1898.[93] The poet John Young provided further proof of the slow pace of imperial cultural transmission by publishing his twenty-three canto, up-to-date account of the trial at Cape Town in 1902, by which time in all but South Africa Orton was an out-of-date curiosity.[94]

Briefly celebrated as they were, Corder and Orton were merely sensational up-to-date facets of a public fascination which made spring-driven penny peep shows exceedingly popular in London.[95] These competed with itinerant lantern lecturers who worked a weekly circuit of town halls, assembly rooms and penny gaffs with their slides illustrating familiar stories. Lecturers altered the bare outlines of well-known nursery tales such as *Hansel and Gretel* to include topical and local allusions. Dangerous woods became nearby parks, coppices or village greens while the farmer's wife in *Three Blind Mice* was given the name of the school mistress.[96]

The macabre popular fascinations evident in these peep shows and lantern lectures survived technological innovation. Cecil Hepworth, one of the most important Edwardian film-makers, was the son of a travelling lecturer, but from childhood he was enthralled by the movies. He bought a job-lot of discarded reels from the film pioneer Robert Paul in about 1898, from which he then spliced together random scenes to form the crude narrative he presented to musical accompaniment in small halls.[97] Hepworth's contemporary and business rival George Pearson first saw the cinematograph as a boy in Kennington when he was lured to invest his sweets money by a patterer standing on a fruit crate outside a local penny gaff.[98] The fascination triggered by this event remained with Pearson in adulthood while he was a teacher. In his thirties, Pearson by-passed the penny gaffs to work in full-scale film production.

Pearson need not have been so reticent to act on his desires, because little capital was required to set oneself up in one of these itinerant businesses. In 1898 W. C. Hughes marketed a £21.1s. street cinematograph machine which accommodated eight viewers, assuring purchasers that the contraption complied with street regulations while easily adapting to present movies on music-hall screens.[99] The following year Hughes brought out a more compact £12.12s. model that could be carried with one hand and assembled in five minutes, which he guaranteed to 'coin money in the villages, seaside [and] market-places'.[100] Machines like these allowed people to conveniently screen movies outdoors and by 1905 these travelling cinemas began replacing peep-show booths at fairs and markets.[101] Even large, established firms such as the London Stereoscopic and Photographic Company advertised their products by displaying 'portraits of the reigning beauties' of the day in the windows of their Cheapside and Regent Street offices, thereby providing pubescent boys with the best free show in town.[102] These peep-show enticements were incorporated directly into music hall in 1900 when the manager of the Prince of Wales Theatre, Soho, installed an elaborate cinematograph machine in his house's doorway to display excerpts from the play then running.[103]

The events and idioms presented in peep shows and lantern lectures were transferred lastingly to Edwardian films which commonly showed malefactors and miscreants being pursued by baying, vengeful mobs.[104] The limited wattage of early electric lights meant that most films were not only shown, but also made on the streets where curious spectators gathered behind costumed actors until 'they suddenly twigged it must be a film because the camera was over the other side of the road taking pictures of these people acting in a suspicious manner'.[105] The least mobile or adventuresome waved excitedly from the verges, but bolder people provided the bulk of the mobs that harried actors speeding along on bicycles and in motor cars.[106] In more confined locations actors were forced to enter scenes by pushing their way through the crowds.[107] Not everyone grasped so readily when they stumbled onto a movie being filmed. For example, a well-dressed man and his dog helped a group of actors attack the star of 1913's *Pimple's Motor Bike.* After a few seconds the intruder's attention was distracted by the sharp words that were directed at him from behind the camera. Mortified with embarrassment, he looked away and briskly walked off.[108]

Hepworth's topical lantern lecture experiences and this public interaction with filming prompted him to advocate that cinematograph companies arouse interest for nightly performances by recording local residents' most mundane activities, such as workers leaving factories. People would attend if they thought they might see themselves and their friends on screen.[109] An existing example of *Workmen Leaving the Factory* shows a long procession of mechanics smiling happily and confidently, obviously aware they were being filmed by the camera they walked towards.[110]

Toys based on music-hall characters were also sold at the turn of the century in both street markets and regular shops. The 'rage of the season' in early 1906 was the 'gazeka' available from Hamley's of Regent Street. Mentioned in George Graves's play *The Little Michus*, this imaginary creature took the form of the winning design submitted for a public contest.[111] 1907 saw a key-wound mechanical doll of 'The galloping major', named for a character in a song published by Francis Day and Hunter, sold from street barrows.[112] On her 1911 American tour, Lil Hawthorne purchased the British performance rights to the song 'The billiken man' which she then had 'brought up-to-date' for its London debut. To publicise the number she threw miniature billikens, mischievous creatures with cherubic bodies, arched eyebrows and pointed heads, into the audience and posted many others to fans who wrote requesting them.[113] More prosaic commercial advertisement lay behind a full-size mechanical model of the twelve-fingered dwarf comedian Little Tich which was used by a Shaftesbury Avenue chemist on the pavement outside his shop to attract business[114]. Similarly, Cyril Maude passed the cartoon mock-up of 'Mr Grumpy', the character he portrayed in a 1914 play, every afternoon as he entered the theatre's front door.[115]

In the midst of these sensational advertisements, the public social welfare provided by street trading and performing was reflected by music-hall owners who fed and fêted needy local children. These examples of music hall's above-mentioned 'peculiar capitalism' were undertaken partly in response to reformers' criticisms of the industry's lax morality, but also in tribute to the coster's cultural dominance. George English wished to make his Sebright music hall the centre of Hackney's social life, so in 1893 he began hosting children's dinners at the theatre in what became an annual event.[116] Sara Lane – the legendary proprietress of the Britannia Theatre, Hoxton, which occupied the prominent position in its locality that English aspired to – was eulogised in 1899 for the great value, estimated at between one and three thousand pounds annually, of her donations to local charities.[117] Her successors upheld the tradition by taking Hoxton youngsters to the countryside for picnics and games.[118] Harry Bawn, another aspirant to music-hall respectability, invited six hundred children to a free Christmas Day party in 1910 at his Edmonton Empire, where they watched the bioscope before being given soup and individual parcels of food and clothing.[119] The South London Palace also operated an annual children's treat. Over 4,500 youngsters attended a matinee in 1911 after which they were each presented with a bag containing buns, sweets and a toy.[120] Oswald Stoll's Shepherd's Bush Empire took children for day trips to the country in spring 1914.[121] In a more intimate gesture, the male impersonator Ella Shields performed at a Christmas Day party for hospitalised children in 1917.[122] Individual artistes also responded to this urge. As the embodiment of coster ideals of self-help, Gus Elen and his wife took such benevolence very seriously. From 1905 to 1909 the pair distributed gifts at Christmas on Clapham Common. Typically, they motored to the Common in a car piled high with gifts which Mrs Elen then doled out while her husband offered seasonal greetings and best wishes, and a local band played Christmas songs.[123]

Two years after Elen retired from this personal public benevolence, one of the most ambitious street charity projects, 'Tag Day', was inaugurated by the Marcate sisters who had seen one of these fund-raisers, where donations were solicited on the streets in return for a decorative lapel badge, while touring America.[124] Once back home, the Marcates convinced the Music-Hall Women's Guild to support a London tag day. With this official recommendation it was easy to interest other music-hall charities and so Charles Douglas Stuart, a journalist who was the secretary of three music-hall benevolent societies, required only a fortnight's notice to launch the event.[125] Up-to-date artistes were evidently not perturbed by such spontaneity as the comedian Harry Tate and his wife were amongst the two hundred and fifty who walked West End streets selling cardboard discs on the third of June. The biggest sensation was caused by the perennial supporter of music-hall charities Charles Coborn, the 'Man who broke the bank at Monte Carlo', dressed as a homeless sandwich board man, a common feature of theatrical and music-hall promotion.[126] Coborn tramped a triangular circuit demarcated by the Strand, Covent Garden and Leicester Square from eleven in the morning until half past five that evening wearing a sign that read

> Kind friends, I am Charles Coborn, comedian
> The man who broke the bank at Monte Carlo.
> See what I have come to – Begging!
> Help the music-hall charities![127]

The syndicate director Oswald Stoll followed this advice, and the artiste stationed on the steps of his Coliseum raised the most money on a day that only partly realised organisers' fiscal ambitions. The novelty of street solicitation, which probably contributed to the low amount accumulated, caused officious constables to question and detain at least one of the participants on suspicion of vagrancy.[128] Irrespective of its shortcomings, an enthusiastic Coborn predicted that over £500 pounds would be raised easily next time.[129]

Less hurried organisers commissioned specially designed brass tags in 1912, while for the first time the Marcates neither helped organise nor participated because they were in the midst of a world tour.[130] The following year a smaller number of 'charming ladies in charming costumes' topped by official blue sashes, unlikely now to be mistaken for mendicants, dispensed with brass tags to sell button holes of forget-me-nots.[131] In 1913 other managers followed Stoll's public support of the event by allowing the participating artistes, most of whom were not first-rank, to roam their halls' aisles. Afterwards organisers realised that improvements were still needed in order for Tag Day to reach its original financial targets.[132] Despite this acknowledgement and the support of more than two hundred performers – including original participants Coborn and Cecilia Marcate, who walked the streets accompanied by a monkey riding on a donkey – only £177.10s.1d. was accumulated by the final Tag Day in June 1914. This was another respectable rise over the previous year, but came nowhere near to fulfilling organisers' fiscal goals for the day.[133]

An event raising more than £150 annually was not abject, yet Tag Day continuously disappointed the committee which oversaw it, partly because of the event's inability to match a close rival. Opting to sell flowers in 1913 was likely an acknowledgement of Alexandra Day's conspicuous success. This annual fund-raiser, held for the first time in June 1912, saw artificial roses sold for charity by peeresses, actresses and ordinary women to commemorate the fiftieth anniversary of Princess Alexandra's arrival in the country. Actresses were marshalled around Harrods' sales floors by Lady Tree, whose husband was the Shakespearean actor Sir Herbert Beerbohm Tree.[134] Stalls were also set up in the lobbies of the Camden Town Hippodrome, and the Pavilion, while the Colman-White automotive company lent one of their cars, suitably bedecked with flowers, to help ferry supplies to rose-sellers as they walked the streets.[135] As the event's titular benefactor, the widowed queen drove through London in an open carriage personally inspecting, greeting and encouraging her supporters.

The discrepancies of scale between the two events tangibly illustrated music-hall artistes' inability to compete with their rival. Between nine and ten thousand women sold millions of roses and raised, on the first Alexandra Day alone, an alleged £30,000.[136] Against this artistes annually mustered but a few hundred pounds and about the same number of, mostly little-known, participants. Tag Day was covered by very short descriptive articles in the daily newspapers which, along with illustrated weekly magazines, conspicuously boomed its rival. Legitimate actresses ignored Tag Day for the publicity, rewards and social exclusivity of its rival. The public also preferred to honour the old queen.

Public performance was important at the end of the century because of the coincident developments of coster culture and professional football in London's streets and public spaces. Since they constantly sought the latest up-to-date interests, music-hall artistes represented on stage the idioms of the markets where haggling with sellers perfected the skills used by audiences when conversing with artistes on stage. Paradoxically, then, while the halls were most completely commercialised, they incorporated 'popular' street elements feverishly. The triumphalist middle-class morality that researchers have seen as concomitant with variety entertainment actually engaged in a continuous dialogue with the streets rather than being arbitrarily imposed from above. Elderly ticket holders for Edwardian variety evenings must have been more comforted by the similarities between what they saw and the music halls of their youths than they were by essentially cosmetic technological changes.

This comfort was possible because the earliest film producers adapted the popular interests in crime that they had seen as youngsters for the screen. They then evicted peep shows and lantern lectures from their traditional pitches in town halls, penny gaffs and marketplaces. Film also moved into the music halls. The songs with which the streets echoed were updated rapidly to reflect popular interests, rather than just hackneyed imperialism. Given how effectively these songs survived, one is tempted to take with a grain of salt the minstrel Richard G. Knowles' declaration that he purposely chose ones without memorable titles in order to avoid 'the fatal popularity of the barrel organ' or those with 'very little refrain so that they don't get whistled in the street'.[137] Pirates eagerly sold football programmes and song sheets on the streets, although part of this trade must have tailed off after gramophones were invented and families listened to music-hall songs indoors.[138] Reformist managers too saw the possibilities of coster culture. Charitable public events effectively ameliorated the social profile of their halls while pre-empting external reform pressures. The constant up-to-date intercourse between stage and street for profit, advertisement and charity was undeniable in London at the turn of the century and will be illustrated more clearly in the chapters that follow.

Notes

1   Ford Madox Hueffer, *The Soul of London: A Survey of a Modern City*, London, J. M. Dent, 1911, p. 27. Hueffer would soon change his name to Ford Madox Ford.

2   At mid-century 60,000 men were employed in the building trades, making it the city's largest single industry Christopher Hibbert, *London: Biography of a City*, London, Allen Lane, 1977, p. 203. See also Donald J. Olsen, *The Growth of Victorian London*, London, Batsford, 1976, *passim*.

3   Roy Porter, *London: A Social History*, London, Hamish Hamilton, 1994, pp. 205–238.

4   Porter, *London*, p. 185; D. A. Reeder, 'A theatre of suburbs: some patterns in development in West London, 1801–1911', in H.J. Dyos (ed.), *The Study of Urban History*, London, Edward Arnold, 1968, pp. 253–271; T.C. Barker and Michael Robbins, *A History of London Transport*, Vol. 2, London, George Allen and Unwin, 1974, *passim*; and John R. Kellett, *The Impact of Railways on Victorian Cities*, London, Routledge and Kegan Paul, 1969, *passim*.

5   London's population expanded by about 15 per cent per decade during the nineteenth century Porter, *London*, p. 186.

6   Lynn Hollen Lees, *Exiles of Erin: Irish Migrants in Victorian London*, Ithaca, Cornell University Press, 1979, *passim*.

7   Jeffrey and Barbara Baum, 'The Jews of Tottenham before the Great War', *Heritage #1*, Jewish Research Group of the Edmonton Hundred Historical Society, undated.

8   H. J. Dyos, 'The slums of Victorian London', *Victorian Studies*, 11.1 (1967) pp. 5–40; Gareth Stedman Jones, *Outcast London*, Harmondsworth, Penguin, 1976; David Feldman, *Englishmen and Jews*, London, Yale University Press, 1994; Christopher T. Husbands, 'East End racism', *London Journal*, 8 (1982) pp. 3–26; David Wohl, 'The housing of the working-classes in London, 1815–1914', in

Stanley D. Chapman (ed.), *The History of Working-Class Housing*, Newton Abbot, David and Charles, 1971, pp. 29–45.

9 John Davis, *Reforming London: The London Government Problem, 1855–1900*, Oxford, Oxford University Press, 1988, *passim*.

10 Charles Booth, *Life and Labour of the People in London*, London, Williams and Norgate, 1892, Raphael Samuel (ed.), *East End Underworld: Chapters in the Life of Arthur Harding*, London, Routledge and Kegan Paul, 1981; Jerry White, *Rothschild Buildings*, London, Routledge and Kegan Paul, 1980, *passim*; and Jerry White, *The Worst Street in North London: Campbell Bunk, Islington*, London, Routledge and Kegan Paul, 1986, *passim*.

11 H. J. Dyos, *Victorian Suburb: A Study of the Growth of Camberwell*, Leicester, Leicester University Press, 1961; Francois Bédarida, 'Urban growth and social structure in nineteenth century Poplar', *London Journal*, 1.2 (1975) pp. 159–188; T.F.M. Hinchcliffe, 'Highbury New Park, a nineteenth century middle-class suburb', *London Journal*, 7.1 (1981), pp. 29–44; Alan A. Jackson, *Semi-detached London*, London, Allen and Unwin, 1973, *passim*; Robert Thorne, 'The White Hart Lane Estate: an LCC venture in suburban development', *London Journal*, 12.1 (1986) pp. 80–88.

12 Dave Russell, *Popular Music in England 1840–1914: A Social History*, Kingston and Montreal, McGill-Queens, 1987, *passim*.

13 Peter Bailey, *Leisure and Class in Victorian England: Rational Recreation and the Contest for Control 1830–1885*, London, Routledge and Kegan Paul, 1978, *passim*.

14 Deborah E. B. Weiner, 'The People's Palace: an image for East London in the 1880s', in David Feldman and Gareth Stedman Jones (eds), *Metropolis London: Histories and Representations Since 1800*, London, Routledge, 1989, pp. 40–55.

15 Booth, *Life and Labour*, Vol. 1, pp. 116–117.

16 'Music-hall gossip', *The Era*, 31 March 1894, p. 17.

17 Thomas Burke, *London in My Time*, London, Rich and Cowan, 1934, p. 76; for the second quotation see 'A girls' east-end club', *The Sketch*, 27 January 1897, p. 37.

18 'Fred Mason, the whistling coster', *The Era*, 26 August 1893, p. 14.

19 Olive Christian Malvery, 'The heart of things, gilding the gutter', *Pearson's Magazine*, Vol. 19 (1905), p. 40.

20 Jenny Billis, oral history interview transcript, Jerry White collection, Tower Hamlets local history archives, London, pp. 1–2. Billis recalled her father's work schedule. For the 'roaring trade' quote see Untitled editorial, *The Tottenham and Edmonton Weekly Herald*, 29 January 1892, unnumbered pages.

21 George Edgar, 'London's Sunday markets', *The World's Work*, 9, December 1906–May 1907, pp. 509–511.

22 'The costermongers in Mare Street', *The Hackney Express and Shoreditch Observer*, 13 November 1886, unnumbered pages.

23 'Hackney and district board of works', *The Hackney Express and Shoreditch Observer*, 16 July 1887, p. 3.

24 'The Kingsland costermongers', *The Hackney Express and Shoreditch Observer*, 23 April 1892, p. 3.

25 'The Farringdon Road costers', *The Graphic*, 24 September 1892, p. 358.

26 'Moved on!', *The Illustrated London News,* 14 December 1907, p. 867.

27 For examples of coster mythologising see 'Work among the costers', *The World's Work*, 17 (1910–11), pp. 423–424 and *The Coster's Wedding*, (1913), viewing copy, British Film Institute, London.

28 Harold Hardy, 'Costers and street sellers', in Booth, *Life and Labour,* Vol. 7, p. 260.

29 Hardy, 'Costers', p. 262. Hardy found that about 15 per cent of the 5,290 licensed barrows in London were tied to a shop.

30 Burke, *London in My Time*, pp. 48–49; Olive Christian Malvery, 'The makers of millions', *Pearson's Magazine*, Vol. 19 (1905), pp. 264–266; Mrs J., oral history interview transcript, Jerry White collection, Tower Hamlets local history archives, London, p. 9; Ralph L. Finn, *No Tears in Aldgate*, London, Robert Hale, 1963, pp. 36–42 and Fred Willis, *101 Jubilee Road: A Book of London Yesterdays*, London, Phoenix House, 1948, pp. 59–61.

31 James Douglas, *Adventures in London*, London, Cassell, 1935, pp. 258–263; Willis, *Jubilee Road*, pp. 59–61 and Malvery, 'The makers of millions', pp. 264–266; Mrs Henderson, oral history interview transcript, Haringey local history archives, Bruce Castle, London, p. 13; Untitled illustration, *The Illustrated London News*, 24 December 1898, p. 957; George R. Sims, 'Kerbstone London', *Living London*, Part 12 (1906), p. 379; and Mrs Ford, oral history interview transcript, Haringey local history archives, Bruce Castle, London, p. 3. Mrs Ford's father believed that no respectable woman would be on the streets after the pub closed.

32 Chirgwin, *Chirgwin's Chirrup*, p. 12.

33 'Variety gossip', *The Era*, 4 November 1905, p. 22.

34 'Variety gossip', *The Era*, 18 August 1906, p. 20.

35 Maurice Willson Disher, *Winkles and Champagne*, London, B. T. Batsford, 1938, pp. 65, 86–87; George Mozart, *Limelight*, London, Hurst and Blackett, 1938, p. 21; 'A chat with Gus Elen', *The Era*, 22 July 1893, p. 15; Ada Reeve, *Take it For a Fact*, London, Heinemann, 1954, pp. 12–13; Chirgwin, *Chirrup*, p. 22; 'A chat with Jenny Hill', *The Era*, 17 June 1893, p. 14; and 'A coster king; a chat with Gus Elen', *The Era*, 10 August 1901, p. 19.

36 'The actor musician – a chat with Auguste van Biene', *The Era*, 22 February 1902, p. 15.

37 'Variety gossip', *The Era*, 21 November 1908, p. 24; 'The Clubman', *The Sketch*, 25 November 1908, p. 200; and 'Variety gossip', *The Era*, 17 December 1910, p. 22.

38 'Variety gossip', *The Era*, 12 September 1908, p. 22.

39 'Variety gossip', *The Era*, 19 September 1908, p. 22.

40 Miss E, oral history interview transcript, Jerry White collection, Tower Hamlets local history archives, London, p. 4, recalled a portable roundabout. Israel Renson, oral history interview transcript, Jerry White collection, Tower Hamlets local history archives, London, p. 20, recalled organ grinders, singers and pianola players. Mick Mindel, oral history interview transcript, Jerry White collection, Tower Hamlets local history archives, London, p. 9, recalled organ grinders. See also Samuel, *East End Underworld*, p. 33; Charles Ward, oral history interview

transcript, Haringey local history archives, Bruce Castle, London, pp. 8 and 13; Annie Ashton, oral history interview transcript, Haringey local history archives, London, p. 14; 'Music-hall gossip', *The Era*, 28 November 1896, p. 20.

41 Bessy Ruben, oral history interview transcript, Jerry White collection, Tower Hamlets local history archives, London, p. 11; Sally Mashlack, oral history interview transcript, Jerry White collection, Tower Hamlets local history archives, London, p. 3; 'Street music', *The Graphic*, 18 January 1890, p. 62.

42 James Coover, *Music Publishing, Copyright and Privacy in Victorian England*, London, Mansell, 1985, *passim*. See also the ongoing campaign for copyright legislation in *Musical Opinion and Music Trade Review*, between 1881 and 1906.

43 Henry Mayhew, *London Labour and the London Poor*, Vol. 3, London, no stated publisher, 1861, pp. 158–159; L. B. O'Brien, 'London street characters', *Living London*, 18 (1906) p. 178 and Margaret Longstreeth, oral history interview, John East collection, Lambeth local history archives, London.

44 George Foster, *The Spice of Life*, London, Hurst and Blackett, 1939, p. 67.

45 'Music-hall gossip', *The Era*, 5 August 1893, p. 15.

46 'A chat with Fannie Leslie', *The Era*, 19 August 1893, p. 9 and for an example of the way spectacular tumbling was incorporated with singing turns see *Will Evans, Musical Eccentric* (1899), viewing copy, British Film Institute, London.

47 Reeve, *Take it for a Fact*, p. 114.

48 Samuel, *East End Underworld*, p. 40.

49 Bransby Williams, *An Actor's Story*, London, Chapman and Hall, 1909, p. 174.

50 'Music-hall gossip', *The Era*, 26 May 1900, p. 18.

51 'London at play', *The Sketch*, 29 August 1900, p. 240.

52 Untitled, *The Era*, 15 October 1913, p. 30.

53 Harry Blacker, *Just Like it Was, Memoirs of the Mittel East*, London, Vallentine, Mitchell, 1974, p. 50; Rogan Taylor and Andrew Ward, *Kicking and Screaming: An Oral History of Football in England*, London, Robson, 1995, pp. 1–4.

54 Blacker, *Just Like it Was*, p. 105.

55 'The Spurs and their prospects, a talk with Mr Buckle', *The Tottenham and Edmonton Weekly Herald*, 20 August 1897, p. 3; Colm Kerrigan, 'London schoolboys and professional football, 1899–1915', *The International Journal of the History of Sport*, 11.2 (1994), pp. 287–297.

56 For encouragement see Untitled, *Hammers' Gazette*, 11 April 1908, unnumbered pages and 'Casual notes from the board room', *The Cottager's Journal*, 3 September 1910, p. 1. Chapman's views are found in Herbert Chapman, *Herbert Chapman on Football*, London, 1934, p. 126.

57 H. Leach, 'Football London', *Living London*, 10 (1906), p. 293.

58 The purchase of the Lea Marshes is discussed in Untitled, *The Tottenham and Edmonton Weekly Herald*, 18 April 1890, unnumbered pages; 'The preservation of Hackney Marshes', *The Hackney Express and Shoreditch Observer*, 24 May 1890, p. 3; 'Our open spaces', *The Hackney Express and Shoreditch Observer*, 2 August 1890, p. 2; and 'Hackney marshes', *The Hackney Express and Shoreditch Observer*, 13 June 1891, p. 2.

59 Mr Henderson, oral history interview, Haringey local history archives, Bruce Castle, London, p. 2.

60 'The Lea Marshes, a recreation ground for the people', *The Hackney Express and Shoreditch Observer*, 22 May 1886, p. 2 and 'The preservation of Hackney marshes', *The Hackney Express and Shoreditch Observer*, 24 May 1890, p. 3.

61 Charles Buchan, *A Lifetime in Football*, London, Phoenix House, 1955, pp. 10–20. See also Charlie Buchan, 'How I got my first chance', *Topical Times*, 17 January 1920, p. 10.

62 Buchan, *Lifetime in Football*, p. 22. For the first study of schoolboy football see Kerrigan, 'London schoolboys'.

63 Raich Carter, *Footballer's Progress*, London, Sporting Handbooks, 1950, pp. 19–25 and 58.

64 Carter, *Footballer's Progress*, p. 36.

65 Jimmy Seed, *The Jimmy Seed Story*, London, Phoenix, 1957, pp. 63–65. For another account of how aspiring footballers studied professional tactics see Jimmy Kain, oral history interview, Martha Vicinus collection, National Sound Archives, London.

66 Norman Douglas, *London Street Games*, London, St Catherine, 1917, p. 81.

67 Iona and Peter Opie, *The Lore and Language of School Children,* Oxford, Oxford University Press, 1959, p. 107.

68 Miss King, oral history interview transcript, Haringey local history archives, Bruce Castle, London, p. 2.

69 Edith Harman, oral history interview, National Sound Archives, London.

70 'A popular song brought up to date', *The Chelsea Football Club Chronicle, Official Programme of the Chelsea Football and Athletic Company Limited*, 3 March 1906, unnumbered pages.

71 'I do like to be beside the seaside', Cartoon, *Oriental Notes: The Official Organ of the Clapton Orient Football Club (1906) Ltd*, 29 October 1910, unnumbered pages.

72 'Club notes', *The Hammers' Gazette: The Official Programme of the West Ham United Football Club*, 19 March 1910, unnumbered pages.

73 M. Tindal, 'Gutter games', *Pearson's Magazine*, Vol. 18 (1904), p. 319.

74 'A chat with Lottie Collins', *The Era*, 10 August 1895, p. 14, and 'A chat with Lottie Collins', *The Era*, 29 June 1901, p. 17. See also Amy Koritz, 'Moving violation: dance in the London music-hall, 1890–1910', *Theatre Journal*, 42.4 (1990), pp. 421–423.

75 Jane Elvin, oral history interview, Martha Vicinus collection, National Sound Archives, London. A broader perspective on the incorporation of the song by children is found in Albert Chevalier, 'On costers and the music halls', *The English Illustrated Magazine*, 10 (1893), p. 480.

76 Opie, *Lore and Language,* p. 108.

77 Opie, *Lore and Language*, p. 107.

78 Opie, *Lore and Language*, p. 109.

79 George Sanger, *Seventy Years a Showman,* London, Pearson, 1910, 1966, pp. 28–30 and 42–43. For another allusion to the popularity of this crime see, Jerome K. Jerome, *My Life and Times*, London, Hodder and Stoughton, 1926, p. 73.

80 V. A. C. Gatrell, *The Hanging Tree: Execution and the English People, 1770–1868*, Oxford, Oxford University Press, 1994, p. 58.

81 Gatrell, *The Hanging Tree*, pp. 256–259.

82 Gatrell, *The Hanging Tree*, p. 159.

83 Mayhew, *London Labour*, Vol. 1, pp. 214–223.

84 For references to the Surrey music-hall murder drama see H. Chance Newton, *Crime and the Drama*, London, Stanley Paul, 1927, pp. 96–97. For Jack the Ripper songs see, Reeve, *Take it for a Fact*, p. 26. The 'sensational offer' was recorded in 'Variety gossip', *The Era*, 28 December 1907, p. 22.

85 Religious causes were stressed in 'Arthur Orton', *Dictionary of National Biography, Supplement*, Ed. Sidney Lee, London, 1901, Vol. 3, pp. 236–238, while Rohan McWilliam felt that the case was at once absurd, but also the most serious flowering of English radicalism between the defeat of Chartism and the advent of socialism: Rohan McWilliam, 'The Tichborne case and the politics of "fair play", 1867–1886', in Eugenio F. Biagini and Alastair J. Reid (eds), *Currents of Radicalism*, Cambridge, Cambridge University Press, 1991, pp. 44–64. Latterly Patrick Joyce made a somewhat too strident argument that the Tichborne claim was a direct assault by the propertied classes on the workers: Patrick Joyce, *Visions of the People*, Cambridge, Cambridge University Press, 1991, pp. 71–73 and 253–255.

86 Foster, *Spice of Life*, pp. 143–144.

87 Louis Bamberger, *Bow Bell Memories*, London, Sampson Low, 1932, p. 155, and Chance Newton, *Crime and the Drama*, pp. 113–116 both recalled the number of Tichborne references on the stage. The songs included M.C. Barter, 'The Tichborne galop' (1870); Alfred Lee, 'The Tichborne trial, comic vocal' (1872); Henry Parker, 'The Tichborne Polka' (1872); W. Archer, 'The Tichborne schottische' (1873); Arthur Lloyd, 'The Tichborne case, a comic medley' (1873); W. Moore, 'The Tichborne polka' (1873), all in the British Library collection of printed music.

88 *Tichborne Gazette*, London, 1872; *The Tichborne Times*, London, 1872; Alexander Cockburn, *Charge of the Lord Chief Justice of England*, London, William Ridgway, 1874; Arthur Orton, *Pictorial Souvenir*, London, Englishman Office, 1874; Guildford Onslow, *A Hundred Facts*, London, Englishman Office, c. 1875; John Bayles, *Tichborne Correspondence*, Newcastle-Upon- Tyne, J. M. Carr, 1876 and Robert Gurnell, *Tichborne Almanack, for 1877*, London, Co-operative Printing and Stationery Co., 1876 are amongst some of the many books and pamphlets published while the case was at court.

89 Michael Roe, *Kenealy and the Tichborne Cause*, Melbourne, Melbourne University Press, 1974, pp. 35–36.

90 Chance Newton, *Crime and the Drama*, pp. 113–116. For the engagement with Sanger and the New York interlude see Douglas Woodruff, *The Tichborne Claimant*, London, Hollis and Carter, 1957, pp. 420–424 and 436–437.

91 David Devant, *My Magic Life*, London, Hutchinson, 1931, p. 64.

92 Mozart, *Limelight*, p. 30.

93 Datas, *Datas, The Memory Man*, London, Wright and Brown, 1932, p. 13.

94   John Young, *Sir Roger Tichborne Up-To-Date – Or the Whirligig of Fate,* Cape Town, Bernard Quaritch, 1902.

95   Thomas Burke, *Son of London,* London, Herbert Jenkins, 1946, p. 36.

96   Burke, *Son of London,* pp. 59–60.

97   Cecil Hepworth, *Came the Dawn,* London, Phoenix House, 1951, pp. 330–337.

98   George Pearson, *Flashback,* London, George Allen and Unwin, 1957, p. 13.

99   Advertisement, 'Street cinematographs', *The Era,* 27 August 1898, p. 28.

100   Advertisement, 'Street cinematograph', *The Era,* 30 March 1901, p. 28.

101   E. V. Lucas, 'The cinematoscope: a power', *Outlook,* 25 November 1905, p. 742 and for the evidence from Hampstead Heath see Douglas, *Adventures in London,* p. 21.

102   Bamberger, *Bow Bell Memories,* pp. 22–23.

103   'Pictures outside theatres', *The Era,* 13 October 1900, p. 11.

104   Lucas, 'The cinematoscope', p. 743. For examples of crowd participation see *The Rival Cyclists* (1908); *Juggins' Motor Skates* (1909) and *Smallest Car in the Biggest City in the World* (1913). For conspiracy and kidnap see *Harry the Footballer* (undated). All are viewing copies at the British Film Institute, London.

105   Robb Smith, oral history interview transcript, John East Collection, Lambeth local archives, London, pp. 2–3 and for another instance of curious spectators coming across a film in production see Stephen Bottomore, 'The coming of the cinema', *History Today,* March 1996, p. 20.

106   *Juggins' Motor Skates* (1909), viewing copy, British Film Institute, London.

107   *The Lure of London* (1914), viewing copy, British Film Institute, London.

108   *Pimple's Motor Bike* (1913), viewing copy, British Film Institute, London.

109   Hepworth, *Came the Dawn,* pp. 58–59.

110   *Workmen Leaving the Factory* (1900), viewing copy, British Film Institute, London.

111   'The gazeka', *The Era,* 24 February 1906, p. 13.

112   'Moved on!', *The Illustrated London News,* 14 December 1907, p. 867. For information on the song see John Abbott, *The Story of Francis Day and Hunter,* London, Francis Day and Hunter, 1952, p. 19; Reeve, *Take it for a Fact,* p. 146 and Williams, *Actor's Story,* p. 260.

113   'The billiken man', *The Era,* 29 July 1911, p. 23.

114   Untitled photographs, *The Sketch,* 20 April 1908, p. 80.

115   'Mr Maude and Grumpy', *Daily Chronicle,* 12 June 1914, p. 9.

116   'A chat with George English', *The Era,* 10 November 1894, p. 16. For an indication of the moral forces to which English was directly responding, see Mrs Ormiston Chant, *Why We Attacked the Empire,* London, Marshall and Son, 1895, *passim.*

117   'Death of Miss Sara Lane', *The Era,* 19 August 1899, p. 9 and 'Personal', *The Illustrated London News,* 26 August 1899, p. 275. Also Jim Davis and Tracy C. Davis, '"The people of the people's theatre": the social demography of the Britannia Theatre (Hoxton)', *Theatre Survey,* 32.2 (1991) pp. 137–172.

118   'Variety gossip', *The Era,* 7 September 1907, p. 22.

119   'Variety gossip', *The Era,* 31 December 1910, p. 24.

120   'Variety gossip', *The Era,* 7 January 1911, p. 22.

121   'Variety gossip', *The Era,* 4 March 1914, p. 18.

122 A. S. Jasper, *A Hoxton Childhood*, London, Barrie and Rockliff, 1969, p. 93.

123 'Variety gossip', *The Era*, 30 December 1905, p. 22; 'Variety gossip', *The Era*, 22 December 1906, p. 20; 'Variety gossip', *The Era*, 29 December 1906, p. 20; 'Variety gossip', *The Era*, 21 December 1907, p. 22; 'Variety gossip', *The Era*, 19 December 1908, p. 24; 'Variety gossip', *The Era*, 25 December 1909, p. 20.

124 'Variety gossip', *The Era*, 3 June 1911, p. 22.

125 'Variety gossip', *The Era*, 20 May 1911, p. 22.

126 'A chat with Mr J. L. Graydon', *The Era*, 8 July 1894, p. 14, and William Smith, *Advertise, How? When? Where?*, London, Swan, 1863, p. 103.

127 Charles Coborn, 'Tagging the tag', *The Era*, 10 June 1911, p. 24, and '"Tag-day" collection', *Daily Chronicle*, 18 July 1912, p. 1.

128 'Success of tag-day', *Daily Express*, 5 June 1911, p. 5; 'Music-hall tag-day', *Daily Mail*, 5 June 1911, p. 3; and 'Music-hall beggars', *Daily Chronicle*, 5 June 1911, p. 7.

129 'Variety gossip', *The Era*, 10 June 1911, p. 20.

130 '"Tag-day" collection', *Daily Chronicle*, 18 July 1912, p. 1; 'Variety gossip', *The Era*, 21 June 1913, p. 18.

131 'Variety gossip', *The Era*, 10 May 1913, p. 200.

132 'Variety gossip', *The Era*, 20 July 1912, p. 18.

133 'Variety gossip', *The Era*, 14 June 1913, p. 18, and 'Variety gossip', *The Era*, 28 June 1913, p. 18; '"Tag-day," 1913', *The Era*, 28 June 1913, p. 19.

134 'Variety gossip', *The Era*, 10 June 1914, p. 14.

135 'Alexandra day', *Daily Chronicle*, 25 June 1913, p. 1; 'The rose girls', *Daily Mail*, 26 June 1913, p. 3, and 'Roses all the way', *Daily News and Leader*, 25 June 1913, p. 5; 'Alexandra day', *Daily Chronicle*, 24 June 1913, p. 9.

136 'London a city of roses', *Daily Chronicle*, 27 June 1912, p. 1, and 'Roses all the way', *Daily News and Leader*, 25 June 1913, p. 5.

137 'A chat with R. G. Knowles', *The Era*, 29 September 1894, p. 10, and for 'whistling' see T. H. L., 'Mr. R. G. Knowles at home', *The Sketch*, 28 November 1894, p. 218. Also Andy Medhurst, 'Music-hall and British cinema', in Charles Barr (ed.), *All Our Yesterdays: 90 Years of British Cinema*, London, British Film Institute, 1986, pp. 168–188; Sarah Street, *British National Cinema*, London, Routledge 1997, pp. 117–119.

138 Dorothy Burnham, *Through Dooms of Love*, London, Chatto and Windus, 1969, p. 65.

2

Carriages

From the 1830s the streets of London had witnessed a revolution in commercial advertisement. Until that decade products had most often been boomed by posters, bills and hoardings which had covered the capital's walls. However, an enterprising and prescient tradesman had captured the public's attention by parading huge mock-ups of his products through the streets on horse-drawn carts. He was soon being emulated by his competitors, so that by the 1840s the streets of London groaned under the weight of enormous papier-mâché cheeses, brushes, boots, sides of bacon and hats all bearing the names of their manufacturers.[1] The conspicuous, spectacular advertising of this nascent 'commodity culture' forced saleable items into the public consciousness in an entirely new way. Wall-posters had been lost easily and quickly amid over-laying and adjacent sheets, and had always been inaccessible to the large illiterate section of the populace. Potential customers in mid-Victorian Britain, though, were shown products individually, directly and in increasingly spectacular ways.[2]

It was against this backdrop that the American impresario Phineas T. Barnum arrived in England in January 1844 accompanying Tom Thumb, the dwarf singer and dancer. Barnum understood that in order for Thumb to succeed in London he had to intrigue the curiosity and secure the custom of fashionable society. Through their patronage, Barnum hoped to attract the attention of the royal family, believing that a private performance before the Queen and Prince Consort would ensure Thumb's theatrical success. The sight of London's new street advertising coupled with Barnum's experience as an American circus promoter to make him well aware of the utility of public spectacles and parades in drawing attention to his exhibits. Consequently, he adapted these advertising techniques for his new performer. Tom Thumb rode daily from the house Barnum leased in St James's about town in an opulent carriage making a public spectacle of his presence. London society visited Barnum and eventually Victoria and Albert summoned Thumb for a private performance at Windsor Castle, where the young Prince of Wales was fascinated by the midget.[3]

The sensation created by this widely reported royal command ensured Thumb's success at the Egyptian Hall, Piccadilly. From London the American duo travelled to France where Barnum had a splendid scale-sized carriage built for his ward, which was pulled by ponies and driven by dwarf outriders, inverting the emphasis on incredible size seen until then in London advertisements. Barnum was then permitted to drive this carriage in the sovereign's progression to Longchamps race course.[4] The coach was subsequently used in London, before Thumb and Barnum returned to America, though they made several more tours of Europe before their deaths at the end of the century. Their greatest impact, though, remained the adoption of these new commercial advertising techniques, especially by theatrical figures who created public spectacles with immaculate carriages.

The second important nineteenth-century development in trade was the Great Exhibition of 1851, which took place mid-way between Barnum and Thumb's first visit and their equally successful 1858 return. This enormous fair was the most significant development in the commodification of goods in the nineteenth century. The booths displaying the end products of industry in the Crystal Palace that year gave manufactured items a charisma and appeal that they had not before enjoyed.[5] It was the finished products of industry – individual, identifiable, marketable items – rather than the manufacturing processes that were celebrated. Such items were easily packaged, promoted and sold by increasingly sophisticated advertising to a newly identified element in society, the consumer.[6] In 1863, after witnessing these developments and reading Barnum's books, William Smith, manager of the Adelphi Theatre, published the most popular Victorian treatise on advertising. In *Advertise How? When? Where?* Smith distilled the important elements in London advertising as brevity, direct emotional appeal and the sensational representation of everyday objects.[7]

Because Barnum's London sojourns and the Great Exhibition also coincided with the earliest days of the music halls, one can see his direct impact on theatrical publicity. Sensing an affinity with British showmen, Barnum had entertained his English peers while in the country.[8] Though there is no evidence to link him directly with Barnum or Smith, in 1868 William Holland, 'the people's caterer', compelled his singer George Leybourne to appear in public enacting the 'swell' character he portrayed on stage while singing his immensely successful song 'Champagne Charlie'. Holland felt that this continuous public performance would generate unparalleled publicity.[9] This dictate proved that the new idea of marketable, advertisable consumer goods and American circus promotions had coalesced in Holland's music-hall sensibilities. Every evening that summer Leybourne – clad in striped trousers, flash waistcoat, Dundreary whiskers, enormous cigar and surfeit of lace ruffles – sat smugly atop his splendid barouche as it paraded from Islington to Westminster Bridge. Nor did Holland neglect to plaster London's walls and railings with 'long quasi-legal placards' which stated that 'George Leybourne shall every day, and at all reasonable times and places when required so to do, appear in a carriage, drawn by four horses, driven by two postillions and attended by his grooms'.[10] These posters emphasised Leybourne's lavish lifestyle, while encouraging Londoners to anticipate and await his public appearances. These advertisements made Leybourne music hall's first great star, though his unrepentant public embracement of the swell's hedonistic dissolution was an omen of his subsequent penury and early death because this contract 'at twenty-five pounds a week gave him a taste for champagne, a glistening topper, and a great-coat with the largest fur collar in London'.[11] No matter, because the advertisement was inordinately successful, helping to create the myth of the swell whom enrapt observers believed roistered with the '"dooks" and "markises"' of whom he sang.[12]

Leybourne's public boulevardier persona reflected topical commercial developments. In the 1850s champagne, long an expensive indulgence restricted to the very wealthy, came into the reach of the up-to-date middle classes, who formed the bulk of the new Victorian consumer group. At the same time quality control that allowed the wines to be drunk much younger, thus minimising storage costs, had been mastered meaning that large quantities could be produced to meet the new demand. Parliament, led by Gladstone who drank a quart nightly with his supper, reduced import duties on champagne in 1861 and the resulting competitive cash-sales business solidified the British love for the drink.[13] Champagne Charlie was, therefore, one of the very earliest instances of up-to-date music hall.

Within this burgeoning luxury marketplace Leybourne's impact on fellow artistes was obvious. Commercial advertisement was most overtly tied to the halls when the Great Vance, a rival artiste, sang the praises of a renowned château in 'Cliquot, Cliquot! that's the wine for me' and subsequent imitators praised almost every tipple that a large and well-stocked drinks cupboard could hold.[14] Vance was a 'showman throughout' who 'adopted every conceivable device to make his personality sensational wherever he went' and claimed to have been the first performer to use his own personal brougham when driving between turns in the evenings. These public performances attracted more people to the halls Vance played than did his inconsiderable voice.[15] Many performers acquired their own private, though less lavish, conveyances in order to secure a patina of Leybourne and Vance's charisma.[16] Holland's great rival Charles Morton hired a pair of broughams to convey the artistes performing at his two halls: The Canterbury, Lambeth, and the Oxford in Tottenham Court Road.[17] The minstrel E. W. Mackney, the corpulent soubrette Annie Adams and Arthur Lloyd all began using broughams, while comedian Harry Liston followed Leybourne about London in a cart drawn by four donkeys.[18]

The introduction of the 'turns' system in the 1880s and 1890s, when artistes performed a short set of songs or jokes nightly in several halls, made coaches necessary for dashing between London halls. By the end of the century Londoners had become accustomed to seeing costumed artistes flitting between halls in their coaches. Two incidents in the 1890s concerning Marie Lloyd, a Hoxton publican's daughter who became music hall's most popular female performer, illustrated some consequences of these public performances. After alighting at the start of an engagement in the Isle of Man, a popular holiday resort that boasted several sumptuous halls, Lloyd publicised her engagement by driving in cabs repeatedly between Douglas and the hall at Derby Castle in which she was appearing just to 'show the blighters that Marie Lloyd's in town'.[19] Back in London Lloyd was easily recognised travelling between shows in her brougham and at least once, in December 1895, she was injured by gifts flung at the carriage by her admirers in the Mile End Road.[20] When necessity and promotion intersected, carriages were adopted by almost every performer.[21] The Six Brothers Luck paraded through towns on foot or in coaches dressed identically in the ostentatious suits they wore on stage while portraying successful race-course gamblers.[22] Similarly, the comedian and magician Carlton hired a coach and four to drive round the city in full stage costume and enacted free preview performances in school playgrounds.[23] Belatedly the comedian Arthur Roberts claimed in his 1895 memoirs, appositely titled *The Adventures of Arthur Roberts by Rail, Road and River*, that he had been the first artiste to own a brougham. Chung Ling Soo, a trick artiste who caught bullets in his teeth, drove in a state coach through London wearing Chinese robes accompanied by his 'translator'. As late as 1910 when the comedian Billy Merson first played the London halls he engaged a brougham to take him on his forty- to-fifty mile nightly drives through the capital.[24]

Fred Karno, the illiterate West Country acrobat who was music hall's most successful sketch-writer, was also its astutest judge of the value of such public previews. Karno never blinkered his promotional vision and it is to him that many of the most spectacular advertisements were due. From 1901 Karno was based at his 'Fun Factory' in Vaughan Road, Kennington from which building troupes of comedians processed nightly through the streets of South London and north across the Thames in their costumes, enacting tantalising previews of their routines. Because they knew about these street shows, spectators gathered outside the Fun Factory in the early evenings to see Karno's companies depart for the capital's music-halls.[25] This culminated in 1901 with the London pre-mière of the prison sketch *Jail Birds* at the Paragon, Stepney, when Karno used a real Black Maria to transport his actors to and from the hall. The actors wore their costumes as they progressed through the streets performing a repeating burlesque of chase, arrest, imprisonment and escape.[26] The Birds' sketches, which launched the careers of both Charlie Chaplin and Stan Laurel, were long, acrobatic, slap-stick mimes that proved Karno's most profitable and enduring offerings. These skits were easily adapted for public promotion because their plots were conveyed through the characters' physical movements rather than dialogue.

Three years later Karno purchased two ornate state coaches at the sale of the Duke of Cambridge's effects. The heraldic ciphers were removed from the doors and remounted on the walls of Karno's office while advertising signs were affixed in their stead. Karno himself then drove through London's streets and even once tagged along behind a military procession. This form of brash, overt advertisement was deemed to be *lèse-majesté* by the government who, Karno claimed, forced him to sell his coaches.[27] Such parliamentary dictates could not dampen Karno's love of street advertisements because at the time of this official demand his garage housed a small fleet of motor-cars, omnibuses, broughams, lorries and traps which conveyed his artistes about London and the provinces.[28]

The employment of coaches as a public medium of transportation by music-hall stars over these sixty years did not occur during a period of technological stasis. Whereas when Tom Thumb had first appeared in London in 1844 the coach had been the most up-to-date and fashionable form of transport, by 1901 it had been relegated to its present use during ostentatious state, military and royal pageantry.[29] When the Prince of Wales purchased 'an electric brougham' for trav-elling in London in early 1903 it was considered 'a distinct innovation' because the royal family had hitherto only used motors in the country whilst preferring the dignity of their carriages for public duties in town.[30] Spectacular fashion took its cue from the royal family and automobiles soon displaced coaches. Horse-drawn carriages were expensive to maintain, and so they were more exclusive than their descendants. Whereas Leybourne had aped foppish swells in his carriage, in the early years of the century Karno's troupes crossed north over Vauxhall Bridge on any number of different petrol-powered vehicles in more proletarian parodies of life. When the assets of Lord George Sanger's Circus were sold in 1905, a coach which had once belonged to Queen Anne was sold for a sovereign and the carriage in which the Duchess of Kent had ridden to Victoria's coronation fetched only thirteen shillings.[31] It was a Chinese Mandarin who bought and shipped home Karno's royal coaches in the same year.[32]

Notes

1   William Smith, *Advertise, How? When? Where?*, London, Swan, 1863, pp. 122–148.
2   Thomas Richards, *The Commodity Culture of Victorian England*, London, Verso, 1990, pp. 40–49.
3   Phineas T. Barnum, *The Life of P.T. Barnum, Written by Himself*, London, Sampson Low, 1855, pp. 228–237.
4   Phineas T. Barnum, *The Struggles and Triumphs of P.T. Barnum Told by Himself*, London, MacGibbon and Kee, 1967, pp. 47–48.
5   Richards, *Commodity Culture*, p. 53.
6   Smith, *Advertise*, p. 13, and Richards, *Commodity Culture*, p. 53.
7   Smith, *Advertise*, pp. 15–30. Smith quotes Barnum on p. 112.
8   Albert Smith, 'A go-a-head day with Barnum', *Bentley's Miscellany*, 21 (1847), pp. 522–527 and 623–628. For Barnum's own list of those he met see Barnum, *Struggles and Triumphs*, p. 103.
9   'A chat with William Holland', *The Era*, 6 January 1894, p. 18.
10   'London music halls', *The Era*, 12 July 1868, p. 6.
11   Maurice Willson Disher, *Winkles and Champagne*, London, B. T. Batsford, 1938, p. 18.
12   Percy Fitzgerald, *Music-hall Land*, London, Ward and Downey, 1891, p. 6; Arthur Roberts, *Fifty Years of Spoof*, London, John Lane, 1927, pp. 98–99.
13   André L. Simon, *History of the Champagne Trade in England*, London, Wyman and Sons, 1905, *passim*.
14   Peter Bailey, 'Champagne Charlie: performance and ideology in the music-hall swell song', in J. S. Bratton (ed.), *Music-Hall: Performance and Style*, Milton Keynes, Open University Press, 1986, pp. 49–69, p. 52.
15   William Morton, *I Remember: A Feat of Memory*, London, Goddard, Walker and Brown, 1934, pp. 115–116; Henry J. Jennings, *Chestnuts and Small Beer*, London, Chapman and Hall, 1920, p. 203.
16   Louis Bamberger, *Bow Bell Memories*, London, Sampson Low, 1932, pp. 160–161; William H. Boardman, *Vaudeville Days*, London, Jarrolds, 1935, pp. 225–226; Disher, *Winkles and Champagne*, p. 18; George Foster, *The Spice of Life*, London, Hurst and Blackett, 1939, p. 73; H. Chance Newton, *Idols of the Halls*, London,

Heath Cranton, 1928, pp. 57– 59; Charles Douglas Stuart and A. J. Park, *The Variety Stage*, London, T. Fisher Unwin, 1895, p. 56; Roberts, *Fifty Years of Spoof*, pp. 98–99. These memoirs all recall the impact of Leybourne riding around London.

17 W. H. Morton and H. Chance Newton, *Sixty Years' Stage Service, Being a Record of the Life of Charles Morton, 'the Father of the Halls'*, London, Gale and Polden, 1905, p. 68.

18 'A chat with Mr. J. L. Graydon', *The Era*, 8 July 1893, p. 14. For descriptions of Mackney and Adams' acts see Colin MacInnes, *Sweet Saturday Night*, London, MacGibbon and Kee, 1967, pp. 136–137; Foster, *Spice of Life*, p. 78; Morton, *I Remember*, p. 88.

19 Foster, *Spice of Life*, pp. 61–62, the quote is found on p. 62. Foster was an intimate friend of Lloyd's and accompanied her on this Isle of Man engagement.

20 'East and west with Marie Lloyd', *The Sketch*, 25 December 1895, p. 452.

21 Arthur Roberts, *The Adventures of Arthur Roberts by Rail, Road and River, Told by Himself and Chronicled by Richard Morton*, London, Bristol and Co., 1895, p. 49.

22 Boardman, *Vaudeville Days*, pp. 167–168.

23 Carlton, *Twenty Years of Spoof and Bluff*, London, Herbert Jenkins, 1920, p. 160.

24 Boardman, *Vaudeville Days*, pp. 160–161; Billy Merson, *Fixing the Stoof Oop*, London, Hutchinson, 1925, p. 89.

25 Robb Smith, oral history interview transcript, John East collection, Lambeth local history archives, London, p. 1. For a photograph of Karno's troupes lined up on Vaughan Road see Charles Chaplin, *My Autobiography*, London, Bodley Head, 1964, photographic plate, unnumbered pages.

26 Edwin Adeler and Con West, *Remember Fred Karno? The Life of a Great Showman*, London, John Long, 1939, pp. 73–74. This is the illiterate Karno's autobiography.

27 Adeler and West, *Fred Karno?*, pp. 138–141 and for the cost of redecoration see 'Music hall gossip', *The Era*, 22 October 1904, p. 22.

28 'The Karno combine: a chat with Mr Fred Karno', *The Era*, 12 August 1905, p. 22.

29 David Cannadine, 'The context, performance and meaning of ritual: the British monarchy and the invention of tradition, c. 1820–1977', in Terence Ranger and Eric Hobsbawm (eds), *The Invention of Tradition*, Cambridge, Cambridge University Press, 1983, pp. 111–112 and 123–124.

30 'Metropolitan notes', *The Hackney Express, Shoreditch Observer and Bethnal Green Advertiser*, 2 May 1903, p. 3.

31 'A sovereign for a sovereign's coach: Queen Anne's carriage sold at the sale of Sanger's Circus', *The Sketch*, 15 November 1905, p. 136.

32 Adeler and West, *Fred Karno?*, p. 141.

3

Parades

American Circus traditions were allied intimately with the music hall throughout the period before the First World War under the continued influence of Barnum and Smith's advertising techniques. Once again, some of the influence came from the United States. The bronco riders, cowboys, native warriors, stage coaches, cavalry troopers and sharp-shooting Amazons of Buffalo Bill Cody's Wild West Show landed at Gravesend in April 1887. Cody, the legendary American frontier scout, soldier and Pony Express rider, whose long yellow hair, Napoleonic waxed moustaches and exquisitely beaded buckskins commanded people's attention easily, was aware of how Barnum had exploited public performances. He set about doing the same for his troupe.[1] Arriving alone and incognito, Cody reconnoitred the busiest and potentially most sensational route into town. Then, special coaches met the company at the dock and drove them to their Earls Court showground through streets lined with spectators who, though they had read tuppenny western pulp adventure stories, had never seen real cowboys. Crowds of curious Londoners watched Cody's men as they pitched camp and ate dinner under the stars on their first night in the capital. The Shakespearean actor Henry Irving attended one of the first performances after which the Americans repaid the compliment by parading to Irving's Lyceum Theatre in the Strand in the ornate western regalia that Cody insisted they wear in public. The company remained in the metropolis until October, during which time they played before the Queen, Prince of Wales, prominent peers and even William Gladstone, an unlikely admirer of gun fights and rough-riding.[2] Cody's troupe then toured provincial cities, parading through the streets at each stop. Almost completely reflecting 1868's mix of public and stage performances, the immense sensation caused by this western show was saluted simultaneously on the halls in a 'Cody' song by the male-impersonator Vesta Tilley.[3] To be extolled in song was one thing, but

Cody was soon forced to take protracted legal measures in order to compel Lord George Sanger to desist from presenting his own up-to-date 'Scenes from Buffalo Bill'.[4]

After imprinting himself in the public imagination so sensationally, Cody brought his stirring vision of America's wild west to Europe regularly for the next twenty years. Cody's techniques were later copied almost exactly by Charles B. Cochran, one of the most famous Edwardian promoters. This Brighton lad, who had trained as a theatre producer in America for seven years, staged a wild west rodeo at the White City Exhibition Grounds just after the First World War. Cochran had obviously studied Buffalo Bill. He hired a launch to ferry journalists who met his elaborately dressed cowboys as they prepared to disembark at Tilbury, from where twenty charabancs took the show to Wembley in 'one of the most picturesque and also one of the noisiest and most exciting parades that London has ever seen'. Cowboys with lariats ensnared unsuspecting passers-by throughout downtown London and caused sufficient excitement to ensure that the rodeo was greatly publicised.[5]

The importance of parades and spectacles in national pageantry increased in the last years of Victoria's reign. This stemmed originally from Benjamin Disraeli's acute sense of public ceremonial's power for emotional persuasion. Disraeli wished to rehabilitate a Queen who was seen by the public as a bitter, reclusive widow by having her open parliament in person, and declaring her Empress of India in 1876.[6] Though these ceremonies were held in private, the parades which accompanied them were overwhelmingly successful and led directly to the 1887 Golden Jubilee. This was the first 'modern' royal event because of the way that it was staged and choreographed as much with the needs of the spectators in mind as those of the participants. Previous royal ceremonies had always been private and hidden from public view, but the jubilee parade and its attendant celebrations took place on London's streets in the midst of Cody's triumphs.[7]

No matter what these ceremonies were meant to achieve, or their unanticipated outcomes, the public recognised them to be part of a wider popular culture. The 1896 Jameson Raid, which Cecil Rhodes had financed and condoned in the hopes of expanding South Africa's northern borders, was commemorated by a commando of twelve horsemen accoutred in appropriate uniforms, who paraded nightly through London from Holborn to a Surrey-side music hall.[8] With such patriotic processions as a precursor, the Diamond Jubilee in June 1897 saw a file lasting two and a half hours of colonial leaders, princes and troops, peers and royals – all of this offset by a tiny Queen clad in black bombazine, holding a simple parasol, seated in a carriage drawn by cream-coloured ponies – marching through the streets from Victoria Park to the Mansion House.[9] Thousands of spectators bought maps of the route and all manner of programmes, souvenirs, crockery, books and silverware, including an immensely popular 'flicker book' whose stout pages each contained an individual photographic image that gave the sensation of continuous motion when flipped rapidly with the thumb.[10] Spectators could thus relive the parade in suburban sitting rooms. These private pageants could be accompanied by any of the myriad music-hall tunes which celebrated the occasion. Film of the Diamond Jubilee parade was screened immediately in London's music halls and within the year was being watched in the farthest corners of the empire.[11] Music halls and theatres in all parts of the capital then staged patriotic plays which lauded the Queen's achievements. Colonial troops appeared on stage at both the Alhambra and the South London music halls where Victoria was portrayed as a protector and imperial grandmother.[12]

After witnessing the success of the Jubilee, Walter Gibbons, the manager of Charing Cross's Palace Theatre, one of London's most sumptuous halls, secured six vantage points between Cowes and Windsor from which to film Queen Victoria's funeral in 1901. Aware that up-to-dateness was evanescent, he ensured that the film would be ready for exhibition at the Palace on Monday night, the first night of the music hall's weekly run.[13] Nine years later droves of Londoners witnessed Edward's funeral procession, with the sight of the king's dog, Caesar, being a particularly maudlin sight. Audiences filled music halls throughout the empire the following year to watch a film of the coronation parade of Victoria's grandson George V.[14]

Such national and imperial ceremonies were also reflected at a lower level. Managers who desired to establish middle-class, respectable entertainments in their halls participated in local carnivals that accompanied these national celebrations, for as John Bolitho, a Tottenham grammar school pupil at the turn of the century, recalled 'that was just the general atmosphere all around us'.[15] These parades and advertisements did more to instil a belief in the Empire, nation and monarch than written manifestos because they used William Smith's direct appeal. Much of that sense of envelopment must have come from the halls which briefly promoted up-to-date imperial themes in the streets during the Boer war and Edward's coronation.

Boys like Bolitho would have seen many different parades in London. For instance, on Victoria's birthday in May 1900 carnivals were held all over the metropolis in aid of the Boer War Soldiers' Widows' and Orphans Fund. The newly opened Hippodrome, Leicester Square, paraded a car decorated at the astonishing cost of £260. This float depicted the ancient Roman Hippodrome with dancing girls, Victory holding a laurel wreath, warriors and a chariot drawn by lions. This whole was pulled by six horses bedecked in gilt trimmings.[16] Meanwhile, Finchley saw bicycle riders dressed as football and cricket players share the road with Boadicea, pierrettes, Don Quixote, North American Indians, jockeys, Vikings and colonial troops in that district's bicycle parade to celebrate the Queen's birthday (Figure 2).[17]

The Hippodrome's float subsequently paraded in an Islington pageant in June 1900, alongside one sponsored by the Islington Empire. This latter car, entitled 'Islington in ye olden times' recounted scenes of local history from a maypole, which was electrically illuminated at night, to actors representing neighbourhood notables such as Sir Hugh Myddleton, who had overseen the provision of fresh water in seventeenth-century London, Sam Collins the popular Irish singer and early music-hall star who had founded the Empire, and the bailiff of Islington and his daughter, who were the subjects of a local folk song.[18] Though the car's allusions were intended to cement the relationship between the hall and the locality, it was preceded by a more national 'procession of various characters' of whom John Bull was prominent. Shoreditch held a carnival on the same day to which the neighbourhood's London Music-Hall sent a car displaying the district's medieval legend of Jane Shore begging through the streets of the town. This car was appropriately preceded by pikemen in historical costume.[19]

The Hackney coronation procession in July 1902 witnessed a pageant of floats depicting 'the crown and the empire'.[20] A fortnight later the Hackney Empire car, depicting the crown and the empire, paraded through Tottenham and Stamford Hill, collecting funds for the Tottenham Hospital. The Hackney Empire's manager John Christie photographed the procession and displayed the pictures in his hall.[21] Christie's idea must have been remunerative because he entered another car for the following year's pageant which was carried out on a much grander scale. The Biograph Company filmed the show and the result was screened at the Hackney Empire a few days later.[22]

In 1903, with the Boer war ended and Edward crowned, imperialism was dropped and street carnivals were updated to collect money for charity. In May the Empress, Brixton, sponsored a coachful of famous artistes to parade the neighbourhood, accompanied by Lottie Lennox's brougham and Mignon Tremaine appearing as the 'Milliner Duchess' in a motor car.[23] The main group of stars were conveyed in an open coach, while others rode in hired omnibuses.

A typical suburban street carnival in 1900 celebrating history by way of up-to-date   **2**
inventions like the bicycle.

Even when parade decorations depicted patriotic subjects, the names of spon-soring theatres were displayed on the floats of which photographs were mounted subsequently outside the halls where topical films of the parade could be seen.[24] The nationalist and imperialist nature of some of these parades should not be overly emphasised because they were simply one up-to-date facet in the incorporation of public fascinations with parades.

As with other sensational events, music-hallers soon realised how to update public processions. On a Wednesday afternoon in 1906 the telepathist Ahrensmeyer drove a coach and four from The Bedford, Camden Town, through Tottenham Court Road, Oxford Street, Regent Street, Piccadilly and back whilst blindfolded.[25] Two years later Unthian, 'The Armless Wonder' who manipulated things with his feet, travelled from the Shepherd's Bush Empire across London to the Bank of England at the reins of a carriage and pair. Before setting out, Unthian posed for photographs in a motor car which it was reported that he could also drive.[26]

The accomplishments of such unusual human coachmen were surpassed by the mechanical dolls who drove carriages and cars through the metropolis. Whether truly mechanical wonders or disguised humans, these robots were rooted in the craze for automata which had grown in the capital after 1875 when the card-playing 'Psycho' had given its début at the Egyptian Hall, Piccadilly.[27] Shepherd's Bush was again the starting point in August 1905 when Enigmarelle, 'The Man of Steel', more likely a normal man of flesh, emerged from the Empire to the cheers of a vast crowd and took his seat on the dickey before Frederick Ireland, the 'inventor' who manipulated his controls for the journey to Temple Bar and back.[28] Charcot, another mechanical doll, began blindfold driving in the provinces in 1908 thereby generating excitement for his London début. His appearance in the streets of Bolton that autumn mingled two eras of spectacular transportation when his carriage and pair was preceded by the soubrette Kate Carney and some friends riding in her motor car.[29] Charcot played the Lancashire halls throughout the autumn of 1908 and was booked for early 1909 in London. His very rapid rise to popularity was 'ascribed to the fact that he possesses personality and originality, and his up-to-date sensation, the driving blindfolded of a 48 h.p. motor car through the busiest thoroughfare of a town, is right out of the beaten track for nothing like it has ever been seen on the variety stage'.[30] After such sensational drives Charcot's advertisements, in which he was pictured beside his 'inventor', proclaimed him to be 'bang right up-to-date' because of his sensational presence on the streets.[31]

For female artistes, sexual suggestion was never far removed from music-hall promotion. Paris' *outré* reputation was confirmed in English eyes in May 1908, when women appeared at Longchamps races wearing scandalously low-cut 'merveilleuse' dresses. Marie Lloyd reflected this sensation at Brixton that year when she sang about the girl who 'showed the boys much more than they ever saw before'.[32] Simultaneously, equestrians in Rotten Row, including Winston Churchill, were distracted by a young woman rider wearing one of these dresses: La Belle Titcombe – who was then appearing at the Hippodrome, Leicester Square, in an equestrian act – caused much alarm.[33] Titcombe's ride from the Hippodrome to Hyde Park reflected the way Leybourne's coach had parodied the capital's fashionable riders. On the heels of her London success Titcombe toured the provinces where, like Charcot, her daily ride was preceded by a motor-car which cleared a trail through the crowd for her. She was followed by a uniformed groom who controlled any unduly forthright spectators.[34]

A remarkable physique worked as well for Carlton the comic magician. Carlton was extremely tall and gangly with a high forehead and long legs. Because music-hall comedians loved to ludicrously juxtapose fat and skinny people, one of Carlton's staple advertisement techniques was to parade Bobby Dunlop, a member of his company who weighed more than forty stones, through the streets on the back of a lorry knowing that Dunlop's mountainous flesh beside his own spare figure would prompt attention. On one occasion Dunlop was driven down the Strand, one of London's busiest and most fashionable streets, at midday in order to stop at a tailor's shop that offered hand-made men's suits, in any size, for only thirty shillings. Dunlop had himself publicly measured for one.[35]

One can still glimpse the effect of these sensational advertisements. The miniature Cadillac ordered by Queen Alexandra as a present for one of her Norwegian nephews was paraded through the streets of London in 1913, filmed and presented in music halls.[36] The film is interesting in that it shows crowds of people, aware of the camera's presence, following the car through the streets.

These parades and processions sparked a craze for music-hall sketches, especially those involving horses, being enacted on the streets. The earliest case of this incorporation of horse racing by the stage was that of Philip Astley, whose 'Circus' in Westminster Bridge Road, had first staged racing dramas in 1822. This Epsom Downs meeting saw the stage filled with cabs, carriages, pickpockets, singers and pie-men.[37] Racing scenes became more popular and spectacular at the end of the century after managers saw the impact of Barnum, Smith and Cody's advertising techniques.

In 1895 Fred Karno employed the spectacle of the Epsom Derby to publicise his sketch *Dandy Thieves*. The procession of carriages to the Surrey Downs was called a 'minor festival peculiar to south London' because people lined the suburban high streets in order to see the 'decorated vehicles from the noble to the ridiculous, the staid to the eccentric'.[38] Hawkers sold balloons, confetti, water squirters and other trinkets on the curbs as the carnival passed.[39] With performers dressed as drivers, warders and inmates, Karno's party caused a remarkable sensation as they drove through the concourse of people to the race track in the authentic Black Maria that he had purchased from Wandsworth prison.[40] Some moralists were alarmed by this sketch because they feared that its contents might corrupt the minds of impressionable spectators. However, Karno, one of the most astute publicists of his generation, stewarded this hysteria by writing to *The Era*, the leading music-hall newspaper, to deny the 'rumour' that one of his players was a discharged prisoner. Instead he attributed the realism of *Dandy Thieves* to his visits to Portland prison while doing research for the sketch.[41] This is probably bluster, but Karno's dramas immediately inspired many imitators like Tom Shaw, manager of the South London Theatre, who included real horses in a stage play the next year.[42]

Theatre manager Albert Douglass's memoirs also proved that co-opting the Derby procession was not simply a south London phenomenon manufactured by Karno at the end of the nineteenth century. The isolated location of the Douglass family's Standard Theatre, Shoreditch, with a long lane on one side and a piece of open ground on the other, allowed him to stage *Daybreak*, in which the Derby itself was enacted by jockeys riding real horses. At the announced hour the streets around the theatre were cleared by a constable who acted as the 'racecourse's' chief book maker. Each time the horses completed a circuit of the neighbourhood they sped across the Standard's stage.[43] Some people paid to see the race from the theatre's seats while many others watched outdoors. Douglass followed this success with *The Road Home From the Derby*, which showed the parade of 'real hansom cabs [of course motor traffic was unknown] donkey barrows, waggonettes, coal carts and a couple of four-in-hands, all crowded with noisy revellers and pleasure seekers cheered by a swaying and exciting multitude'. [44] The lanes and open ground outside the theatre were again employed by Douglass and once more they were 'nightly thronged with spectators eager to obtain a view of the procession in the street'.[45]

This fascination survived technological developments. The Epsom Derby was the most popular horse races in Victorian Britain and the subject of perhaps the most exciting and dramatic film made in this country during the nineteenth century. Robert W. Paul was a manufacturer of scientific instruments in Hatton Garden, who in his spare time built a motion picture camera. After quitting his trade, Paul made many films on the streets of London before establishing a studio in the grounds of the Alexandra Palace in 1896.[46] That July he decided to make a topical film of the Derby. He arrived at the course early in the morning and set up his camera twenty metres from the winning post. The one minute and forty-five second film Paul shot that day captured the Prince of Wales's horse Persimmon winning the race in one of the most dramatic finishes in memory. Sensing the value of the exposed film in his camera, Paul abandoned his assistant and equipment and sped to the railway station clutching the valuable spool. The negative was hung up to dry that evening and the film was screened the next day at both the Alhambra, Leicester Square, where the band accompanied it with *God Save the Queen*, and the Canterbury, South London.[47] Audiences in both houses demanded that it be screened repeatedly to quench their appetite for a film whose tense drama and furious action must have eclipsed anything yet captured on camera.[48]

The same race then reverted to the stage. The Coliseum opened in St Martin's Lane, Trafalgar Square, in 1904 with a play called simply *The Derby*.

The picnickers, crowds and carriages, who were revealed as the curtain opened for the first scene, were eventually cleared away by mounted police before post-time when horses galloped on to the stage. A special platform fitted into the stage that revolved at between fifteen and twenty miles per hour checked the horses' forward movement.[49] In the summer of 1912 *The Chance of a Lifetime*, billed as 'the greatest of all racing plays', took the stage at the Kennington Theatre, South London. Advertisements showed the company's horses being off-loaded from a railway wagon and ridden five-abreast to the theatre by their jockeys down streets that were crowded with onlookers.[50]

Horse racing, along with royal and patriotic spectacles, was an extension of the Victorian craze for public parades. Jingoistic patriotism should not be overly stressed when examining these public spectacles because they were updated continually to represent seasonal and topical events. These traditional parades and processions were only challenged in the decade before the First World War by the technological innovations which displaced carriages as the flashy symbols of up-to-dateness in London, because both bicycle riders and motorists adopted them when promoting their hobby. Artistes, as with everything else topical, were not slow to incorporate these ideas.

Notes

1 Victor Weybright and Henry Sell, *Buffalo Bill and the Wild West*, London, Hamish Hamilton, 1956, p. 158.
2 First-hand accounts of Cody's London shows are found in Henry Llewellyn Williams, *Buffalo Bill*, London, Routledge, 1887 *passim*; Helen Cody Wetmore, *The Last of the Great Scouts*, London, Methuen, 1901, pp. 243–253; and Dan Muller, *My Life with Buffalo Bill*, Chicago, Reilly and Lee, 1948, pp. 138–140. Further information is found in Rupert Croft-Cooke and W. S. Meadmore, *Buffalo Bill, the Legend, the Man of Action, the Showman*, London, Sidgwick and Jackson, 1952, pp. 185–191; Weybright and Sell, *Buffalo Bill*, pp. 148–161; and Joseph G. Rosa and Robin May, *Buffalo Bill and His Wild West*, Lawrence, Kansas, University of Kansas Press, 1989, pp. 102–129.
3 Croft-Cooke and Meadmore, *Buffalo Bill*, p. 190; Rosa and May, *Buffalo Bill*, p. 127; and Maurice Willson Disher, *The Greatest Show on Earth*, London, G. Bell, 1937, pp. 265–266.
4 Rosa, *Buffalo Bill*, p. 125.
5 Charles B. Cochran, *I Had Almost Forgotten*, London, Hutchinson, 1932, p. 49.
6 Richard Shannon, *The Crisis of Imperialism 1865–1915*, St Albans, Paladin, 1974, p. 109. Robert Blake, *Disraeli*, London, Eyre and Spottiswoode, 1967, pp. 562–563.
7 Thomas Richards, *The Commodity Culture of Victorian England*, London, Verso, 1994, pp. 74–78.

8 'Music hall gossip', *The Era*, 14 March 1896, p. 19.

9 Mitchell A. Leaska (ed.), *Virginia Woolf, a Passionate Apprentice: The Early Journals, 1897– 1909*, London, Chatto and Windus, 1990, pp. 104–105; 'The east end procession', *The Hackney Express, Shoreditch Observer and Bethnal Green Advertiser*, 19 June 1897, p. 4. The quote is found in 'The jubilee celebrations', *The Hackney Express, Shoreditch Observer and Bethnal Green Advertiser*, 26 June 1897, p. 3.

10 John M. Mackenzie, *Propaganda and Empire*, Manchester, Manchester University Press, 1984, p. 28.

11 Ada Reeve, *Take it for a Fact*, London, Heinemann, 1954, p. 60.

12 Tori Smith, '"Almost pathetic … but also very glorious": the consumer spectacle of the Diamond Jubilee', *Social History/Histoire Sociale*, 58 (1996), pp. 333–356.

13 'Music hall gossip', *The Era*, 2 February 1901, p. 20.

14 Anthony Powell, *Infants of the Spring*, London, Heinemann, 1976, p. 7; 'Packed theatres and music halls', *Daily Chronicle*, 23 June 1911, p. 10.

15 John Bolitho, oral history interview transcript, Haringey local history archives, Bruce Castle, London, p. 7.

16 'Music hall gossip', *The Era*, 26 May 1900, p. 18.

17 'Cycling carnival at Finchley', *Cycling*, 2 June 1900, p. 420.

18 'Sir Hugh Myddleton', in Sidney Lee (ed.), *The Dictionary of National Biography*, Vol. 39, London, Smith Elder, 1894, pp. 436–438.

19 'Music hall gossip', *The Era*, 16 June 1900, p. 18.

20 'Music hall gossip', *The Era*, 21 June 1902, p. 18.

21 'Music hall gossip', *The Era*, 19 July 1902, p. 18.

22 'Music hall gossip', *The Era*, 11 July 1903, p. 20.

23 'Music hall gossip', *The Era*, 16 May 1903, p. 20.

24 'Music hall gossip', *The Era*, 14 July 1900, p. 16.

25 'Music hall gossip', *The Era*, 11 April 1903, p. 18.

26 'Music hall gossip', *The Era*, 4 March 1905, p. 20.

27 Conrad William Cooke, *Automata Old and New*, London, privately printed, 1893, p. 86.

28 'Music hall gossip', *The Era*, 12 August 1905, p. 20.

29 'Variety gossip', *The Era*, 24 October 1908, p. 22.

30 'Variety gossip', *The Era*, 19 December 1908, p. 24.

31 'Charcot and his automatic man', *The Era*, 2 January 1909, p. 47.

32 'Variety gossip', *The Era*, 4 July 1908, p. 22. Lloyd's song was most likely John P. Harrington, 'The directoire girl' (1908), British Library catalogue of printed music. Also James Laver, *Costume and Fashion: A Concise History*, London, Thames and Hudson, 1992, p. 219.

33 'Variety gossip', *The Era*, 23 May 1908, p. 22.

34 'Variety gossip', *The Era*, 8 August 1908, p. 20.

35 Carlton, *Twenty Years of Spoof and Bluff*, London, Herbert Jenkins, 1920, p. 74.

36 *Smallest Car in the Biggest City in the World* (1913), viewing copy, British Film Institute, London

37 Disher, *Greatest Show on Earth*, p. 86.

38 Thomas Burke, *Son of London*, London, Herbert Jenkins, 1946, p. 39.

39 Burke, *Son of London*, pp. 39–40. For another description of the Derby procession see Frederick Willis, *London General*, London, Phoenix, 1953, pp. 151–154.

40 'Variety gossip', *The Era*, 14 December 1907, p. 22.

41 'Music hall gossip', *The Era*, 9 October 1897, p. 19.

42 'Music hall gossip', *The Era*, 15 February 1896, p. 19.

43 Albert Douglass, *Memories of Mummers and the Old Standard Theatre*, London, The Era, 1925, p. 90.

44 Douglass, *Memories*, p. 91.

45 Douglass, *Memories*, p. 91.

46 Robert Paul, 'Kinematographic experiences', in Raymond Fielding (ed.), *A Technological History of Motion Pictures and Television*, Berkeley, University of California Press, 1967, pp. 42–48, *passim*.

47 'The Prince's Derby', *Strand Magazine*, August 1896, pp. 135–140 and Colin Sorensen, *London on Film*, London, Museum of London, 1996, pp. 22–25.

48 Sorensen, *London on Film*, p. 25.

49 Felix Barker, *The House That Stoll Built: The Story of the Coliseum Theatre*, London, Frederick Muller, 1957, pp. 26–27.

50 Untitled, *The Era*, 25 May 1912, p. 35.

4

Bicycles

Though the first amateur cycling club was founded in 1869, it was three decades before the sport boiled over in sensation.[1] The corpulent Prince of Wales was a keen, though unathletic, tricyclist whose patronage set the fashion for cycling by society in the middle of the 1890s.[2] At about the same time middle-class ladies took up the sport for pleasant recreation, and leading manufacturers opened showrooms in Holborn Viaduct that were patronised 'by crowds of "smart" people'.[3] 1896 was cycling's British *annus mirabilis* when anyone who wished to appear up-to-date and fashionable learned to ride.[4] The boom had hit the United States somewhat earlier meaning that American manufacturers had sufficient stocks to supply the new demand while advertising their products using 'more original and attractive methods than had been the custom with English cycle makers'.[5]

Actors and artistes were equally quick to associate themselves with the craze; however, they did so in a manner that was becoming commonplace. The London pantomime star Fred Leslie had pioneered this trend, cycling enthusiastically until his premature death in 1894, while comedian Tom Costello took up the sport the following year.[6] Artistes responded immediately once the craze began. The sword-swallowing dandy Chevalier Cliquot, whose name updated both swells and champagne by associating them with bicycles, appeared at the Aquarium, Westminster, at the beginning of 1896.[7] Simultaneously, Lottie Collins hoped to recapture the success she had enjoyed with 'Ta-ra-ra-boom-de-ay' four years earlier with a new song called 'Marriage on a bicycle'.[8] That spring music-hall cyclists began advertising sensationally in public. In March the unicyclist W. Salmon, whose turn was featured in *Dick Whittington* at the Royal, Coatbridge, rode from Glasgow to that theatre on his seat-less machine. He followed this feat by riding the same cycle up the steepest hill in town.[9] Links with the halls soon included those who did not cycle themselves. In

March the rotund Sir Augustus Harris, the legendary manager of the Drury
Lane Theatre who had created the modern Christmas pantomime, was photographed outside his home dressed in a business suit leaning uneasily against a
bicycle.[10]

Further evidence of the up-to-date transference of cycling from street and
park to stage was provided that October by the acrimonious quarrel in *The Era*
between the playwrights E. M. Stuart and Herbert Barrs over who owned the
name *The Bicycle Girl.* Barrs claimed he had produced a musical comedy with
this title at Wolverhampton's Grand Theatre in 1896, while Stuart rebutted that
his play, salaciously subtitled *The Scorcher*, an allusion to the fast morals of
women who sped along astride a bicycle seat, antedated the craze, before Barrs
conceded that the same title may have been thought of independently as an up-
to-date 'case of *A Bicycle Girl* made for two'.[11] The result of this dispute was
never reported though the young H. G. Wells acted on the same topical
impulses that had inspired Stuart and Barrs and chronicled the romances and
adventures of a London clerk cycling through the south of England in *The
Wheels of Chance*, probably the first cycling novel, that same year.[12]

Back on the streets the passion for cycling grew. In November a crowd
watched Salmon cycle up the most formidable hill in Stirling.[13] During the
Christmas pantomime season Salmon awed Coventry, where many worked
building bicycles, by unicycling through streets that were heavily covered in
slush.[14] Meanwhile the Grover family of artistes publicly promised to balance a
human pyramid atop a single cycle for the Manchester pantomime.[15]

Seeing how readily audiences adored these pantomime turns, 1897 saw the
magazine *Cycling* ally itself to music hall. In February they published a cartoon
of 'Widow Twankey', Dan Leno's character at the Drury Lane pantomime,
cycling in a 'rational' dress.[16] Throughout the spring *Cycling* published other
such cartoons under the rubric 'Cycling versions of plays of the day' in which
the main characters of current West End hits, such as the kimono-clad star of
The Geisha or the kilted piper from *The MacHaggis*, were pictured on bicycles
(Figure 3).[17] The magazine revisited pantomime at the end of the year, by pre-
dicting what the 1897 Christmas pantomimes, a genre always full of topical
allusions, would require. It was a scene showing the principal boy clad as
Robinson Crusoe wheeling his bike past the devil disguised as a policeman,
intent on enforcing traffic regulations (Figure 4).[18]

The off-stage adoption of cycling by artistes continued apace that year. The
German strongman Eugene Sandow – who popularised modern body-building
and was a prolific showman, entrepreneur, journalist, and author of exercise

3   As the craze escalated in 1897, artists anticipated the bicycle's appearance in 'legitimate' theatre.

4   It was not hard for artists to imagine what up-to-date pantomimes would include at Christmas 1897.

books – posed with his bicycle in March 1897 when expounding his views
about riding for fitness. He had initially attracted public acclaim in 1889 by
emerging from the audience at the Royal Aquarium, Westminster, to answer the
strong-man Samson's challenge to best his feats of strength. Unluckily for
Samson, Sandow and his agent had trained secretly and mastered the
Frenchman's technique while they awaited Sandow's opportunity to claim the
crown as strongest man in the world.[19] Sandow was a widely acknowledged
authority on fitness who cycled often in the country for his health and included
a bicycling feat of strength in his act in 1896, in which he held aloft a mounted
rider in each hand; an accomplishment that was 'always sure of a warm welcome' from the strongman's spectators.[20] Sandow was followed by the playwrights Arthur Pinero and Henry Jones and the actor William Terriss who were
also pictured in stately poses with their bicycles.[21] The coster impersonator Gus
Elen was then photographed in the conventional Victorian cycling attire of
Norfolk jacket, cap and trouser-clips. Despite his sober appearance, in the
accompanying interview Elen evoked the ludicrous figure he presented cycling
in the streets around his house at Clapham where he could be seen 'coming
home with a parcel under each arm, and the handle-bars of my machine fes-
tooned with onion nets'.[22] Though there is no evidence of her having cycled,
Queen Victoria was co-opted by the craze in 1897, when, in honour of her
Diamond Jubilee, cycling caps bearing her portrait were popular.[23]

Lottie Collins was soon joined by other artistes who celebrated cycling in
songs. 'The bicycle quadrille' and 'The bicycle galop' had been published in
1877, after which titles appeared sporadically until 1895 when four were
written.[24] That 'The bicycle barn dance' and 'Salute my bicycle' of that year
were composed by George Le Brunn, one of the most prolific music-hall songwriters, was further proof that the most established artistes adopted the craze.[25]
Five songs celebrating bicycle belles and parades were published the next year
and five in 1897.[26] From then on a handful of cycling songs appeared every year
until 1905's 'The bicycle who loved the fiddle' when their frequency abated,
suggesting that this was when public fascination truly waned.[27]

Given the immense public interest in cycling and the corollary pressure for
artistes to identify themselves with the sport, whether they actually rode or not,
many celebrities, such as Sir Augustus Harris posed for cycling photographs. This
was an era when people sat for photographs in fanciful costumes before dioramas
depicting everything from the African veldt to Aegean temples and arctic ice
floes. Despite this widespread pastime in 1897 the journalist Raymond Raife
wrote that 'on very few subjects indeed have so many journalistic untruths been

told as concerning "Celebrities Who Cycle". To-day probably the majority of notables go a-wheel; but a season or two back the case was very different. Accordingly, not a few writers manufactured their cycling celebrities whole-sale'.[28] According to Raife, famous performers like Mrs Patrick Campbell, Forbes Robertson, Charles Wyndham and the prima donna Nellie Melba animated the refrain of T. W. Connor's 1897 song 'I'm going to ride a bicycle' without heeding its injunction.[29] During portrait sessions photographers would invite their subjects to 'sit or stand for a wheeling picture, which will go very well in any of the illustrated journals just at present'.[30] As in the halls, even the most prominent names in the theatre, whose careers did not rely on them generating such publicity, felt it necessary to assert their up-to-dateness by tying themselves publicly to this craze. At the same time, studios updated their props.[31]

In June 1898 Dan Leno was again depicted as a cyclist though this time in a photograph with his wife and children. In an accompanying interview Leno claimed to have introduced Sir Augustus Harris to the sport, and that he relaxed by riding between his Brixton home and Hampton Court.[32] This interview coincided with an issue of *Dan Leno's Comic Journal,* a short-lived half-penny weekly filled with comics and adventure stories, that depicted six Lenos, all wearing different costumes, atop the same bike.[33] Leno the cyclist was a popularly promoted and acknowledged figure. Cycle companies were the most prominent advertisers in his *Comic Journal* and in November a correspondent to the editors of *Cycling* about new types of head lamps for bikes signed himself 'Dan Aceti-Leno'.[34] It is not surprising then that amongst several films Leno made for the Warwick Biograph Company was an up-to-date one shot in 1900 entitled *Dan Leno's Attempt to Master the Cycle* in a cinematic adaptation of his new hobby.[35] Against the backdrop of these cycling antics Jerome K. Jerome updated his cherished book *Three Men in a Boat,* by sending his trio of London clerks, to say nothing of Montmorency the dog, on a Continental cycling holiday.[36]

In 1901 the weekly illustrated magazine *The Sketch* carried portraits of famous artistes on their bikes, ranging from the obvious advertisement of Dan Leno, Walter Munro and George Robey posing in full pantomime costume, to the male impersonator Vesta Tilley in a dress, while popular American minstrel Eugene Stratton appeared once in blackface and then again in mufti.[37] In that year Sandow made his bicycling act more perilous by raising a pair of riders above his head.[38] Just as before, Sandow also used his bike more conventionally by cycling for recreation in a Norfolk jacket and breeks. Some artistes were apparently still unable to ride five years into the craze. The comedian Harry Randall improbably and shakily mounted his machine in an immaculate tweed suit, leather gloves and homburg whilst smoking a cigar.[39] These photographs once again showed that performers at the very top of the music-hall and theatrical professions allied themselves with this craze in order to be seen as up-to-date.

Bikes were ridden sensationally by artistes and managers at the turn of the century. In April 1898, Harry Black one of the 'Two Bees' troupe, suggested to Harry Lundy – manager of the Oxford, Leicester Square, and director of the Music-Hall Sports – that a bicycle parade should be added to the day's entertainment. Black suggested that this parade assemble in Lambeth Road, a district in which many artistes lived. Artistes and audience members would then cycle to the Herne Hill grounds where those wearing the prettiest, funniest and most original costumes would be awarded prizes in a carnival sure to attract London's leading bicycle clubs 'besides giving great advertising scope to boom the Sports'.[40] By the middle of June the Water Rats, the largest artistes' fraternal organisation, endorsed this parade whose route was lengthened to begin in Kennington. *The Era*'s editors were especially optimistic about the parade's success as the Water Rats included some of the most famous comedians of the day, such as Leno and George Robey, whose wheeling antics could be relied upon to attract crowds.[41]

In the end an even more ambitious route was followed. Beginning at Cleopatra's Needle on the Embankment, the parade crossed Westminster Bridge, before proceeding through Kennington and Brixton to Herne Hill.[42] Alas, the parade was a disappointing fiasco as the leading members of the Water Rats were absent and

> the cavalcade formed but a small pageant of pros, and a Highlander, a tailless Mephisto, a donkey, a monkey, an owl, and other fearful wild fowl, attracted some notice. Of course, the ladies wore nattier and more becoming costumes, and their bicycles were prettily decorated. The procession was started by Mr Harry Lundy at 10:30 and his smart cob and trap was followed by the Alhambra coach, with its assemblage of handsomely dressed girls and a few gentlemen, Fregoli among them.[43]

The appearance of Fregoli, an immensely popular Italian mimic and quick-change music-hall and cinema performer who was about to appear at the Alhambra, shows the close links between cycling and sensational advertising.[44] One can excuse the Water Rats' misjudgement of public interest in the parade because bicycling festivals were enormously popular in London. One month before the Sports, the Woodford cycle parade in north-east London was attended by over two thousand riders, many of them in costume. Perhaps the Water Rats had read the journalist who observed with 'wonder at the vast development of the cyclist craze by which alone so immense a gallery could be rendered possible' as the Woodford club members gathered on the village green.[45]

Given the popularity of the sport, it is understandable that artistes continued to court cyclists even after the Embankment parade had failed. In March 1899 Fred Holden organised a 'variety and theatrical cycle parade' in order to make a film for exhibition at the Canterbury, Lambeth. An hour before the parade was supposed to begin the Canterbury's lobby was spilling over with cyclists. When the crowd moved, it proceeded through local streets to Kennington Park where additional shots were filmed. At least eight individual turns and six troupes took part riding tandems, racers, unicycles and trick riders' bikes, while less energetic representatives of various halls rode in coaches. Echoing Harry Black's reasons for prefacing the Sports with a parade, representatives of 'nearly all the most popular cycling clubs in and around London' rode before the cameras.[46]

The Woodford carnival attracted over two thousand participants and raised £200 for charity in 1900, though only about half as many cyclists took part the following year. Nevertheless, promoters were optimistic.[47] Sam Gerthing, the acting manager of the Stratford Empire, filmed the Woodford meet in 1903 because once again thousands of cyclists took part in the costume derby, and then encouraged riders to come and see themselves on the Empire's screen.[48] Cecil Hepworth, one of the most prominent Edwardian film-makers, understood the drawing power of such films because 'bicycles in those days were still so new that the riding of them attracted attention and people flocked in quantities to see these gymkhanas'.[49]

Despite the craze, cycling's most important impact on London was less sensational. Even though the middle and upper classes rode less often in Battersea and Hyde Parks after 1897, bicycles remained popular with the lower middle classes for much longer.[50] An examination of the stock flotations by cycle companies showed that the boom of 1896-1897 was followed by a decline in investment after the turn of the century. However, investors' confidence gradually returned, perhaps with the realisation of the bicycle's resilience and ongoing popularity.[51]

The importance of the bicycle for the lower middle classes remained as important as it had been when Wells had written *Wheels of Chance*. Cycling never disappeared and it was not only the making or screening of cycling films which brought riders to the halls. The cheap mobility offered by bicycles, especially in emancipating women, was resolutely most popular with the lower middle classes.[52] Calls for the provision of free cycle lock-ups to accommodate these patrons at every music hall were heard at the height of the craze in 1896.[53] Five years later the Holloway Empire installed bicycle storage sheds at the theatre because so many ticket-buyers cycled from the emerging lower-middle-class neighbourhoods of Enfield, Barnet and Potter's Bar. This service was advertised along with other amenities such as a sliding roof and free fans for ladies as an inducement to attendance on hot summer evenings.[54]

By 1906 the bicycle was an important method of transport for suburban commuters, and a leisure activity enjoyed by both sexes, while racing tracks had been erected at Herne Hill, Crystal Palace and Wood Green.[55] The result was that for many years after the boom music-hall stages were replete with cyclists racing on banked tracks, Australians pedalling bamboo machines, trick-riding troupes carrying one another in all manner of precarious poses and even a one-legged performer who manipulated his pedals sufficiently well to cycle off the Hippodrome's roof into a tank of water on the street ninety feet below.[56] As we have seen, cycling songs remained popular until the mid-Edwardian era. Despite its continued service on the roads as an efficient and inexpensive form of transportation, the bicycle was updated in the early years of the century by the more sensational motor-car.

Notes

1　F. Neville Piggott, 'Sport in the Victorian era', *Sandow's Magazine of Physical Culture*, Vol. 6 (1901), pp. 187–190.

2　Selwyn Francis Edge, *My Motoring Reminiscences*, London, G. T. Foulis, 1934, p. 257.

3　A. C. Pemberton, *The Complete Cyclist*, London, C. P. Sisley and G. Floyd, 1897, p. 33.

4　David Rubinstein, 'Cycling eighty years ago', *History Today*, August 1978, p. 545.

5　Pemberton, *Complete Cyclist*, p. 38. For an interesting cinema bicycle advertisement see *Rudge Whitworth, Britain's Best Bicycle* (1900), viewing copy, British Film Institute, London.

6　'Music hall gossip', *The Era*, 5 October 1895, p. 17, and W. T. Vincent, *Recollections of Fred Leslie*, London, Kegan Paul, 1894, Vol. 1, p. 145.

7　'Music hall gossip', *The Era*, 29 February 1896, p. 17.

8　'A new cycling song', *Cycling*, 29 February 1896, p. 110.

9　'Music hall gossip', *The Era*, 21 March 1896, p. 19.

10　Will o' the Wisp, 'The music hall sports', *Cycling*, 25 July 1896, p. 28; and 'Sir Augustus Harris', *Cycling*, 16 May 1896, p. 307.

11　'The bicycle girl', *The Era*, 17 October 1896, p. 13; Letter, 'The bicycle girl', *The Era*, 31 October 1896, p. 12; Letter, 'The bicycle girl', *The Era*, 24 October 1896,

p. 13; Letter, 'The bicycle girl', *The Era*, 7 November 1896, p. 13; For the supposed promiscuity of women awheel see Mrs Humphrey Ward, *Manners for Women*, Whitstable, Pryor, 1993, p. 21.

12   H. G. Wells, *The Wheels of Chance*, London, J. M. Dent, 1896.

13   'Music hall gossip', *The Era*, 24 October 1896, p. 19, and 'Music hall gossip', *The Era*, 7 November 1896, p. 19.

14   'Music hall gossip', *The Era*, 12 December 1896, p. 19.

15   'Music hall gossip', *The Era*, 12 December 1896, p. 19.

16   'Purely imaginary', *Cycling*, 20 February 1897, p. 5.

17   'Plays of the day – I, "The Geisha"', *Cycling*, 13 March 1897, p. 5; 'Cycling versions of plays of the day – II, "The Saucy Sally"', *Cycling*, 20 March 1897, p. 5; 'Cycling versions of plays of the day – III, "Black Ey'd Susan" at the Adelphi', *Cycling*, 27 March 1897, p. 5; and 'Cycling versions of plays of the day – IV, "The MacHaggis" at the Globe', *Cycling*, 3 April 1897, p. 5.

18   'What we must expect in this year's pantomimes', *Cycling*, 25 September 1897, p. 221.

19   David L. Chapman, *Sandow the Magnificent*, Urbana, Illinois, University of Illinois Press, 1994, pp. 23–24.

20   'Sandow and his cycle – a chat with the monarch of muscle', *Cycling*, 13 March 1897, pp. 180–181. The quote is found on p. 180.

21   'Notable cyclists – Mr A. W. Pinero', *Cycling*, 27 March 1897, p. 222; 'Notable Cyclists – ten minutes with Mr. Henry Arthur Jones, playwright and wheelman', *Cycling*, 3 April 1897, p. 252; and 'Notable cyclists – Mr. William Terriss', *Cycling*, 10 April 1897, p. 281.

22   'Notable cyclists – Mr Gus Elen', *Cycling*, 24 April 1897, p. 334. For another view of Elen cycling see 'Mr. Gus Elen', *The Sketch*, 26 February 1902, p. 237.

23   Tori Smith, '"Almost pathetic", but also very glorious: the consumer spectacle of the Diamond Jubilee', *Social History/Histoire Sociale*, 58 (1966,) p. 338.

24   Charles Davieson, 'The bicycle galop' (1877); Jacques N. Kart, 'The bicycle quadrille' (1877); Thomas Gregory, 'Charley, the bicycle pet' (1878); Stanislaus Elliot, 'The bicycle sonata' (1881); James Castle, 'The bell of the bicycle' (1884); J. W. Hall, 'Does anybody want to buy a bicycle?' (1893); all in the British Library catalogue of printed music.

25   George Le Brunn, 'The bicycle barn dance' (1895) and 'Salute my bicycle' (1895), both in the British Library catalogue of printed music.

26   Dox Cruger, 'Bicycle parade march' (1896); Walter Goold, 'The bicycle meet' (1896); C. Ormsby Gregory, 'Bicycle galop' (1896); Richard Hoffman, 'A bicycle ride' (1896); George A. Watts, 'The bicycle belle march' (1896); T.W. Connor, 'I'm going to ride a bicycle' (1897); Gerald Deane, 'Queen of the wheel' (1897); Annie Forder, 'My bike' (1897); Albert Perry, 'On my bicy-icy-bicycle' (1897); and W.G. Workman, 'The bicycle club parade' (1897); all in the British Library catalogue of printed music.

27   John Pridham, 'Bicycle belle polka' (1898); A. M. Thatcher, '"His whiskers" on a bike' (1898); Clarence Hunt, 'Pat Casey's tandem bike' (1900); Julius Borges, 'My

bike' (1903); and George A. Stevens, 'The bicycle who loved the fiddle' (1905); all in the British Library catalogue of printed music.

28   Raymond Raife, 'Non-wheeling theatrical cyclists – inventing celebrities who ride', *Cycling*, 28 August 1897, p. 127.

29   T. W. Connor, 'I'm going to ride a bicycle' (1897), British Library catalogue of printed music; Raife, 'Non-wheeling cyclists', p. 127.

30   Raife, 'Non-wheeling cyclists', p. 127.

31   Raymond Raife, 'Doing chats with cycling celebrities', *Cycling*, 19 March 1898, pp. 220–221.

32   'The king of mirth makers', *Cycling*, 11 June 1898, p. 524.

33   'The Leno family out for a spin', *Dan Leno's Comic Journal*, 4 June 1898, p. 1.

34   Letter, 'Acetylene lamps', *Cycling*, 11 November 1899, p. 345. For cycle adverts see Advertisement, *Dan Leno's Comic Journal*, 5 March 1898, p. 7 and Advertisement, *Dan Leno's Comic Journal*, 18 March 1899, p. 7.

35   Stephen Herbert and Luke McKernan, *Who's Who of Victorian Cinema*, London, British Film Institute, 1996, p. 81.

36   Jerome K. Jerome, *Three Men on the Bummel*, Bristol, J. W. Arrowsmith, 1900.

37   All of these references are found in *The Sketch*: 'Mr Eugene Stratton about to take the air from his cycle', 13 March 1901, p. 325; 'George Robey, Walter Munro and Dan Leno amuse themselves and others', 15 May 1901, p. 157; 'Miss Vesta Tilley', 5 June 1901, p. 279; 'Harry Randall who is nightly discussing drink at the Tivoli', 12 June 1901, p. 319; 'Mr. Eugene Stratton at "The Coon's Rest"', 19 June 1901, p. 359; and 'Mr. Eugene Sandow the celebrated "strong man"', 20 November 1901, p. 191.

38   'An interview with Sandow', *Cycling*, 12 October 1901, p. 266.

39   'Harry Randall – cyclist', *The Sketch*, 12 June 1901, p. 319.

40   Letter, 'A suggestion for the sports', *The Era*, 2 April 1898, p. 20.

41   'Music hall gossip', *The Era*, 11 June 1898, p. 19.

42   'Music hall sports', *The Era*, 2 July 1898, p. 17.

43   'Music hall sports', *The Era*, 9 July 1898, p. 20.

44   Herbert and McKernan, *Victorian Cinema*, p. 53. For the announcement of Fregoli's Alhambra date see 'Music hall gossip', *The Era*, 11 June 1898, p. 19.

45   'Epping Forest and the cycle parade', *The Hackney Express, Shoreditch Observer and Bethnal Green Advertiser*, 11 June 1898, p. 3.

46   'Music hall gossip', *The Era*, 25 March 1899, p. 19.

47   'Snapped at the Woodford meet', *Cycling*, 23 June 1900, pp. 478–479. For the amount of money raised see 'Cyclists and charity', *Daily Express*, 6 September 1901, p. 8; 'The Woodford meet', *Cycling*, 15 June, 1901, pp. 494–495.

48   'Music hall gossip', *The Era*, 27 June 1903, p. 18.

49   Cecil Hepworth, *Came the Dawn*, London, Phoenix House, 1951, p. 43.

50   Frederick Alderson, *Bicycling: A History*, Newton Abbot, David and Charles, 1972, p. 86.

51   A. E. Harrison, 'Joint-stock company flotation in the cycle, motor-vehicle and related industries, 1882-1914', *Business History*, 23 (1981), pp. 165–168.

52 Anonymous, *Narrow Waters*, London, W. Hodge, 1935, pp. 160–161.

53 'Bicycles and theatres', *The Era*, 14 November 1896, p. 20.

54 'Music hall gossip', *The Era*, 27 July 1901, p. 16.

55 C. Duncan Lucas, 'Cycling London', *Living London*, 32 (1906), pp. 248–252.

56 For racing see 'The Jones-Hiliard bicycle sensation', *The Era*, 31 August 1901, p. 19; 'The Jones-Hiliard bicycle sensation', *The Era*, 7 September 1901, p. 18; and 'Empire theatre: more sensational cycling', *Daily Chronicle*, 5 September 1901, p. 6. 'Music hall gossip', *The Era*, 5 December 1896, p. 18 talks of a troupe who rode bamboo bicycles. A. E. Johnson, 'Across the footlights', *Sandow's Magazine of Physical Culture*, 4 (1900), pp. 191–192 discusses trick riding. A photograph of the Hippodrome's one-legged cyclist is featured in Untitled, *The Sketch*, 12 March 1902, p. 319.

5

Automobiles

Just as with cycling, the public had shown a passing interest in motor-cars after they were invented in Germany during the 1880s, though they were not often seen in Britain until about 1895.[1] The earliest engines were unreliable and prone to frequent breakdowns, and subject to severe legal speed and safety restrictions. Automobile design and construction matured in about 1905 and it is from this date that the car established itself as a dependable form of transport.[2] The failure of Sanger's coaches to realise anything more than a pittance at auction and the sale of Karno's pair of coaches to China that same year symbolised this new confidence in the automobile.

Almost as soon as bicycling boomed in London it was threatened by an automobile craze that swept the country from north to south. The inaugural London to Brighton motor rally was staged in 1896 to celebrate the repeal of many restrictive speed and safety laws.[3] Automobiles made their first, tentative appearances on the halls that same summer, when the 'novelty' of the Anglo-French motor carriage mesmerised Tyneside audiences as it was driven across the stage.[4] Meanwhile, people in sitting rooms and parlours danced 'The motor car polka' while the first 'original and up-to-date' automobile songs were performed in the halls.[5] Given such inducements it was not long before people like the cycling champion Selwyn Edge forsook the craze of the bike for the folly of the automobile.[6] Edge became the most famous Edwardian motor-racer, automobile dealer and celebrity chauffeur.

In April 1900 the 'Thousand Miles Trial', a race promoted by the publisher and motoring enthusiast Alfred Harmsworth – later Lord Northcliffe – and the engineer Claude Johnson made a circuit of Britain from London to Edinburgh and back in order to convince the country that automobiles were both safe and innocuous. The rally's start at Hyde Park Corner was attended by a huge crowd – including many cyclists who followed the entrants, apparently unaware that the car would soon supplant them – as they drove to the western edges of London.[7] The automobile's triumph in the halls was sealed seven years later when *The Sketch* eschewed bicycling photographs for those showing leading stage personalities with their cars. Ellaline Terriss, whose father William had posed for photographers with his bike in the 1890s, provided convincing personal evidence of this evolution by appearing with her automobile.[8]

Bicycles had never directly replaced broughams because they did not perform the practical function of transporting artistes between their nightly engagements. Leybourne and Mackney had emphasised ostentation as well as efficiency with their coaches: something which, as Harry Randall and Eugene Stratton had proved, could not be replicated on a bike. Significantly, bicycles came within the purchasing power of many Londoners and were therefore sometimes used to publicly integrate audiences and artistes. But automobiles, like carriages, were too expensive for most music-hall patrons, an inaccessibility that imbued both as icons of wealth and status.

Artistes appeared simultaneously on the halls and in the streets in their automobiles. E. J. Coles exhibited his driving skills at the Alhambra, Leicester Square, in 1900 and at the Agricultural Hall, Islington, on the eve of the Thousand Miles Trial. London audiences demanded a more advanced show than those that had been held in Newcastle four years earlier. Coles responded by driving his vehicle up and down steps before demonstrating its braking capabilities by racing, at the plodding top speed that early motor-cars mustered, across the stage towards an assistant only to stop at the last moment. In order to make the act even more daring Coles then performed these feats with his arms folded across his chest and his feet upon the controls.[9] The earliest surviving automobile movie, Hepworth's one minute-long *Explosion of a Motor-Car*, also dates from 1900.[10] Meanwhile, automobile songs took off. A few had appeared yearly between 1896 and 1900 from which time they proliferated on both sides of the Atlantic. Titles like 'All the girls loved Bertie when he had a motor car' emphasised the driver as a symbol of daring and romance, while 'My hundred-pound motor car' proclaimed wealth and social prestige (Figure 5).[11]

Just like carriages, automobiles wove together utilitarian transportation and dandified public spectacle. The most perceptively up-to-date artistes employed cars to shuttle between engagements and, just as with Arthur Roberts' claim about broughams and Leno's about cycling, a number of them insisted that they had initiated music-hall motoring. Tom Wootwell claimed that in 1900 he had been the first artiste to motor between London turns in a car, attracting crowds wherever he drove.[12] George Foster countered Wootwell's assertion and insisted

In the early days of motoring Londoners flocked to watch such 'fancy driving'.   **5**

that he had introduced Gus Elen, Harry Tate and Walter de Frece, the agent and husband of Vesta Tilley, to motoring.[13] The comedian T. E. Dunville toured the provinces by motor-car in 1901.[14] Arthur Roberts retired his brougham and declared his membership of the London car brigade in the motoring press in early 1902.[15] Such was the public demand to know about motor-cars and their drivers at the turn of the century that celebrated motorists did not only come from the halls. For instance Edward, the Prince of Wales, was an early adherent of motoring, who refused to be driven at anything less than top speed and in motor-cars that bore royal ciphers on the doors, while Arthur Balfour, another former cyclist, bought his first motor, 'a huge machine of the road-racing type' in the summer of 1902.[16]

No matter who had been first, Wootwell and Foster unleashed a flood of motoring artistes. In 1902 Gus Elen chained up his bike in favour of a car. Feeling slighted by reports that his new automobile cost only £650, Elen posted a curt letter to *The Era* stating that he had paid over one thousand pounds, a much more spectacular amount.[17] This ostentatious purchase was confirmed publicly the following month when Elen and his wife were photographed in the same journal descending the steps of their London home to a waiting chauffeur-driven car.[18] Moreover, the couple annually carried their Christmas charity presents to Clapham Common in their motor-car, but Elen would take a more reactionary stand at the Coliseum in January 1908 when he gave the début of 'The coster's pony' in which the beast proved more reliable than the automobiles he derisively referred to as a 'thousand guinea animated paraffin can'.[19] Having encountered Elen for so many years as a motorist, Londoners must have perceived the song's irony.

Public interest in motor-cars intensified in 1903 prompting the marmoreal Oswald Stoll, owner of the London Coliseum and manager of one of the biggest national syndicates, to describe George Robey as the 'automobile of comic singers' in an acknowledgement of the latter's up-to-dateness.[20] Not willing to let his reputation as a motorist rest on Stoll's pronouncements, the only photograph of George Robey's family included in his 1908 autobiography showed them seated in their car.[21]

Dr Walford Bodie, a Scottish artiste who used electricity to achieve spectacular effects, was naturally, given the inherent up-to-dateness of his act, drawn to the automobile and quickly became one of its greatest music-hall patrons. At the end of 1902 he purchased an 'up-to-date' five hundred guinea car that was intended 'for advertising purposes' as well as convenience and luxurious indulgence.[22] By April, Dunville was touring the provincial halls in his motor-car, while the itinerary for Elen's national tour that year included a detailed description of his route and the places where and times at which he his wife and favourite dog Tiddles would stop.[23] Fans could then meet them and see the car. At the end of the year Bodie emphasised the status accorded to him by motoring in a photographic advertisement for his turn which showed him leaving his Scottish residence for a chauffeured drive.[24] The Charles Dickens impersonator Bransby Williams depended on a motor car for speed, reliability and convenience after his first drive, in one of the king's automobiles, *en route* to Sandringham for a command performance in 1903.[25] He too drew attention to this passion by including a photograph of his family with Selwyn Edge in his autobiography.[26]

In the spring of 1905 Sam Mayo and Tom Pacey were accompanied in their Mercedes by Ted Cowan on a motorcycle for a provincial tour.[27] Jenny Hill's daughter and imitator Peggy Pryde emulated the up-to-dateness that her mother had expressed by owning a carriage when she toured by car in 1907.[28] Such was the public's infatuation with the automobile by then that enthusiasts watched a film in a music hall which showed a motor-car being assembled followed soon after by one entitled *Purchasing an Automobile*.[29] People leaving these films might then have encountered Vasco, 'the mad musician', who drove through the streets of London in a car emblazoned with his name and that of the theatre circuit to which he was engaged, when he appeared at the Empire, Leicester Square in, 1908.[30]

In the unlikely event of Vasco slipping past unnoticed, Harry Lauder repeatedly boomed his pinch-penny Scotch persona from the seat of his car. After dining at the Argyle and Sutherland Highlanders' Chatham barracks in 1906 he was paraded from the hall to his train by the regimental band who encouraged his return with the Jacobite lament 'Will ye no come back again'.[31] Two years later the pipers of the London Scottish paraded Lauder's car, over the bonnet of which the Saltire had been draped, from his home to Euston Station where he caught the New York boat-train. Four more pipers played him up the gangway at Liverpool.[32] The scenes at Euston and Liverpool were repeated a year later.[33] Finally, a kilted Lauder, escorted by two pipers and a troupe of cyclists, drove through London's northern suburbs to the Gramophone Company's recording studios in Hayes, Middlesex in May 1913. He arrived at the plant only to see its workers leaving for their dinner break. They insisted that Lauder complete this public preview of his performance and he was made to sing his latest hit in the roadway.[34]

Subsidiary references to artistes in their cars are very common and need only be briefly mentioned. The Nottingham comedian Billy Merson held out obstinately against the pressure to motor by using a brougham in London as late as 1910.[35] This attitude softened some time between then and 1922 when he published an autobiography that included a photo of him applying his make-up in the back seat of his car.[36] In 1910 Seymour Hicks and Gertie Millar, two of London's most popular actors, advertised the '20 h.p. Metallurgique car with Vanden Plas body' while undertaking promotional Christmas shopping tours of Mayfair and the West End for the *Daily Mail*, a newspaper owned by Harmsworth, one of motoring's earliest patrons.[37] The minstrel George Chirgwin was another enthusiastic motorist whose 1912 autobiography proved his passion by including the obligatory up-to-date photograph of him riding with his family. His motoring anecdotes had been published in *The Era* a decade earlier.[38] On the eve of war the operatic tenor and recording star Enrico Caruso patriotically used an Italian Lancia automobile in 1913 for professional and 'social' purposes whilst in London and the acrobat, comedian and dancer Albert Le Fre declared that he always drove to his engagements.[39]

Because automobiles were so expensive they represented wealth and luxury and, unlike bicycles, they never became quotidian vehicles. Even when they were divorced completely from any practical function, their proximity conferred glamour and up-to-dateness on artistes. Therefore, the soubrette Kitty Loftus racily posed with one, both on and off stage, while acting as 'Naughty Nancy' in late 1902 (Figure 6)[40]. The sensation of automobiling alternated

6   Kitty Loftus booms her up-to-dateness from the seat of an automobile in 1902.

continually between stage and street, as in 1903 when a lady appeared at the London Hippodrome 'hooping the hoop' by racing her motor car through an elevated track's vertical loop. Though her performance lasted only a few seconds 'even the most apathetic spectators must confess that her exhibition of pluck is sufficiently thrilling'.[41] In 1903 Herr Julius Seeth, an animal trainer who played the Hippodrome, employed a luxurious Daimler automobile in an unlikely promotion for his act.[42] Initially his lions were bashful about entering the car to have their photographs taken with Seeth at the wheel, so he induced their co-operation by placing beef steaks on the seats. Fresh meat warmed the cats to the idea of posing, but after the photographs were taken they tore off the tyres whilst 'generally playing havoc with the vehicle' in a vain search for other edible parts.[43] Edgar Romaine sang a specially written song celebrating the one thousand pound car he took on to the stage with him in 1905, greatly impressing his audience. Romaine dressed in an all-white motorist's outfit to extol the virtues of his machine and salaciously invited ladies in the audience to join him in the passenger seat.[44] Six years later a revue called *The Winner* staged by Seymour Hicks at the Hippodrome prominently advertised that a 'motor-brougham' was one of the props employed.[45]

The most famous incorporation of automobiles was *Motoring*, a sketch devised by Harry Tate and Wal Pink in about 1900. Ronald Hutchinson was a Scottish clerk with London's Tate and Lyle sugar company who had been

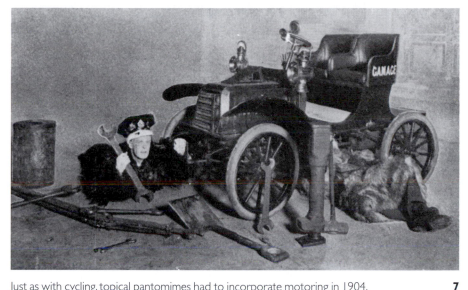

Just as with cycling, topical pantomimes had to incorporate motoring in 1904.   **7**

encouraged to try the stage by Marie Lloyd. Thereafter he performed under his employer's surname as Harry Tate. Tate made his London debut at the Oxford Music-hall in 1895 with the first of his series of topical comic sketches based on popular pastimes. *Motoring's* premise was simple: a father, clad in the elaborate driving costume of the day, and his 'know it all' son set out for a ride in the country where they were beset by incessant mechanical breakdowns. The son and several passers-by made ever-more absurd and annoying suggestions about how to repair the vehicle while the father, played by Tate, worked to repair the engine. Each time that Tate fixed the car he cranked the ignition, climbed up behind the wheel and with a gleeful optimistic cry of 'good bye-ee!' commenced, unsuccessfully, to drive away. As his annoyance and frustration rose, Tate's ludicrously exaggerated moustaches spun like a pin-wheel in a pathetic fallacy for his feelings. The sketch was immensely popular.

Tate had a genius for promotion. He was publicly recognisable in his own lavish automobile to which were affixed number plates, made necessary under the terms of the Motor Act of 1902, bearing the personalised legend 'T8', which 'spelt his name, and he kept that number always' until his death.[46] Such number plates recalled the royal ciphers which Karno's coaches had borne, and those same insignia sported on King Edward's equally conspicuous motor-car. Promotional posters and advertisements for Tate's appearances referred to these plates through such phrases as 'Harry T8 presents his GR8 *Motoring* sketch. Up to D8'.[47] Tate remained 'up to D8' by developing subsequent sketches, though none lasted so well as *Motoring,* which the public demanded until the Second World War.

Like Karno, Tate exploited the streets of London for publicity. In June 1908 he convinced the Water Rats to organise a London to Brighton motor rally for artistes.[48] Like Harry Lundy's bicycle parade, this was to be a music-hall version of existing pastimes. Interest grew quickly once the idea had been mooted and in early June between seventy and one hundred cars had been pledged for the run. As with the original London to Brighton rally and the Thousand Miles Trial, the event was promoted to a public who were sceptical about the motor-car's reliability as a way of proving that so many automobiles could appear at once without causing inconvenience or exceeding the 20 mph speed limit.[49] When entrants arrived at the Vaudeville Club in Leicester Square for the start of the race they found that the fifty cars present were not sufficient to convey all of them to the coast, so the organisers impressed the services of taxis from the ranks in the streets nearby. In the end sixty-three vehicles – including those lent by Gladiator, Hills Martin, Darracq and Rolls-Royce – carried artistes past huge crowds on the way to Brighton.[50]

In 1909 the second edition of Tate's rally included about twenty-four automobile manufacturers, and their directors.[51] Cars were conspicuously numbered, in order to help spectators identify passengers while fans along the route obtained the signatures of their favourite artistes. The press was driven to Brighton in a specially reserved motor bus.[52] The Brighton run was never repeated, though Tate continued his public driving performances with comedic attempts to break the speed record during the music-hall football carnivals held in north London on the eve of the First World War.[53] Just as on his number plates, Tate favoured word-play to promote these events. In February 1914 he challenged the mile record in a 90 horsepower 'Dudner' automobile at an artistes versus jockeys football match at Stamford Bridge.[54] Amidst a great list of performers this turn remained 'one of the most thrilling events of the afternoon'.[55] Tate then attempted 'the 2,000 Kill'em metre speed record in his 37 candle power hardpan car' in March at a White Hart Lane carnival. This car's name was a malapropism for the French marque Panhard-Levassor, one of the leading automobile manufacturers.[56]

Cars were inaccessible badges of wealth and social prestige to most people until well into the twentieth century because the British motor industry produced very limited numbers of high-quality models, only grudgingly introducing Henry Ford's concept of mass-production on an 'assembly-line'.[57] Even after automobiles had become more common, the Scots comedian Dave Hunter recalled that his audiences were impressed by the prestige of seeing him drive around town in a sports car during an engagement. Moreover, such motor-cars were always parked by their owners near a theatre's public entrance in order that the customers could marvel at them and argue over which artiste owned which car. The public looked upon an artiste incredulously unless he possessed such a tangible token of his success.[58] A flash car and a large wad of cash were Hunter's latter-day equivalent of a chairman's diamond shirt studs, Leybourne's carriage or Elen's bicycle in that it proclaimed his success to spectators while at the same time reassuring creditors and employees that they would be paid.[59]

As carriages had, motor-cars also produced material benefits for up-to-date artistes who earned more money at the turn of the century. Those like Sam Mayo exploited this facility to increase the number of turns he gave in an evening due to the reliability and speed of his transport around the capital.[60] The automobile's increasing speed and reliability allowed artistes to incorporate the suburban theatres into the same twice-nightly circuit that operated in the centre of the metropolis.[61] Even those performers who were too poor to purchase a car could hire one to usher them between their London turns from a firm aiming its business directly at these professionals.[62] Finally, the motor industry capitalised on the connection with the halls. Dan Leno's son-in-law ran Balham's Dan Leno Motor Works, Sidney Lawrence, brother of the popular male impersonator Vesta Victoria, sold Darracq and Minerva automobiles to many artistes, while Cecilia Loftus advertised C. B. Whittaker's dealership in Great Russell Street.[63] J. A. Lawton of Orchard Street supplied Vesta Tilley, Marie Lloyd and had 'also had the pleasure of doing business, both in connection with motor cars and carriages', with Claire Romaine, Chirgwin, Elen, Stratton and others, while L. M. Brew of Kennington supplied the Scottish comedian Jock McKay in 1914.[64] Even firms that did not directly invoke artistes' names, like A. C. Wright Motors of Camberwell, thanked the music-hall trade generated by their continuous advertisements in *The Encore*.[65] In addition, in 1907 *The Era* commenced publishing a 'Motor gossip' column which detailed the cars purchased by artistes who also sold their old motor cars, sometimes offering preferential rates to fellow professionals through its pages.[66]

Though audience members might have been too poor to purchase a car they enjoyed the status of ownership vicariously through the depiction of luxury vehicles. These aspirations were summed up in the title of the 1904 song 'If you can't buy a motor car, buy a motor cap'.[67] Though Londoners saw cars in the streets every day, they remained impressed with the opulence of Edgar

Romaine's, Gus Elen's and latterly Dave Hunter's. But there must also have been a constituency who were both music-hall audience members and possessed of a great enough disposable income to purchase an automobile. For these the endorsement of a star might sway their decision about which model to choose.

Notes

1 Lionel Rolt, *Horseless Carriage: The Motor Car in England*, London, Constable, 1950, pp. 71–73.
2 Rolt, *Horseless Carriage*, p. 83.
3 Rolt, *Horseless Carriage*, p. 41.
4 'Music hall gossip', *The Era*, 26 September 1896, p. 19.
5 Felix Dumas, 'The motor car polka' (1896), British Library catalogue of printed music; 'Music hall gossip', *The Era*, 6 June 1896, p. 17. For the quote see 'Music hall gossip', *The Era*, 29 August 1896, p. 19.
6 Selwyn Francis Edge, *My Motoring Reminiscences*, London, G. T. Foulis, 1934, pp. 11–22.
7 Paul Tritton, *John Montagu of Beaulieu, 1866–1929, Motoring Pioneer and Prophet*, London, Golden Eagle/George Hart, 1985, pp. 61–64.
8 Untitled photograph, *The Sketch*, 16 October 1907, p. 27.
9 Edge, *Reminiscences*, pp. 80–81.
10 *Explosion of a Motor Car* (1900), viewing copy, British Film Institute, London.
11 John P. Long, 'All the girls loved Bertie when he had a motor car' (1914) and Sam Richards, 'My hundred-pound motor car' (1901), both in the British Library catalogue of printed music.
12 'Mummers and motors', *The Era*, 6 July 1907, p. 23.
13 George Foster, *The Spice of Life*, London, Hurst and Blackett, 1932, pp. 137–138. A photograph of one of de Frece's automobiles is found in Untitled, *The Autocar*, 21 January 1911, p. 91.
14 'Music hall celebrities', *The Era*, 11 April 1908, p. 23; T. E. Dunville, *The Autobiography of an Eccentric Comedian*, London, Everett and Co., 1912, p. 96.
15 'A well known comedian's car', *The Autocar*, 4 January 1902, p. 4, and 'Music hall gossip', *The Era*, 11 February 1905, p. 20.
16 Christopher Hibbert, *Edward VII: A Portrait*, Harmondsworth, Penguin, 1982, pp. 198–199; 'Metropolitan notes', *The Hackney Express, Shoreditch Observer and Bethnal Green Advertiser*, 26 July 1902, p. 2. Photographs of Balfour's car are found in 'Balfour's new car', *The Autocar*, 26 July 1902, p. 82, and 'A. J. Balfour's car', *The Autocar*, 13 December 1902, p. 620.
17 'Music hall gossip', *The Era*, 4 April 1903, p. 20.
18 'Mr and Mrs Gus Elen leaving Edith villa in their motor "The Idler"', *The Era*, 30 May 1903, p. 21.
19 'Variety gossip', *The Era*, 18 January 1908, p. 22.
20 'Music hall gossip', *The Era*, 26 March 1904, p. 20.

21 George Robey, *My Life Up Till Now*, London, Greening, 1908, p. 22. In one of the more unlikely examples of up-to-dateness, in November 1910, Clive Bell referred to Bertrand Russell as an 'automobile of intellect'. Clive Bell, as quoted in Peter Stansky, *On or About December 1910: Early Bloomsbury and its Intimate World*, London, Harvard University Press, 1997, p. 208.

22 'Music hall gossip', *The Era,* 29 November, 1902, p. 22.

23 'Music hall gossip', *The Era*, 18 April 1903, p. 20; 'Music hall gossip', *The Era*, 3 October 1903, p. 20.

24 'Walford Bodie MD', *The Era*, 28 November 1903, p. 35.

25 'Bransby Williams, Motorist', *The Era*, 2 January 1909, p. 27.

26 Bransby Williams, *An Actor's Story*, London, Chapman and Hall, 1909, photographic plate, unnumbered pages

27 'Music hall gossip', *The Era*, 11 March 1905, p. 20.

28 'Variety gossip', *The Era*, 12 October 1907, p. 22.

29 'Variety gossip', *The Era*, 10 August 1907, p. 20; Untitled, *The Era*, 9 November 1907, p. 40. For an existing copy of a film showing the construction of an automobile see *Building a Motor Car* (1913), viewing copy, British Film Institute, London.

30 Untitled, *The Era*, 6 June 1908, p. 35.

31 'Variety gossip', *The Era*, 14 July 1906, p. 20.

32 'Variety gossip', *The Era*, 10 October 1908, p. 22.

33 'Variety gossip', *The Era*, 9 October 1909, p. 22.

34 'The age of records', *The Illustrated Sporting and Dramatic News*, 31 May 1913, p. 656.

35 Billy Merson, *Fixing the Stoof Oop*, London, Hutchinson, 1925, p. 89.

36 Merson, *Fixing the Stoof*, photographic plate, unnumbered pages.

37 'Mr Seymour Hicks spends a strenuous day in town', *Daily Mail*, 20 December 1910, p. 8, and 'The Quaker girl goes shopping', *Daily Mail*, 15 December 1910, p. 8.

38 'Chirgwin and some of his family motoring', *The Era*, 24 January 1903, p. 2. For his motoring stories see Untitled, *The Era*, 7 February 1903, p. 24, and 'Music hall gossip', *The Era*, 6 June 1903, p. 20.

39 'Variety gossip', *The Era*, 10 September 1913, p. 20; 'The car of Caruso', *The Illustrated Sporting and Dramatic News*, 18 October 1913, p. 304.

40 Miss Kitty Loftus, *The Autocar*, 22 November 1902, p. 515.

41 'The playhouses', *The Illustrated London News*, 6 June 1903, p. 853.

42 'Music hall gossip', *The Era*, 2 May 1903, p. 20, and S. Gordon Hunter, 'Physique at the Hippodrome', *Sandow's Magazine of Physical Culture*, 12 (1904), pp. 307–308.

43 'Music hall gossip', *The Era*, 2 May 1903, p. 20.

44 'Variety gossip', *The Era*, 25 November 1905, p. 20.

45 Untitled photograph, *The Sketch*, 5 April 1911, p. 401.

46 'Variety gossip', *The Era*, 28 June 1913, p. 18; W. MacQueen-Pope, *The Melodies Linger On,* London, W. H. Allen, 1951, p. 364.

47 Advertisement, *The Edmonton and Tottenham Wednesday Herald*, 5 March 1913, p. 1.

48 Charlie Chester, *The Grand Order of Water Rats,* London, W. H. Allen, 1984, p. 14, and 'Variety gossip', *The Era,* 16 May 1908, p. 22.

49 'Variety gossip', *The Era,* 6 June 1908, p. 20.

50 'The Rats motoring', *The Era,* 4 July 1908, p. 23.

51 'Variety gossip', *The Era,* 26 June 1909, p. 20; 'Variety gossip', *The Era,* 3 July 1909, p. 20.

52 'Rats' run to Brighton', *The Era,* 10 July 1909, p. 22; William Boddy, 'The motor-course', in Charles Gardner (ed.), *Fifty Years of Brooklands,* London, Heinemann, 1956, p. 47.

53 Reynard, 'Fun and frolic: a merry meeting at White Hart Lane', *Daily Chronicle,* 6 March 1914, p. 8. These sporting spectaculars are discussed in detail in later chapters.

54 Reynard, 'All sorts of sport at Chelsea', *Daily Chronicle,* 19 February 1914, p. 8. This match is discussed in detail in later chapters.

55 'Referee joins the game', *Daily Express,* 19 February 1914, p. 8.

56 'The charity sports day at Tottenham', *The Encore,* 12 March 1914, pp. 16–17. This match is also discussed in detail in later chapters.

57 S. B. Saul, 'The motor industry in Britain to 1914', *Business History,* 5.1 (1962), pp. 41–43.

58 Frank Bruce, '"You had to be game to stay in yon business": a working life in variety theatre, 1920-1950', *Oral History,* Autumn 1996, p. 70.

59 Bruce, 'You had to be game', p. 69.

60 'Music hall gossip', *The Era,* 12 September 1903, p. 20.

61 'Variety gossip', *The Era,* 26 February 1910, p. 22.

62 Advertisement, *The Era,* 7 June 1913, p. 15.

63 'Variety gossip', *The Era,* 16 December 1905, p. 22; 'Variety gossip', *The Era,* 31 March 1906, p. 22; 'Variety gossip', *The Era,* 17 October 1908, p. 22.

64 'Motor gossip', *The Era,* 9 November 1907, p. 15; Advertisement, *The Encore,* 7 May 1914, p. 24.

65 'Music hall world', *The Encore,* 30 January 1913, p. 9.

66 'Motor gossip', *The Era,* 2 November 1907, p. 15. For artistes selling automobiles see 'Variety gossip', *The Era,* 10 March, 1906, p. 22; Untitled photograph, *The Era,* 4 June 1910, p. 22 and 'Variety gossip', *The Era,* 15 October 1910, p. 22.

67 Charles Collins, 'If you can't buy a motor-car, buy a motor cap' (1904), British Library catalogue of printed music.

6

Aeroplanes

The aeroplane was the last major technological development in transportation before the First World War. The Wright brothers first flew at Kitty Hawk, North Carolina, in December 1903, culminating a global fascination with mechanised flight. Ballooning from the lawns of the Crystal Palace and Earls Court Exhibition Grounds was popular amongst some, like the pantomime star Fred Leslie, who could afford the pastime, and as early as 1875 writers of melodrama had incorporated this passion by making foreign spies attempt to escape their pursuers by balloon in climactic stage scenes, while 'professors' of parachuting had performed at the Crystal Palace and Alexandra Palace in north London where they had leapt from balloons that were tethered above the watching crowds.[1] Disregarded in Britain, the Wrights were given an accommodating welcome from the French who quickly took the lead in European flight.

As increased attention was devoted to the problems of sustainable, mechanised flight, engineers and inventors shifted their focus away from dirigibles to man-carrying kites, the real precursors of aeroplanes. Because there was very minimal government sponsorship for aircraft development and construction in England, advances were made, as with the Wrights in America, by self-funded men working alone, often without direct contact or knowledge of one another. As a result, early flight in England was identified very closely in the public imagination with the individual exploits of these few widely idolised aviators. Pioneer aeronauts designed, cobbled, sewed and spliced together fragile machines. If they did not possess sufficient private capital they were forced to use their inventions to garner money from the public. The need to generate funding through public performances caused tensions up until the First World War between those who believed in a sober, scientific approach to flight where pilots would be 'notabilities, not notorieties' and a faction who were forced to take up passengers in order to continue flying.[2] The public were not so avidly interested in flight as a scientific concept governed by empirically tested laws as they were in the exploits of individual engineers, pilots and promoters. This was not wholly positive as many pioneer pilots died in their planes through an ignorance of, and inability to calculate, the critical structural loads and stresses to which machines were subjected.

The careers of several of the most prominent of these men followed fairly closely popular culture's continuous incorporation of technological innovations. The Honourable Charles Rolls was the Eton- and Cambridge-educated younger son of a Monmouthshire aristocrat. Born in 1877, he grew up fascinated by mechanics and after matriculating at Trinity College in 1896 he won a half-blue as a member of the University bicycle club. Rolls forsook cycling during his second year at college when he was given an automobile.[3] His interest in motoring was sustained and in 1900 he helped his friend Claude Johnson organise the Thousand Miles Trial. Two years later Rolls opened a car dealership in Fulham selling the most technically advanced and luxurious French marques. He was ubiquitous as a motoring journalist and from 1904 produced cars in partnership with Henry Royce.[4] Driving successes in races staged both in England and on the continent made Rolls a national celebrity by 1905, the year in which the automobile attained its maturity.[5]

Rolls was a restless, physically active man and when automobiles became his business he took to ballooning as his hobby. The Aero Club, whose offices were in Piccadilly, was co-founded by Rolls in 1901 to promote this sport, which one of the club's earliest members contended was 'the only way to go into the air like a gentleman'.[6] However, Rolls tempered ballooning's patrician posing with business acumen by prominently displaying examples of his firm's cars during his sporting weekends at the family seat in Wales. Whenever the opportunity offered, Rolls used these parties to make a sale to one of his aeronaut guests.[7] Neither was the motor-racing Rolls satisfied with the plodding pace of ballooning. He undertook his first aeroplane ride in France, as a passenger of Wilbur Wright, in 1908 and thereafter limited his involvement with the daily administration of his car company in order to fly, taking little direct interest in automobiles until his death in July 1910 at Bournemouth when his plane's wings buckled in mid-air.[8]

The life of Tommy Sopwith mirrored that of his elder colleague. Sopwith was born in London into a wealthy family in 1888 and as a boy spent his school holidays cycling through the capital and sailing in the sea off the family's Scottish estate. Rejected by the Navy, Sopwith attended engineering college and in 1903 opened an automobile showroom in Albermarle Street, Piccadilly. Sopwith bought his first motorcycle in 1904 and, thanks to Rolls' encouragement, began ballooning two years later. But balloons could not hold Sopwith's mechanical fascinations for long and so he purchased his first aeroplane in 1910, after which he toured the United States for two years in pursuit of prize money before returning to open an aviation school at Brooklands aerodrome, near Weybridge, Surrey.[9] From the outset Sopwith approached flying as a profit-generating business as well as a hobby and he successfully manufactured aeroplanes for sale at his Brooklands works, the daily management of which forced him to engage test pilots and retire from flying.

Rolls and Sopwith had the endowments, business acumen and leisure to pursue flying in a country where public funds were scarce. They were also two of the most recognisable and important figures in British aviation before the First World War, but three of their contemporaries, 'Colonel' Samuel Franklin Cody, Claude Grahame-White and Alliott Verdon-Roe were equally famous and important. Colonel Cody was an American-born showman whose music-hall wild west act was the greatest British rival to that of Buffalo Bill Cody, to whom he was not related. At the turn of the century Cody retired from the stage to concentrate on building flying machines. From their hyphenated family names it is possible to deduce that Grahame-White and Verdon-Roe followed in Rolls' and Sopwith's tradition of genteel flyers. However, Grahame-White was also a keen businessman who exploited flying's spectacular potential whilst Verdon-Roe, who was chronically under-funded and excluded from leading aerodromes, established his flying base on the Lea Marshes, before he too accumulated a fortune from designing and selling planes.

Born in Texas in 1861, Cody spent much of his youth building and flying box-kites. In early adulthood he worked in the saddle on his family's property, drove cattle herds across-country to distant rail-heads, becoming an expert rider and rifle-shot and spent 1883 and 1884 in the Klondyke prospecting for gold. On his return to Texas he was engaged to ferry a cargo of horses to England. In London he and his fellow cowboys went sightseeing dressed in their gaudy clothes only to provoke bemused attention from the fashionable riders in Rotten Row who were aware of the American west through cheap novels but did not see many real cowboys until Buffalo Bill's first visit in 1887.[10]

Cody met and married an Englishwoman before returning to live in America where he developed a trick-shooting show. He was eventually persuaded by his wife to capitalise on Buffalo Bill's popularity by trying his act on the British music halls. The show was an immense success at the Alhambra, Leicester

Square. Initially Lela Cody alone held the glass targets for her husband, but later their sons were skilled enough to be included in an act where glasses were shot from atop one another's heads and out of each others' hands. These feats were usually accomplished under some severe impediment to the marksman such as hanging upside down from a trapeze or sighting with the aid of a hand-mirror a rifle that was cradled backwards over the shoulder. Cody advertised the family act by riding through the streets in full costume on a mustang at the head of his small troupe, much as Buffalo Bill had done with his grander wild west show.[11]

The Codys toured Europe successfully and were especially popular in France where the show was expanded to accommodate the bicycle craze with races between the Colonel on horseback and champion cyclists over long distances. Obviously a galloping horse was much faster than even the quickest cyclists but Cody was a master at feigning injuries during the race which forced him out of the saddle for long periods of recuperation. These convalescences allowed his opponent to pass into the lead. Cody's sense of theatre was impeccable for at the last possible moment he recovered miraculously, mounted up and charged to victory. During his time on the continent Cody grew his black hair to his shoulders and adopted the goatee and waxed moustaches worn by French dandies in emulation of the late emperor Napoleon III before returning to England looking like his namesake cowboy rival.

The family combined these two acts on their return to London where they devised an outdoor wild west show at their base at the Alexandra Palace. This remained an impecunious version of Buffalo Bill's show as the only North American Indians to be seen were impersonated by the Englishman Edward Leroy.[12] Nevertheless, these initial outdoor events were very popular and earned a great deal of money for Colonel Cody. In the wake of the family's appearance at the Wood Green, north London track during London's cycling boom of 1896 commentators wished 'that there were more of this sort of thing going on in London, for it draws a gate and pleases the crowd – a state of things pleasing to the promoter and to the pleasure-seeker'.[13] The show's success led the Codys to develop a condensed stage version and to embark on a national tour.

When a vast gold field was discovered in the Klondyke in 1896 Cody decided to reset his cowboy show in the Canadian tundra. *Klondyke Nugget* had seven elaborate scenes depicting prospectors fighting a malevolent sheriff played by Cody. It was immensely popular from its début at the Alexandra Palace in 1898 and thereafter toured Britain endlessly, generating the fortune that Cody invested in flying.[14] Cody's childhood interest in kites was re-ignited in Edinburgh on the earliest stages of the *Klondyke Nugget* tour in 1899 when he saw a group of boys flying them in a park. He became obsessed with the idea of building a man-lifting device. Initially, by flying his experimental kites at every provincial date and at the Alexandra Palace, Cody coupled his renewed hobby with his performances of *Klondyke Nugget,* with which he toured until 1904. While the show played London, Cody spent the early mornings with his sons, clad in their cowboy clothes, experimenting with kites.[15] Cody also flew his enormous box-kites in parks, fields and from the roofs of provincial halls. Eventually Cody, Lela and their sons all flew from a wicker chair suspended below these kites to demonstrate their potential use for transportation, and though these machines never bore aloft the name *Klondyke Nugget* they were immensely successful in attracting crowds to the halls.[16]

As early as 1903 the posters for Cody's act displayed one of his box-kites and billed him as the 'inventor of the famous war kite'.[17] In the same year Cody announced in *Pearson's Magazine* 'I do not wish to assert that I have produced a flying machine in the full sense of the term, but I must confess that I have ambitions in that direction; and I hope at no very distant date to play an important part in the complete conquest of the air'.[18] Apart from a public announcement of his intentions, Cody did something equally dramatic but more subtle by uttering these words because with them he declared that he would seriously and publicly undertake what had until that time been only his hobby. Cody formally retired from the stage in 1905, returning to the Alexandra Palace where he tested his kites extensively, while travelling companies of *Klondyke Nugget* meant that he continued receiving regular royalty payments.[19] Though he was now a professional aviator, the popular idea that he was 'a theatrical cowboy sort of person' clung to him.[20]

Cody then joined a War Office project, based at Salisbury, evaluating airships for military purposes. Despite the patina of respectability, these government-sanctioned trials were underwritten by the *Klondyke Nugget.* It was only with the successful and sensational flight of the experimental military dirigible *Nulli Secundus,* which flew lumberingly across central London in 1907, that Cody was accepted by the public as a legitimate pilot.[21] The marriage was not ideal because military authorities preferred to develop dirigibles while Cody favoured developing winged aircraft. Eventually Cody left the project, though the War Office allowed him to maintain his hangars at Salisbury. It was there that he made the first mechanically powered flight in the British Empire, in a plane of his own design, on the sixteenth of October 1908, barely five years after the Wright brothers' first flight.[22] Britain's first pilot had originally been a music-hall artiste.

Though his work was laudable and he was the first aviator on British soil, Cody found it difficult to win continued public acceptance for the seriousness of his flying career. Unlike 'gentlemen' flyers, Cody was suspected of being an untalented publicity-seeking showman.[23] This criticism was to some extent apt: Cody's aeroplanes were mocked by critics as 'flying cathedrals' because their enormous silk wings were buttressed by a gothic elaboration of spars, struts and wires. Penury forced Cody to construct his frames of bamboo while other builders used metal. These machines were ungainly, extremely difficult to fly and, because Cody adamantly refused to incorporate new technology, increasingly outmoded. Moreover, Cody's striking appearance at six feet three inches tall dressed in a flying suit consisting of a 'ten-gallon' stetson hat, shoulder length hair, waxed moustaches, goatee, cravat and high-heeled cowboy boots, leant itself to self-promotion, but also to mockery.

Because of the difficulty he encountered in publicly legitimising his flying, Cody maintained an ambivalent and often truculent relationship with the music halls. Circumstances also forced Cody to exploit his fame, because when the financial returns from *Klondyke Nugget* were depleted he depended on winning prizes, giving flying lessons to eager undergraduates and military officers and charging for passenger rides. The Cody aeroplane works always hovered on the cusp of bankruptcy because very few of his temperamental cathedrals were sold. Salisbury was a remote base for someone relying on public subscriptions and so Cody was a regular participant at the Hendon, north London aeroplane rallies from their beginning. Despite these efforts, the Colonel was unable to disavow his past completely. Edward Leroy and the Cody family, essentially the same company with which he had worked the halls, staffed his Salisbury hangar.[24] Because Cody remained friends with many people in the industry he demonstrated his kites at select halls like the London Palladium, in order to further expound the seriousness of his work, but also to keep his name before the public.[25] He began concealing his hair in his hat, because it better suited a sober pilot. His head was eventually shorn. However, Cody's music-hall promotional experiences remained with him in 'the hoarse husky voice in which he would address waiting crowds, his instinct for the audience, his liking for handbills, display, and brass bands'.[26] The cash crisis must have come to a head in 1911 when he agreed to release pamphlets advertising the appearance of a 'turn' over Aldershot.[27]

Cutting his hair was an overt sign of Cody's unease about recalling his showman past after his acceptance as a serious flyer. When Salisbury accorded him a benefit reception at the local music hall where he saw an exhibition of photographs depicting a cowboy's daily life, he pointed to the screen and commented that 'there you see my boyhood days – but this is a fake'.[28] It was only when a woman with whom he had worked in the early part of his career came on stage that he allowed himself to become nostalgic about his previous persona.[29] Salisbury's celebration of Cody's achievements reflected the public's blending of both halves of his life. Sometimes the showman was emphasised while at others the crowds hailed him as a flying pioneer. Cody was less comfortable with this dual basis for public fascination.

Colonel Cody and his young passenger were killed at Salisbury in August 1913 because of the mid-air structural collapse of a sea plane he was developing for a round-Britain rally. Just like the serious half of his life that he romantically devoted to flying, his sacrificial, imperially heroic death scene was worthy of anything boys read in *Chums* or *The Magnet*. His sons Leon and Frank were working nearby in the family hangar and ran to the scene where they knelt over his prostrate body pitifully sobbing 'oh, dad, dad, dad!'.[30] Colleagues from both of his careers honoured their dead friend. A matinee performance at the Hippodrome, Leicester Square with forty-five top music-hall artistes was held in the traditional professionals' manner of raising money for distressed families. Two passenger flights for Hendon were auctioned from the stage in a confident, if somewhat macabre, tribute to the public's unshakeable fascination with flying.[31] A similar memorial performance was held at Aldershot, while leading pilots then honoured Cody with an aerial exhibition above Aintree racecourse in Liverpool.[32]

If Cody was the artiste who linked the halls most directly with flight in England, then Claude Graham-White was early flying's greatest and most up-to-date promoter and showman. Grahame-White was born in 1879 to a comfortably wealthy Hampshire family. Like Rolls, he was interested in mechanics as a boy, and he was as keen a sailor as Sopwith. He and his brother built their own bicycles and were champion riders throughout their teens though Claude graduated to automobiles after seeing the 1896 London–Brighton rally.[33] In 1905 he opened an automobile dealership in Albermarle Street nearby Sopwith's and began ballooning the following year.[34] This growing interest in flying meant that he gradually shifted the emphasis of his showrooms at Albermarle Street from automobiles to aeroplanes.[35] He flew initially from Brooklands but in 1910 Grahame-White bought more than two hundred acres of land at Hendon in North London to develop into a commercial aerodrome. The elaborate plans drawn up for Hendon required a great deal of capital to realise and so, because the prize-purses available to flyers were greater in the

United States, Grahame-White crossed the Atlantic in 1910 to compete in rallies, winning $250,000.[36]

When he returned home the next year, Grahame-White entered into partnership with the French aviator and aeroplane designer Louis Blériot and the Anglo-American inventor Sir Hiram Maxim, and floated a public company to develop the land at Hendon. The three men envisaged this north-London airfield as a sort of aviation luna park which would capitalise on the craze of flying. Hendon lay only six miles north of Marble Arch and the promoters felt – like Oswald Stoll's lawyers when his syndicate planned a new suburban hall, or like football club directors – that convenient access by road, rail and Underground would establish it as a successful rival to other popular resorts. When less than half the necessary capital was raised Grahame-White decided personally to underwrite the initial phase of construction consisting of seventeen hangars, grandstands and refreshment rooms.[37]

The London Aerodrome was conceived at a time when promoters were developing permanent popular entertainment 'theme parks' in London. The first and most successful of these venues was Imre Kiralfy's Exhibition Grounds at White City, which opened in 1908. White City hosted a profitable annual series of Imperial and World's Fairs that glorified the products of scientific and mechanical progress. Kiralfy, a onetime associate of Barnum, amassed a Byzantine fortune from these shows whose run ended only when the site was requisitioned by the government as a training base during the First World War.[38] Fred Karno attempted to develop a similar venue for music hall when he ruinously opened his Karsino on Tagg's Island in the Thames at Hampton Court in 1913. Launches ferried patrons up the river from central London to this music hall, restaurant, casino, amusement park and hotel where people could socialise with artistes. Even with Karno's theatrical sensibilities behind the project, inflated construction costs, constantly inclement weather, an inability to attract sufficient customers and the outbreak of war doomed both it and his empire. After several failed attempts to remain in the music-hall business and a stint in Hollywood living on Chaplin and Laurel's charity, Karno retired to run an off-licence in his native Exeter.[39]

Grahame-White's business acumen was as astute as Kiralfy's while his promotional instincts rivalled Karno's. He and Pauline Chase, the actress who originally played Peter Pan, had been friends for many years and this personal proximity to the entertainment industry may have given Grahame-White much of the inspiration for the development of Hendon. He flew several popular young stars on his American tour during which he also landed his plane on one of Washington's broad avenues for a scheduled visit with President Taft. Citing his personal safety the president refused the offer of a ride, which was perhaps wise given his legendary girth and the limited horsepower of the first aeroplane engines.[40] Such promotional devices, coupled with his successes in the cockpit, made Grahame-White a popular idol in the United States. During his American stay he was also very publicly engaged to marry Chase who was then starring on Broadway, although the betrothal did not last. Links between the skies and the stage were more durable in the United States, for while in Boston, flying, Grahame-White attended a production of an up-to-date comedy entitled *The Aviator* by George M. Cohan where he was recognised and applauded by the audience.[41] Even the most casual or flippant comments by celebrity pilots were reported by an eager American press and facetious, Bertie Woosterish sayings attributed to Grahame-White like 'I say, old fellow, what a splendid show!' boomed current plays from public placards.[42]

With these experiences behind him, considerations about flying's potential as entertainment were never far removed from Grahame-White's vision for Hendon. Partly out of economic self-interest, Grahame-White co-operated with Lord Northcliffe on a campaign to 'Wake up England!' in 1912 by which they hoped both to demystify and popularise flight and to make the authorities aware of the need for a military air corps. *The Daily Mail* reported enthusiastically on the activities of Grahame-White's group of pilots who visited the biggest cities and most popular resorts throughout July and August to demonstrate the aeroplane's potential.[43] Meanwhile, the government which had at one point relied on Cody's funding, awakened, slowly, to flight. Much of this was due to the efforts of Colonel John Seely, the soldier, sportsman and politician who, after going up with Grahame-White in 1909, boasted of having been the first cabinet minister to fly.[44] Seely took over the War Office in 1912 and collaborated with his fellow reformer and flying enthusiast Winston Churchill, after the latter became First Lord of the Admiralty the next year, in a brief to build up Britain's air defences.[45] Whitehall's interest in and financial backing of aviation dated from these ministerial investitures.

Meanwhile, spring 1911 saw the opening of the comedy *The Belle of the Skies*, perhaps the very first British aviation play, at Birmingham's Theatre Royal.[46] Grahame-White simultaneously brought his 'American' acumen to London when he publicly announced he would fly a Bioscope Company cameraman over the Coronation procession, though he was prevented from doing so by a nervous government's intervention.[47] The dramatists of the Women's Aerial League then adapted the play *Mona Vanna* to centre on female flyers.

They presented Grahame-White with a medal during the 'friendly, if incongruous' interlude to the performance, during which his work in promoting the sport as a pastime for women was cheered.[48] Capitalising on this female interest, Hendon then hosted its first Ladies' Day, at which Christabel Pankhurst, a member of the Women's Aerial League, was the most memorable guest.[49]

This was not purely altruistic interest in the advancement of science, because the popularity of Northcliffe's 'new journalism' rested on sensational publicity stunts which capitalised on current public fascinations.[50] By nature these stunts were of short duration and topically mirrored public opinion. Hence Northcliffe's initial support for motoring. In the years before the First World War, aviation was the central 'talking point' boomed by Northcliffe's papers.[50] Northcliffe's biography was very similar to those of many early pilots as he cycled around London in his youth and was an enthusiastic motorist in the 1890s. He had helped to finance the Thousand Miles Trial for automobiles and had written the volume on motoring for the popular *Badminton Library of Sports* in 1900. He switched his allegiance to aviation after seeing the Wright brothers fly at Pau, France. In 1909 his £1,000 prize induced Blériot, after a suitably publicised nationalistic duel with the English pilot Herbert Latham, to fly the Channel fly on 25 July after which the Frenchman was fêted at a dinner and his monoplane was displayed in the window of Selfridges department store on Oxford Street.[52] After paying out the prize for the first man to fly the Channel, Northcliffe hoped to repeat the sensation of that duel by offering another one for the first man to fly non-stop between London and Manchester, the cities in which the *Daily Mail* was printed. As planes grew more reliable Northcliffe endowed a competition for the first flight around the British Isles and on the eve of the war he announced a prize for the first transatlantic flight.

While the skies hailed the first airborne suffragette, Harry Tate performed his newest disaster-laden sketch, *Flying*. *Flying* was an updated version of *Motoring* in which Tate's plane disintegrated in mid-flight in a flash of smoke and fireworks. This sketch topically commented on the frantic pursuit of aerial prizes and the macabre unreliability of early aeroplanes. *Flying* was boomed by posters bearing the legend 'Aviation Week'. When Tate arrived these advertisements were updated 'by two men with bills resembling a "rush" contents bill of a newspaper with "descent of an aviator"', in the music hall in which Tate was appearing.[53]

Northcliffe's *Daily Mail* sponsored a 'Circuit of Britain' air race in 1911; at the first stage on Saturday thirty to forty thousand people saw the twenty-one entrants take off from Brooklands for Hendon.[54] As the second leg of the race only began at first light on the Monday, the contestants attended the Hippodrome, Leicester Square, on Saturday evening to watch film of their day's flying and to hear a speech from Grahame-White. In that film the competitors were each shown sitting in their cockpits, taking off and circling above the aerodrome; while the flyers were in the theatre a crowd camped out at Hendon to be sure of witnessing the planes taking off at dawn on Monday.[55] Several theatrical celebrities also braved the uncommonly early hours to watch their new friends take off.[56] After the end of the race, on the following Saturday, artistes were reunited with their aviator chums when the latter appeared on the Hippodrome stage, under Grahame-White's leadership.[57]

1912 was the year that the 'Hendon habit', relentlessly promoted by Grahame-White, finally took off and his vision of aviation as a remunerative public spectacle was predominant. The summer season opened at Easter after which meetings were held every Saturday. Tournaments and special 'theme' days were interspersed with these regular racing derbies throughout the year. As a mundane, strictly commercial enterprise hangars were hired out to other aviators.[58] Much of Hendon's success was captured in *With the Airmen*, a book written by Grahame-White to advertise Hendon in 1913. After extolling the aerodrome's amenities, the author announced that one could reserve tickets in advance through the offices of a leading West End theatrical booking agency with which a direct telephone line had been established. On the chosen day one simply rang the aerodrome to ensure that planes were flying, and then took the underground to Hendon.[59] Brooklands, which was never as aggressive as its rival, then hired its own West End wicket.[60]

Under Richard Gates's daily management Hendon developed neither as an élitist venue for sporting flyers, nor as a place where scientific experiments were carried out. Rather, the London Aerodrome reflected Gates's ability to understand the public mood. Gates pioneered 'crazy', or 'ragtime' flying in which pilots put their machines through perilous twists and turns in the air in an effort to reflect syncopated jazz dances. During the week Gates oversaw Grahame-White's operations conscientiously, but at the weekends he led the stunt pilots from the air, causing the editors of *The Aeroplane*, who were normally antipathetic to all but scientific and gentlemanly flying, to concede that Gates was the most talented show pilot of the day.[61]

The second Alexandra Day, in June 1912, was selected as the date for one of these special promotional meetings and so Grahame-White loaded his plane with rose petals and flew across London dispersing them on the crowds below.[62]

Grahame-White next linked industry with his venture, by inviting publicity-conscious firms to sponsor open days at the aerodrome. The most famous pilots of the day, many of whom lacked funding and needed public patronage to continue, attended these meetings where their abilities were scrutinised by the crowds. The earliest planes flew at well below sixty miles per hour and so they could easily be watched from the tea rooms and grand stands. One did not have to remain on the ground at Hendon because a standard set of prices ranging from £2.2.0d. for 'two circuits of the aerodrome' to the £5.5.0d. 'special flight' going 'outside the aerodrome, in the direction of Edgware', were charged by pilots to more adventurous spectators.[63] Other impecunious flyers, but 'expert aviators and aeronauts', also advertised their flight services for 'public and private entertainments' in the pages of *The Era*.[64]

The last member of the trio of fliers introduced above, Alliott Verdon-Roe, was born in Manchester in 1877. His father was a motoring enthusiast who had helped to found the Automobile Club in London. Alliot was a passionate cyclist, who left St Paul's School at fifteen to work in British Columbia, and later studied marine engineering at King's College, London, before working as a ship's officer with the British South Africa Royal Mail Company. Over time he became fascinated by sea birds in flight, quit his job and joined the motor industry as a draughtsman, but he designed model aircraft, by then his sole passion, in the evenings.[65]

Roe graduated from scale-models to pilot his first aeroplane from his base at Brooklands, then not normally open to flyers, in 1907, when he and John Brabazon were lured to Weybridge by the £2,500 prize offered by the circuit's directors for the first man to fly around the motor track. Neither succeeded.[66] Even though its directors publicly supported flight, Roe was only grudgingly permitted to build a wooden hangar at Brooklands, and so he was compelled to leave the race-track the following year. After being refused permission to re-erect his hangar either alongside Cody's at Salisbury, or in London at Wormwood Scrubs or Wimbledon Common, Verdon-Roe realised that he did not need permission to fly from the Lea Marshes.[67]

On an initial inspection tour he hired two nearby railway arches as his base and moved his plane there in early 1908.[68] But the Marshes were only ever a temporary stop for Verdon-Roe as the ground near his workshop was dotted with tree stumps, to which local inhabitants tethered their animals. The Marshes were also replete with football pitches and were bordered tightly by a fence to one side and the River Lea on the other. Such physical obstacles were augmented by the angry drunkards and homeless people who were roused from sleep by Roe's early morning flights and also the sarcastic comments of more lucid observers. Roe was then forced to take off at inconveniently early hours in order to avoid the bailiffs dispatched by a nervous local authority to prevent him from flying on the Marshes.[69] His schedule may not have allowed many Londoners to see him fly, but Verdon-Roe's experiments were the most intimate public facet of early flight in the capital.

When, from July 1909, he did fly on the Marshes, it was generally for short 'hops' of between 10 and 120 yards. Even then Verdon-Roe's aeroplane was followed by a man on a bicycle carrying a fire extinguisher and others afoot laden with tools to repair the inevitable crash damages. As Verdon-Roe later told his biographer 'a 50 yd. hop, a crash and then two weeks' work' was the normal schedule on the Marshes.[70] Flying required money, which he could not garner on the Marshes, and so with his brother Alliott founded A. V. Roe Aviation to manufacture aeroplanes commercially in 1909. He accompanied Grahame-White on the money-generating tour to America the following year where theatre placards displayed the laudation 'It's a jolly good play!', attributed to Verdon-Roe, but worthy of any member of the Drones Club, on the pavement outside.[71] On his return Verdon-Roe settled once again at Brooklands.

Grahame-White's earnestness in developing Hendon on his return from America reflected his desire to exploit the ways in which he had seen flight shows staged in that country. As Verdon-Roe recalled of his own return from that tour;

> On arriving at Brooklands I produced the Boston newspaper. The word 'stunt' was used frequently; it was unknown here at the time. This was just the word Brooklands had been waiting for. It was soon in universal use at Brooklands and then the racing drivers got hold of it, and so it went. The journalese of those days for flyers was 'Intrepid Birdmen', so 'intrepidity' was the word often used jokingly by us.[72]

American promoters and reporters showed British airmen how to develop the entertainment aspect of flying and also gave them the language with which to promote their shows. The etymology of the word stunt roughly bears out Roe's chronology as the first instance of its usage in the sense of an event designed to attract attention was in 1901. 'Stunt' was first applied to aerobatics in a September 1909 article in *Flight* magazine.[73]

Amidst this excitement, commercial advertisers remembered William Smith's mid-Victorian admonition to incorporate popular interests. Boots the Chemists' 1909 Christmas advertising campaign in the *Daily Mail* reflected Northcliffe's stunts and the popular fascination with technology. Full-page promotions featured Father Christmas piloting a 'Wright Flyer' laden with presents on its wings with the slogan 'straight as a bird from Boots, with Xmas [sic] gifts suitable for all'.[74] The turf accountant Douglas Stuart advertised his company's services with a picture of an aeroplane and the reassuring slogan, 'The man who flies is no use to you'.[75] Beecham's pills, a patent medicine that claimed to cure most ills, were taken with 'water (plain)' and promoted in 1913 by a picture of a sea-plane taking off.[76] Amalgam Tyres capitalised on Hendon's popularity at the end of 1913 when they flew a couple of kites bearing their company motto at the entrance to the aerodrome.[77] Finally, in 1914, Players' Navy Cut cigarettes featured drawings of the latest aircraft with accompanying written descriptions in their newspaper advertisements.[78] The number of examples of these advertisements is only limited by the amount of time devoted to finding them (Figure 8).

Because of the excitement flying generated, forward-looking painters took it up as a subject. Spencer Gore was one of the leading members of the Camden Town group of artists who gathered at the turn of the century around the Fitzroy Street studio of Walter Sickert to record post-impressionist scenes of ordinary London life.[79] These artists were always acutely aware of popular sensations, and the most famous Camden Town studies remain those painted by Sickert and Gore of the performers at the Old Bedford, Middlesex and Alhambra music halls. The Camden Town painters were fascinated by popular culture and so on 6 July 1912 Gore led a party to Hendon where they went up in Blériot aeroplanes and admired the trick flying. Gore was inspired by this excursion

(Camera Portrait, Hoppé)

Nerve Strain—

Mr. B. C. HUCKS (the well-known Flying Man), of 5, Queen's Gate Terrace, London, S.W., writes:— "I really must express my appreciation of Phosferine. Some time back I felt myself in a curious state of nervous tension, brought on, no doubt, by the severe strain caused by flying under all sorts of weather conditions for the "Daily Mail" tour last summer. I had an idea that my nerves were becoming shaken. I was advised to try Phosferine, and was quite astonished at the beneficial effect produced by even the first few doses. I am now feeling more 'fit' than ever and ready to start upon a season's flying that promises to be considerably more arduous than the last."

No other medicine has received such absolute proof of its extraordinary properties in restoring Shattered Constitutions, and in giving back to the prematurely aged New Life and Energy.

CAUTION

There is only one Phosferine—beware of illegal imitations— do not be misled by *Phosph This* or *Phosph That*, but get

PHOSFERINE
THE REMEDY OF KINGS

Phosferine has been supplied by Royal Commands

To the Royal Family	H.M. the Queen of Spain
H.I.M. the Empress of Russia	H.M. the late King of Greece
H.M. the King of Spain	H.M. the Queen of Roumania, etc.

The 2/9 size contains nearly four times the 1/1½ size.

8   Pilots become celebrities as B. C. Hucks advertises patent medicine.

to paint what may be the earliest depiction of an aeroplane. *Flying at Hendon* showed the concourse of people assembled before their motor cars. Above them a plane banked as it turned. The aeroplane's representation was simplified and flattened by Gore who reduced the machine to its essential mechanical features; a short grey-green brush stroke for the tail stabiliser and two longer ones, one slightly protruding over the other, for the main wings.[80] As Gore painted that July, the actors of the *Princess Caprice* company watched the flying at Hendon from a special enclosure. After the display they were taken up in the planes.[81]

Artistes, including a large number of motor-car parties, turned out at Hendon Aerodrome in May 1913 for a Vaudeville Aviation Sunday during which Jane Wood of the Hippodrome company was awarded a free flight as the winner of an *Era* readers' ballot.[82] The middle of June saw an equivalent Theatrical Aviation Sunday with another readers' poll in *The Era*.[83] Grahame-White saw clearly that legitimate actresses and their patrons were better customers by again holding an Alexandra Day pageant. A parade of over 100 flower-bedecked cars mustered in front of judges in Connaught Square before driving in a parade to Hendon where flower-covered planes raced one another and bombed the audience with petals.[84]

Advertisement was mutually beneficial for aviators and artistes. Marie Dainton toured the Earls Court arena atop a donkey to collect money for Cody's memorial in September 1913.[85] Later in September the entire cast of Dainton's revue *I Should Worry?* attended the meet at Hendon to watch flights by leading aviators.[86] In a pattern audiences recognised from music-hall sports matches, the competitors attended the Empire that evening as the guests of the management 'and had a big reception from a crowded house'.[87] It was not long before *Queen of the Air, the Monoplane Drama* premiered and, as with *Jail Birds*, the writers of this play advertised that the accuracy of their piece had been drawn from a week of research – in this case at the London Aerodrome.[88]

Throughout this period many songs celebrated flying and aeroplanes, which helps to explain the public reluctance to accept Cody's second career. The earliest 'aeroplane' songs were six published in 1906, two years before the Colonel brought flight to Britain. These ranged from the romance of Fred d'Albert's 'Who'll come with me for a ride in my aeroplane?' and Tom Mellor's 'In my aeroplane for two' to a pair of celebratory songs entitled simply 'In my aeroplane'.[89] Aeroplane songs were printed in each year from then until 1914. As with bicycles and motor-cars, most of their titles reflected the public's romantic associations with flying, as people danced to aeroplane waltzes and, like Hendon flyers, ventured into syncopated jazz rhythms with 'That aeroplane rag'.[90] Love was celebrated above all else, though given the noise, acrid fumes, oil sprays and the inherent brittleness and unreliability of aircraft, 1910's declaration that 'There's an aeroplane air about you' may have been a somewhat qualified avowal of amorous intentions.[91] 1914 saw the publication of 'The aeroplane march' a fittingly martial title to send the plane off to the war which saw its emergence as the dominant force in battle, though, as we have seen, this song's antecedents came as much from the long tradition of bicycle, automobile and aeroplane love and celebratory songs as from any specific militarist intent.[92]

The fear of invasion and destruction from the air grew as the war neared. In 1909 the first aerial invasion melodrama was staged: Charles Urban's *The Airship Destroyer*, in which a young man won his love's heart by single-handedly saving the country from an air attack.[93] Military dirigibles were in the forefront of the public imagination in 1910. In July the army airship *Beta* was watched by the king and queen as it flew from Aldershot past St Paul's Cathedral and on to Parliament in the early evening. Traffic stopped in the streets while drivers stared at the airship, and rooftops along the route were crowded with photographers and curious spectators.[94] Music-hall performers soon drew on this public inspiration and the Coliseum stage saw 'the wireless wonder of the world' that year when Raymond Phillips stood behind an electric control panel on the stage and guided a twenty-foot-long dirigible through the proscenium out over the audience. Astonished people gaped at the craft as it manoeuvred above the middle of the stalls. It stopped suddenly and Phillips asked his listeners to think of the havoc that the full-size version of such a machine could bring to enemy cities if it carried bombs instead of the paper toys he released by throwing a switch.[95]

George Dangerfield, who aptly called this the 'airship melodrama', charted the public perception of England's vulnerability that followed Winston Churchill's successful negotiations to limit Germany's naval construction policy. In February 1913 the threat of the Kaiser's Baltic dreadnought fleet was replaced by a series of hysterical sightings of wraith-like airships silently reconnoitring the English coast. The press disseminated news of these nocturnal visits and exploited the fears they engendered to increase circulation throughout the first half of the year.[96] Cynical Fleet Street publishers were not the only ones to utilise this public concern for their own financial benefit. In their advertisement, British and Mercantile Insurers warned that 'the real peril', as written on the sides of a (presumably German) military airship, was the misfortune caused by burglary, accident, old age, death and fire.[97]

In 1913 London's stages saw aviation melodramas which reflected this fear of imminent, unstoppable invasion. *War in the Air*, a play designed to arouse the nation to the hovering peril, whose cast included a young Noël Coward, detailed the heroics of Tommy Vincent the commander of Britain's fictional Central Aerial Station. As in many melodramas, female weakness caused the trouble. Vincent's fiancée had unwittingly allowed Britain's enemies to dupe his pilots into believing that the north-east coast was being invaded. As the British squadron headed north, the enemy's aircraft attacked Kent. Needless to say, such an evil, ungentlemanly ruse was discovered when the emboldened fiancée cabled a new warning and was avenged unsparingly as Vincent's planes destroyed the enemy fleet over Dover. These aerial battles were carried out between planes suspended on wires above the audience.[98] Subsequent performances in Willesden and Shoreditch proved to Londoners that British pilots would protect them, from both air and seaborne invasions.[99]

Meanwhile, patrons at Hendon that same month saw planes and warships, their two bogeys, oppose each other in a night attack by pilots on the wooden silhouette of a dreadnought. The aeroplanes were followed through the sky by the audience with the aid of powerful search lights. Pilots dropped dummy bombs on the ships in a scenario designed explicitly to demonstrate an air corps' ability to protect Britain from a naval invasion.[100]

The culmination of these relations between melodrama and flight came at Drury Lane in September 1913 with the production of the spy thriller *Sealed Orders*. This drama saw a Hatton Garden clerk forced, because of an addiction to gambling, to assume a false identity and spy for an unnamed foreign power. He then persuaded the dissolute daughter of a senior admiral to steal official communiqués from her father's safe for him in return for money. The finale was a 'big sensation scene' where the spy, the hero and the admiral's daughter all boarded the foreign power's airship as it landed furtively on the Downs. While the two men fought in the gondola, a British battleship fired at them from the Channel below. At the climax the dirigible was brought down and the government's secrets were retrieved (Figure 9). Because it combined so many up-to-date elements reviewers appreciated the play's status as 'the most ingenious dove-tailing together of contemporary actualities with an admirably contrived plot'.[101]

As authors had done with *The Bicycle Girl* in the 1890s, playwright George Degray sent an irate letter to *The Era* protesting that he had been the first to devise a plot which culminated with a fight on the deck of an airship in flight.

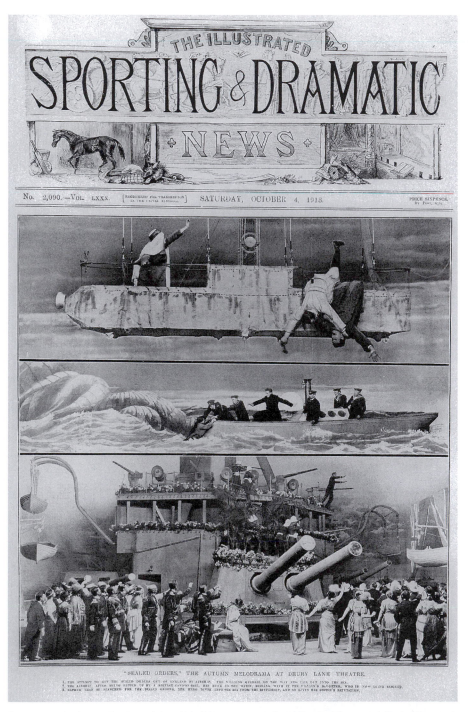

THE ILLUSTRATED SPORTING & DRAMATIC NEWS

No. 2,090.—Vol. LXXX. [REGISTERED FOR TRANSMISSION IN THE UNITED KINGDOM.] SATURDAY, OCTOBER 4, 1913. PRICE SIXPENCE By Post, 6½d.

"SEALED ORDERS," THE AUTUMN MELODRAMA AT DRURY LANE THEATRE.

1. THE ATTEMPT TO GET THE SEALED ORDERS OUT OF ENGLAND BY AIRSHIP. THE VILLAINS QUARREL ON THE WAY AND FALL OUT INTO THE SEA.
2. THE AIRSHIP, AFTER BEING RIPPED UP BY A BRITISH CANNON-BALL, HAS SUNK TO THE WATER, BEARING WITH IT THE VILLAIN'S DAUGHTER, WHO IS NOW BEING RESCUED.
3. RATHER THAN BE SEARCHED FOR THE SEALED ORDERS, THE HERO DIVES INTO THE SEA FROM THE BATTLESHIP, AND SO SAVES HIS SISTER'S REPUTATION.

9   Londoners begin to learn that the country can be defended from aerial invasion.

Degray's production was, so he claimed, already well known to provincial managers and had prospective bookings well into 1914.[102] Such letters proved once again that playwrights, like musicians, publishers and artistes were aware of how profitable it was to be the first to incorporate current hysteria into popular drama and spectacle.

The eve of the war saw the final stage in music hall's incorporation of popular culture. In May 1914 crowds watched as pilots circling at 300 feet dropped 'bombs' on a 100-foot-wide chalk target.[103] Amid fears that there were not enough flyers to defend the country adequately, some artistes, like Cody, were not content to let others pilot them around. In 1913 Ruth Vincent, an actress at the Palladium, began studying for her pilot's licence, unlike most other female performers who merely posed with an aircraft for the publicity.[104] Again the parallels with bicycling are clear. Vincent hoped to emulate Grahame-White and the Hendon professionals by dropping 'bombs' of sweets into the schoolyards she passed over during a flight from Hendon to the Green Park at the completion of her training in September 1913 (Figure 10).[105] If the flight took place, it was not well reported, but the juggler T. Elder Hearn claimed billing as the first artiste to qualify as a pilot when he helped to fly a plane from London to Paris in early 1914.[106]

In order to undertake military flight training Hearn returned to England where he began touring the provinces by air when he travelled from London to Liverpool in his Blériot monoplane.[107] This flight, which was lauded as 'the latest record in the variety world', was the last part of the development of music hall that had begun with the use of carriages to speed between London halls, and evolved to provincial tours by motor-car.[108] Because such an 'aviation tour' would be extremely expensive, Hearn asked Oswald Stoll to back a 'flying scheme'. Though Stoll was initially interested, one must assume because he understood that the first flying artiste would generate enormous publicity, he refused to underwrite Hearn.[109] This indicated that, despite Hendon's success, British theatrical promoters were less ready to identify themselves with costly flying than were their American counterparts. Hearn's initial air tour was announced the way Elen's early provincial automobile circuits had been because he scheduled a public stop-over at Wolverhampton. Hearn also attracted attention to himself by giving flying exhibitions whilst in Lancashire.[110]

Meanwhile, the crowds at Hendon were huge during 1914, but this created difficulties for the aerodrome's administrators because much of the flying could be seen clearly from outside the perimeter fence by those not paying admission. In retaliation a programme was printed containing photographs illustrating the

10   Actress Ruth Vincent demonstrates her up-to-dateness in 1913.

latest topical sensations such as 'looping the loop' that were shielded from public view.[111] The programme was then distributed free to the non-paying crowds in order to induce them inside.[112] Looping the loop had been first exhibited at Brooklands by Adolphe Pégoud. Most pilots felt that upside-down flying was impossible, but Pégoud silenced all doubters on the first of September 1913 outside Paris. He performed his sensational and up-to-date 'turn' in London three weeks later.[113] In the immense London publicity for the stunt Pégoud described himself as primarily an aviator but also as 'a music-hall performer' in response to the public demand for trick flyers.[114] Once Pégoud had proved the trick was possible, pilots throughout London and the British Isles were forced to include this up-to-date sensation in their performances.[115]

As with other sensations, music-hall flight was not confined to London. The comedian and contortionist Carlton, who had once used carriages, advertised by plane at Lincoln.[116] In that same city in the spring of 1914, Helena Millais and her cowboys, who were on a provincial tour with their revue *Silver Creek*, assisted at the aviator B. C. Hucks's derby at the local aerodrome. Photos of the event were in great demand in local shops for some time after.[117] Hucks was a celebrity in his own right from the time he became the first Englishman to both loop the loop and fly upside down, in emulation of Pégoud's stunts. After mastering this trick in France, Hucks was met at Charing Cross by fellow British aviators who hoisted him on to their shoulders upside-down. He later gave exhibitions of looping the loop and upside-down flying at Hendon.[118] Hucks then advertised the patent medicine Phosferine, the only product strong enough to combat the undefined 'nerve strain' which a fascinated public believed to be inherent in these difficult aerial stunts (Figure 11).[119] In April 1914, under the auspices of *The Sphere* magazine and the Coliseum, Hucks flew a cameraman across the Channel to film the king and queen's journey to France aboard the royal yacht. As the royal couple landed at Calais he circled the quay before heading home to Hendon. Processing the negative quickly was the key, just as it had been with Robert Paul's film of the thrilling Derby finish almost two decades previously, and so the Coliseum audience saw the film at 5:30 the same evening.[120] At the end of the film Hucks took the stage amid loud applause.[121]

During the last summer before the war the links between the halls and flying were at their most profound. The Music-Hall Convalescent Home Fund grafted flying to charity when they arranged for a 'grand music-hall carnival and flying day' to be held at Hendon in July.[122] Spectators were treated to an aerial derby by eight pilots including the up-to-date Reginald Carr who looped the loop, while a 'comedy carnival by the élite of the variety profession' was carried on below. Passenger spots in the aeroplanes were auctioned off and, despite the participation of some of Britain's most famous professional pilots, the most sought-after tickets on the day were flights with Hearn who was still 'the only music-hall aviator'.[123]

The attraction of this marriage of stage and flying forced the carnival's organisers to find a greater role for artistes. Even if they did not appear at the planes' controls the public retained an insatiable desire to see pretty soubrettes, like Pauline Chase, as passengers. To satisfy this wish the comedian Wilkie Bard donated a cup that was awarded for a race in which pilots flew a prescribed course with a female passenger, landed, ran to a machine awaiting with another

11   Juggler T. Elder Hearn, the first music-hall pilot and the first artiste to tour by air.

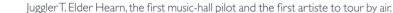

female passenger and flew a second circuit.[124] The chorus girls of Harry Tate's Hippodrome revue *Hullo Tango!* dressed in blue bathing costumes and challenged the Kilburn Empire's *Fancy Meeting You!* chorus who donned red swimsuits for the race.[125]

In April 1913 Lord Northcliffe had attempted to spur on aeroplane development by offering a £10,000 prize to the first pilot to cross the Atlantic Ocean.[126] Inspired by the knowledge that the public were aware of how much money was at stake, the improbable trio of Harry Tate, capitalising once again on popular technological interests, along with the comedians Harry Weldon and Joe Elvin updated *Flying*, by attempting to 'fly' the Atlantic during the music-hall show. Their machines disintegrated around them as smoke crackers ignited, just as Tate's cars and planes regularly did. This 'burying of the aviator – life helmet and all – in the debris, and the summoning of the ambulance corps was quite the funniest incident of the afternoon' to onlookers.[127] But the artistes did not allow their transportation heritage to be subsumed completely by technological marvels as the entertainment on the ground included a 'return to the seventies' in the form of a race for four-wheeled horse-drawn cabs.[128]

Aviation journalists that afternoon saw Hearn as a symbol of the way that Grahame-White's promotions led flying away from scientific research and gentlemanly sporting sensibilities towards 'spectacle' and music hall. *The Aeroplane*, the most influential pre-war flying magazine, said Hearn's plane was badly aligned. Hearn's flying was rough and unsteady and when he touched down, by almost dropping vertically to the ground with a loud, bone-rattling smack, the crowds were relieved that no one was hurt. Given that Tate, Weldon and Elvin burlesqued flight on the ground for the spectators and that Richard Gates regularly flew ragtime, it is possible that Hearn did the same thing, much more dangerously, in the air. In July 1914 Hearn was an experienced pilot and holder of the most exacting licence then available. He must surely have been aware of the necessity to assemble his machine properly. However, a plane that bounced, bumped and 'flew worse than most decent models' would have invariably held the spectators' attention, and promotion of this sort, no matter how riskily achieved, was always a basic requirement of up-to-date music-hall transportation (Figure 11).[129]

The Aeroplane commented further that lending the London Aerodrome to music-hall artistes led to 'an advertisement which will do it more harm than half a dozen fatal accidents' because such shows were 'repellent to the better class people whom one wishes to interest in aviation'.[130] The editors argued that Hendon should ideally be a genteel place through 'an aerial combination of Ranelagh or Hurlingham and Sandown Park' where gentlemen would compete against one another as they did in Germany.[131] The journalists feared the Aerodrome's inclination to become a sort of Coliseum, Hippodrome or Hampstead Heath. This last reactionary call went unheeded as few noblemen flew in the war. The middle classes staffed the most junior service and there was no English equivalent of the genteel *Junker* Manfred von Richthofen.[132] Not even the 'Red Baron' could escape this democratic tendency. National sentiments still cloud the debate about whether in the spring of 1918 he was downed by an Anzac gun battery below him, or by the bullets from the pursuing Sopwith-designed 'Camel' of Roy Brown, a Canadian businessman.[133]

Music hall's relations with the aeroplane never fully matured. Even though Samuel Cody was the first pilot in the British Empire, the difficulty he experienced in establishing an identity as something other than an opportunistic showman caused him moments of reticence about openly associating with the halls. Though this was occasionally his public demeanour, old colleagues and

artistes were always welcome at Laffan's Plain, and music-hall money under-
wrote his later work. This adulation of Cody in itself is very interesting because
it placed him and other pilots in a position in the public imagination that they
could exploit for their own financial needs.

Aviators who experienced the early days of flight in the United States learned
how to manipulate this sensational new technology for profit effectively. They
were joined in their endeavour by Lord Northcliffe and his newspaper's publicity,
patronage and money. Many of the earliest flights occurred in public places like
the Lea Marshes, Brooklands and eventually Hendon which site was chosen for
its ease of access to the centre of London. Despite this legacy, during the summer
of 1914 flying was yet a sufficiently rare and unreliable curiosity with an
expanding list of stunts like looping the loop to draw large crowds. Hearn's use of
a private plane for touring foreshadowed the post-war use of aircraft for continental and then world tours. All of these elements might have been the prelude to
a boom in flying artistes, but the war interrupted this relationship.

Notes

1 Vincent, *Recollections of Fred Leslie*, Vol. 1, p. 204. For the Crystal Palace see Fred
   Willis, *Peace and Dripping Toast*, London, Phoenix House, 1950, p. 19, and for
   Earls Court see 'Music hall gossip', *The Era*, 15 February 1896, p. 19. For provin-
   cial ballooning centres see 'Music hall gossip', *The Era*, 11 July 1896, p. 14, and
   'Music hall gossip', *The Era*, 26 September 1896, p. 19; Joe Graham, *An Old Stock
   Actor's Memories*, London, John Murray, 1930, pp. 35–42; 'The Alexandra Palace',
   The Tottenham and Edmonton Weekly Herald, 10 August 1888 and 'Royalty at the
   Alexandra Palace', *The Tottenham and Edmonton Weekly Herald*, 24 August 1888,
   both unnumbered pages. Further references to parachuting displays are found in
   'Parachuting', *The Era*, 26 July 1890, p. 15, and 'Music hall gossip', *The Era*, 25
   July 1896, p. 14.
2 'Sport or spectacle', *The Aeroplane*, 15 July 1914, p. 60.
3 John Rowland, *The Rolls Royce Men – The Story of Charles Rolls and Henry Royce*,
   London, Lutterworth, 1969, pp. 10–11.
4 Rowland, *Rolls Royce Men*, pp. 17–24 and 61.
5 Paul Tritton, *John Montagu of Beaulieu, 1866–1929: Motoring Pioneer and Prophet*,
   London, Golden Eagle/George Hart, 1985, p. 136.
6 Lord Brabazon of Tara, *The Brabazon Story*, London, Heinemann, 1956, p. 40.
7 Rowland, *Rolls Royce Men*, pp. 64–65.
8 Charles S. Rolls, *An Aeroplane Flight with Wilbur Wright*, Esher, Tabard, 1964,
   unnumbered pages; Rowland, *Rolls Royce Men*, p. 102.
9 Alan Bramson, *Pure Luck: The Authorised Biography of Sir Thomas Sopwith,
   1888–1989*, London, Stephens, 1990, pp. 14–39.

10 George A. Broomfield, *Pioneer of the Air: The Life and Times of Colonel S. F. Cody*, Aldershot, Gale and Polden, 1953, pp. 1–11. Broomfield was one of Cody's mechanics at Laffan's Plain.

11 Harold Ashton, 'Colonel Cody', *Daily News and Leader*, 8 August 1913, p. 4; Broomfield, *Pioneer*, p. 20.

12 Arthur Gould Lee, *The Flying Cathedral*, London, Methuen, 1965, photographic plate, unnumbered pages.

13 'The wild west at Wood Green', *Cycling*, 7 August 1897, p. 77.

14 'The late Colonel Cody', *The Era*, 13 August 1913, p. 22.

15 Ashton, 'Colonel Cody', p. 4.

16 Lee, *Flying Cathedral*, pp. 101–104.

17 Lee, *Flying Cathedral*, preface, unnumbered pages.

18 Samuel F. Cody. 'The kite that lifts a man', *Pearson's Magazine*, 16 (1903), p. 106.

19 Untitled letter, *The Era*, 13 August 1913, p. 22.

20 H. Hamilton Fyfe, 'The optimism of Colonel Cody', *Daily Mail*, 8 August 1913, p. 4.

21 Fyfe, 'Optimism of Colonel Cody', p. 4.

22 Lee, *Flying Cathedral*, p. 157, and Broomfield, *Pioneer*, pp. 60–63.

23 Ashton, 'Colonel Cody', p. 4.

24 Lee, *Flying Cathedral*, p. 168.

25 'The late Colonel Cody', *The Era*, 13 August 1913, p. 22.

26 'Colonel Cody killed', *Daily Chronicle*, 8 August 1913, p. 1.

27 Broomfield, *Pioneer of the Air*, p. 102.

28 F. D. Bone, 'Picturesque career', *Daily Express*, 8 August 1913, p. 2.

29 Bone, 'Picturesque career', p. 2.

30 Lee, *Flying Cathedral*, p. 252.

31 'Cody matinee', *Daily Chronicle,* 17 September 1913, p. 5.

32 'For Mrs Cody', *The Aeroplane*, 2 October 1913, p. 383; Broomfield, *Pioneer*, p. 149.

33 Graham Wallace, *Claude Grahame-White: A Biography*, London, Putnam, 1960, pp. 14–17.

34 Wallace, *Claude Grahame-White*, pp. 25–26.

35 Wallace, *Claude Grahame-White*, p. 77.

36 Wallace, *Claude Grahame-White*, p. 96.

37 Wallace, *Claude Grahame-White*, pp. 131–132; A. J. Crowhurst, 'The music-hall 1855–1922: the emergence of a national entertainment industry in Britain', unpublished Ph.D. dissertation, University of Cambridge, 1992, p. 10.

38 John M. Mackenzie, *Propaganda and Empire*, Manchester, Manchester University Press, 1984, pp. 102–117.

39 Edwin Adeler and Con West, *Remember Fred Karno? The Life of a Great Showman*, London, John Long, 1939, pp. 198–250.

40 Wallace, *Claude Grahame-White*, pp. 110–111.

41 Wallace, *Claude Grahame-White*, p. 103.

42 L. J. Ludovici, *The Challenging Sky: The Life of Sir Alliott Verdon-Roe*, London, Herbert Jenkins, 1956, p. 70.

43 Wallace, *Claude Grahame-White*, p. 171. See also 'The Daily Mail flying men', *Daily Mail*, 16 July 1912, p. 4; 'The Daily Mail flying men', *Daily Mail*, 17 July 1912, p. 3; and 'The Daily Mail flying men', *Daily Mail*, 18 July 1912, p. 5.

44 John E. B. Seely, *Adventure*, London, Heinemann, 1930, pp. 135–136.

45 Churchill first became interested in flying in 1909 Martin Gilbert, *Churchill: A Life*, London, Heinemann, 1991, pp. 202 and 248–249.

46 'The belle of the skies', *The Era*, 27 May 1911, p. 13.

47 'Flying prohibited', *Daily Chronicle*, 13 June 1911, p. 7. Grahame-White's boast is found in Wallace, *Claude Grahame-White*, pp. 138–139.

48 'Flying and the theatre', *Daily Mail*, 2 June 1911, p. 8.

49 Wallace, *Claude Grahame-White*, p. 139.

50 Max Pemberton, *Lord Northcliffe: A Memoir*, London, Hodder and Stoughton, 1922, pp. 187–196.

51 Harry J. Greenwall, *Northcliffe: Napoleon of Fleet Street*, London, Allan Wingate, 1957, p. 76.

52 Greenwall, *Northcliffe*, pp. 72–73. The banquet was also recalled in Hamilton Fyfe, *Northcliffe: an Intimate Biography*, London, G. Allen and Unwin, 1930, pp. 148–149.

53 Variety gossip', *The Era*, 29 July 1911, p. 20.

54 L' Ancien, 'Brooklands as an aerodrome', in Charles Gardner (ed.), *Fifty Years of Brooklands*, London, Heinemann, 1956, p. 74.

55 Wallace, *Claude Grahame-White*, p. 144.

56 Untitled photograph, *The Era*, 29 July 1911, p. 12.

57 'Variety gossip', *The Era*, 29 July 1911, p. 20; *Weybridge Aviation* (1913), viewing copy, British Film Institute, London; C. C. Turner, *The Old Flying Days*, London, Sampson and Low, 1927, p. 49.

58 Wallace, *Claude Grahame-White*, pp. 132–133.

59 Claude Grahame-White and Harry Harper, *With the Airmen*, London, Hodder and Stoughton, 1913, p. 225; J.B. Priestley, *The Edwardians*, London, Heinemann, 1970, p. 86.

60 L' Ancien, 'Brooklands as an aerodrome', p. 78.

61 Turner, *Old Flying Days*, pp. 46–48; 'A fine day's flying', *The Aeroplane*, 13 February 1913, p. 172; L. A. Strange, *Recollections of an Airman*, London, John Hamilton, 1933, pp. 14–15.

62 'To-day's wild rose fete', *Daily Chronicle*, 26 June 1912, p. 1.

63 Wallace, *Claude Grahame-White*, pp. 164–166. The quote is found on p. 166.

64 'Aeroplane flights on land and sea', *The Era*, 11 May 1912, p. 35.

65 Ludovici, *Challenging Sky*, pp. 19–32.

66 L' Ancien, 'Brooklands as an aerodrome', pp. 63–65.

67 Ludovici, *Challenging Sky*, p. 54.

68 Turner, *Old Flying Days*, p. 75.

69 Ludovici, *Challenging Sky*, pp. 56–57.

70 Ludovici, *Challenging Sky*, p. 55.

71 Ludovici, *Challenging Sky*, p. 70.

72 As quoted in Ludovici, *Challenging Sky*, p. 71.

73 *The Oxford English Dictionary*, 2nd Ed., Oxford, Oxford University Press, 1989, Vol. 16, p. 997. Eric Partridge's chronology for the word stunt is somewhat askew. He felt that it had been introduced to Britain in about 1912, but only adopted to aeroplanes in 1915. Eric Partridge, *A Dictionary of Slang and Unconventional English*, Vol. 1, London, Penguin, 1974, p. 844.

74 Advertisement, *Daily Mail*, 9 December 1909, p. 1.

75 Advertisement, *The Illustrated Sporting and Dramatic News*, 14 June 1913, p. 767.

76 Advertisement, *Daily Chronicle*, 3 September 1913, p. 4.

77 'Flying at Hendon', *The Aeroplane*, 18 December 1913, p. 668.

78 Advertisement, *Daily Mail*, 1 July 1914, p. 9.

79 Wendy Baron, *The Camden Town Group*, London, Scolar Press, 1979, pp. 3–4 and 13–30.

80 Frederick Gore and Richard Shone, *Spencer Frederick Gore*, London, Anthony d'Offay, 1983, unnumbered pages and plate 21.

81 'Theatrical aviation', *The Era*, 27 July 1912, p. 13.

82 'Vaudeville aviation Sunday', *The Era*, 24 May 1913, p. 21.

83 'Theatrical aviation Sunday', *The Era*, 14 June 1913, p. 10.

84 'Flower day at Hendon', *Daily News and Leader*, 20 June 1913, p. 5 and 'Aeroplanes to join in floral battle', *Daily Chronicle*, 24 June 1913, p. 1.

85 Untitled, *The Era*, 17 September 1913, p. 30.

86 'Variety gossip', *The Era*, 24 September 1913, p. 22.

87 Untitled, *The Era*, 24 September 1913, p. 33.

88 Advertisement, *The Era*, 1 October 1913, p. 4.

89 Fred d'Albert, 'Who'll come for a ride with me in my aeroplane?' (1907); Fred Godfrey, 'In my aeroplane' (1907); Tom Mellor, 'In my aeroplane for two' (1907); and Fred Murray, 'In my aeroplane' (1907); all in the British Library catalogue of printed music.

90 Violet King, 'Aeroplane waltz' (1909); Ezra Read, 'Aeroplane waltzes' (1910); and Berte C. Randall, 'That aeroplane rag' (1911) all in the British Library catalogue of printed music.

91 Louis Achille Hirsch, 'There's an aeroplane air about you' (c. 1910–12), British Library catalogue of printed music.

92 Albert Maurice, 'The aeroplane march' (1914), British Library catalogue of printed music; Mackenzie, *Propaganda and Empire*, p. 31.

93 Matthew Paris, 'The rise of the airmen: the origins of Air Force elitism, c. 1890–1918', *Journal of Contemporary History*, 28 (1993), p. 129.

94 'Airship over St Paul's', *Daily Mail*, 13 July 1910, p. 7, and 'Beta's flight', *Daily News and Leader*, 13 July 1910, p. 7.

95 Felix Barker, *House that Stoll Built: the Story of the Coliseum Theatre*, London, Frederick Muller, 1957, pp. 170–171.

96 George Dangerfield, *The Strange Death of Liberal England*, London, Constable, 1936, pp. 114–117.

97 Advertisement, *The Illustrated Sporting and Dramatic News*, 9 August 1913, p. 1151.

98   'War in the air', *The Era*, 28 June 1913, p. 19.

99   Sheridan Morley, *A Talent to Amuse: A Biography of Noël Coward*, London, Heinemann, 1969, pp. 21–22.

100 'The finale of the night flying meeting at Hendon – the attack on a battleship', *The Illustrated Sporting and Dramatic News*, 21 June 1913, p. 797.

101 'Sealed orders', *The Era*, 17 September 1913, p. 14. For photographs of the climactic scenes see 'Sealed orders', *The Illustrated Sporting and Dramatic News*, 20 September 1913, p. 89, and 'Sealed orders', *The Illustrated Sporting and Dramatic News*, 4 October 1913, p. 173.

102 'Another airship sensation', *The Era*, 17 September 1913, p. 19.

103 Strange, *Recollections*, p. 25.

104 'From the Palladium to Hendon, Miss Ruth Vincent', *The Illustrated Sporting and Dramatic News*, 27 September 1913, p. 137.

105 'Actress as airwoman', *Daily Chronicle*, 20 September 1913, p. 6, and 'Songstress as aviator', *Daily Express*, 20 September 1913, p. 2.

106 'Variety gossip', *The Era*, 1 April 1914, p. 18.

107 'Music hall world', *The Encore*, 26 February 1914, p. 7. The flight to Liverpool is described in 'Variety gossip', *The Era*, 20 May 1914, p. 18.

108 'Variety gossip', *The Era*, 20 May 1914, p. 18.

109 'Variety gossip', *The Era*, 27 May 1914, p. 18.

110 'Variety gossip', *The Era*, 20 May 1914, p. 18.

111 'Music hall world', *The Encore*, 7 May 1914, p. 16.

112 'Music hall world', *The Encore*, 7 May 1914, p. 16.

113 L' Ancien, 'Brooklands as an aerodrome', pp. 78–79.

114 Adolphe Pégoud, 'How I fly upside down', *Daily Express*, 24 September 1913, p. 4.

115 Strange, *Recollections*, pp. 29–31.

116 Carlton, *Twenty Years of Spoof and Bluff*, London, Herbert Jenkins, 1920, pp. 198–200.

117 Untitled, *The Era*, 15 April 1914, p. 17.

118 Turner, *Old Flying Days*, p. 56.

119 'Nerve strain', *Daily News and Leader*, 27 May 1913, p. 4.

120 'Their Majesties' aerial flight', *The Aeroplane*, 30 April 1914, p. 511.

121 Barker, *House that Stoll Built*, pp. 174–175.

122 'Variety gossip', *The Era*, 10 June 1914, p. 14.

123 'Fun at Hendon', *Daily News and Leader*, 8 July 1914, p. 5; 'Variety gossip', *The Era*, 17 June 1914, p. 14.

124 'Variety gossip', *The Era*, 1 July 1914, p. 14.

125 'Flying matinee – Stars in the sky for sweet charity', *Daily Chronicle*, 8 July 1914, p. 7.

126 Lee, *Flying Cathedral*, p. 243.

127 'Fun at Hendon', *Daily News and Leader*, 8 July 1914, p. 5.

128 'Variety gossip', *The Era*, 1 July 1914, p. 14.

129 'London–Paris–London', *The Aeroplane*, 15 July 1914, p. 68.

130 'Sport or spectacle', *The Aeroplane*, 15 July 1914, p. 60.

131 'Sport or spectacle', *The Aeroplane,* 15 July 1914, p. 60.

132 David Cannadine, 'Nobility and mobility in modern Britain', in David Cannadine, *Aspects of Aristocracy*, London, Yale University Press, 1994, p. 69.

133 Bramson, *Pure Luck*, p. 57; Chaz Bowyer, *The Encyclopaedia of British Military Aircraft*, London, Arms and Armour, 1982, p. 45.

7

Sport

Topicality and up-to-dateness were not only conferred through public association with transportation technology, because four spectator sports that became popular in London during the 1890s were just as readily co-opted by artistes. This interaction closely followed the chronology of the capital's emergence as the pre-eminent English sporting centre when ever-more numerous stadiums and arenas were constructed to contain the huge crowds who regularly attended matches. Because of this need for a sophisticated infrastructure, many music-hall sporting events were developed originally in the provinces where professional spectator sports had first evolved. This national context is not yet entirely clear because not even the most introductory work on music-hall sports has been undertaken, though the alleyways mapped in this section should lead interested researchers into rewarding areas for further study. Neither has the history of the annual London music-hall charity sports – a day of egg-and-spoon, three-legged and costume races, which sometimes incorporated up-to-date elements – yet been written.[1]

It is clear, however, that no middle-class managerial cabals, if they existed, could have harnessed this interaction. Rather, analysis of the evidence contained in newspaper reports, biographies and team line-ups suggests strongly that music-hall sports emerged in London because of the continuous mass immigration of provincially trained managers, performers and athletes. People who had been apprenticed in this provincial atmosphere of interaction between stage and pitch recreated it subsequently in London. There was little place in commercialised football for managerial scruples about employing only local performers, because talent was the only criterion for selection. Therefore the foremost London-based sports clubs recruited players from throughout the country, just as the variety syndicates did with artistes.[2] Of the other three sports examined in this section, baseball was the least successful because it was neither topical nor convenient for artistes. Cricket's nascent mass popularity was quickly stunted by the overwhelming emergence of London association football. Only boxing saw a stridently *dirigiste* management, though as we shall see, this was continuously knocked off kilter and eventually emasculated by the rage of music-hall up-to-dateness.

This dynamic relationship between pitch and stage evolved rapidly because up-to-dateness necessarily mirrored the public's often fickle esteem. Music-hallers' interest in any sport withered quickly when outside the public gaze. Caprice is more glaring here than in the preceding section because successful events were almost casually discontinued at the first indication of waning public support. Individual matches ceased but the process of updating acts through sports remained, as artistes, syndicate managers and professional club directors exploited this interaction actively by sponsoring spoof events and afternoon-long festivals in order to increase their fame and business. But this interaction was not limited to these carnivals and galas, because some individual sporting artistes became imbued with a very modern form of celebrity by appearing constantly on the pitch. That is to say they enjoyed, like pilots, a level of popularity and public identification which rested on their personalities rather than their mastery of any single activity. Quotidian sporting artistes such as Datas and Chirgwin were content to recall the latest matches and bouts in their stage acts while others performed songs and skits, but the most athletically talented people pursued serious sporting careers by appearing regularly in the uniforms of leading sides. Once the link between stage and pitch had been firmly established the most popular sportsmen earned vast salaries on the halls, usually acting in plays whose flimsy plots were merely excuses to introduce exhibitions of sparring, dribbling or batting. The transition from fame resting exclusively with one activity to comprehensive sporting celebrity was not always seamless, it was often frankly absurd, but Londoners saw an admittedly small number of men move constantly between athletic fields and stages. Those not talented enough to follow spoofed these endeavours in whichever arena they could.

Notes

1 For the best surviving picture of the sports see R. W. Paul's *Comic Costume Race* (1896), viewing copy, British Film Institute, London and a commentary about them is heard in Annie Hartley, oral history interview, Martha Vicinus collection, National Sound Archives, London.

2 For football see, for instance, William J. Baker, 'The making of a working-class football culture in Victorian England', *The Journal of Social History*, 13.2 (1979), pp. 241–251, *passim.*

8

Baseball

This American game may seem an odd sport to include in this study. However, London flirted with the sport twice in the twenty years before the First World War. Baseball was first played in England in 1874 when the Boston Red Stockings and Philadelphia Athletics made a tour of provincial cities that culminated with a number of games in London. This visit had very little lasting effect, because the teams attracted scant interest either as the ambassadors of a reconstructed, confident United States, or as sportsmen.[1] Baseball's subsequent English venture was much more significant. In 1889 A. G. Spalding, a player-turned-sporting-goods-manufacturer and manager of the Chicago White Sox, embarked with his team on a promotional world tour, playing matches in the Sandwich Islands, New Zealand, Australia, the pyramids at Giza, in the Coliseum at Rome and in the shadow of the Eiffel Tower. When they finally reached London in March 1889 the baseballers' presence was so sensational that their first game at the Oval, the biggest sporting venue in the capital, attracted between seven and eight thousand fans, including England's greatest sporting patron, the Prince of Wales.[2] Missionary work was taken up that summer when American undergraduates conducted introductory clinics in London, the home counties and Birmingham. The first native response was heard in October 1889 when 'several gentlemen prominently identified with outdoor sports, chiefly with football' formed the National Baseball League of Great Britain.[3]

That winter, football, hockey and harriers clubs, located predominantly in the football-mad north and midlands at Preston North End, Aston Villa, Birmingham, Stoke County Cricket Club and Derby, allied themselves to the new sport as a means for their members to keep fit over the summer. The following summer the Baseball Association of Great Britain and Ireland was formed to oversee the amateur game, with Reverend W. Marshall (an official of the Yorkshire Rugby Union) as president. The association's eight-member council included representatives of Birmingham, Derby, the south of England, Newcastle, Cleveland, the Potteries, Lancashire, Belfast and two Scots members. The sole London representative was Newton Crane, an American expatriate.[4] Sensing his opportunity for publicity and profit, Spalding donated a trophy to the league that targeted football clubs, because they owned fields and stadiums large enough to host the new game, while American collegians concentrated their efforts on the north and industrial midlands, the areas where baseball was initially most popular.[5]

Neither association football nor professional spectator sports had overwhelmed London by 1890. Therefore, the impetus for baseball in the capital came from the minstrel Richard G. Knowles and a small group of fellow American music-hall artistes.[6] Knowles was a keen athlete who, for a time at least, spent a good deal of his leisure promoting baseball amongst his companions.[7] He had first arrived in London from America in 1891, settled and led this group who played their matches on Clapham Common, Battersea Park and Dulwich in South London, near to where its members lived, for a cup he donated.[8] Games attracted bemused attention from local spectators, but it was only when George Dare led a team to Earls Court to counter the cowboys of Buffalo Bill Cody's Wild West Show at the end of June 1892 that London took notice of its baseballers. This sensation was created because Buffalo Bill's promoters performed their jobs admirably and attracted large crowds to the games, which were umpired by American theatrical manager John D. Hopkins.[9]

This Clapham Common Nine re-christened themselves the Thespians and joined the National Baseball Association of England in 1893, which enabled them to compete against the best clubs in the country, all of whom were still found in the north.[10] That spring Knowles tried to attract more members for the club by writing to *The Era* asking any professional artistes who played the game and wanted to join the Thespian Baseball club to contact him as he was organising matches against the principal north of England teams.[11] The level of play that summer cannot have been too advanced as, in a game where a final score of 4-2 is considered a respectable outcome, the Thespians won their first match against favoured Stockton 27-19 after which the visiting team attended the Canterbury music hall where the baseball cup was displayed.[12] Music-hall baseball appeared at an auspicious time as it coincided roughly with the founding of the artistes' sporting fraternity, the Jays, whose decision to sponsor a team indicated baseball's burgeoning popularity within the theatrical world. Not surprisingly, though, they lost their inaugural match to Thespians 38-8.[13]

Knowles then helped found the London Baseball Association in February 1894. Under the guidance of Newton Crane, president of the English National Association, Eugene Stratton, another popular American minstrel, was elected president while the English acrobat and Jay Albert Le Fre and John Sexton of Remington Typewriters were vice-presidents. The Jays, Thespians, Remingtons, Electrics and Clapham Postmen represented London, while delegates from Liverpool, Derby, Stockton, Darlington, Middlesborough and Newcastle also attended.[14] About 3,000 people attended the inaugural match at Thespians' new home ground at Hyde Farm, Balham, in May 1894, but in spite of these efforts, London baseball remained identified with Knowles who was 'the leading spirit of the association'.[15] The American-dominated Thespians again won the championship by beating Stockton.[16]

In 1895 London baseball ended its peripatetic days by playing at Crystal Palace and Wembley Park, but principally at Brixton, its third home in as many seasons, in the heart of a wealthy suburb favoured by the music-hall community. It was hoped that baseball's popularity would soar at this permanent home because Brixton was well serviced by trams and trains from north of the river, one of the reasons it was so popular with artistes, though most ticket buyers remained American residents of London.[17] Sir Joseph Renals, the Lord Mayor, was honorary president, and the American ambassador, along with six or seven hundred others including 'many notables in the theatrical and music-hall world', attended the first game.[18] The president was Thomas Dewar, the distiller, politician and social reformer who had been captivated by baseball whilst travelling across the United States in 1892 at the start of a convalescent world tour.[19] Dewar sponsored a team from amongst his workers and provided a trophy. As the league grew artistes were displaced on the executive increasingly by businessmen like J. Walter Earle, a former player who directed the European expansion of Remington Typewriters, and the American confectioner William B. Fuller, who sponsored a works side and ran the stadium tea rooms. William E. Geddes – whose company manufactured St. Jacob's Oil, a liniment for sore muscles – advertised his goods by funding a factory team.[20]

A derelict grandstand was purchased and transported to the Brixton baseball park during the closed season. It was then painted by Knowles and the artiste T. Reed Pinaud who also erected a perimeter fence with what Dewar extolled as commendable parsimony, suggesting little capital was being committed to the League.[21] Pre-season matches helped officials distribute the most talented players throughout the league so that games would be more evenly and excitingly contested.[22] Knowles was unable to attend the season opener because he was performing in Edinburgh in a portent of his decreasing involvement.[23] Despite this, Knowles confidently proclaimed that the game drew increasing numbers of British fans.[24]

Baseball's stage connections climaxed in August 1895 with a charity match that raised £30 for the Music-Hall Benevolent Fund.[25] But the sport signally failed to establish a wider popularity that afternoon as Thespians appeared in their stage costumes to play Fullers before an audience composed mostly of people from the variety profession.[26] Not even cavorting artistes could induce Londoners to attend. Crystal Palace also hosted matches when the first amateur teams appeared that autumn, by which time, with the Lord Mayor's two sons playing, Knowles had 'so completely identified himself with baseball in England that he has made this fascinating game a part of the variety stage'.[27]

Baseball never firmly established itself in London and 1896 was the last year it was played under the aegis of the music halls. Knowles was mercurial, for though he invested much energy into the game he left for an extended tour of Australia in the autumn of 1895 and did not return to London until part-way through the following summer. From then on he was no longer in London regularly enough to preside over baseball. The loss of an ardent patron was compounded by the sport's inability to attract Londoners who would not journey to a makeshift Brixton stadium in order to watch a game whose rules they did not understand and 'the consequence was that our games were between purely American players, chiefly Music Hall artists [sic], and our spectatorate were drawn from the same sources'.[28]

Baseball was London's first music-hall sport and as such it showed many weaknesses from which its successors would not suffer. Despite continual managerial manipulation the game's rules remained obscure, meaning that artistes played before stands filled with their friends. Such arrangements made the sport vulnerable to the constant travel demanded by stage careers which prevented artistes from participating in regularly scheduled league games. The lack of a permanent home handicapped the sport further by failing to accommodate spectators comfortably. Finally, despite its music-hall trappings, baseball was played, sponsored and watched almost exclusively by London's American colony. Baseball was never topical.

Yet the game was not inexorably doomed to failure; indeed, it attracted increasing sponsorship with each season. The memory of its brief success prompted Spalding to attempt a revival in 1906 when Chelsea, Fulham, Clapton, Arsenal and Tottenham Hotspur football clubs fielded teams in a short-lived summer league.[29] Spectacular baseball exploded once more in pre-war London. At the end of February 1914, the King, the American ambassador, various members of 'society', and between fifteen and thirty thousand others saw the Chicago White Sox face the New York Giants at Stamford Bridge stadium. The event bore all the trappings of music-hall sport. In the two evenings before the game, the teams had attended West End melodramas. On match day they paraded in full uniform from the Cecil Hotel in the Strand to the stadium, in cars that were bedecked with American flags. The audience had also been primed for the match by up-to-date sport, calling for the Giants' star player to 'strike appropriate attitudes when sensational catches were affected. Moreover, he obliged with comic walks as he made his way out to the centre field position'.[30]

Even if their sport had never been greatly popular, Knowles and his friends had not been fundamentally misguided because, as we shall see, sporting events sponsored by music-hall artistes and managers were immensely popular in provincial cities during the 1890s. Baseball failed because neither comedians nor businessmen could induce Londoners to accept a foreign game, but throughout England artistes updated their turns by burlesquing existing popular sports. It is to three more successful music-hall ventures that we must now turn.

Notes

1   Newton Crane, *Baseball*, London, G. Bell and Sons, 1891, p. 12.
2   Crane, *Baseball*, pp. 13–14.
3   Crane, *Baseball*, p. 17.
4   Crane, *Baseball*, unnumbered end pages.
5   Crane, *Baseball*, pp. 17–23.
6   Richard G. Knowles and Richard Morton, *Baseball*, London, London and Co., 1896, p. 44.
7   'A chat with R. G. Knowles', *The Era*, 29 September 1894, p. 10.
8   'Benevolent baseball', *The Era*, 17 August 1895, p. 15.
9   Knowles and Morton, *Baseball*, pp. 46–48.
10 Knowles and Morton, *Baseball*, p. 48.
11 Letter, 'Theatrical baseball', *The Era*, 8 April 1893, p. 16.
12 'Music hall gossip', *The Era*, 15 July 1893, p. 14.
13 'Music hall gossip', *The Era*, 29 July 1893, p. 15.
14 'London baseball association', *The Era*, 24 February 1894, p. 15.
15 'Music hall gossip', *The Era*, 12 May 1894, p. 17; 'Mr. R.G. Knowles at home', *The Sketch*, 28 November 1894, p. 218.
16 'Music hall gossip', *The Era*, 1 September 1894, p. 15.
17 Advertisement, *London American*, 14 June 1895, p. 13, and for a description of the crowds see 'Baseball notes', *London American*, 28 June 1895, p. 7.

18 'Music hall gossip', *The Era*, 4 May 1895, p. 17, and the quote is found in 'Music hall gossip', *The Era*, 11 May 1895, p. 16.

19 'London baseball association', *The Era*, 14 March 1896, p. 18, and see Thomas R. Dewar, *A Ramble Round the Globe*, London, Chatto and Windus, 1894, *passim*, for his fascination with the United States.

20 Knowles, *Baseball*, pp. 64–68; 'Benevolent baseball', *The Era*, 17 August 1895, p. 15.

21 'London baseball association', *The Era*, 14 March 1896 p. 18.

22 Balham Hyde, 'Baseball in London', *London American*, 1 May 1895, p. 6.

23 Balham Hyde, 'Baseball in London', *London American*, 10 May 1895, p. 5.

24 Richard G. Knowles, 'Baseball in England: past present and future', *The Windsor Magazine*, 2 (1895), p. 517.

25 'Music hall gossip', *The Era*, 10 August 1895, p. 15, and for the total raised see 'Music hall gossip', *The Era*, 31 August 1895, p. 17.

26 Knowles, *Baseball*, pp. 52–53.

27 'Music hall gossip', *The Era*, 2 November 1895, p. 16.

28 Henry Chadwick (ed.), *Spalding's Official Baseball Guide*, London, no stated publisher, 1906, p. 55.

29 J. Sharp, 'Baseball', *C. B. Fry's Magazine*, 5 (1906), pp. 457–463; 'Summing Up', *Stage and Sport*, 12 May 1906, p. 3; '"Glorified rounders" comes into fashion in England', *The Sketch*, 8 August 1906, supplement, p. 8; 'The United States' national game in Britain: The base-ball championships', *The Illustrated London News*, 18 August 1906, p. 235; 'Baseball, a suitable sport for women', *The Sketch*, 17 July 1907, supplement, p. 10; *Oriental Notes: The Official Organ of the Clapton Orient Football Club (1906) Ltd.*, 9 May 1908, *passim*; and 'The editor's effort', *Oriental Notes*, 29 April 1911, unnumbered pages.

30 For the quote see 'Royal baseball', *Daily Mail*, 27 February 1914, p. 7; see also 'The King and baseball', *Daily Mail*, 26 February 1914, p. 7; 'King George at a baseball game', *Daily News and Leader*, 27 February 1914, p. 1; 'The invasion of baseball', *Daily News and Leader*, 27 February 1914, p. 10; 'The King at the baseball match', *The Times*, 27 February 1914, p. 8; 'The American baseball teams', *The Times*, 26 February 1914, p. 12; 'Baseball: 30,000 Britons see American baseball', *New York Times*, 27 February 1914, p. 1; John P. Rossi, 'A glorified form of rounders: baseball in Britain, February 1914', in *Cooperstown Symposium on Baseball and the American Culture (1990)*, Westport, Connecticut, Meckler, 1990, pp. 243–255.

9

Cricket

Artistes' cricket traced its descent from a Kennington Oval match in 1873 when over £70 had been realised for the Music-Hall Sick Fund in what was called 'the first healthy reunion to lift the music-hall artiste above beer and skittles'.[1] The Thespian Cricket Club was founded to play other London teams eight years later and from at least the middle of the 1890s men like George Robey, a passionate cricketer who was elected to the Marylebone Cricket Club in 1905, and Harry Randall occasionally organised charity matches in provincial cities.[2] Artistes were not the only ones who enjoyed the sport, though, as the staffs of various London halls competed against one another as early as 1894 when the Tivoli and Oxford met at the baseball stadium while the London Syndicate Halls vied for their own challenge cup.[3] These staff leagues survived and expanded with new suburban theatres sponsoring teams at the turn of the century, though we will examine the way artistes updated their acts at this time through comic cricket matches.[4]

Before doing so we must briefly reconstruct the atmosphere which prompted music-hallers' interest in this sport. Victorian cricket attained great prominence in the public schools, universities and in all parts of the empire, making the turn of the twentieth century the sport's most mythic age. Epics are incomplete without both inspired strategists and compelling heroes. Cricket had both. From the 1880s the Etonian Lord Hawke created the modern test match system by managing and captaining English teams which regularly travelled the globe to face increasingly prodigious colonial sides. Up-to-date West End music-hall directors capitalised on this interest by first inviting the Australians to watch the Alhambra ballet in 1893 and then the Pavilion acrobats six years later during which tour the cricketers were also issued complimentary season passes to the Empire.[5] Nor were fans ever isolated from the English team as from 1897 cinema films recorded its progress during protracted overseas tours.[6]

The domestic game was dominated through almost four decades by the Bristol doctor W. G. Grace: physically by his prodigious batting – at a time when fifties were uncommon and centuries rare he tallied them by the brace – his long beard and enormous girth, and institutionally by his national captaincy. Pavilions throughout the country were built or enlarged as a result of the interest Grace stimulated in the game.[7] He retired aged fifty-one in 1899 from both the England and Gloucestershire squads to manage a Crystal Palace team that had been established especially so that he could play regularly in London. His final first-class innings occurred in 1908. Though Grace was a Victorian stalwart, the English squad at the turn of the century contained handsome, emerging legends like Prince Ranjitsinhji, the Cambridge-educated maharajah who revolutionised batting with the leg-glance. 'Ranji' played for Sussex and England in a billowing silk shirt alongside his celebrated partner C. B. Fry.[8] As a batting partnership the pair exhorted one another to enormous scores. As a mark of Ranji's celebrity, in late 1901 *The Autocar* published a photograph of him learning to drive (Figure 12)[9]. The capital physically reflected cricket's popularity as Lord's private sanctum in St John's Wood shared London with the Kennington Oval and Crystal Palace; newer, bigger, stadiums designed to accommodate massive crowds.

Music hall incorporated this interest during the 1890s under the guidance of Dan Leno, England's most popular comedian. His 'Danites' first appeared in June 1898 when they played Camberwell Tradesmen in aid of the Camberwell and Dulwich Pension Society. Leno's initial eleven included several of the day's most popular entertainers such as Eugene Stratton, who after several years' residency in England had dropped baseball's hickory for cricket's willow. George Robey also played as did Herbert Campbell, the adipose giant who annually partnered the slight Leno in pantomime at the Drury Lane Theatre.[10] Spectators adored these initial music-hall cricket matches and the idea took hold. Leno presented prizes for a ladies' match at the Music-hall Sports at Stamford Bridge, Chelsea in September 1898.[11]

The staging of London charity matches developed significantly that September when Leno's Eccentrics played a team of Sir Thomas Dewar's kilted employees at the Grove Hotel, Dulwich.[12] London newspapers were cautious about praising the quality of the comedy.[13] The *Daily Mail* correspondent felt that 'the fooling, as is usually the case on these occasions, was for the most part certainly of poor quality, but as, according to Mr W. S. Gilbert, an accepted wit has but to say "pass the mustard" and people roar their ribs out, so it happened that the spectators at Dulwich yesterday were thoroughly satisfied with the fun

12   Cricketing up-to-date 1901: Prince Ranjitsinhji learns to drive.

provided'.[14] The innate quality of the humour at charity matches was facile but 'a capital burlesque of the aggressive type of county cricketer was given by Little Dando, who took middle, patted the ground, and looked round at the field-smen in the most approved fashion'.[15] Dando's exaggerated performance at the wicket illustrated that artistes parodied popular sporting figures on the pitch. Despite its apparent success, this match raised a desultory £12.1s. each for the Music-Hall Benevolent Fund and the Licensed Victuallers.[16]

The pace quickened in 1899 as Leno again led his team to Stamford Bridge where they faced Chelsea, Fulham and Kensington charities in aid of the Music-Hall Benevolent Society.[17] Public interest was much greater this year and so receipts totalled £144.[18] This public interest was reflected in a cartoon in *Leno's Comic Journal* that July which chronicled Dan's alleged prowess with the bat; meanwhile, Leno and Dewar raised a further £35 at Dulwich in October 1900.[19] *Dan Leno's Cricket Match*, the first of two such movies, both sadly now lost, boomed the sporting Leno throughout England in 1900.[20]

Stamford Bridge hosted another of Leno's cricket matches in June 1901, and the popularity for mimicking the sport climaxed in early autumn 1901 when music-hall cricketers appeared at the Kennington Oval.[21] As they had already raised substantial sums for charity it is not surprising that Leno and Dewar, now a conservative MP, produced a comic cricketing gala at the Oval that September in aid of the Music-Hall Benevolent Fund, Licensed Victuallers' schools and the New Belgrave Hospital for Children, Clapham. This was the largest game of its kind yet staged, as about 18,000 people attended on a warm sunny day. The bands of the Irish Guards, L Division of the police and the Licensed Victuallers' Schools performed.[22] Fred Karno's convict band boomed *Jail Birds* by leading the 'grand military parade': this started the day by ushering Leno, clad in a field marshal's uniform, on to the pitch.[23] Leno then dressed as an undertaker to open the batting at 11.00 a.m. in a partnership with the pirate Bob Hutt. However, because Leno was no athlete the opposition, which included several Surrey professionals, bowled

> slow balls that bounded gently in front of the bat. But captain Leno was not to be disconcerted. Every now and then he caught the ball a hard hit with his bat, sometimes sending it – the ball – right away to the boundary. So that his score leapt up, and still up, the creditable total of 176 being amassed in the first five minutes. At other times the ball eluded his vigorous aim and either fouled with the wicket or collided with his boots. Several times, too, he sent it a little way up in the air, and a member of the other team caught it.[24]

Luckily, Herbert Campbell umpired and allowed Leno's innings to continue until the batsman was carried off to the pavilion by Dewar's exasperated team.[25]

Cinematograph cameras recorded the players when they returned to the field after the lunch interval.[26] Female artistes sold programmes in the stands throughout the day while performers amused the crowd with their turns, including Harry Tate who circled the arena on a motorcycle during Dewar's innings, adding motoring up-to-dateness to this match.[27] In the midst of this pandemonium, Leno was the afternoon's star as 'the chief incident of the game was the difficulty of dismissing' him.[28] He garnered further laughs after being retired by chasing a pantomime lion and romping around the field dressed initially as a schoolgirl riding a camel and then as a North American Indian fighting a lion.[29] The match was a public tribute to his genius at improvisation though his comic cricketing skills were equally well honed. The images captured by the cinema cameras toured the halls as *Dan Leno's Record Score* but, as we have seen with baseball, this conspicuous identification of a single personality with the event was dangerous.[30]

Leno's Eccentrics were updated the next summer when they were re-christened the Komical Koronation Kricketers to honour Edward's enthronement, before a September rematch with Dewar's team was set for the Oval.[31] Memories of the previous year's success induced the principal artistes appearing in London to volunteer their services for the carnival.[32] An annual Kennington match was almost stillborn when Leno was impersonated on the pitch by Syd May because he was 'suffering somewhat from nervous break-down' in a foreshadowing of the alcoholism that killed him aged forty-three in November 1904.[33] Organisers feared that public knowledge of their star's indisposition would make the match less attractive and so 'his illness was kept a profound secret and to the last he hoped to be there' but he was not and therefore May deceived the audience into thinking that Dan was present.[34] May's costume and make-up made it difficult to tell it was not Leno in even the clearest photographs taken that afternoon (Figure 13).[35] This elaborate physical and comedic disguise proved how much the event relied on Leno for success. The false Leno did not play for long, perhaps because it was feared the deception would be uncovered if he were too conspicuous, but 'cheers were raised at the supposed advent of Dan Leno, and many people believed that a figure in wide pantaloons, who wielded a brush and insisted on rolling the pitch with the fattest player present, was Dan Leno in the flesh'.[36]

May's prolonged comedic turn that day emulated Leno and Campbell's pantomime jokes which relied on the physical disparity of their statures. At other times he stood at the boundary rope in the military officer's uniform familiar from the previous year, using his sword to direct play. Batting opened with a partnership between the dwarf Little Dando and sixteen-stone giant Bumper Mott, which also recalled the physical disparity between Campbell and Leno that was so famous from Drury Lane and previous cricket matches.[37] Though the weather was gloomy, music-hall turns were enacted continuously on a stage that had been installed at the side of the pitch.[38] Female artistes again sold programmes and collected money in the stands. Despite organisers' attempts to provide a compelling show, the threatening rain and Leno's indisposition made the afternoon 'a case of *Hamlet* without the prince'.[39]

Dewar and new partner Frank Allen, one of the directors of the Moss Empires circuit, were not deterred by the more limited success of the 1902 match when they organised a third, final one which took place in 1903 without even a suggestion of Leno's involvement. The public were aware that Leno was permanently incapacitated and so only about one-third as many spectators as the previous year bought tickets, prompting the *Daily Express* to comment that

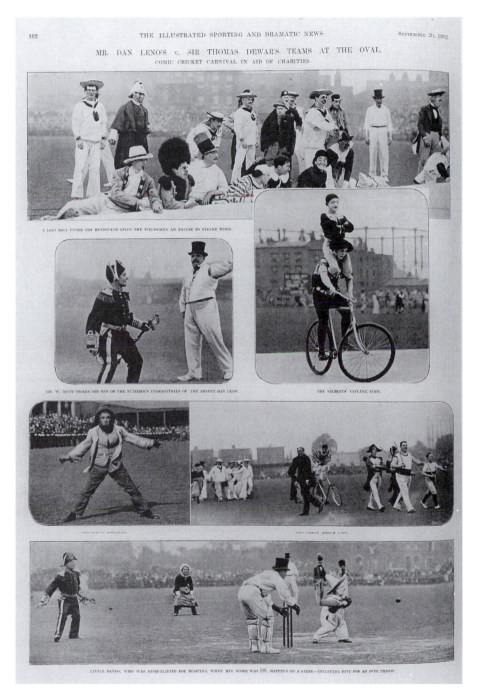

MR. DAN LENO'S v. SIR THOMAS DEWAR'S TEAMS AT THE OVAL.
COMIC CRICKET CARNIVAL IN AID OF CHARITIES.

A LOST BALL UNDER THE BANDSTAND GIVES THE FIELDSMEN AN EXCUSE TO STRIKE WORK.

MR. W. MOTT ORDERS OFF ONE OF THE NUMEROUS UNDERSTUDIES OF THE ABSENT DAN LENO.

THE SELBINIS' CYCLING TURN.

LITTLE DANDO, WHO WAS DISQUALIFIED FOR BUMPING WHEN HIS SCORE WAS 195, HAPPENS ON A SIXER—INCLUDING FIVE FOR AN OVER THROW.

Syd May, in naval uniform, impersonates the dying Dan Leno in the 1902 Oval charity match.

13

there is no doubt that the great comedian's name has been responsible for the good attendances and heavy money-bags in the past. Last year everybody thought 'Dan' would be present, and nearly all thought he was there. Result, a gate of 24,000 people. Yesterday everybody knew of his absence, and at no time did the attendance reach more than 8,000 persons all told.[40]

Nor could organisers obliterate memories of Leno's play at the event he founded because 'his great feats in the past were talked of with awe' by spectators.[41]

This nostalgic link was visible on the pitch where Johnny Danvers, Leno's uncle, led his Moore and Burgess Minstrel Comic Cricketers.[42] Many artistes reinforced the sense of loss by reverting to gags they had tested in previous years. Little Dando's partner Bumper Mott, dressed as the hirsute W. G. Grace, captained the artistes from behind a fulsome beard, white flannel trousers, striped blazer and a public school cap. Karno's *Jail Birds* were chased repeatedly across the pitch by policemen, apprehended and locked securely in a Black Maria only to escape anew. Harry Tate drove an automobile beset with mechanical problems around the pitch as in his up-to-date sketch *Motoring*.[43] Nell Lynch displayed her marksmanship with a rifle, and the bands of the Irish Guards, L Division of police and Licensed Victuallers' Schools appeared.[44] Less energetic lady artistes again sold programmes in the stands.[45] Spectators, by now acutely aware of Leno's absence, heard a message from his wife who 'accompanied by her little daughter Alice arrived on the scene, after visiting her distinguished husband' just before four o'clock, when rain ended the day's play. The wild applause she faced, testimony to how greatly her dying husband was missed, fittingly closed the last edition of a match that had once been so popular.[46]

But music-hall cricket did not end abruptly that afternoon, for two weeks later Miss Sable Fern announced that she would enact *My Cricket Girl* on stage.[47] Oswald Stoll produced a cricket match between county professionals from Middlesex and Surrey behind a safety net raised across the Coliseum's proscenium in 1908.[48] In the same year seven-year-old Greville Stevens impressed music-hall critics with his 'novel exhibition' imitating famous cricketers at the wicket.[49] Harking back to Dewar's days, Harry Lauder wore a kilt on the pitch in 1910 to play the Newcastle press as music-hall comic cricket gasped its dying breath (Figure 14).[50]

Leno succumbed to alcoholism a little more than one year after the third Oval gala when his emotive sway over fans permanently disappeared. Herbert Campbell passed away suddenly thereafter. Thus two cricket clowns died as their sport faced new challenges, but enthusiastic players like George Robey now allied themselves with boxing and association football, London's emerging

Harry Lauder, Kilted Komic Kricketer.   **14**

sporting passions. Dewar's attentions, as we shall see, were also drawn away while Moss Empires were evidently disappointed enough with the final Oval match not to sponsor another. Even if Leno's sanity had returned, most artistes would probably have abandoned a game that interested them only so long as it updated their turns. Though charity receipts remained laudable, cricket paid devaluing personal promotional returns in the face of newer sports, and so we must now look more comprehensively at its more enduring successors.

Notes

1 'Music hall gossip', *The Era*, 16 November 1901, p. 20.
2 Letter, 'Acting and cricketing', *The Era*, 19 April 1890, p. 9; 'Music hall gossip', *The Era*, 29 September 1894, p. 17; 'Music hall gossip', *The Era*, 4 April 1896, p. 17; and 'Charity cricket carnival at Newcastle', *The Era*, 22 August 1896, p. 11. For Robey see George Robey, *Looking Back on Life*, London, Constable, 1933, pp. 123–128;

James Harding, *George Robey and the Music-Hall*, London, Hodder and Stoughton, 1990, pp. 64–65; and Edward Robey, *The Jester and the Court*, London, Kimber, 1976, p. 26.

3 'Music hall gossip', *The Era*, 17 May, 1894, p. 17, and 'Music hall gossip', *The Era*, 27 April 1895, p. 17.

4 'Music hall gossip', *The Era*, 23 July 1904, p. 18.

5 'Music hall gossip', *The Era*, 6 May 1893, p. 17; 'Music hall gossip', *The Era*, 6 May 1899, p. 19; and Untitled, *The Era*, 19 August 1899, p. 17.

6 'Music hall gossip', *The Era*, 16 August 1902, p. 18; Barry Anthony, 'Earliest cricket on film', *Wisden Cricket Monthly*, December 1993, pp. 32–33.

7 Albert Knight, *The Complete Cricketer*, London, Methuen, 1906, pp. 68 and 265–269.

8 Roland Wild, *The Biography of Colonel His Highness Shri Sir Ranjitsinhji*, London, Rich and Cowan, 1934, pp. 30–43.

9 'The first lesson', *The Autocar*, 21 December 1901, p. 616.

10 'Music hall gossip', *The Era*, 18 June 1898, p. 17.

11 'Music hall gossip', *The Era*, 10 September 1898, p. 18, and for the total raised see 'Music hall gossip', *The Era*, 24 September 1898, p. 19.

12 'Music hall gossip', *The Era*, 1 October 1898, p. 19; 'Cricket extraordinary: The Danites scoring for charity', *Daily Mail*, 29 September 1898, p. 6.

13 'Music hall cricket', *Daily Chronicle*, 29 September 1898, p. 7.

14 'Cricket extraordinary: The Danites scoring for charity', *Daily Mail*, 29 September 1898, p. 6.

15 'Cricket extraordinary: The Danites scoring for charity', *Daily Mail*, 29 September 1898, p. 6.

16 'Music hall gossip', *The Era*, 14 January 1899, p. 19.

17 'Music hall gossip', *The Era*, 3 June 1899, p. 19.

18 'Music hall gossip', *The Era*, 17 February 1900, p. 18.

19 'Daniel does a little bit off his own bat', *Dan Leno's Comic Journal*, 29 July 1899, p. 313; 'Music hall gossip', *The Era*, 6 October 1900, p. 18.

20 Stephen Herbert and Luke McKernan, *Who's Who of Victorian Cinema*, London, British Film Institute, 1996, p. 81.

21 'Music hall gossip', *The Era*, 8 June 1901, p. 18, and for the total raised see 'Music hall gossip', *The Era*, 15 June 1901, p. 18.

22 'Music hall gossip', *The Era*, 24 August 1901, p. 18, and 'Comic cricket at the Oval', *Daily News*, 6 September 1901, p. 8.

23 'Cricket by comedians', *The Era*, 7 September 1901, p. 19.

24 'Comic cricket at the Oval', *Daily News*, 6 September 1901, p. 8.

25 'Mr Leno plays cricket', *Daily Mail*, 6 September 1901, p. 3.

26 'Dan Leno at the Oval', *The Sun*, 5 September 1901, unnumbered pages.

27 '"Cricket" at the Oval: Mr Dan Leno makes a record score', *Daily Chronicle*, 6 September 1901, p. 8; 'A charity match', *Licensed Victuallers' Gazette and Hotel Courier*, 6 September 1901, p. 586.

28 'Mr Leno plays cricket', *Daily Mail*, 6 September 1901, p. 3.

29 'Comic cricket at the Oval', *Daily News*, 6 September 1901, p. 8, and '"Cricket" at the Oval: Mr. Dan Leno makes a record score', *Daily Chronicle*, 6 September 1901, p. 8.

30 Anthony, 'Earliest cricket on film', p. 33.

31 'Music hall gossip', *The Era*, 9 August 1902, p. 20.

32 'Music hall gossip', *The Era*, 16 August 1902, p. 18.

33 'Music hall gossip', *The Era*, 13 September 1902, p. 20.

34 '"King's jester" ill', *Daily Mail*, 11 September 1902, p. 3.

35 'Mr Dan Leno's v. Sir Thomas Dewar's teams at the Oval; comic cricket in aid of charities', *The Illustrated Sporting and Dramatic News*, 20 September 1902, p. 102.

36 'Cricket gone mad', *Daily Chronicle,* 11 September 1902, p. 6.

37 'Comical cricket', *Daily News*, 11 September 1902, p. 11.

38 'Comic cricket', *Licensed Victuallers' Gazette and Hotel Courier,* 12 September 1902, p. 632, and 'The Leno carnival', *Daily Express*, 11 September 1902, p. 8.

39 'The Leno carnival', *Daily Express*, 11 September 1902, p. 8.

40 'Comic cricket match: absence of Dan Leno makes difference in gate', *Daily Express*, 19 September 1903, p. 7.

41 'Sensational cricket', *Daily Chronicle*, 19 September 1903, p. 9.

42 'Music hall gossip', *The Era*, 22 August 1903, p. 20. Danvers' team is also mentioned in 'Music hall gossip', *The Era*, 28 June 1902, p. 16.

43 'The comic cricket carnival at Kennington Oval on behalf of music hall and other charities', *The Illustrated Sporting and Dramatic News*, 26 September 1903, p. 150.

44 'Comic cricket carnival', *Daily News*, 19 September 1903, p. 11.

45 'Sensational cricket', *Daily Chronicle*, 19 September 1903, p. 9.

46 'Comic cricket match: absence of Dan Leno makes difference in gate', *Daily Express*, 19 September 1903, p. 7.

47 Advertisement, *The Era*, 3 October 1903, p. 39.

48 Felix Barker, *The House that Stoll Built: The Story of the Coliseum Theatre*, London, Frederick Muller, 1957, pp. 165–166, and 'Variety gossip', *The Era*, 22 February 1908, p. 22.

49 'Why not this new method of imitation in the halls', *The Sketch*, 17 June 1908, p. 298.

50 'Kilted for the fray', *The Sketch*, 10 August 1910, p. 144.

10

Boxing

Cricket's golden age was parallelled by that of boxing which was transformed from brutal, semi-legal origins to middle- class respectability during the two decades before the First World War. The most important early bases for this new game were the National Sporting Club in Covent Garden, which opened in 1891; the music halls; the Ring, Blackfriars, which opened in 1895; and the cinema after 1897. This progress culminated in the 1914 'boxing boom' that was staged before enormous audiences, primarily at the Olympia in Kensington.

Victorian prizefighting had seen hulking men adopted by aristocrats, publicans or gamblers who housed, fed and employed them, arranged contests and paid purses from side wagers. Though fought under an eighteenth-century code of rules, the viciousness of bare-knuckle fights made them illegal and so they were held secretly in public house gardens before a local clientele. National championships took place in secluded fields which spectators approached stealthily lest they be discovered by vigilant local authorities out to arrest both the crowd and combatants. Fights lasted until one contestant was knocked unconscious; there was no referee to intervene and protect an insensible man from the finishing blow.

Pugilism was replaced by modern boxing at the end of the century through the foundation of a strident regulatory agency enforcing the Queensberry rules of 1867, which insisted upon referees, gloves and a counted ten-second knock-out. This body, the National Sporting Club (NSC), was founded in 1891 out of the ashes of its roistering predecessor, the Pelican Club, which had occupied the same Covent Garden building. The Pelicans had been a mixture of peers, gentlemen, journalists and actors, including the sports-mad Prince of Wales, who had assembled to watch fights, gamble and carouse in premises that had once housed Evans' Song and Supper Rooms, one of the earliest music halls. The club had converted the 1,300-seat basement auditorium into a private boxing venue.[1]

On the Pelican's bankruptcy in early 1891 John Fleming and 'Peggy' Bettinson took over the premises and renamed the building the National Sporting Club. No longer a home to privileged spendthrifts, this private club 'was a businesslike undertaking of business men for other business men'.[2] Bettinson's capital had underwritten much of the new venture and he ruled the club as an opinionated, outspoken patriarch of British boxing for the next thirty-two years. From 1891 Fleming and Bettinson courted middle-class patrons to their establishment. White ties were no longer required; smoking at ring-side was banned. The club guaranteed the honesty of its bookmakers, while its board of directors acted as a *de facto* national supervisory agency for the sport. Given boxing's uncertain legal status, the NSC acted circumspectly as a private venue. As such it was tolerated by the local magistracy. However, the club's directors were prosecuted unsuccessfully four times after boxers had died in the ring; the final acquittal, in 1901, legalised boxing in Britain.[3]

The comedian Arthur Roberts and George Edwardes, manager of the Gaiety Theatre, had been the most prominent of many stage members of the Pelican Club, and the connection between stage and ring was not severed by the NSC, which hosted musical and dramatic evenings at which actors from both the halls and legitimate drama performed.[4] King Edward's continued patronage was celebrated when American and British fighters met at the Albert Hall under the NSC's banner in 1901 in a Coronation Tournament. Encouraged by the popularity of this show, Bettinson organised the NSC's first weekend gala where fighting was interspersed with performances by leading music-hall artistes. Walter de Frece – the syndicate owner, club member and husband of Vesta Tilley – chaired this event at which Harry Lauder and the Scottish international rugby footballer W. A. Peterkin were the star non-fighting attractions.[5]

By such means as the Coronation Tournament, the NSC adapted to an expanding, open boxing world at the turn of the century. Small London halls had staged furtive sparring contests to promote local fighters from the 1890s in a relic of the role pubs had played during the prize ring era. After the 1901 judgement, they too were able more openly to present prominent men, both nationally and internationally.[6] Until it burned down in 1911, Wonderland in Whitechapel Road held weekly tournaments for local and national fighters, while The Ring in Blackfriars Road opened 1908 as a more proletarian rival to the NSC. These new arenas continued the democratisation of the sport. Women were not officially barred, as they were from the NSC, though their presence was rare. Finally, music-hall and theatrical promoters such as Charles B. Cochran and the Australian Hugh D. 'Huge Deal' Macintosh soon perceived

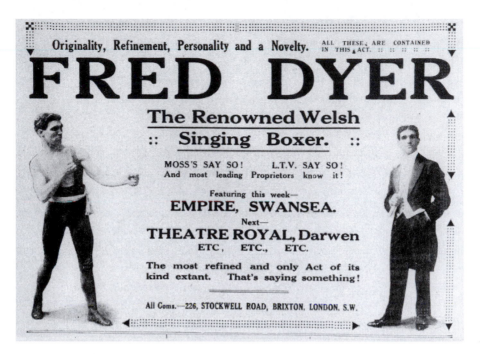

Originality, Refinement, Personality and a Novelty. ALL THESE ARE CONTAINED IN THIS ACT. :: :: :: :: ::

FRED DYER

The Renowned Welsh
:: Singing Boxer. ::

MOSS'S SAY SO!   L.T.V. SAY SO!
And most leading Proprietors know it!

Featuring this week—
EMPIRE, SWANSEA.
Next—
THEATRE ROYAL, Darwen
ETC, ETC., ETC.

The most refined and only Act of its
kind extant.   That's saying something!

All Coms.—226, STOCKWELL ROAD, BRIXTON, LONDON, S.W.

15   During the boxing boom any excuse was permitted to introduce the sport on to the music-hall stage.

these changes and leased the capital's largest arenas like the Olympia where they offered enormous purses to the world's best fighters. These new boxing venues accommodated thousands of spectators, boosted prize money enormously and effectively eclipsed the NSC, which responded briefly by leasing a large skating rink in Holland Park to host public fights, but retreated soon after to the cloisters of Covent Garden.[7]

The displacement was not complete as newer arenas did not copy the NSC's role as a paternalistic boxing academy where entertaining fighters like the immensely popular 'Pedlar' Palmer of Canning Town were trained, developed and promoted. Palmer was a gregarious lightweight who had boxed in London's penny gaffs.[8] Palmer's flair attracted the NSC who oversaw his training and scheduled fights for him. By these means club favourites were guaranteed regular matches from which they earned comfortable, though not extravagant, livings. However, Palmer was unable to restrain his spending and so like many Edwardian fighters reared by the NSC, he decamped for Wonderland's money.

The NSC's position at the top of British boxing was jeopardised by financial inducements for fighters to leave and so the directors mortgaged the club's most valuable remaining asset: historic prestige. In 1908 the committee began awarding Lonsdale championship belts to the best fighters in specific, regulated weight categories. These trophies were named for Lord Lonsdale, one of the most famous amateur sportsmen of the day and a long-serving official of the club. This was the NSC's reasoned, fiscally responsible alternative to public boxing spectacles. Lonsdale belts did not carry with them big purses because they could only be won at the NSC; however, fighters retained them permanently after a third successful defence and retired champions were entitled to an annual £50 pension.[9]

Not surprisingly the Lonsdale belts failed to keep boxers within the NSC's stable. Palmer's career exemplified the way canny fighters gained experience and fame at the club, which they then exploited in other arenas, only returning to the NSC for the minimum number of title defences. Though British champions could only be crowned at the NSC, they refused to grant its directors monopolistic control of their careers and were enriched elsewhere. The NSC committee was not wholly misguided though, because there could have been no effective Edwardian inducement to amateurism once heavyweights – with their tremendous punches, constant maulings and threats of permanent injury – defected from the club at the end of the century when their division became the most glamorous and popular in the world.

One must look to the United States for other crucial developments of spectacular fighting. John L. Sullivan punched himself out of the Irish ghettos of Massachusetts to become the United States' heavyweight champion in 1882 and one of that country's most recognisable and idolised men. Success gave Sullivan a taste for high living and so he supplemented his income throughout the next decade by touring incessantly with vaudeville shows, where he earned five hundred dollars per night boxing local braggarts. He spent his wages courting chorus girls.[10] Sullivan's shift from sports arenas to music halls changed boxing. Sullivan toured Britain only once, in 1888. Buffalo Bill had only just left London and so Sullivan supplanted him as the ambassador of American up-to-dateness. A huge crowd met his train at Euston and saw him box at St James's Hall, Piccadilly, before embarking on a national tour that culminated in a twelve-night engagement at the Westminster Aquarium, election to the Pelican Club, and a private bout before the Prince of Wales. Throughout his stay Sullivan dressed like a vulgar spendthrift – or music-hall swell – in striped trousers, frock coat and top hat, parading through the streets and challenging all British heavyweights. Before leaving the country he defeated the Britsh Champion, Charlie Mitchell, at Portsmouth.[11]

Two years later Sullivan changed the way boxing was presented in the halls by commissioning the melodrama *Honest Hearts and Willing Hands*, in which he played an amorous blacksmith who knocked out the villain in the final scene. Sullivan's income soared to as much as $50,000 per year with this move away from the traditions of the carnival boxer who dared all-comers, though vaudeville life permanently compromised the champion's physical stamina as he gorged, drank excessively and boxed primarily in exhibitions with untrained amateurs during his ten-year reign.[12]

Sullivan lost his crown to San Francisco's 'Gentleman' Jim Corbett in 1892. Corbett was an affable, attractive San Francisco bank clerk whose career was managed by Broadway impresario William Brady. Brady crafted a refined persona for his fighter: where Sullivan mingled with fans in taverns, Corbett haunted the poshest hotels. Brady masterminded a prolonged campaign during which Corbett taunted the champion from vaudeville stages all across the country. Corbett faced local fighters in the halls, where he also sang up-to-date songs such as 'Ta-ra-ra-boom-de-ay'. Sullivan was eventually forced to meet this challenge. The two then sparred clad in formal white-tie outfits – Corbett was after all a 'gentleman' – in California, where Sullivan's theatrical company was awaiting passage to Australia. After this bout Corbett travelled with a popular minstrel troupe, where he sparred between turns, and then starred in a Broadway boxing melodrama. By virtue of Corbett's touring, Americans were able to assess his skills and Sullivan could no longer only fight him in a stagey manner. The flabby, dissolute Sullivan was eventually sufficiently pressured to meet the 'aspirants for fistic fame and championship honours'.[13] Corbett accepted this open challenge and, so as not to conflict with Sullivan's music-hall tour, a bout was scheduled for New Orleans in September 1892. Corbett won the first world championship between gloved men adhering to the Queensberry rules.

The new champion then emulated Sullivan by demonstrating his skills in music halls on his way home to New York. Once at home he commissioned the play *Gentleman Jack*, in which he portrayed a Princeton student vying with the nasty Charlie Twitchell for the love of the female lead. Naturally, the play's climax saw Corbett knock Twitchell out.[14] The villain's name had been chosen by Brady to taunt Sullivan's one-time opponent, Charlie Mitchell, who insisted Corbett fight him. Corbett then took the play to London's Drury Lane Theatre where he benefited once again from Brady's theatrical nous. The showman distributed free passes to the 'Champion's Box' to pubs and sporting clubs throughout the capital. Bearers of these tickets were, if space permitted, allowed to sit in a special box on stage for the fight. On stage these punters rubbed shoulders with prominent sportsmen who had been publicly invited to appear. After its London engagement the play toured the provinces and Europe.[15] Corbett then returned home in 1895 to introduce *The Naval Cadet*, in which he perpetuated his gentlemanly image by playing a Harvard undergraduate. In his absence, Corbett's challengers had been touring American theatres to show off their prowess. In a segregated land, his most redoubtable opponent, the West Indian Peter Jackson, kept his name before the public by touring as Simon Legree in a production of *Uncle Tom's Cabin*, to which boxing scenes had been added.[16] Corbett relinquished his crown in 1896 when promoters could not find a venue for a bout with the tall, spare, red-haired Cornishman Robert Fitzsimmons. This was no rash measure, as the abstemious Corbett's stage salary and investments were far greater than what he earned in the ring.[17]

The two men were eventually persuaded to meet in Carson City, Nevada, in March 1897. Carson City was so remote that few fans attended the fight. However, it was the first title bout to be filmed, by three cinema cameras installed in the stadium. Perhaps in order to mollify his famous vanity, Corbett announced in his autobiography that he had agreed to the bout partly because a cinematic record of the fight would make it an historic affair.[18] Film of this exciting match, which Fitzsimmons won by a fourteenth-round knock-out, was screened to adulation in New York and Chicago over the summer and then re-edited to improve the action before its London début in September 1897. The soubrette and pantomime principal-boy Ada Reeve, who toured Melbourne Australia in 1897, recalled that music-hall patrons in that city could choose between three sensational films, depending on the hall they attended: fight fans watched the Corbett–Fitzsimmons bout, while cricketers evaluated the batting form of Prince Ranjitsinhji who was then in the country with the English team, and monarchists witnessed the Queen driving through the streets of London at her Diamond Jubilee celebrations.[19] Fitzsimmons then lifted a page from Corbett's book. A blacksmith by trade, Fitzsimmons spent two years touring the world's music halls with *The Honest Blacksmith*, in which he made horseshoes that he inscribed with his name and distributed to the audience.[20] Seeking a less punishing living, Corbett permanently retired after losing the fight to concentrate on stage plays while Fitzsimmons also took up acting full time after he quit the ring six years later. For the rest of their lives both men toured the halls extensively and prominently attended major heavyweight fights.[21]

Corbett's appearances at music halls had demonstrated his skills to boxing fans for whom no compelling visual account of his fights were available. These appearances also fostered and promoted Corbett's cultivated image, thus helping to raise boxing out of the gloom of saloons. Films completed this evolution, and as the best heavy weight fighters were drawn away from the ring to the music-hall stage they became celebrities. Not even the biggest American prize purses matched the steady income from theatrical receipts. Real fighting was no longer the sole, safest or easiest way for boxers to make money.

The effect was soon felt in England. George Gray proved – by preaching fundamentalist muscular Christianity in *The Fighting Parson*, one of the most popular Edwardian music-hall melodramas – that British artistes quickly co-opted the emerging craze for spectacular heavyweight boxing. Harry Lundy of the Royal, Holborn, obeyed his up-to-date theatrical sense by backing a new sketch which starred the popular clerical hero of the earlier playlets *Road to Ruin* and *Parson Gray*. The play climaxed when the boxing clergyman trounced the local evil-doer.[22] *The Fighting Parson* premiered at the Royal in January 1903 where it ran for 159 performances before commencing a decade-long tour.[23] It is clear that, despite twenty years between John L. Sullivan's stage début and this play, music-hall fight fans' tastes had not greatly matured; they wanted to see uncompromisingly bad men decisively bested in the final scene by unimpeachably good heroes.

British audiences were primed by these fights, plays and films for the emergence of Jack Johnson, a gigantic, gold-toothed, garrulous man from the docks of Galveston Texas who was the next great American heavyweight. After defeating Fitzsimmons's successor, James J. Jeffries, and the best opponents at home Johnson arrived in Britain in 1908 in pursuit of Tommy Burns, the reigning world champion. Burns was an American of Quebecois extraction who had earned a reputed £10,000 when he defeated Britain's pug-faced, tattooed Gunner Moir for the Lonsdale title at the NSC in December 1907.[24] The NSC recouped some of its expenses by filming the fight, which was screened at the Alhambra in Leicester Square.[25] An American approach to boxing, still novel to London, raised awareness of the fight as the two men trained publicly while Burns regularly and conspicuously relaxed in the evenings at London music halls.[26] Having taken Moir's belt, in February 1908, Burns bested Jack Palmer in East London before embarking on a fighting tour of the British Isles, while simultaneously publishing an illustrated book of training tips for aspiring boxers. Moir had published such a book the year before, but nothing outdated a champion's feints and training tips as quickly, it seems, as losing the title.[27] These new promotions also paid dividends to Moir who earned £44 for one week at the Oxford Music Hall two months after the contest, where he sparred and presented a film of himself boxing.[28]

Despite the intense interest in matching them, Johnson and Burns, the two most prominent fighters of the day, demanded far more money than the NSC was able to offer. Like Corbett before him, Johnson maintained the pressure on Burns partly by giving boxing demonstrations at the Oxford.[29] Burns was then lured to Sydney Australia by Hugh D. 'Huge Deal' Macintosh's financial guarantees, to which city Johnson pursued him. The two fought that December at Rushcutter's Bay in a specially constructed open-air stadium. The champion was not equal to Johnson, who spent the first twelve rounds casually fending off his opponent's challenges whilst grinning at the cinema cameras at the side of the ring.[30] After making a sufficiently compelling spectacle, Johnson knocked Burns out – but the glory was not solely his, as sporting fans were urged as a consolation to see 'the awful punishment Tommy receives and the plucky way he takes it' when the film was shown at the Hackney Empire in May 1909.[31] Edwardian boxing fans learned again and again to appreciate a defeated man's determined heroism.

Jeffries was then prompted out of retirement by people who hoped he could stop Johnson. The two men fought a patriotic battle in Nevada on 4 July 1910, when Johnson's swift, efficient knock-out forced people in the arena, and those who saw the film, to acknowledge that he was indisputably the best fighter in the world. But his advent from national to international renown created a new, frantic boxing climate as fans and promoters the world over sought a successful challenger.[32] This activity was spurred by the reality, unsettling to many at a time when eugenic theories of race enjoyed widespread credibility, that the best fighter in the world was black.

Boxing had deep racist roots.[33] John L. Sullivan had refused to fight black men throughut his career. Such feelings caused film of the Johnson–Burns bout to be banned from many American cinemas.[34] Nevertheless, films of Johnson fights, which were always entertaining because of the champion's flair and showmanship, were *succès de scandale* and so he was offered huge sums by film producers for exclusive rights.[35] Johnson, who had had trouble finding venues in the US for his bouts, hoped England would be more accommodating to black fighters. The NSC tried unsuccessfully to bring Johnson into their fold by offering him one-third of all revenue generated by a film of his first London championship bout.[36] This was the only way the Club's small auditorium could compete with stadium purses. When the best, most famous fighter alive spurned Bettinson's approach the NSC was effectively displaced as the foremost boxing centre.

Film and stage appearances made Johnson one of the planet's most recognisable men, while frantic promoters the world over sought a suitable challenger, the initial 'great white hope', to take the Texan's title. Up-to-date music-hall cinema parodied the hunt for the new challenger by promoting Willie Sanders in 1910's *The Man to Beat Jack Johnson*. In this film, Sanders, a blonde-headed Scouse four-year-old, boxed an adult who sat on the floor. Hard, swift punches were delivered by both fighters, but Willie flexed his biceps in triumph and smiled at the camera after knocking out his opponent in the third round.[37] Johnson's endeavours were equally ludicrous. Because he was invincible and unavailable in the ring Johnson was in demand as a music-hall performer. This was the persona that most Londoners saw because Johnson fought only once in England, as a precursor to the Burns match. Music-hall tours also provided him with a reliable income. The champion was also a skilful clown who stopped his best punches millimetres short of George Robey before being downed by the comedian's desperately flailing arms in charity bouts at the Palladium.[38] Johnson regularly appeared on British stages right up to the outbreak of the First World War, when he was starring in a London revue called *Seconds Out.* [39]

This tension between an NSC-led sport where 'honour' accounted for more than prize money, the development of the boxer as music-hall celebrity and the search for Johnson's challenger provided the background for the emergence of Bombardier Billy Wells, Edwardian Britain's most popular fighter and one of the first modern celebrities. A review of his rather mediocre career statistics confirms that Wells was 'at once the greatest favourite and the greatest disappointment the sporting public of this country has known'.[40] He fought in only twenty-six irregularly spaced bouts during the four years before the war. Losses in important fights were followed hastily by victories over less renowned opponents which restored Wells's public image. But Wells's celebrity and career in top-level boxing lasted much longer than was accounted for by his prowess, thanks to his 'subtle magnetism that attracts the interest of even those who care little for boxing' and the ways in which he exploited this status.[41]

Wells was born in Stepney in August 1887, represented his school at football and subscribed to *Sandow's Magazine* while working as a message runner. The young athlete strengthened his muscles for sports and taught boxing at a local youth club, but resisted developing a body-builder's mass.[42] He enlisted in 1906, a decade after the inaugural army boxing championships, and was posted to an artillery company in India where three years later he won the force's heavyweight title at Simla. From the latter nineteenth century, military leaders had endorsed inter-regimental boxing tournaments as a means of promoting physical fitness and martial spirit in the ranks.[43] Because of this patronage, at the turn of the century a force's title-holder was probably equal in skill to a professional national champion. Promoters regularly poached the best fighters from the regimental rosters and so an Edwardian roll call of British boxers lists many 'privates', 'gunners', 'bandsmen' and 'stokers'. Wells was not immune to this system. Jim Maloney, an army boxing instructor stationed in India, recognised the bombardier's talents, befriended him and sent photos and encouraging reports to London's boxing press. Billy then purchased his discharge in April 1910 and returned home, to train for a professional game that was 'shrieking for a "White Hope"'.[44] After only nine fights, in one of which he was convincingly defeated by the ageing Gunner Moir before cinema cameras, Wells won the first of his three Lonsdale belts in the spring of 1911.

Relatively few professional fights established the Bombardier as the apotheosis of the boxer/artiste. Tall, muscular and blonde, this shy but affable man's face had not been ravaged by years in the ring. As a result of the route which had brought him to boxing Wells had the graceful, symmetrically proportioned body of an all-round athlete, rather than that of an experienced fighter.[45] He was lithe and fair when other heavyweights looked fleshy and battered. Wells's personality belied his physical appearance as virtually all Edwardian commentators blamed the glaring defeats of his career on stage fright, anxiety, shyness and lack of self-belief. Despite these deficiencies, any one of which might have precluded a fighting career, Wells was extolled, as Tommy Burns had been, for exemplifying character traits which the British middle-classes lauded, such as the pluck to stand up to formidable opponents, perseverance in the face of adversity and graceful good humour in defeat. Despite this romanticism, Wells assessed his vulnerability more prosaically by saying that he was 'naturally of a nervous and quick disposition'.[46]

Billy first fought in London at Wonderland in 1910, after which his career was guided by Hugh D. Macintosh. Having lost to Moir in a filmed bout, Wells set out almost immediately on the first of many music-hall engagements by sparring nightly at the Euston Palace and the Canterbury in order to promote himself to the public as the coming champion.[47] Wells secured the Lonsdale belt after a year-long series of matches on the London halls during which time he trained with a body-builder to increase his strength and was boomed heavily by the boxing and athletic presses.[48] Possession of the Lonsdale belt, which he won from 'Iron' Hague, cemented Wells's claim to be Johnson's next opponent.

The two men agreed to fight at the Earls Court arena in October 1911 for the biggest British purse ever, which would be financed by film revenues.[49] Agitation against the bout – led by the Reverend F. B. Meyer, the newly appointed secretary to the National Free Church Council – began almost immediately. Meyer promoted this non-sectarian issue as a balm to salve schismatic tensions within his organisation. Council deputies canvassed widely for a public campaign aimed at preventing a display of Johnson's reputed savagery. The testimonial's goal was enunciated with suitably religious imagery, given its authors, as a merciful crusade to protect Wells from facing a vastly superior opponent 'before he has come to his full strength and is out of his noviciate'.[50] Within a week colonial clerics and administrators complained to *The Times* that the bout and the film of it intended for the halls would cause racial problems throughout the empire, especially if, as expected, Johnson won.[51] At home, Meyer obtained the support of prominent politicians, academics and ecclesiastics, including the Archbishop of Canterbury, for his memorial against the fight.[52] By the end of September the government could not ignore this appeal by a broad section of middle-class opinion and the Home Secretary issued writs against Wells and Johnson for attempted breach of the peace. While a judge considered the matter, the owners of Earls Court obtained an injunction against the fight's promoters. The pair never boxed one another, and Johnson began an itinerant life, appearing on stage and, whenever possible, in the ring.[53]

Preparations for the match were as public as the demonstrations against it, with Wells training initially on a Blackpool stage.[54] However, he moved back home after Eugene Corri, the Eastbourne stockbroker who was the most prominent Edwardian boxing referee, announced that Wells would win the fight, an encomium that prompted London music-hall managers to book Wells, who was then advertised as 'The man Mr Eugene Corri thinks will beat Johnson'.[55] Audiences demanded more than endless exhibition rounds and so Wells commissioned the play *Wanted, a Man* with roles for himself, his younger brother Syd, an accomplished fighter in his own right, and Billy's manager Jim Maloney. This melodrama – in which Wells's character, the servant Jack Bandon, fought a bare-knuckle contest with the rakish Squire Hazelton – reflected London's mood (Figure 16). The Tottenham Palace filled with wild cheers when Wells's character boasted 'I'm afraid of no man white or black' in a thinly veiled challenge to Johnson.[56] Wells appeared subsequently at six other London halls as well as the Ardwick Empire, Manchester, in pre-fight promotions.[57] Once speculation about Billy's chances had been whipped up to a peak he published his personal training tips for young fighters.[58] Meanwhile, Johnson pitched camp at the Royal Forest Hotel, Chingford where he starred at the local hall and for three weeks in succession at the Oxford.[59] Both men were also contractually required to work out publicly twice daily in the fight venue at Earls Court, while the promoter covered London with advertisements.[60] Meanwhile, the

The Great White Hope is launched in London. Billy Wells takes to the stage during the
run-up to his aborted fight with Jack Johnson.   **16**

boxing press carried photos of both fighters relaxing in their motor-cars, along
with one of Wells developing his lungs and agility by playing an informal game
of football with his trainers.[61]

As a result of this unprecedented promotion, Wells's career was nearly eclipsed
when the Johnson bout fell through. He fought only one more time, at the NSC,
that year. The denouement lasted throughout 1912. Though he had been cast as
the villain in this melodrama, Johnson's immediate fortunes were somewhat
easier. He was booked by Sir Edward Moss for the Palladium immediately after
the fight had been prohibited. Moss explained to his critics that it was his duty to
his shareholders to present up-to-date acts that drew large crowds.[62] Continued
speculation about which white fighter would take the title from Johnson
prompted the film *The Night I Fought Jack Johnson* in which the champion was
portrayed by a man in a dark leotard with burnt cork on his face while his white
opponent wore a boating jacket and tie in the ring. After a few initial blows the
comedian approached the near-side ropes where he appealed lamentably to
viewers for mercy, while 'Johnson' was fanned by seconds who whitened his face
with shaving foam in an overt comment on the racist objections to the Wells

fight. The white fighter's appeals to the audience intermingled with rounds in which the demonic Johnson stalked his fleeing opponent about the ring.[63] This was the cinematic equivalent of a 1911 topical song of the same name by Harry Castling.[64] As this film made the rounds of London cinemas, George Gray, who was wearying of stage sparring, decided to film *The Fighting Parson*, with a cast of two hundred and fifty in a critically acclaimed and popular 3½ minute spectacular.[65] After a brief sabbatical the clerical stage hero joined up in 1914 for the topical wartime sketch *Parson Gray VC.*

As British champion Wells sailed to New York in May 1912, intending to arrange lucrative fights with America's best boxers. Unfortunately, in his first contest he was knocked out in the third round, before defeating a less- esteemed opponent and returning home. London always proved a welcoming haven for Wells whose September 1912 marriage to the sixteen-year-old daughter of a Tooting publican was reported in sporting and national newspapers.[66] Police marshalled the hundreds-strong crowd of both sexes that assembled outside the South London church, where the couple were photographed many times by the press, while sandwich-board men circulated announcing that scenes from the wedding would be presented that night at a local music hall.[67] Having reclaimed his fame, Wells toured the London halls that autumn, sparring and exhibiting a film of his training sessions.[68] Billy then re-established his fighting name when he needed just two rounds to beat the South African champion George Rodel at King's Hall in December, his first London fight in twelve months.

Cinema also helped rehabilitate Wells's image. In a film released at the time of the Rodel bout, an incensed Billy raced to Paris after hearing the child-boxer Willie Sanders' usurping public claim to his title. Both fighters scoffed indignantly when French promoters offered only fifteen thousand francs each to meet in the ring. They countered by demanding fifteen, but eventually settled for ten, million francs a piece. Wild cheers from a female chorus, tribute to his real-life barrackers, filled the room when Wells climbed into the ring to face his challenger. The first round saw Sanders knocked down though he recovered sufficiently in the second round to stamp on Billy's toes and punch him repeatedly while he hopped about in agony. A hobbling Wells then granted Sanders' request to fight the rest of the round whilst seated on the floor. Wells obviously did not attend the cinema often enough to recognise his opponent's favoured methods. Repeated blows dazed and dropped Billy who struggled to a sitting position after a count of six. 1912's ignominy plumbed its profoundest depths for Wells when Sanders crept through the distracted referee's legs to deliver the knock-out punch just as his opponent righted himself (Figure 17). The fighters' contrasting

Music hall, cinema and boxing converge as Billy Wells faces Willie Sanders.   **17**

statures, 'already enough to make a dead hyena laugh' had been emphasised as they entered the ring and were recalled again in the final scene of this movie when Wells held Sanders in his arms so that the two could, literally, kiss and make up.[69]

Despite his stage and screen bravado and Corri's boasting, Wells was not, strictly, a great boxer. He met his most accomplished opponents in 1913, mirroring the previous year with its swift, disappointing defeats to Gunboat Smith in New York in March and to the youthful French light-heavyweight Georges Carpentier at Ghent, Belgium, in June.[70] July saw Wells fight twice in London to yet again restore his public image, which he accomplished in September by beating the now senescent Gunner Moir – the only Englishman who had ever bested him.

Georges Carpentier was Wells's nemesis. The Londoner was married, while the ebullient, handsome and slight Carpentier dressed well and flirted continuously with women. France was the unlikely incubator of this great boxer as there was little history of the sport in a nation where *la savate*, in which men struck with both arms and legs, remained popular. Carpentier had been born amid the north-eastern coal seams of the country where a travelling wrestler had noticed the child's potential, convinced his parents of their son's future and put the lad into training. At eighteen Carpentier was French champion, and parlayed his popularity into theatrical tours, advertising automobiles and all sort of cures and training aids. The French craze for this handsome youth was noticed by Jimmy White, the promoter of the Wells–Johnson match, who brought Carpentier to London to spar with Wells.[71]

Only weeks after his Ghent defeat, Billy appeared in the stalls of the London Opera House, where the Frenchman was appearing in a sketch. In mid-performance he challenged Carpentier to a re-match.[72] This NSC bout in December lasted just seventy-three seconds. Carpentier attacked Wells's famously vulnerable midriff immediately. Wells could not compose himself during this frenzy and was knocked out. The audience jeered, but Billy succeeded in reclaiming their admiration by an address he made from the ring after regaining consciousness. In this speech, Wells was said to have articulated the innately British qualities he was believed to embody: he admitted that though he could not match Carpentier's skill and strength, he had fought honestly.[73] This match sealed 1913's ignominy and effectively precluded Wells from ever again competing for the world title, though he remained the British champion until 1919.

Wells reigned supreme against British opponents, both in the ring and on stage, although he was never either European or world champion, primarily because his self-doubts became more pronounced in bigger bouts. But more importantly bashful Billy and gregarious Georges momentarily changed their misogynist sport by attracting significant numbers of women to the stadium, who came to see these handsome idols.[74] Women's greatest ever interest in the sport came with the boxing boom, when as many as one thousand saw Wells fight Colin Bell at Olympia in July 1914.[75]

Carpentier competed with Wells's popularity on the halls as well as in the ring. Between their two bouts in 1913 he starred, as we have seen, at the London Opera House, at a reputed salary of £500 per week, in a French revue at the New Middlesex, and in cinema.[76] The two men were almost interchangeable in the public's affections as Wells 'appeared with great success in the place of his conqueror' when, immediately after their December fight, Carpentier broke his £800 per week contract with the Palladium.[77] The popular boxing journalist Charlie Rose saw Wells when he subsequently deputised for Carpentier at the

Kingsway Opera House. According to Rose, Billy was 'shockingly nervy' in the wings about the reception he would get, given the NSC audience's jeering, but as he stepped on to the stage 'the crowd rose as one, every man, woman and child cheering, cheering, cheering'.[78] By such measures was Wells's fleeting self-confidence restored. Meanwhile, Carpentier continued to box the best British fighters, like the London Irishman Pat O'Keefe, a onetime opponent of Wells, whose happy personality made him a fixture of the boxing boom.[79]

Jimmy Wilde's career leads us first from stage appearances and movies into boxing by artistes and in turn to the 1914 boxing boom. Wilde was the good-looking Welsh lightweight world champion who, along with Carpentier and Wells, was one of the most popular fighters in Britain before the war. He was also friends with many music-hall singers and comedians and sparred on the Oxford's stage from the earliest days of his career.[80] Wells repeated the success of his Willie Sanders' spoof by facing Wilde for a charity show, where the audience delighted in the bigger man's inability to land a punch on his opponent.[81] Wilde also starred in one film before the war, called *From Pit-Boy to World's Champion*, in which he boxed Tommy Noble.[82]

As the boom began, boxing artistes emerged. Wilde's theatrical peers had been aware of boxing as early as 1899 when the retired music-hall fighter Abe Daltrey had offered to instruct artistes. Boxing acts appeared regularly in the halls, but it was not until 1914 that men like the lanky comedian Carlton adopted the sport to update their turns.[83] Carlton's interest in boxing began when he toured Australia and befriended Charlie Griffin, that country's feather-weight champion. They returned together to London where Carlton and Tommy Burns seconded Griffin in a championship bout at the NSC. This fight re-affirmed the NSC's intimacy with the stage, and in early 1914 Walter de Frece approached Carlton about boxing the strongman Apollo at the Club. Carlton agreed and *The Era* promised that artistes would 'be there in full force' when the men fought to raise money for music-hall charities.[84] The delight in matching disproportionately sized people underpinned the fight's humour. Bettinson introduced the boxers entering the auditorium as 'Carlton, the Human Hairpin' and 'Apollo, the Ideal Athlete'. Apollo bested his opponent in the fourth round.[85]

Afterwards Carlton forsook Billy Wells's grace in defeat, and wrote to *The Era* to defend his performance by claiming that he had never felt confident because he was much lighter than his opponent. In addition, Apollo had been seconded by the former British champion Charlie Mitchell, another fighter who had retired to the halls, in breach of the contest's spirit.[86] But this mismatch had been arranged deliberately in order to amuse spectators. Carlton then fought Jimmy Wilde at the NSC and finally a comedy match with the ex-featherweight champion Jim Driscoll.[87] Presumably these fights, in which he was by far the taller and heavier man, better emboldened Carlton's confidence.

But Carlton was not the only music-haller to box in 1914, as a growing public interest in the sport carried over into the halls. In February, Bandsman Blake sparred at the Islington Empire in the run-up to his heavily publicised March fight with Billy Wells at the Palladium. Blake was challenged on the Empire stage by the American comedians Friend and Downing. Blake accepted and so Al Friend fearfully kissed his seconds 'good-bye' before getting into the ring, when he comedically knocked Blake out in the third round.[88] Friend and Downing boomed themselves and their achievement in the following issue of *The Era* by boasting of challenges from Johnson, Carpentier, Wells and the American fighter Sam Langford.[89] That March, encouraged by his success, Friend promoted himself as 'the champion 8st. 4lb. boxer of the music-hall profession'.[90] The idea of a music-hall title took hold and he faced Apollo for the crown at the NSC in June before fighting at the Ring, Blackfriars, that month to raise money for the Variety Artistes Benevolent Association.[91]

Carpentier and Wells's effects on boxing crowds were also celebrated on stage. In May a troupe of English, French and Norwegian 'muscular, well built girls' along with female seconds and a lady referee began touring the biggest syndicates.[92] On stage and in posters the champion Mlle Carpentier, one of these boxers, defied any woman in the world to meet her in the ring.[93] Audiences were not sated by a female version of the European champion and so the diminutive Kid Johnson, billed as the 'The Wandering Pugilist', also profitably worked the halls that spring.[94]

The immense public and professional interest in fighting had been first noted by the boxing-mad youth Charles B. Cochran when he saw Corbett in *Gentleman Jim* at Drury Lane.[95] Cochran later emigrated to New York where he trained for seven years as a theatre promoter before returning home to produce West End revues and wrestling at Olympia. Like Fred Karno, Cochran's talent lay in capturing current fancies. He poached boxers from the NSC's 1901 Coronation Tournament for the London halls, dabbled occasionally thereafter in the sport, and in early 1914 realised that huge profits could be made by selling thousands of inexpensive seats to attractive bouts, but 'boxing connoisseurs alone would never fill Olympia. One of the contestants must have a personality that influences the public outside boxing circles, and there must be an intense desire to see him win, or an intense desire to see him beaten'.[96]

Therefore, that summer women, couples and children were encouraged to watch handsome, immensely popular fighters like Wells and Carpentier act out pugilistic pantomimes in which companionable men met malevolent opponents just as they had regularly done in boxing stage plays.

Wells was once again rebuilding his career just as the London halls took a keen interest in boxing. Handsome, and willing to fight, he became the boxing boom's biggest star. He faced Colin Bell at the top of Cochran's fight-card in a match at the end of June 1914 that was seen as the Imperial heavyweight championship. Bell was a balding, snarling Australian who had handily defeated a succession of English fighters after arriving in the country early that spring. The British champion was equally resurgent. In the six months following his decisive loss to Carpentier he had boxed more frequently than he ever had in his professional career, soliciting support from new quarters with appearances in Belfast, Liverpool and Cardiff early in the year. Wells then returned to London in March when he beat Bandsman Blake at the Palladium. This first metropolitan appearance, three months after his convincing defeat by Carpentier, was heavily promoted. Victory was capitalised upon quickly and Billy beat Albert Lurie at the Canterbury in April.

Though Wells no longer pretended to the world crown, these five victories emphatically re-asserted his position as the best and most celebrated British fighter. He was also the handsomest, most pleasant man in the ring. Therefore, all Olympia's seats were filled and the cinema cameras turned as Bell was knocked out in the second round and London saw 'the real Wells again'.[97] Billy capitalised on his celebrity in the week after the fight by appearing at the Oxford where film of him training preceded a lecture extolling the Bombardier's fighting qualities. Once the crowd's desire to see their hero had been heightened, Wells appeared to immense applause and sparred several rounds on stage.[98]

Back in the ring, in July, Carpentier faced the American Gunboat Smith in another Cochran-produced match at Olympia billed as the 'heavy-weight championship of the world in the ranks of white men'.[99] Carpentier trained out of the limelight in Paris, but Smith did so publicly at Harrow.[100] A huge crowd of Londoners, anxious about the pending fight, met Carpentier at Charing Cross on his arrival. The 1914 boxing boom climaxed as a band played 'La Marseillaise' when he emerged from the station to see thousands of people in the streets.[101] The supportive mob harried the Frenchman's coach as it sped around the corner to a hotel in Northumberland Street where Carpentier himself had to tell the fans to disperse. Neither Carpentier nor

London had ever seen such a reception given to a boxer.[102] Carpentier then sparred at the Empire where he earned over £100 per night and was contractually obliged to give a special performance for his female admirers.[103] Smith promoted himself equally sensationally by boxing a couple of rounds before the crowds who gathered to see Tate, Elvin and Weldon fly the Atlantic at the Hendon music-hall carnival, which was held just days before the bout.[104] The frenzy these events induced was cemented in the public imagination by controversy when Smith was disqualified in the ring for hitting a prostrate Carpentier in the back of the neck.[105]

Like Wells, Carpentier went on the London stage, at the Empire, immediately after his pyrrhic victory to demonstrate his training techniques and spar a few rounds. This choice of boxing material was apt for 'coming on top of his latest triumph, it certainly drew a large crowd, and consequently fulfilled its purpose'.[106] The most successful music-hall boxers were those, like Wells and Carpentier, who alternated between stage personae. They demonstrated physical accomplishments when booming fights or boasting victories, but in the fallow between bouts they acted, spoofed and sang (Figure 18).

Gunboat Smith's appearance at the London Aerodrome in July 1914 had other effects. The Lancashire comedian Harry Weldon, 'Stiffy the Goalkeeper' in Fred Karno's immensely successful play *The Football Match*, was 'flying' the Atlantic with Harry Tate. Friendship with Jimmy Wilde had brought Weldon into the fighting world and so he appeared on the halls as 'Stiffy the Boxer', challenging any lady in the audience to a fight. Militant suffragettes, Oxbridge lady blues and any similarly emancipated boxing fans likely to accept his offer were soon dissuaded by Weldon's recitation of his athletic prowess in the song 'What I did to Colin Bell!'[107] After the war Weldon comically proclaimed himself 'England's last hope for the heavy-weight championship' and dreamed publicly of a chance to fight the elusive Carpentier.[108]

A passage published at the height of the boxing craze provided a concise description of the emergence of celebrity in Edwardian England: 'in the old days (good old days too, in many respects) the boxer was photographed at his job, because it was mainly his job that interested people. To-day he is photographed more or less like everybody else, as well as at work, because people like to assure themselves that the boxer is no longer a man apart, but one of them'.[109] Music-hall appearances helped create this demand to see champion boxers on stage at the same time that international heroes predominated in large arenas, where previously men popular in their neighbourhoods had fought one another. It has been argued that international competitions and

Georges Carpentier adapts to London boxing promotion and becomes a favourite.   18

large purses removed champions permanently from tenements and terraces in an estrangement characterised by a fighter's 'inability to accidentally tread on your toe' as you passed him in daily life.[110] But this impersonal relationship between fighters and audiences was then made closer by the novel and diverse ways they displayed their talents and personalities. Even if people could not shake Billy Wells's hand, they saw him spar, fight and frolic constantly on local screens and stages and even attended his wedding thanks to cinema's proxy. One can look at the Oxford, one of London's most prestigious music halls, for a cursory indication of boxing's hold on the stage. This hall alone booked twenty-seven weeks of boxing, from burlesques to international-calibre fighters, in the four years before the first world war.[111] Artistes were not strangers to boxing either, and they updated their turns by identifying with the sport at the height of the craze.

Notes

1 Guy Deghy, *Noble and Manly: The History of the National Sporting Club*, London, Hutchinson, 1956, pp 18–19.
2 Deghy, *Noble and Manly*, p. 97.
3 Deghy, *Noble and Manly*, pp. 145–161.
4 Deghy, *Noble and Manly*, pp. 101–102.
5 A. F. Bettinson and B. Bennison, *The Home of Boxing*, London, Odhams, 1922, pp. 52–53.
6 Stan Shipley, 'Tom Causer of Bermondsey: a boxer hero of the 1890s', *History Workshop Journal*, 15 (1983), pp. 28–53.
7 Bettinson and Bennison, *Home of Boxing*, pp. 40–41.
8 'Music hall gossip', *The Era*, 7 November 1896, p. 19, and Joe Palmer, *Recollections of a Boxing Referee*, London, John Lane, 1927, pp. 20–37. Joe Palmer was Pedlar's cousin.
9 Deghy, *Noble and Manly*, pp. 167–174.
10 Nat Fleischer, *John L. Sullivan*, London, Robert Hale, 1952, pp. 57–58 and 127.
11 Charlie Rose, *Life's a Knock-out*, London, Hutchinson, 1953, p. 20; Michael T. Isenberg, *John L. Sullivan and His America*, Urbana Illinois, University of Illinois, 1988, pp. 240–244; and Fred Henning, *Fights for the Championship: The Men and Their Times*, London, Licensed Victualler's Gazette, 1902, pp. 511–514.
12 Fleischer, *John L. Sullivan*, pp. 126–127, and for Sullivan's earnings see p. 135.
13 Excerpt from Sullivan's challenge as reported by the Associated Press, printed in James J. Corbett, *The Roar of the Crowd*, London, G. P. Putnam, 1925, p. 165.
14 Corbett, *Roar*, p. 207.
15 Charles B. Cochran, *Cock-a-Doodle-Do*, London, J. M. Dent, 1941, p. 151, and Corbett, *Roar*, pp. 233–235; William A. Brady, *Showman*, New York, E. P. Dutton, 1937, p. 80.
16 David K. Wiggins, 'Peter Jackson and the elusive heavy-weight championship: a black athlete's struggle against the late nineteenth century color-line', *The Journal of Sports History*, 12.2 (Summer 1985), pp. 143–168, p. 161; Charles B. Cochran, *Secrets of a Showman*, London, Heinemann, 1925, pp. 156–157.
17 Corbett, *Roar*, pp. 245–248. Much of the information about Corbett's relationship with Brady is drawn from Alan Woods, 'James J. Corbett: theatrical star', *The Journal of Sport History*, 3.2, Summer 1976, pp. 162–175.
18 Corbett, *Roar*, p. 249.
19 Ada Reeve, *Take it for a Fact*, London, Heinemann, 1954, p. 60 and Barry Anthony, 'Earliest cricket on film', *Wisden Cricket Monthly*, December 1993, p. 32. Anthony felt that the film of the Corbett–Fitzsimmons fight directly inspired one of Ranjitsinhji practising in the nets at Sydney.

20 Brady, *Showman*, p. 82.

21 Eugene Corri, *Gloves and the Man*, London, Hutchinson, 1927, pp. 34 and 42. For a report on one of Corbett's London music-hall appearances see 'Variety gossip', *The Era*, 31 July 1909, p. 20.

22 George Gray, *Vagaries of a Vagabond*, London, Heath Cranton, 1930, p. 148.

23 Gray, *Vagaries*, pp. 147–149.

24 *Boxing Match for the Championship of the World*, (1907), viewing copy, British Film Institute, London.

25 James Douglas, *Adventures in London*, London, Cassell, 1935, p. 79.

26 Eugene Corri, *Thirty Years a Boxing Referee*, London, Edward Arnold, 1915, p. 143.

27 Gunner Moir, *The Complete Boxer*, London, Health and Strength, 1907; Tommy Burns, *Scientific Boxing and Self Defence*, London, Athletic Publications, 1908; Murray Greig, *Going the Distance: Canada's Boxing Heritage*, Toronto, Macmillan, 1996, pp. 9–20.

28 Booking register of the Oxford Music Hall, 17 February 1908, Theatre Museum, Blythe House, London, unnumbered pages.

29 Booking register of the Oxford Music Hall, 22 June 1908, Theatre Museum, Blythe House, London, unnumbered pages.

30 Harry Furniss, *By Ways and Queer Ways of Boxing*, London, Harrison, 1920, p. 57.

31 'Hackney Empire', *Oriental Notes*, 27 March 1909, unnumbered pages.

32 Billy Wells, 'My life and my fights', *Thomson's Weekly News*, 24 April 1920, p. 16.

33 See for instance Wiggins, 'Peter Jackson', pp. 143–168, and William H. Wiggins Jr, 'Boxing's Sambo twins: racial stereotypes in Jack Johnson and Joe Louis cartoons, 1908–1938', *The Journal of Sport History*, 15.3 (1988), pp. 242–257.

34 Stuart Mews, 'Puritanicalism, sport and race: a symbolic crusade of 1911', in G. J. Cuming and Derek Baker (eds), *Studies in Church History*, 8 (1972), pp. 310–311; see also E.B. Osborn, 'The revival of boxing', *Nineteenth Century and After*, LXX (1911) pp. 771–781.

35 John G. B. Lynch, *Prominent Pugilists of To-day*, London, Max Goshen, 1914, p. 25.

36 Charles B. Cochran, *Showman Looks On*, London, J. M. Dent, 1945, p. 259. The British Film Institute archives contain films of three entire NSC championship bouts, suggesting that they were all filmed to generate revenue for the club. *Boxing Match for the Championship of the World, Tommy Burns versus Gunner Moir*, (1907); *Thomas V. Sullivan at the National Sporting Club*, (1910) and *The Lightweight Championship of the World and £1900 at the NSC, Packy McFarland Versus Freddy Welsh*, (1910); all viewing copies, British Film Institute, London.

37 *The Man to Beat Jack Johnson*, (1910), viewing copy, British Film Institute, London.

38 Cochran, *Showman Looks On*, p. 258.

39 Jimmy Wilde, *Fighting Was My Business*, London, Michael Joseph, 1938, p. 131; 'Variety gossip', *The Era*, 27 August 1913, p. 20; and Stan Shipley, 'Boxing', in Tony Mason (ed.), *Sport in Britain, A Social History*, Cambridge, Cambridge University Press, 1989, p. 95.

40 Eugene Corri, *Fifty Years in the Ring*, London, Hutchinson, 1933, p. 12.

41 Billy Wells 'My life and my fights', *Thomson's Weekly News*, 24 April 1920, p. 16.

42 Stan Shipley, *Bombardier Billy Wells: The Life and Times of a Boxing Hero*, Whitley Bay, Berwick, 1993, pp. 1–21, and Billy Wells, 'My life and my fights', *Thomson's Weekly News*, 17 April 1920, p. 16.

43 Shipley, *Billy Wells*, p. 24.

44 The quote comes from Billy Wells, 'My life and my fights', *Thomson's Weekly News*, 24 April 1920, p. 16. His last days in the army are chronicled in Billy Wells, 'My life and my fights', *Thomson's Weekly News*, 1 May 1920, p. 16.

45 Lynch, *Prominent Pugilists*, p. 14.

46 Billy Wells, 'How I came back as a boxer', *Lloyd's Sunday News*, 18 April 1920, p. 9.

47 Shipley, *Billy Wells*, p. 34.

48 Shipley, *Billy Wells*, p. 42.

49 Shipley, 'Boxing,' p. 95; Shipley, *Billy Wells*, p. 50 and a photograph of the fighters endorsing the contract is found in 'Jack Johnson and Bombardier Wells signing articles', *The Mirror of Life*, 22 July 1911, p. 4.

50 'Johnson and Wells: a study in style', *The Times*, 12 September 1911, p. 8.

51 'The Johnson–Wells match', *The Times*, 16 September 1911, p. 8.

52 For lists of subscribers to the memorial see 'Mr Meyer and the Johnson–Wells match', *The Times*, 19 September 1911, p. 5; 'The primate and the Johnson–Wells match', *The Times*, 20 September 1911, p. 4; 'The Johnson–Wells match', *The Times*, 23 September 1911, p. 5; and 'The Johnson–Wells match', *The Times*, 26 September 1911, p. 4.

53 Mews, 'Puritanicalism', *passim,* and for Billy's post-war career see Shipley, *Billy Wells*, pp. 140–196.

54 Billy Wells, 'My life and my fights', *Thomson's Weekly News*, 12 June 1920, p. 16.

55 Eugene Corri, *Refereeing 1000 Fights*, London, Edward Arnold, 1919, p. 54.

56 Shipley, *Billy Wells*, p. 56. For photographs of the actors in costume see Untitled, *Boxing,* 22 July 1911, p. 283. Wells rather unconvincingly related that the lines quoted were in the play by coincidence in 'Why I am fighting Jack Johnson', *Boxing*, 5 August 1911, pp. 329–330.

57 Advertisements found in, *Music Hall and Theatre Review,* 6 July 1911, p. 423; *Music Hall and Theatre Review*, 20 July 1911, p. 457; 3 August 1911, p. 489; and 10 August 1911, p. 505.

58 Bombardier Wells, *Modern Boxing*, London, Ewart, Seymour, 1911 An advertisement for the book is found in *Boxing*, 26 August 1911, p. 416.

59 Shipley, *Billy Wells*, p. 52; and booking register of the Oxford Music Hall, 10 July 1911, Theatre Museum, Blythe House, London, unnumbered pages.

60 Mews, 'Puritanicalism', p. 321, and Shipley, *Billy Wells*, p. 56.

61 Untitled photographs, *Boxing*, 2 September 1911, pp. 424–425, show Wells and Johnson and their automobiles. Untitled photograph, *Boxing*, 16 September 1911, p. 474, shows Wells playing football.

62 'Pugilism and the Palladium', *Music Hall and Theatre Review*, 5 October 1911, p. 633.

63 *The Night I Fought Jack Johnson,* (1912), viewing copy, British Film Institute, London.

64 Harry Castling, 'Diabolo mad!', (1907), and Harry Castling, 'The night I fought Jack Johnson', (1911) both in the British Library catalogue of printed music.
65 Advertisement, *The Bioscope*, 19 December 1912, p. 878, and Gray, *Vagaries*, p. 214; 'The Fighting Parson', *The Bioscope*, 9 January 1913, p. 141.
66 'The Bombardier and his bride', *Boxing*, 14 September 1912, pp. 465 and 467–468; 'Champion boxer and his young bride', *Lloyd's Weekly News*, 8 September 1912, p. 2, 'Champion boxer's wedding', *Daily Express*, 9 September 1912, p. 6; 'Bombardier Wells's bride', *Daily Mail*, 9 September 1912, p. 6; 'Saturday's weddings at Tooting and St. George's', *Daily News and Leader*, 9 September 1912, p. 12.
67 'Champion boxer and his young bride', *Lloyd's Weekly News,* 8 September 1912, p. 2, and 'The editor's ideas', *Boxing*, 14 September 1912, p. 467.
68 Shipley, *Billy Wells*, p. 67.
69 'Bombardier Wells' first contest in France', *Boxing*, 7 December 1912, pp. 146–147.
70 Peter Heller, *In This Corner: Forty World Champions Tell Their Stories*, New York, Simon and Schuster, 1973, pp. 32–38.
71 Corri, *Fifty Years,* p. 28; also F. Hurdman-Lucas, *From Pit-Boy to Champion Boxer: The Romance of Georges Carpentier,* London, Ewart Seymour, 1914, pp. 53, 66–69.
72 Rover, 'About the halls', *The Sketch*, 18 June 1913, p. 344.
73 Shipley, *Billy Wells*, p. 88.
74 Corri, *Thirty Years*, p. 49; Furniss, *By-Ways and Queer Ways*, pp. 182–183; and Shipley, 'Boxing', p. 89.
75 'Witnessed by a thousand women', *The Sketch*, 8 July 1914, p. 10, and 'Women at the Wells v. Bell match', *Daily Mail*, 1 July 1914, p. 8.
76 Untitled, *The Era*, 5 July 1913, p. 25; Hurdman-Lucas, *From Pit-boy*, pp. 69–70.
77 'Variety gossip', *The Era*, 17 December 1913, p. 18.
78 Rose, *Life's a Knockout*, p. 86.
79 Georges Carpentier, *My Fighting Life*, London, Cassell, 1920, p. 99.
80 Wilde, *Fighting*, pp. 84–85 and 193.
81 Corri, *Fifty Years,* p. 104.
82 Wilde, *Fighting*, p. 283.
83 'Music hall gossip', *The Era*, 21 October 1899, p. 19. See also the booking register of the Oxford Music Hall, Theatre Museum, Blythe House, London, *passim*.
84 'Variety gossip', *The Era*, 15 April 1914, p. 16.
85 Carlton, *Twenty Years of Spoof and Bluff,* London, Herbert Jenkins, 1920, p. 112.
86 Letter, 'Carlton versus Apollo', *The Era*, 19 May 1914, p. 18.
87 Carlton, *Twenty Years*, pp. 111–118.
88 'Variety gossip', *The Era*, 4 February 1914, p. 18.
89 'Variety gossip', *The Era*, 11 February 1914, p. 18.
90 'Variety gossip', *The Era*, 4 March 1914, p. 18.
91 'Variety gossip', *The Era*, 6 May 1914, p. 18; 'Variety gossip', *The Era*, 19 May 1914, p. 18; and 'Variety gossip', *The Era*, 10 June 1914, p. 14.
92 'Music hall musings', *The Umpire*, 3 May 1914, p. 7.
93 Advertisement, *The Encore*, 14 May 1914, p. 12.

94 Advertisement, *The Encore*, 14 May 1914, p. 13.

95 Cochran, *Cock-a-Doodle-Do*, p. 151.

96 Charles B. Cochran, *The Secrets of a Showman*, London, Heinemann, 1925, pp. 156–157, and for the quote see p. 299.

97 John Murray, 'The real Wells again', *Boxing*, 4 July 1914, p. 238.

98 Rover, 'About the halls', *The Sketch*, 15 July 1914, p. 58.

99 Corri, *Thirty Years*, p. 25.

100 Carpentier, *My Fighting Life*, p. 108, and 'Fun at Hendon', *Daily News and Leader*, 8 July 1914, p. 5.

101 Corri, *Thirty Years*, p. 234.

102 Carpentier, *My Fighting Life*, p. 108. A photograph of the crowds, estimated to number five thousand, can be found in 'The clubman', *The Sketch*, 22 July 1914, p. 71.

103 'Variety gossip', *The Era*, 22 July 1914, p. 14.

104 'Fun at Hendon', *Daily News and Leader*, 8 July 1914, p. 5.

105 For Smith's version of events see Heller, *This Corner*, p. 43.

106 Rover, 'About the halls', *The Sketch*, 5 August 1914, p. 156.

107 Bettinson and Bennison, *Home of Boxing*, p. 166; W. J. Makin, *The Story of Twenty-five Years*, London, George Newnes, 1935, p. 43; and Wilde, *Fighting*, pp. 84–85.

108 Harry Weldon, 'My favourite dream', *George Robey's Christmas Annual, 1921*, p. 29.

109 Lynch, *Prominent Pugilists*, p. 36.

110 Shipley, 'Tom Causer', p. 45.

111 Booking register of the Oxford Music Hall, Theatre Museum, Blythe House, London, *passim*. The register ends in April 1914, making it possible that further acts appeared during the summer boom.

Football

ootball followed a similar route to respectability as boxing. An often brutal, traditional pastime was claimed by the middle classes for the 'cult of games' of the reformed public schools in the middle of the nineteenth century. These schools each developed rules for the new sport which were roughly divisible between those like Rugby, where players handled the ball, and the 'kicking game', where athletes were restricted to striking it with their feet. Clubs were established throughout the country by young men when they left school and so the myriad forms of football expanded nationally. Differing rules did not present any immediate difficulty to a localised sport centred around factories, rectories and country houses. However, Cambridge undergraduates were unable to organise an intramural football league, despite much enthusiasm, because supporters were divided into small groups that each adhered to their particular school's game. A synod of these various sects was convened in October 1863, where they debated and compromised on specific features before codifying the rules of a new game.[1]

These difficulties were experienced by men outside college walls and so in the same month as the Cambridge meeting, representatives of thirteen London clubs assembled at the Freemason's Tavern, Lincoln's Inn Fields and founded the Football Association (FA), with the aim of establishing a national code of laws.[2] The resulting rules were gradually accepted as standard for the kicking game throughout England. A national championship, the Football Association Cup, was first competed for during the 1871–72 season by clubs adhering to this code. Association football's founders conceived of their creation as an uplifting and moralising game, just as it had been in their schools. Gentlemen who subscribed to this ideology did not play for pay or intentionally break the rules. These middle-class beliefs dominated the early years of the game just as London, with many teams composed of public school and university men, owned the FA Cup for the first twenty years.

It was propitious that association football was introduced to the country during the 1860s just as successive factory acts reduced the length of the working week. Increasing numbers of labourers shared a common day or day-and-a-half rest per week which allowed them to play regularly scheduled organised games for the first time. The formal segregation of work and leisure also allowed for the creation of 'spectacular' sports because those not inclined to play themselves might be induced to watch others do so. Moderately rising wages secured the relationship by giving men the disposable incomes to spend on match tickets.[3] Because these factory acts were industry-specific, football gained its greatest initial popularity in the single-manufactory towns of northern England, Scotland and Wales. Spectacular football developed comparatively slowly in London where work reforms did little to help clerks, artisans, casual labourers and shop-keepers on whom the capital's economy was based.[4]

Wherever it took hold, spectacular football changed the middle-class game. In 1876 or 1877 the first professionals appeared for Sheffield. Hired in Scotland, where men did not share the middle-class contempt for earning a wage with their football skills, these men were not paid directly, but were hired to work in the factories of their club's wealthy supporters.[5] The trend was soon established and Lancashire teams advertised in local Scottish newspapers offering mill jobs for those who could play the game well.[6] 'Shamateurism', a system by which players were paid covertly or given sinecures by club backers, grew dramatically in just a few years as talented men from penurious areas were not inclined to balk at being paid to play. Soon the supremacy of London teams was challenged by professional provincial sides who did not heed amateur ideals. Such tension over professionalism was to cleave the game of rugby in 1887, into mutually antagonistic amateur and professional wings, but the FA avoided repeating this schism when it voted narrowly to allow professionalism in 1885.

The Football League (FL) was established in September 1888 as another response to the game's growing popularity in northern and midland industrial areas. The FL arranged and oversaw match fixtures throughout the season because gate receipts were the only way to meet professional wages and so games, once arranged, had to be played. Before FL regulation many teams had blithely failed to appear for seasonal fixtures in order to concentrate on more popular and profitable cup-ties. Players' wages were also strictly controlled by the FL though by the 1890s players like Tottenham Hotspur's James Collins, who earned £2 in the weeks he turned out for the team and half that when remaining on the bench, earned about as much as skilled artisans.[7] Salaries were relatively stable, as three years later Spurs paid Leonard Hyde £2.10s. per week during the playing season and £1.10s. over the summer.[8] Historians have argued lately that with the advent of professionalism the running of teams, associations and leagues was left to the lower middle classes in 'an often fractious alliance between clerks, self-made business men and the like' in a dynamic relationship whose strident advocacy of professionalism parallelled Bettinson's control of the NSC.[9]

Tactics evolved quickly to suit a spectacular sport played by professionals who were reproached for being 'performers' in the contemporary middle-class vernacular.[10] Public school games masters had celebrated undeviating, forward rushes by the man on the ball whose team-mates had followed closely behind to collect the ball if it came loose. Defenders had legally 'hacked' these strikers by kicking them repeatedly on the shins as they approached. Players had worn no leg guards and hobbled stoically about the pitch until too bruised to continue in a 'dashing and audacious' strategy that suited the public schools' role as the incubators of heroic, independent men.[11] Late-Victorian professionals played a less 'manly' version of the sport which stressed attacking in strategically manoeuvring combinations. Dribbling, passing, heading and tackling the ball, rather than the man, spread players across the entire field in fluid, co-ordinated attacks on goal which were better suited to a game designed to entertain paying spectators.

Much of the unease between amateur and professional conceptions of the game coalesced around these new tactics because 'the public become so accustomed to the 'fiddling' tactics of professionals who perpetually indulge in short passes and play about with the ball instead of going straight for the goal, that when they see the amateurs rushing down on the goal they say it is not football and call it "selfish play"'.[12] Professional strategies were equated with stealth and deceit by middle-class commentators, especially as these teams had to win consistently in order to attract fans. This chase for cups and victories was thought to lead men to commit fouls purposefully and feign injuries, something absent from elegiac memories of the amateur game.[13] The Football Association was mindful of how the game was evolving and so in 1891 referees appeared for the first time.[14] Such on-field arbitration marked the final development of a game that used the entire pitch in plays spread out by accurate passing. Top-class late-Victorian and Edwardian football was entertainment for spectators who practised its tactics in the streets.

Some reacted against these developments. The London Football Association (LFA) was founded by Nicholas Lane Jackson in 1882 as a bulwark against the capital being overwhelmed by professionalism.[15] Jackson – a journalist, sports promoter and FA secretary – then established the Corinthian Football Club to assemble the best amateurs from throughout the country under one uniform. Continually training and playing together was expected to help the national side, which contained a majority of public school and university men, defeat the overwhelmingly professional Scottish teams.[16] C. B. Fry played for Corinthians. The Lord Mayor patronised a London match between the FA Cup winners and Corinthians in hopes of annually asserting the resilient strength of gentlemanly play. While supporting music-hall cricket, Sir Thomas Dewar sponsored this trophy during his term of office in 1898.[17] Professional football first arrived in the capital in 1891 when Woolwich Arsenal opted to pay players. The team was then ostracised by the LFA and in response convened a meeting in Fleet Street with a view to establishing a professional league for southern England. Attending delegates refused to ratify this initial proposal but after further discussion the Southern League (SL) was formally constituted in 1894 with seven affiliated clubs.[18] Competition in the new league was originally as fierce as in the FL, though it eventually stagnated because by the turn of the century northern professional teams clearly dominated the country.[19] Every ambitious London team turned professional eventually, in order to play regular fixtures with these northern clubs. As they did so these teams deserted the SL for the FL. By the First World War the SL was a parochial league composed of the reserve sides of FL clubs.

Tracing the ascents of several prominent clubs will demonstrate more fully the development of London football while also providing a background for the rest of this section. Most clubs were initially sponsored either by parish churches or local businesses to provide workers with an alternative to public-houses and gambling.[20] Ecclesiastical clubs included Fulham, founded in 1879 under the sponsorship of Fulham St Andrews Church, and Queen's Park Rangers, who trace their history to St Jude's Institute in 1882.[21] Other London clubs were originally connected to businesses. In 1885 workers at Morton's marmalade factory on the Isle of Dogs formed Millwall Rovers.[22] Ten years later Alfred Hills, a Harrovian and Oxonian who exemplified the ethos of the university missions, established West Ham United at the Thames Ironworks Shipbuilding Company.[23] Arsenal were founded in 1886 by Scotsmen employed in the royal munitions factory at Plumstead and in 1904 workers at the Crystal Palace, which annually hosted the FA Cup final, founded a team which joined the SL the following year.[24] Two other teams were founded by cricket clubs. Tottenham Hotspur was established in 1882 by members of the Hotspur Cricket Club while Clapton Orient (which would later change its name to Leyton Orient) dates to 1888 when Hackney's Glyn Cricket Club organised a football squad in order to keep in training during the close season.[25]

Each of these clubs came to predominate London because their directors worked in similar ways to make them the outstanding teams in the metropolis. They employed talented players from Scotland, the north and midlands, and trained formally in order to win consistently. Directors dropped men who did not give their utmost in every game, reducing the average length of top-level careers.[26] Gate receipts helped to pay players, and so luring and housing spectators became the central dilemma faced by expansion-minded football clubs. But like suburban music halls, bigger stadiums had to be accessible by public transportation to compete in a metropolitan football 'marketplace' where fans attended the most attractive fixture on any given day, rather than supporting one side unswervingly.[27] Each prominent London club fulfilled these conditions in the two decades before the First World War.

Fulham played in various London leagues during the 1880s and 1890s and purchased Craven Cottage in 1894, where rubble from Hammersmith Underground was used to create the banking around the pitch.[28] In 1898 the team joined the Southern League and adopted professionalism.[29] Despite the directors' aspirations, Fulham languished until trams and the Underground arrived in West London in 1909, making the stadium easily accessible.[30]

Millwall bought their own stadium in 1889. This attracted better players with the promise of regular fixtures. Close association with the nearby busy docks was a blessing for the directors, who lured skilled players to the team with the promise of employment, until 1893, when Millwall turned professional. They moved to the Isle of Dogs in 1901; however, because this ground was ill-served by public transportation the team languished until they moved south of the river in 1910.[31] West Ham's course to professionalism was less easy because of Hills' paternalist control. This patronage benefited the club in 1897 when Hills financed the Memorial Stadium, but the district around the Thames Ironworks, popularly known as the 'Far East' because of its endemic poverty, could not support an ambitious team.[32] Nevertheless, they moved to their present address at Upton Park in 1904.[33] Clapton Orient played initially on a strip of waste ground, joined the third division of the London League and moved to a new fenced-in home in 1893, turned professional ten years later, imported better players and raised admission charges to help cover the new expenses. Queen's Park Rangers turned professional in 1898, thereafter wandering from pitch to pitch until purchasing their present ground at Loftus Road in 1917.[34]

By December 1886 Dial Square had adopted the name Royal Arsenal and, according to their founding secretary Elijah Watkins played home games on a bedraggled pitch sandwiched between back-garden walls and a festering open sewer, before moving to a permanent home at the Manor Ground, Plumstead in 1888.[35] The next year they vied for the FA Cup for the first time and leased a bigger Plumstead ground. Arsenal were ejected from the LFA when they became London's first professional club in 1891 and so they were compelled to concentrate on northern and midland opponents.[36] In 1893 Arsenal became a public company to raise the rent for the Invicta Ground at Plumstead, which held 20,000 people. South London was an increasingly obscure home for an ambitious club because it was forty minutes further by train from central London than Millwall, the Arsenal's closest rivals. Therefore in 1912 the directors hired Alfred Norris, a businessman and politician who sat on Fulham's board, to help it secure a new home. Norris championed a merger between Fulham and Arsenal, but when it failed Norris joined Arsenal. Despite opposition from Spurs and Orient, who feared the increased local competition, Arsenal moved to Highbury in 1913 where they built a 9,000 seat stadium.[37]

Spurs played on Tottenham Marshes until 1887 when increasing numbers of spectators forced them to use ropes and stakes to control crowds, which regularly numbered around 4,000. Spurs built their first permanent stadium in 1888 at Northumberland Park. The carpet manufacturer John Oliver employed players in his factories and guided the team on the road to professionalism.[38] Spurs turned professional and joined the FA in 1895.[39] They joined the SL in 1896 and the next year they were hailed in the local press because 'the pet football club of the northern suburbs are ever proving to the public their prowess, not alone in the field of football, but also in the field of commerce'.[40] In 1899 White Hart Lane stadium opened with grandstand accommodation for 1,300 spectators, and seventeen rows of terracing.[41] They won the SL championship in 1900 and were the first Southern professional team to win the FA Cup in 1901 by fielding three northerners, two Welshmen, an Irishman and five Scots.[42] Spurs joined the FL in 1908.

Chelsea's directors compressed this evolution from local to national prominence into a few months. In 1905 Mears Brothers, who had built Craven Cottage for Fulham, bought Stamford Bridge Athletic Grounds, along with some adjacent market gardens. With a £100,000 budget and the slag mountains produced by the extension of the District Line at their disposal, they built the biggest sports stadium in London. When Fulham refused the lease the Mears founded Chelsea Football Club.[43] The team entered the FL six months later with the discreet but cajoling support of the newspaper publisher Horatio Bottomley. This expediency carried over to the field where Chelsea's first two managers, both Scots, were allowed enormous sums to assemble winning teams by assiduously using the transfer market.[44] Because they were able to hire many of the ablest players in the country and oppose the most revered teams in a conveniently reached stadium, Chelsea soon attracted amongst the largest gates in London.

In summary, London clubs emerged because their directors adopted a commercial approach to winning. These men built or secured long-term leases on grounds and stadiums which allowed them to charge admission to bigger crowds. Secure incomes then enabled directors to import talented northern professionals, but only by drawing large crowds consistently could success be guaranteed. Stadiums had to be located near efficient public transport links and in relatively prosperous areas in order to ensure fan support. It was stated that some London clubs – principally the city's most important modern teams – had risen through the enterprise and energy of directors but that 'the question is of vital importance whether other of the clubs have not gone too far in the way of enterprise' in areas unable to sustain such growth.[45] Such clubs never prospered, and withered before attaining national predominance.

Ambitious London teams asserted their position as top-flight football clubs during the 1890s. Arsenal's 1893 election to the Football League was followed by five other clubs over the next sixteen years, each of whom faced the same northern squads that had once been Woolwich's monopoly.[46] If Spurs' 1901 Cup triumph signalled the arrival of first-class football in London, then this continual increase in FL membership showed the sport's permanency at the expense of other sports. Football's resilience was signalled in 1906 when Tottenham, Millwall, Southampton and Woolwich were cited as the most competitive southern sides because, as in many northern districts, their players and fans 'knew the passions which imbue a district on match day'.[47]

London football clubs were also influenced by the provinces in ways which have not yet been explored. Stage, music-hall and pantomime representations of the game came to the metropolis from the provinces on the heels of Tottenham's 1901 FA Cup victory. It was then that the links between stage and sport that had been attempted with varying success by baseball players and cricketers came to fruition in London. Music-hall football first appeared in the provinces. In an echo of disputes we have already seen, in 1895 John Humphries announced in *The Era* that he intended to include a match in a play called *The Football King* (Figure 19). Humphries' production was announced

MESSRS HUMPHRIES and GRAY'S
New Sensational Drama,

"THE   FOOTBALL   KING,"
" THE FOOTBALL KING,"
" THE FOOTBALL KING,"   " THE FOOTBALL KING,"
" THE FOOTBALL KING,"   " THE FOOTBALL KING,"
" THE FOOTBALL KING,"   " THE FOOTBALL KING,"

by George Gray.
Tour under the Direction of Mr A. A. BARCLAY.
Autumn, 1896. Bookings include :—
THEATRE ROYAL, BRADFORD (Bank Holiday) ;
AVENUE THEATRE. SUNDERLAND ;
THEATRE ROYAL, HUDDERSFIELD ;
GRAND THEATRE, HULL ;
PRINCE OF WALES'S THEATRE, GRIMSBY ;
COLOSSEUM THEATRE, OLDHAM ;
THEATRE ROYAL, NOTTINGHAM ;
THEATRE ROYAL, LEICESTER ;
GRAND THEATRE, PLYMOUTH ;
THEATRE ROYAL, PORTSMOUTH ;
THEATRE ROYAL, CARDIFF ;
GRAND THEATRE, WOLVERHAMPTON ;
OPERA HOUSE, NORTHAMPTON ;
ELEPHANT AND CASTLE THEATRE ;
NEW BOROUGH, STRATFORD.
The Entire elaborate Plant (Four Acts) of Scenery carried.
Magnificent Printing by Allen and Stafford.
Three original Sensational Scenes, including
Kennington Oval,
the Final for the English Cup,
in which will appear the celebrated
Preston North End Player,
DAVE RUSSELL,
Mr JOHN HUMPHRIES, Mr GEORGE GRAY,
and Company of Twenty acknowledged Artists.
All Applications for Dates, address A. A. BARCLAY,
" Don Juan." en route ; or,
2, Duke-street, Portland-place, London, W.

19   Football plays migrate to the city as the game becomes more popular in London.

with fifteen bookings for the autumn of 1896, of which eleven were in northern districts where football was as yet far more popular than in the south, where it played Plymouth, Portsmouth and London, roughly corresponding to the centres of southern English football.[48] The Football King's centrepiece was the 'three original sensational scenes, including Kennington Oval, the final for the English Cup in which will appear the celebrated Preston North End player, Dave Russell'. George Gray, of Manchester's Theatre Royal, then claimed that he had pioneered such football scenes in For England, while Bristol's E. J. Lampard asserted that he had originated this stage device in Bootle in

December 1894 and was currently reviving it in a new drama entitled *The Secret Service,* while Widdicombe Hartley of Tring claimed his 1891 play *The Football's Flash,* which had been set at Kennington Oval during the FA Cup final, had been the first football drama. Finally, J. P. Sutherland claimed to have staged the *Football, Or Life As It Is,* another drama set at the Oval in 1883 with 'productions in London, Liverpool and elsewhere'. Its hero had been played by an unnamed famous footballer.[49] Given their patriotic titles, it appears that *For England* and *The Secret Service* were espionage adventure melodramas in which the heroes were footballers. Continental countries took up football at the end of the century so there were ample ways to indulge fantasies about visiting teams bent on espionage. *The Football King* was a great hit at Stratford's Theatre Royal in 1896 and 1897.[50]

These disputed plays were the first popular productions to incorporate football scenes, but many comedians used the game to update their acts, a link that was apparent initially during private entertainments. Performers like Arthur Roberts had gained valuable experience early in their careers by singing at London football club smoking concerts where they were asked inevitably to include topical references in their songs. On an evening when he had brought the music for the operatic aria 'Il Bacio' Roberts was pressed to include 'something about forwards and half-backs or full backs', Roberts 'moaned dismally how will this do? … It's "Il Back-io"'.[51] Though the joke was strained it could have been no more improbable to audiences than footballers saving national secrets.

It is likely that other artistes had similar experiences, because these football club fund-raisers were reported regularly in local newspapers at the end of the century, though historians have yet to examine this aspect of early club financing. It is also clear that these concerts were not only used by clubs during their earliest financial struggles, as the chronically impoverished Clapton Orient were established members of the FL when they produced a pierrot concert at the King's Hall, Hackney, in early 1910 to fund the players' summer wages.[52] That December, ladies were 'especially invited' to a benefit concert for West Ham's Fred Blackburn and George Kitchen.[53] The concert was not simply a side-show to a benefit match because its substantial receipts provided about one-fifth of the £345 raised for the players.[54] Such concerts created business relationships between London football directors and artistes that were more fully exploited in the twentieth century.

The FA, who resolutely controlled investment in the game lest it be overwhelmed by financially unstable clubs, was not completely happy with spectacular stage football. The biggest test of this policy came in autumn 1905 when 'an ambitious syndicate' proposed to hold indoor games featuring top-level players vying for a new national trophy, at Olympia on a specially woven £5,000 green carpet.[55] By this time all of the most prominent clubs in the country were members of the FA, giving that body a monopolistic sanction in its ability to bar players from appearing with any of these teams. FA banishment could effectively end careers because the best British footballers were far too skilled to play in fledgling foreign leagues. The Olympia project threatened the FA because it was not simply a stage representation of the game, but a profit-making rival competition run at the same time of year. Within two months the FA Council banned the new game and all current players from taking part. Despite the sanction, organisers posted hoardings all over the capital.[56] Some undeterred footballers defied their controllers and appeared, only to be barred permanently from FA clubs.[57] The Olympia league collapsed because of public indifference in the spring of 1906, leaving these destitute men at the mercy of Chelsea's manager, who organised a fund to pay for their transportation home.[58] Spoof and melodrama were permissible, but direct competition was not.

Fred Karno, whose *Football Match* débuted in late 1906, created the most successful and popular of the football plays. *The Football Match* was first announced to the public when Karno asked retired footballers, who were immune to FA sanctions, with 'good big reputations' to audition for his Christmas pantomime show.[59] This sketch recreated a game between the Midnight Wanderers and Middleton Piecans who were seen training in the first scene. Gamblers then attempted to bribe Stiffy the Goal-Keeper, played by Harry Weldon, into throwing the match. Weldon's popularity was cemented in the finale when his character refused to submit to the fraudsters and won the game for his side. The sketch toured relentlessly, launching Charlie Chaplin's stardom in 1910 when he replaced Weldon at the Oxford.[60] Meanwhile, the *Football Match* teams boomed the sketch by playing in charity games with professional clubs and music halls in London and at every tour stop.

The Football Match's stage setting reflected the influence of Corbett's boxing plays as the teams played before a painted backdrop depicting a vast crowd. Members of this concourse had holes cut where their heads should be through which the well-known professional footballers showed their faces, while a compère clad as a referee introduced them.[61] London loved the sketch; it played the Hackney Empire in early 1908, while its production at the Chelsea Palace over Christmas 1909 was advertised prominently in the local football club's programme, which announced that eight first-class professional players, including two former members of London teams, would appear.[62]

There was not always even a cursory attempt to portray football in a formal, realist manner on the halls. When Fulham hosted Nottingham Forest in February 1906 both teams were invited by the *Football Chat* to spend the evening at the Pavilion, Piccadilly. In order to prepare for this visit Jock Whiteford, the comedian whose five-minute-long recital of events at a Scottish cup-tie was that hall's star feature, attended Craven Cottage during the afternoon. About seventy footballers and many guests laughed as every turn on the bill mentioned the day's play, culminating with Whiteford adding a coda set at Fulham. This addendum lampooned those athletes in attendance, before Whiteford took a curtain call clad in the jersey of victors Nottingham Forest while clutching a Fulham shirt.[63] The Lyceum Theatre in the Strand would not be upstaged by its West End rival and so three weeks later Tottenham Hotspur attended as they prepared for a Cup-tie replay with Birmingham. Successive turns recalled Spurs' achievements and saluted Birmingham's directors. Film of Spurs' previous game against Birmingham would have been screened but for a technical hitch, though such movies were promised for a second music-hall evening, at the Birmingham Hippodrome, after the match.[64]

Similarly, in 1909 the stage of the Huddersfield Hippodrome was the setting when the local club, winners of the Yorkshire Football Cup, attended. The trophy, bound in the club's colours of claret and gold was displayed and J. W. Rowley, the artiste who had introduced somersaults to the halls forty years before, updated his current act by wearing the team's uniform to sing 'The football song'.[65] Two years later George French performed another football song at the Grand Theatre, Glasgow, pantomime while increasing local interest by wearing the jersey of Partick Thistle's Alex Raisbeck, James Quinn of Celtic's shorts, Sunderland's Ronald Orr's boots and the hose of Billy Minter of Spurs.[66] According to theatrical journalist Dion Calthrop, when the Lancashire dialect singer appeared 'the audience become football enthusiasts to a man'.[67] Sporting turns were popular in London where the Stratford Empire hosted 'The Football skating girls' at the start of 1913, and Sammy Shields portrayed a Scotsman watching a football match at a March 1914 Palladium royal charity performance.[68] Finally, the revue *A Year in an Hour*, in which a female troupe portrayed the year's main events, opened in 1914 at the Palladium with league fixtures and the FA Cup final forming an entire 'season' of the five enacted.[69]

Inviting sports teams to music halls was another provincial development of the 1890s. Sunderland Football Club went to the Derby Alhambra before they played the local side in October 1894. After the show George Ripon entertained the team at their hotel with his football song before the performers attended Sunderland's football match.[70] The Alhambra, Leicester Square, was perhaps the first London hall to host football when the French national squad attended in February 1893. The French and British flags adorned the balconies and the band saluted the guests by playing their national anthems.[71] When Sheffield United and the Corinthians attended after playing the first-ever match for the Thomas Dewar Cup five years later, fans were urged to be present because 'the teams will once more face one another that evening from private boxes on opposite sides of the auditorium'.[72] Similarly, Oxford and Cambridge scullers, music-hall sportsmen, American university athletes, boxers and Australian cricketers all watched themselves on the screens of West End music halls at the end of the century.[73]

FA Cup fever hit London in 1901. The Warwick Trading Company arranged to film and screen that year's match between Sheffield United and Tottenham Hotspur on the same evening in London's leading music halls.[74] Smaller halls received their prints a few days later. Warwick's engineers processed the two-minute-long negative and delivered it to the capital from the venue at Bolton in time for the evening performance. Interest in the match's final outcome was palpable in London and even though Warwick owned the game's cinema rights, Edison-Thomas Vitascope, one of their staunchest competitors, announced Spurs' victory on the screen of the sports-mad Harry Lundy's Royal, Holborn, when the city first received the news.[75] 1902 was another important year for southern football because Southampton appeared in the Cup final, on Spurs' victorious heels. Consecutive southern finalists must have boosted Urban's commercial expectations for this film, which they supplied to a very limited number of halls on match day.[76]

The Alhambra's habit of inviting sportsmen to occupy the hall's seats was linked to screening football movies in 1906 when Cup finalists Everton witnessed Urban's film of their match.[77] The entire 1907 final, again filmed by Urban, was presented at the Alhambra during the second house on match evening.[78] This 'turn' was repeated the following week when the Sheffield Empire hosted the victorious local team after the players had dined with the Lord Mayor at the town hall.[79] Wolverhampton beat Newcastle in 1908 before attending the Alhambra where Urban again presented the entire match.[80] As with Sheffield the year before, the defeated Newcastle team attended a music hall after returning home, to hear Maidie Scott sing 'I couldn't come home in the dark' which the crowd updated as 'I couldn't come home with the cup'.[81] Swindon and Barnsley reassembled in Leicester Square to see themselves play after the Cup semi-final at Chelsea in 1912.[82] Similarly, Billy Boardman, who managed the Brighton Hippodrome, advertised that his patrons would be informed of the score during the matinée when the local Seagulls played in a 1914 Cup tie at Sheffield.[83]

Neither Leicester Square palaces, cinema companies nor the Cup final monopolised the appearance of footballers in the audience, as Spurs discovered in November 1901 when they played West Norwood. On this occasion E. V. Page, manager of the Empress, Brixton, offered them two boxes and forty seats in the stalls.[84] This visit came five months after Spurs won the FA Cup, meaning the astute and up-to-date Page not only capitalised on the presence of a popular metropolitan team at his hall, but also that of the national champions. Provincial hall managers like the Middlesborough Empire's Johnny Thornborrow also regularly supported local clubs in this manner.[85] Managers had to be wary of these promotions, as footballers celebrating after a match were not always their sport's meekest ambassadors. Chelsea attended the Burton Hippodrome in October 1906 after which the London press reported that drunken players had stumbled riotously through the streets when the hall closed. The team were still establishing their reputation with fans and the press at the start of their second season and so the directors denied these reports in the subsequent match-day programme.[86]

Supporters' behaviour could be equally troublesome. Chelsea directors feared street disturbances after a Cup-tie derby with Spurs in 1910 and so they implored people to go home immediately after the match in order to have tea with their wives, while unmarried men were advised to take their 'best girl' out to a music hall.[87] Courting fans on their best behaviour were steered to the halls, but so too were both teams, along with their directors and officers, who went to the Alhambra.[88] The Chelsea Palace kept pace with the Alhambra by screening film of the game during the second house that evening and all through the following week.[89] Similarly, Orient's president Horatio Bottomley took his players to the pantomime at their local music hall, the Britannia, Hoxton, in February 1912 where the group posed for photographs with the actors George Lupino and Daisy Goldsack (Figure 20).[90] Cup-final day regularly saw the capital invaded by northerners barracking for their teams. The Euston, situated near to London's northern terminus, advertised itself in *The Era* as a stop-over for spectators as they awaited their homeward trains.[91]

Cinema companies often filmed matches to screen at halls near a team's home ground as a way to attract customers.[92] The local Palace Theatre showed a Fulham home match in front of a record audience on game night in 1907.[93] In 1912 small local music halls screened films of West Ham matches the following

20   Clapton Orient at their local theatre with team president Horatio Bottomley.

week while the players were invited to attend.[94] Topical football movies were another manifestation of the way Edwardian producers filmed local scenes, which is evidence that music-hall managers were aware that football fans were a good potential source of revenue.

A relationship based on screening match films and team appearances occasionally in music halls could not be very profound. However, music halls also courted football fans' patronage actively by advertising regularly in the match-day programmes which London football clubs first published in 1906. Cartoons and drawings abounded, although photographs rarely appeared in these pamphlets where short press cuttings conveyed national news, while extended editorials and dressing-room gossip sections did the same for team affairs. The middle pages named the players appearing for each side in a large box surrounded by advertisements. It is safe to assume that this border carried the most important and expensive advertisements in programmes which must have been opened at the players' page throughout the afternoon for easy reference.

The East Ham Palace advertised in *The Hammers' Gazette* from its inaugural issue 1907–08 season, followed by six other local halls over the next four years.[95]

From its first issue in 1907 Clapton's *Oriental Notes* contained notices for the Hackney Empire above the team line-up, along with occasional critical appraisals of the artistes appearing both there and at the Dalston Theatre.[96] The Empire's manager watched a match with Wolves in December 1907, hoping Orient's supporters would reciprocate this patronage. In order to persuade them, the following season's first programme contained a banner from the hall above the team line-up and a supporting article detailing 'where to go tonight'.[97] Seven months after the Orient had been photographed at the pantomime, in 1912, the Britannia advertisements appeared, along with the Clapton Rink Cinema and the Dalston Theatre.[98]

The Granville advertised in the *Chelsea Chronicle* from October 1907 while the Chelsea Palace hired space at the start of the next season.[99] Fans purchasing Arsenal's programme from October 1909 saw Royal Artillery Theatre advertisements decorating one half of the front cover.[100] Tottenham halls were less forthright with their promotions as it was not until 1910 that the Edmonton Empire and Tottenham Palace first advertised in Spurs' *Programme*.[101] Finally, Fulham's Grand Theatre advertised in the *Cottager's Journal* from the beginning of the 1912 season with both banners and pictures of the week's prettiest actresses.[102] Though they were the last club to feature music-hall advertisements, Fulham's programme published George Robey's story *Football in the Year 2000* in which he predicted that players would be paid in tobacco and flown to matches which, rather than wars, would resolve national rivalries.[103] This piece appeared one year after a pavilion forecasting life at the end of the twentieth century had been mounted at the Crystal Palace Festival of Empire.[104]

Directors understood that attendance by popular sportsmen attracted bigger audiences to their halls where football melodramas, spoofs and films represented the sport on the stage. This patronage was not limited to Cup celebrations though because music halls continually reserved the most prominent advertising spaces in match-day programmes. These relationships proved the consanguinity of football and music-hall audiences. Not all of this courtship happened on stage and so we must now look at how artistes used football venues.

Victorian Christmas pantomime companies engaged in charity football matches with local clubs from at least 1890 when *The Era* published a seasonal 'Theatrical football' column. As with football on the stage, the origin of these games is moot. However, such matches originated most likely in the provinces, given spectacular football's initial locus. A Sheffield music-hall proprietor donated a competition cup in 1867 in the earliest instance of this patronage.[105]

Whether he had immediate imitators is unclear, but by 1890 press and pantomime companies played annual costume matches in Leicester, Glasgow, Liverpool, Bradford and Birmingham.[106] These day-long carnivals followed a standard pattern. They were kicked-off by pretty soubrettes, watched by civic dignitaries, and ended with a trip to the local theatre. From 1893 until 1899, pantomime matches were held in Huddersfield, Leeds, Newcastle, Derby, Lancaster, Reading, Bury, Bixley Heath, Glasgow, Northwich, Bristol, Birmingham, Kendal, Liverpool, Wolverhampton and Cheltenham.[107] In September at Melbourne, Australia, a country with very little history of association football, over £1,000 was raised for the Australian Dramatic and Musical Association in a match where players dressed as characters from the most popular music-hall songs.[108]

Though the basic premise of these matches was adopted by London music-hall baseballers, and cricketers, football was a far more popular sport. The potential for personal advertisement was consequently greater. Leslie Henson, one of the top music-hall comedians toured the provinces with *The Quaker Girl* as part of a fourteen-person company in 1911 and 1912. At most stops the actors proceeded from the station to their hotel where they changed into football gear to play fixtures which had been arranged in advance.[109] Just as with Leybourne's carriage, or Tate's car, these matches announced the company's arrival. Albert Douglass of the Standard Theatre, Shoreditch, demonstrated another way that such a game could be arranged. One day the police dropped by and talk turned to football. The male actors bragged of their superiority to local favourites Tottenham Hotspur. The police would not let such a boast go unanswered and so a charity match, at which soubrettes sold programmes, was readily agreed upon.[110]

Such accounts show that artistes gained enjoyment, altruistic benevolence and publicity from these matches. However, a more compelling story comes from Billy Merson, a popular Nottingham-born comedian, whose London engagements were interrupted by provincial holiday pantomime tours. In the annual Birmingham carnival between Aston Villa and local pantomime companies Merson wore 'an old brown Homburg hat, a disreputable creation that had been in my possession for years and years. I picked it out just because I thought it looked so ludicrous'.[111] He became annoyed while running about because his hat kept falling on to the muddy pitch. Merson created one of his most popular gags when he exasperatedly warned one of the opposition to 'mind my velour!' because 'It's on the flo-or!' The defender laughed and so Merson wore the hat and repeated the joke in his performance on the stage that night. It is not clear whether the spectators in the stadium heard his initial impromptu remark, but the audience at the hall shrieked with laughter and 'the gag rushed through the Midlands like a flash of lightning; and everywhere one heard people asking about a fictitious "velour" that was "on the flo-or!"' I kept the gag in the show till the pantomime ended; and later I introduced it to London when I played in *Brighter London* at the Hippodrome'.[112] Merson, like Jock Whiteford, incorporated the day's play into his act. This was not the funniest jest ever devised, but its genesis clearly showed that pantomime matches attracted artistes partly because they could provide material for stage turns. Because this hat gag was transposed easily to other settings it may have lasted longer than most football jokes.

Despite being keen and active footballers neither Henson, Douglass nor Merson brought these pantomime matches to London. That was accomplished by George Robey, the most ardent music-hall athlete. Robey, 'the prime minister of mirth', was one of the most popular Edwardian comedians. Born into a middle-class London family in 1869, he was raised partly in England and Germany, while as a Birmingham engineer's apprentice he took up association football.[113] Robey's London stage breakthrough came in 1891 after which, as his career progressed rapidly, he made pantomime appearances especially in Birmingham, Manchester, Liverpool and Glasgow, cities which hosted annual football matches.[114] Sports may not have been foremost in Robey's mind when accepting these extended seasonal engagements, for his son recalled that, with two constantly touring artiste parents, pantomime season was almost the only time the family spent together.[115] These bookings in northern football centres, along with Robey's involvement in Leno's cricketers, are substantial clues as to where he learned to manage his own teams. Another is the way he nurtured his sporting passions by turning out as an amateur for Hull City, Glasgow Rangers and Millwall.

Robey first organised a sports match in 1902 while playing in a Manchester pantomime when his team met prominent cricketers to help the family of Lancashire batsman Johnny Briggs.[116] From then on Robey raised money for charity assiduously, but unlike Leno he was 'boldly competitive', though not always with the results he anticipated.[117] Though Robey played for several professional clubs he was dismayed that spectators did not come to laud his skill, but in the hopes that he would add comic touches to otherwise serious matches. Crowds roared with laughter as his shots on goal honestly defeated keepers in 1903 when he played for Millwall reserves because his 'professional reputation debars the public from regarding his efforts as any other than farcical'.[118] A wag had only to shout one of his signature stage sayings during quiet moments for the spectators to erupt in laughter and generally 'all George's clever bits of play were treated as humorous turns, especially arranged for the entertainment of the crowd'.[119] One year later Robey, though 'a strong and effective footballer', was still not taken entirely seriously by the Millwall fans. Untoward play directed at him was seen by the mirthful spectators as pre-arranged complicity with opponents to facilitate his clowning antics.[120] In Glasgow Robey collided at full speed with the opposing goalkeeper who was attempting to punch the ball away, was struck in the head and broke his ribs. However, 'the next thing I saw was a hundred grinning faces looking down at me from the other side of the touch line, evidently enjoying the joke immensely'.[121]

Robey matched his talents with the most accomplished professionals. He captained a team of national side footballers, including Tottenham's Vivian J. Woodward and four other members of London clubs, in a charity match against Spurs at White Hart Lane in December 1904.[122] On that occasion between six and eight thousand people saw a game 'contested with almost cup-tie keenness from start to finish'.[123] Nevertheless spectators refused to take Robey's playing seriously, and expected him instead to appear, as he did on stage, clad 'in a battered hat, with grease painted face, and a tattered umbrella'.[124]

However, there were dissenting views of his ability. When Robey turned out for Shepherd's Bush football club while appearing at the local Empire in March 1904 his improved play was ascribed to having learned a thing or two from the northerners during a recent pantomime engagement.[125] When he played for Lanark in 1904 while appearing in the Theatre Royal, Glasgow, pantomime the match's kick-off was delayed so that it did not interfere with his matinée.[126] The Scots praised Robey's talent though he 'did not risk much in the way of tackling' and retired at the half, though his athletic contribution had attracted artistes to the stands.[127] Five years later Robey assisted Rangers by scoring one of the team's two goals in a losing effort in a benefit match against Falkirk.[128]

Robey's ubiquitous identification with the game was complete in 1905 when he was described as the 'football comedian', updating his persona less than one year after Oswald Stoll had pronounced him 'the automobile of comic singers'.[129] However, unlike Stoll's booming, Robey felt this new name devalued his sporting achievements. His first autobiography, published in 1908, assuaged his ego by stating that serious matches had, over time, silenced audiences' comedic expectations from him.[130] The statement was an optimistic attempt to amend fans' expectations. Robey gave up the game in 1921, but still vividly and publicly dreamed about winning the FA Cup.[131] In 1920 a second, more insightful and reflective autobiography conceded continual frustration that spectators 'at the beginning of a game at any rate imagined I was being funny'.[132] In 1906 *Stage and Sport*, a short-lived weekly publication aimed at amateur performers, printed a photo of him practising in his flannels on the pitch at Lords while stating that actors and artistes lost 'nothing in the power to amuse by being physically fit, and they can take Mr. Robey as a good example to follow in every way'.[133] Robey averred this view to *C. B. Fry's Magazine* by confessing that football and cricket matches were absolutely essential in calming him before appearing on stage.[134] This photograph was published at the same time that Robey appeared in the Liverpool carnival, evidently alternating, despite his claims, between serious and comedic matches.[135] If his new sobriquet piqued, then Robey could find comfort in these contemporary representations of himself as a serious athlete.

Football was not simply a casually pursued rich man's indulgence, because Robey played regularly with local sides for charity while appearing in provincial pantomime. As part of his association football epiphany of 1899 he had donated a cup to be competed for by his team of personally selected international players and the most prominent local clubs. In addition to the trophy, Robey presented gold medals to every player and sold photographs of himself at the event.[136] The FA assisted Robey with the arrangements for these fixtures by permitting professional footballers to appear.[137]

Just like Merson, Robey played *Jack and the Beanstalk* at the Prince of Wales Theatre, Birmingham in 1903 when he faced Aston Villa in the annual match.[138] Four years later Robey returned with a team of international players to meet Villa before 7,000 spectators.[139] These enormously successful annual matches raised over £25,000 for Birmingham's needy between 1895 and 1905.[140] Robey was evidently fond of the city in which he spent his early adulthood and so he came forward again in 1910 when Birmingham FC was 'in a very bad way financially' to organise a fund-raising match with local rivals Villa.[141] Other stage benefactors emerged and over one thousand people attended a special fund-raising matinée given by all the artistes appearing in Birmingham pantomimes. Rain limited the attendance to some five thousand and so only about £100 was collected, but Robey then entertained his sodden team-mates at the Theatre Royal and the Imperial Hotel.[142] In March Robey met Harry Weldon's *Football Match* team in another benefit for Birmingham Football Club that was kicked off by Ada Reeve and the soubrette Dorothy Ward.[143] The following month Robey played on a stage side at Brentford.[144]

In February 1906 Robey's internationals played Everton. The match took place with 'a certain amount of intentional loose play'; a spirit of which he may not have approved.[145] Nevertheless Robey derived benefits from the publicity when he appeared wearing a football uniform in the illustrated magazine *The Sketch* together with the encomium that he was 'a footballer of considerable skill'.[146] The match realised £405, partly because Robey unexpectedly paid all the expenses incurred, thus whipping up publicity for his benefit evening the following Saturday at the Royal Court Theatre, Liverpool.[147] When Robey introduced Sheffield United at the Canterbury, Lambeth, after they had won the 1907 FA Cup, the Robey Challenge Cup, which had generated £3,000 in eight years, was placed egotistically beside the national trophy.[148] That same spring Billy Meredith, of Manchester United and Wales, one of the most famous footballers of his day, joined Robey and nine members of leading London teams to play at Stamford Bridge.[149]

Ten thousand spectators saw Manchester United meet Glasgow selects at the end of January 1909. Prizes were presented that evening on the stage of the Theatre Royal by Robey.[150] Personal friendships and professional associations melded two years later when Manchester United dined at Robey's Finchley home after winning the FA Cup.[151] Whilst starring at the Olympia, Liverpool, in 1912, Robey led his team against Liverpool and Everton selects.[152] Perhaps inspired by the total raised by this event, the Mexborough Empire aided distressed miners with a fund-raising football match two weeks later.[153] As this litany of matches attests, Robey linked London music-hall football and these annual provincial matches. Though metropolitan pantomime was resurgent at this same time, centring itself in the suburban halls and revitalising scripts by localising its allusions.[154] After 1901 up-to-date allusions were increasingly references to football.[155] The relationship between football and the stage had been fostered in part by the personal ties of stars like George Robey, but other important proponents also appeared.

The first music-hall charity football match in the metropolis occurred, predictably enough, when George Robey and a team of old Millwall players faced the artiste Fred Wright's selected professionals in 1902. About 4,000 people attended a serious match that was followed by a comic costume game. This division of the afternoon into distinct serious and comedic halves, derived from provincial pantomime, was the pattern that promoters adopted for later London carnivals.[156] Robey then took a team of artistes and internationals to Craven Cottage in the fall of 1903 to play Fulham.[157]

Fulham encouraged music-hall matches actively after 1909, the year that tubes and trams reached Craven Cottage and they joined the Football League. The club hosted a comic match that January between Fulham and the artistes from the *Little Red Riding Hood* pantomime at Hammersmith's Lyric Opera House. This event was attended by about 700 spectators who were cadged for donations in aid of local charities by actresses from the pantomime company. Fulham got into the spirit of the day by fielding a back-to-front team, with their goalie and defenders playing forward and attackers in the rear. Arrayed against them were twenty costumed artistes while 'Claude Lipp' kept the club's goal attired in a frock coat and top hat. The Lyric's principal-boy Kittee Rayburn kicked off and scored the first point as Friar Tuck refereed and two police constables – one short and slight, the other tall and fat – were the touch judges. These men chased, arrested and imprisoned Fulham's goal-scorers in the dressing room.[158] The resemblance to Leno's cricket matches must have comforted these audiences.

That evening the Fulham players attended the Lyric for an updated version of *Little Red Riding Hood*, in which three photographs of the match were projected onto a screen and incorporated into the pantomime. The footballers were passive spectators until the final scene's 'procession of notabilities', which included Rayburn holding a gilt trophy, Red Riding Hood carrying a football inscribed 'Lyric' and the entire Fulham team. The hall's manager, Fred S. Jennings, then came on to the stage where he thanked patrons for supporting a match that had been arranged hastily and had not been publicised effectively. However, both Jennings and Fulham's manager announced that they had agreed to an annual event that would be heavily boomed.[159]

Despite the suddenness with which the fixture had been arranged, Fulham's directors were unhappy that so few people had turned out to watch it. A report in *The Cottager's Journal* chastised those who stayed away because 'actors and actresses have big hearts when charity is concerned. We were all very gay. We missed you though'.[160] The weak financial returns increased the club's ire as embarrassed directors augmented funds by £15 after only £35 was raised at the match.[161] This was an abysmal total given that even the most obscure provincial matches regularly collected three times as much. Nevertheless, Fulham directors were optimistic about future music-hall collaborations, and so for a short time in early 1909 the club advertised their forthcoming fixtures and player line-ups in *The Era* – the only FL club to do so.[162] This connection with the halls culminated in a second fixture against the Lyric in January 1910.[163]

Once again, Kittee Rayburn started a game that was, if nothing else, 'worth the 6d. charged for admission'.[164] As in the previous year costumed artistes played a reversed Fulham side and goal scorers were arrested and imprisoned by the touch judges. Play was interrupted by rain showers and so, remarkably, only about half the previous year's total was collected for local charities.[165] That night Fulham's players saw *Aladdin* performed at the Lyric, taking the stage between acts when Jennings thanked them, presented a trophy to Kittee Rayburn and declared his hopes for greater success in the future.[166] These expressions of good will were verbiage given the physical estrangement that was apparent in the failure to incorporate footballers into the show. This was completed the next year when professional footballers were ousted from the match altogether. Instead, the *Dick Whittington* company from the King's Theatre, Hammersmith faced *Cinderella* of the Fulham.[167] Craven Cottage hosted its last pantomime match that year, though Fulham remained very amenable to music-hall football.

C. Aubrey Smith was the 'legitimate' stage's answer to George Robey. He was keenly interested in sports, especially cricket, at which he had captained Charterhouse, Cambridge and England before turning to acting in 1892.[168] Though he was almost fifty years old, Smith gamely brought a 'Church versus Stage' association football game, popular in an era when it was easy to raise a side of clerics who had won blues as undergraduates, to Craven Cottage in late 1910 in aid of the *Daily Mirror* Christmas Pudding Fund.[169] Both elevens included players who had turned out for Football League clubs either as professionals or amateurs.[170] The actor George Alexander kicked off and Robey's friend Vivian J. Woodward appeared as referee. Woodward was an architect and amateur athlete who played for Tottenham and Chelsea, captained England and was 'probably the most popular footballer in the world' before the First World War. Reverend S. J. Childs-Clarke and the actor Rutland Barrington guarded the lines whilst 'a bevy of pretty actresses' sold programmes. Despite this impressive list of participants only £35 was raised.[171]

Lord Lonsdale kicked off at Craven Cottage that December when jockeys met cricketers, scullers and boxers to raise money for Putney Hospital. Billy Wells's appearance was advertised prominently in a two-page cartoon announcing the match in *The Cottagers' Journal* while an unnamed black figure loomed menacingly over the other athletes suggesting that Jack Johnson would also attend.[172] No more sensational, topical advertisement could have been produced that autumn than hinting that Wells and Johnson, whose fight had been cancelled just two months previously, would meet on the pitch. If Fulham's directors had had any scruples about renewing the moribund pantomime match these disappeared at the sight of at least 6,000 spectators for Lonsdale's afternoon. Nor was this game devoid of comedy as the discrepancy in stature between the jockeys and their opponents, a familiar ingredient in music-hall sports, leavened a seriously contested match. Given their disproportionate sizes it was almost inevitable that Billy Wells cantered off the pitch with a jockey on his back.[173] This popular sporting combination was repeated when flat-race jockeys opposed steeplechase riders two months later to raise a fund in aid of 'disabled and necessitous jockeys'.[174]

Craven Cottage was not the sole stadium to host these matches. The *Daily Mail* Christmas Pudding Fund benefited from another Church versus Stage afternoon at Chelsea's Stamford Bridge stadium in December 1909. On this occasion Robey led a team on the pitch of the most famous actors in London, including accomplished footballers like T. Wragg, a sometime member of Nottingham Forest who was then appearing in Karno's *Football Match*, and Basil Foster, 'a forward of almost international class'. Actresses sold programmes in the stands and Woodward again refereed.[175] The different conception which lay behind this match was described overtly when the *Daily Mail* mollified the show's star by deterring anyone who expected a comedy for 'it must be distinctly understood that it is a serious game, and people visiting the ground with the idea of witnessing an open-air variety show will be disappointed'.[176] Between two and three thousand people attended in spite of this warning.[177] The match was not as sober as predicted, for after contesting the first half seriously the teams retired, leaving the comedian Rutland Barrington to conduct the band before serving as a buffoon linesman for the comic second period of play.[178] The participants signed the ball at the close of play and auctioned it off to the highest bidder.[179] Robey's presence, as with his provincial pantomime appearances, was probably not simply the result of personal munificence as he débuted at the Empire on the evening of the match.[180] After the 1910 sequel Billy Williams, 'the man in the velvet suit', purchased the autographed ball in order to update his song 'It's the only bit of English that we've got'.[181]

Tottenham first hosted such a match in January 1909, soon after joining the FL, when professional golfers faced footballers at White Hart Lane.[182] By far the stadium's most popular use occurred four years later when Harry Bawn, who was attempting to revive the doleful fortunes of the Edmonton Empire, secured the ground for a charity match. The idea for such a match had been spawned when Bawn and *The Encore*'s editor had overheard the comedian Sam Mayo and Spurs' Bert Middlemiss chatting.[183] Free use of Spurs' pitch was then granted by club directors while Bawn enlisted the Music-hall Home and the Prince of Wales Hospital, Tottenham, as beneficiaries.[184] It was then necessary to draft players and so artistes 'who can foot the leather' were encouraged to participate.[185]

The idea was booming by the start of February when the *Bloomsbury Burglars* challenged 'Somebody's' Policemen to a comic match on the same afternoon; Spurs furnished the side with a uniform and a list of players was published in late February.[186] Support for the game came from many quarters as London syndicates released artistes from their contracts for the day, Spurs informed their fans through the *Official Programme*, while film companies screened advertisements and the promoters promised a 'beauty stand' filled with female artistes who would bestow kisses on goal scorers.[187] Almost inevitably, George Robey, though he had not created the match, captained an artistes' team. Marie Lloyd kicked off (Figure 21) and just as predictably Vivian J. Woodward refereed. The teams traded goal-keepers at the start of the match, but despite Robey's best instincts, such a grouping of music-hall stars had never been expected to play seriously. Instead, the organisers divided the day's proceedings between a serious match against Spurs and a 'comic costume footer scramble' held afterward.[188] Female artistes were not confined to the stands as Ray's troupe of girls appeared for the comic match clad in a striking costume of regulation jerseys and shorts, with stockings to protect their dignity, and bronzed boots.[189]

About 12,000 people attended and London receipts finally reflected provincial ones when more than £309 was tallied. As with any new event there were organisational problems, especially for scorers who may have received their promised kisses: though 'if this osculatory display took place, it was not in public, whereat the spectators were a little disappointed'.[190] They were opposed by the jackaroos from the *Wild Australia* revue, who armed themselves with lassos and revolvers.[191] Casualty staff attended the many wounded on the pitch throughout this part of the fête, amputating shattered limbs with giant hand saws before fitting the wooden legs which enabled players to carry on. The auction of a football signed by both sides then closed the day.[192]

If Robey reigned in Tottenham, then Fulham belonged to Billy Wells, who played in a charity match against professional golfers one week after his defeat by Carpentier at the NSC.[193] Though his self-esteem was low, just as in the halls that week, he was accorded a 'perfect ovation' on entering and leaving the pitch.[194] Billy's friend, confidant and promoter Eugene Corri, who witnessed the crowd's reaction, felt that it reassured Wells of the public's continuing support and affection.[195] This regenerative tonic had almost instantaneous effect as Billy scored four times against Southampton's professional keeper, which 'opened the eyes of all who did not know him as a footballer', and so he was asked to play for Fulham in an upcoming game against arch rivals Chelsea.[196] These cheers and goals had a talismanic effect on Wells's self-esteem and Craven Cottage became his sanctuary. Such was the champion's fame that his younger

London favourite Marie Lloyd does her bit for charity in 1913.   **21**

brother was given a much-heralded trial by Fulham while Billy trained at
Craven Cottage throughout the spring for his national boxing tour.[197]

During this prolonged training Wells made his first-class début in Fulham's
London derby at Chelsea in February 1914. Though the FA refused to sanction
a cup and medals for the match, Chelsea were still made to agree not to charge
Wells.[198] Even if Wells was sacrosanct, his Fulham team-mate Tommy Laws
recalled that during the game 'I tackled one of their players and he went down
injured. Chelsea players quickly had a go at me, but Billy came in and hauled
them off' thus demonstrating another one of his footballing assets.[199] In March
Fulham's directors asked Billy to join the team for a league fixture in the wake of
his victory over Bandsman Blake at the Palladium.[200]

A second edition of the Tottenham match was announced at the end of
1913.[201] Other clubs saw the potential for extravagant carnivals and so Spurs
and Bawn now had direct competition. In January *The Encore* boomed both the
Tottenham match, known locally as 'big joy day', and the jockeys versus artistes
at Stamford Bridge, which was to be held the month before.[202] The scheduling
of Chelsea's match so close to Tottenham's was obviously designed to capture

the London audience whose interest in these up-to-date events might presently dissipate. Stamford Bridge had hosted successful jockeys' matches in 1911 and 1912 and so organisers reverted to this formula. Racing's aristocratic pretensions attracted ex-king Manuel of Portugal as the gala's patron in the venerated tradition of dethroned European monarchs publicly trading in the tarnished prestige of their birthright, while the Great Eastern Railway ran a cheap train from Newmarket, the traditional home of British racing.[203]

Rain on the eve of the match rendered the pitch unsuitable, not for the football, but for the carnival section of the bill, and so the game was postponed.[204] If the match could not proceed without the comedy, then soccer must only have been the nucleus around which a fuller entertainment revolved. The *Daily Express* recognised this and advised directors to schedule events throughout the afternoon in order to allow late-comers to experience some of the fun and frolic.[205] A straight football match got the day underway. The 'hefty outside left' Sammy Shields was a better player than his team-mate and rival stage describer of Scottish football match crowds, Jock Whiteford, while Arsenal, Chelsea and Fulham players officiated.[206] Robert Whittingham of Chelsea and Fulham's Arthur Collins were linesmen. The Palladium band, representing the venue for the Blake–Wells fight, provided the music. Harry Tate then attempted to set the world record for the mile on the cycle track surrounding the pitch in an automobile that was preceded by a mace-bearer and five-member brass band. His car collapsed amid smoke and fireworks after ten minutes and was towed away by a donkey.[207] In case motorists were dissuaded by this failure, *The Encore* decided to 'withhold the name [of the car] at the request of the makers; they rather question the advisability of the advertisement'.[208] While Tate plodded around the pitch, boxing rings were erected at either end of the stadium, and simultaneously 'Bombardier Wells, in a bout with Sid Wells, showed us what he really can do [and] Bandsman Blake outpointed Fred Drummond'.[209] Wells defeated Blake at the Palladium a fortnight later. The interval concluded with 'a splendid round of comedy turns' in all parts of the stadium.[210]

The jockeys wore their silks and artistes donned stage costumes for a comic second half.[211] Herbert Jones, one of England's most famous jockeys, was induced to try the pantomime horse which predictably collapsed. This was followed by the 'Chelsea Derby Stakes', in which jockeys rode donkeys.[212] The afternoon closed with the riders mounting one of *Wild Australia's* bucking horses: to the crowd's great amusement, 'every jockey who made the attempt was violently thrown off within three seconds' before an Australian upstaged them by maintaining his seat on the same horse for several minutes. Warwick filmed the fun for 'the principal variety theatres'. Mounted photographs were available later.[213] The afternoon raised £506.0.6d. for the Music-hall Home and Rous Memorial Hospital, Newmarket.[214]

Ray's Girls were again announced for White Hart Lane in 1914, however this time they would meet women from the leading West End revues.[215] Salacious expectations for the afternoon were confirmed by newspapers like the *Daily Mail* who published photos of the women, bare-legged in football shorts, training on the eve of the match.[216] The day began with Harry Tate, almost as omnipresent as Robey and Woodward were at charity sports, in a motoring sketch.[217] Bawn's wife, who danced under the stage name 'My Fancy', kicked off and each side was captained by a lady artiste.[218] Woodward, who had recently won his record sixtieth England cap, again refereed while Bandsman Blake and Bombardier Wells were set to recuperate on the touch lines from their bout two days before. When Spurs fielded their best eleven Wells was induced to drop his line flag and join their side.[219] No less adaptable than his opponents during the boxing boom, Spurs' 'Fanny' Walden bravely agreed to box six rounds with any man in variety if the professionals lost.[220] Spectators were not disappointed when they saw goal-scoring kisses publicly bestowed by the chorus girls from the Oxford footballing review *A Year in an Hour* before themselves participating as thirty 'of all that is goodly and beautiful in feminine variety' sold kisses for a sovereign each in the stands.[221] One can only guess the lingering betrayal felt by these puckering fans when they perceived that the 'beautiful belles' of the West End who then met Ray's girls were male artistes in drag.[222] Helena Millais, whose *Silver Creek* cowboy review played the Edmonton Empire that week, also participated.[223] White Hart Lane whetted Millais's appetite for public carnivals and so she assisted B. C. Hucks with his flying afternoon at Lincoln in April. Indeed it was the women who garnered most of the match's residual publicity, as photos of female footballers who were fit and well accoutred, though they had not struck 'the ball with any accuracy or much effect', appeared in London newspapers.[224]

Commentators compared the Chelsea and Tottenham matches in the expectancy of their being played, as well as at their autopsies. An article with the seemingly salutary title 'Fun and frolic, a merry meeting at White Hart Lane', said that Spurs' 'show cannot be said to have equalled that at Chelsea the other week. In the first place, the football match was between full-blown professionals of the Spurs Club and amateurish music-hall artists, [while Spurs] had to do their best to be inept at that which they are paid for being experts. They were not a bit like jockeys'.[225]

Music-hall football, which had originated in the provinces, overwhelmed London at the beginning of the twentieth century. In doing so it cemented two important, emerging entertainment industries in a manner that neither baseball nor cricket had been able to do. Boxers are flamboyant characters who fight alone, stripped to the waist. Their ability to transfer their fame to the stage is therefore not surprising. However, music-hall football drew teams and individual players into the realms of modern celebrity. As First World War popular culture made clear, up-to-date music-hall sport had changed popular culture fundamentally.

Notes

1   Tony Mason, *Association Football and English Society, 1863–1915*, Brighton, Harvester, 1980, p. 15.

2   James Walvin, *The People's Game*, London, Allen Lane, 1975, p. 41.

3   Wray Vamplew, *Pay up and Play the Game: Professional Sport in Britain 1875–1914*, Cambridge, Cambridge University Press, 1988, p. 43; see also Ross McKibbin, 'Work and hobbies in Britain, 1880–1950', in Jay Winter (ed.), *The Working Class in Modern British History*, Cambridge, Cambridge University Press, 1983, p. 130.

4   Walvin, *People's Game*, pp. 53–57, and Gareth Stedman Jones *Outcast London*, Harmondsworth, Penguin, 1976, pp. 21–32.

5   James A. H. Catton, *The Real Football*, London, Sands and Co., 1900, p. 53.

6   Vamplew, *Pay up*, pp. 190–191.

7   Walvin, *People's Game*, p. 82; 'A Tottenham Hotspur man fined', *The Edmonton and Tottenham Weekly Guardian*, 22 May 1896, unnumbered pages.

8   Original player's contract, file 963, Haringey local history archives, Bruce Castle, London.

9   Stephen Wagg, *The Football World: A Contemporary Social History*, Brighton, Harvester, 1984, p. 6.

10 'Notes', *The Outlook*, 3 March 1900, p. 135, and Nicholas L. Jackson, *Association Football*, London, George Newnes, 1899, p. 140.

11 Harold MacFarlane, 'Football of yesterday and to-day', *The Monthly Review*, October 1906, p. 131.

12 'Football', *The Edmonton and Tottenham Weekly Guardian*, 29 October 1897, unnumbered pages.

13 'Football accidents', *Baily's Magazine of Sports and Pastimes*, 55 (1891), pp. 17–19; Charles Edwardes, 'The new football mania', *Nineteenth Century*, 32 (1892), pp. 622–631; Hely Hutchinson Almond, 'Football as a moral agent', *Nineteenth Century*, 34 (1893), pp. 899–911; Creston, 'Football', *Fortnightly Review*, 55 (1894), pp. 25–38; Ernest Ensor, 'The football madness', *Contemporary Review*, 74 (1898), pp. 751–760; Flying Dutchman, 'The professional influence on games', *Baily's Magazine of Sports and Pastimes*, 88 (1907), pp. 355–388.

14 'Current football', *Baily's Magazine of Sports and Pastimes*, 53 (1890), pp. 80–83.

15 Jackson, *Association Football*, p. 253.

16 Nicholas L. Jackson, *Sporting Days and Sporting Ways*, London, Hurst and Blackett, 1932, p. 66, and F. N. S. Creek, *A History of the Corinthian Football Club*, London, Longmans Green, 1933, *passim*.

17 Jackson, *Association Football*, p. 153.

18 Lionel Francis, *Seventy-Five Years of Southern League Football*, London, Pelham, 1969, pp. 20–21.

19 Catton, *Real Football*, pp. 38–41.

20 William J. Baker, 'The making of a working-class football culture in Victorian England', *The Journal of Social History*, 13 (1979), pp. 243–244.

21 Gordon Macey, *Queen's Park Rangers: A Complete Record*, Derby, Breedon Books, 1993, p. 6; Dennis Turner and Alex White, *Fulham: A Complete Record 1879–1987*, Derby, Breedon Books, 1987, p. 9.

22 Richard Lindsay, *Millwall: A Complete Record 1885–1991*, Derby, Breedon Books, 1992, p. 8.

23 John Northcutt and Roy Shoesmith, *West Ham United: A Complete Record 1900–1987*, Derby, Breedon Books, 1987, p. 8.

24 Mike Purkiss and Nigel Sands, *Crystal Palace: A Complete Record 1905–1989*, Derby, Breedon Books, 1990, pp. 9–10.

25 Neil Kaufman and Alan Ravenhill, *Leyton Orient: A Complete Record 1881–1990*, Derby, Breedon Books, 1990, p. 8; Julian Holland, *Spurs: A History of Tottenham Hotspur Football Club*, London, Phoenix Books, 1956, pp. 21–22.

26 Vamplew, *Pay Up*, p. 207. Vamplew cited unpublished statistical material to support his claim that the average career may have lasted about five matches.

27 'Club notes', *Tottenham Hotspur Football and Athletic Company Limited, Official Programme and Record of the Club*, 26 September 1908, unnumbered pages; 'Things heard', *Oriental Notes*, 13 September 1913, unnumbered pages; 'Things heard', *Oriental Notes*, 20 September 1913, unnumbered pages; 'Club notes', *The Hammers' Gazette: The Official Programme of the West Ham United Football Club*, 13 October 1913, unnumbered pages; and 'Chelsea chatter', *The Chelsea Football Club Chronicle, Official Programme of the Chelsea Football and Athletic Company Limited*, 21 and 23 March 1914, p. 2.

28 Turner and White, *Fulham*, p. 40.

29 Turner and White, *Fulham*, p. 11.

30 'From the board room', *The Cottager's Journal*, 16 January 1909, unnumbered pages, and 'From the board room', *The Cottager's Journal*, 23 January 1909, unnumbered pages.

31 Lindsay, *Millwall*, pp. 8–10.

32 Northcutt and Shoesmith, *West Ham United*, p. 9; Blacker, *Just Like It Was, Memoirs of the Mittel East*, London, Vallentine, Mitchell, 1974, p. 18; Charles P. Korr, 'A different kind of success: West Ham United and the creation of tradition and community', in Richard Holt (ed.), *Sport and the Working Class in Modern Britain*, Manchester, Manchester University Press, 1990, p. 147–148.

33   John Moynihan, *The West Ham Story*, London, A. Barker, 1984, pp. 13–18.

34   Macey, *Queen's Park Rangers*, pp. 6–16 and Dennis Signy, *A History of Queen's Park Rangers Football Club*, London, Pelham, 1969, pp. 21–36.

35   Elijah Watkins as quoted in Bernard Joy, *Forward, Arsenal!*, London, Phoenix House, 1952, p. 3.

36   'Royal Arsenal Football Club', *The Illustrated Sporting and Dramatic News*, 10 December 1892, p. 435; Edris A. Hapgood, *Football Ambassador*, London, Sporting Handbooks, 1945, p. 97.

37   Fred Ollier, *Arsenal: A Complete Record 1886–1992*, Derby, Breedon Books, 1992, pp. 19–20.

38   'Football', *The Illustrated Sporting and Dramatic News*, 6 October 1894, p. 167; Rex Pardoe, *The Battle of London*, London, Tom Stacey, 1972, p. 9.

39   Bob Goodwin, *Spurs: A Complete Record 1881–1991*, Derby, Breedon Books, 1991, p. 13; 'Football', *The Illustrated Sporting and Dramatic News*, 6 October 1894, p. 167.

40   'Tottenham Hotspur Football Club tournament', *Tottenham and Edmonton Weekly Herald*, 2 July 1897, unnumbered pages.

41   'Tottenham Hotspur annual military tournament', *Edmonton and Tottenham Weekly Guardian*, 11 August 1899, unnumbered pages.

42   Baker, 'Making of a working-class football culture', p. 244.

43   Scott Cheshire, *Chelsea: A Complete Record 1905–1991*, Derby, Breedon Books, 1991, pp. 9–10.

44   Cheshire, *Chelsea*, pp. 10–11.

45   *The Football Who's Who*, London, C. Arthur Pearson, 1906, p. 5.

46   'Merula', *The Cottager's Journal*, 21 March 1908, p. 10.

47   H. F. Abell, 'The football fever', *Macmillan's Magazine*, February 1904, p. 277.

48   Advertisement, *The Era*, 14 September 1895, p. 3.

49   Letter, 'Football on the stage', *The Era*, 5 October 1895, p. 11; Letter, 'The football king', *The Era* , 28 September 1895, p. 11. The autobiography of George Gray of *Fighting Parson* fame does not mention this play and so the identity of this man must remain open to speculation; Letter, 'Football on the stage', *The Era*, 5 October 1895, p. 11; Advertisement, *The Era*, 14 September 1895, p. 3; Letter, 'Football on the stage', *The Era*, 26 October 1895, p. 13; Letter, 'Football on the Stage', *The Era* , 25 July 1896, p. 8; Letter, 'Football on the stage', *The Era*, 2 November 1895, p. 13.

50   'Theatre Royal Stratford', *The Era*, 25 September 1897, p. 11.

51   Arthur Roberts and Richard Morton, *The Adventures of Arthur Roberts by Rail, Road and River Told by Himself and Chronicled by Richard Morton*, London, Bristol and Co., 1895, p. 95.

52   'Board room bits', *Oriental Notes*, 2 April 1910, unnumbered pages.

53   Charles Coborn, *The Man Who Broke the Bank*, London, Hutchinson, 1928, pp. 30–36; Jackson, *Sporting Days*, pp. 107 and 142–143; and Advertisement, *Football Chat*, 31 (January 1905), p. 3. For fund-raising smokers hosted by Tottenham Hotspur see 'The Hotspur smoking concert', *The Edmonton and Tottenham Weekly*

Guardian, 31 January 1890, unnumbered pages; Untitled announcement, *The Edmonton and Tottenham Weekly Guardian,* 9 December 1892, unnumbered pages; and 'Tottenham Hotspur's smoking concert', *The Edmonton and Tottenham Weekly Guardian,* 16 December 1892, unnumbered pages; 'Club notes', *The Hammers' Gazette,* 24 December 1910, unnumbered pages.

54 'Club notes', *The Hammers' Gazette,* 14 January 1911, unnumbered pages, and 'Club notes', *The Hammers' Gazette,* 25 March 1911, unnumbered pages.

55 'Football as a variety sport', *Football Chat,* 12 September 1905, p. 2.

56 '"Variety" and "show" football', *Football Chat,* 3 October 1905, pp. 1–2, and 'Football at Olympia', *Football Chat,* 12 December 1905, p. 2.

57 'Football at Olympia', *Football Chat,* 23 January 1906, p. 1, and for the public's indifference see Charles B. Cochran, *The Secrets of a Showman,* London, Heinemann, 1925, p. 135.

58 'Appeal for Olympia footballers', *Football Chat,* 6 March 1906, p. 2.

59 'A chance for old "stars"', *Football Chat,* 23 October 1906, p. 2, and Untitled, *Football Chat,* 23 October 1906, p. 8.

60 Charles Chaplin, *My Autobiography,* London, Bodley Head, 1964, p. 119.

61 J. P. Gallagher, *Fred Karno: Master of Mirth and Tears,* London, Hale, 1971, p. 94, and Edwin Adeler and Con West, *Remember Fred Karno? The Life of a Great Showman,* London, John Long, 1939, p. 129.

62 Advertisement, *Chelsea Chronicle,* 25 and 27 December 1909, p. 4. *Football Match* also played at the East Ham Palace; Advertisement, *Hammers' Gazette,* 23 April, 1910, unnumbered pages.

63 'Variety gossip', *The Era,* 3 February 1906, p. 22; 'An amusing football experience', *Football Chat,* 30 January 1906, p. 2; and 'Notts Forest and Fulham fraternize', *Football Chat,* 6 February 1906, p. 2.

64 'The 'Spurs in the West End', *Football Chat,* 27 February 1906, p. 2.

65 Untitled, *The Era,* 4 December 1909, p. 23.

66 'Interesting items', *Tottenham Hotspur: Official Programme,* 28 January 1911, unnumbered pages.

67 Dion Clayton Calthrop, *Music Hall Nights,* London, John Lane, 1926, p. 74.

68 Advertisement, *The Hammers' Gazette,* 1 February 1913, unnumbered pages, and for an appearance by Billy Wells see Advertisement, *The Hammers' Gazette,* 20 April 1912, unnumbered pages; Ian Bevan, *Top of the Bill: The Story of the London Palladium,* London, Frederick Muller, 1952, p. 43.

69 'Round the theatres', *The Illustrated Sporting and Dramatic News,* 21 February 1914, p. 1053.

70 'Music hall gossip', *The Era,* 29 October 1894, p. 17.

71 'Music hall gossip', *The Era,* 18 February 1893, p. 17.

72 'Music hall gossip', *The Era,* 19 March 1898, p. 19, and for the foundation of the Thomas Dewar Cup see Jackson, *Association Football,* pp. 334–335.

73 Untitled article, *The Era,* 1 April 1899, p. 19; 'Music hall gossip', *The Era,* 15 July 1899, p. 17; 'Music hall gossip', *The Era,* 29 July 1899, p. 17, and 'Music hall gossip', *The Era,* 17 May 1902, p. 20; 'Music hall gossip', *The Era,* 8 April 1905, p. 20.

74 'Music hall gossip', *The Era*, 27 April 1901, p. 18.

75 'Music hall gossip', *The Era*, 4 May 1901, p. 18.

76 Advertisement, *The Era*, 19 April 1902, p. 32.

77 'Variety gossip', *The Era*, 21 April 1906, p. 22.

78 'Variety gossip', *The Era*, 20 April 1907, p. 20.

79 'Variety gossip', *The Era*, 27 April 1907, p. 20.

80 'Variety gossip', *The Era*, 25 April 1908, p. 22.

81 'Variety gossip', *The Era*, 2 May 1908, p. 22.

82 'Footballers at the Alhambra', *Music Hall and Theatre Review*, 4 April 1912, p. 217.

83 W. H. Boardman, *Vaudeville Days*, London, Jarrolds, 1935, p. 224.

84 'Music hall gossip', *The Era*, 9 November 1901, p. 20.

85 'Music hall gossip', *The Era*, 5 September 1903, p. 20.

86 'Daisy cutters', *Chelsea Chronicle*, 27 October 1906, unnumbered pages.

87 'Daisy cutters', *Chelsea Chronicle*, 5 February 1910, p. 3.

88 'Daisy cutters', *Chelsea Chronicle*, 5 February 1910, p. 3.

89 Advertisement, *Chelsea Chronicle*, 5 February 1910, p. 4.

90 'Snapped not cinematographed', *The Sketch*, 7 February 1912, p. 134.

91 'Music hall gossip', *The Era*, 26 April 1902, p. 20.

92 Rachel Low and Roger Manville, *The History of the British Film, 1896–1906*, London, George Allen and Unwin, 1948, p. 54, and Cecil Hepworth, *Came the Dawn*, London, Phoenix House, 1951, pp. 58–59.

93 'Variety gossip', *The Era*, 19 January 1907, p. 22.

94 'Club notes', *The Hammers' Gazette*, 13 January 1912, unnumbered pages, and Advertisement, *The Hammers' Gazette*, 24 February 1912, unnumbered pages.

95 Advertisement, *Woolwich Arsenal Football and Athletic Company Limited Official Programme and Record of the Club*, 4 September 1910, unnumbered pages; Advertisement, *The Hammers' Gazette*, 2 November 1907, unnumbered pages, and Advertisement, *The Hammers' Gazette*, 31 October 1908, unnumbered pages; 'Club notes', *The Hammers' Gazette*, 23 September 1911, unnumbered pages.

96 Advertisement, *Oriental Notes*, 2 September 1907, unnumbered pages, and for a critical review see Untitled, *Oriental Notes*, 14 September 1907, unnumbered pages.

97 Untitled, *Oriental Notes*, 21 December 1907, unnumbered pages, and Advertisement, *Oriental Notes*, 12 September 1908, unnumbered pages.

98 Advertisement, *Oriental Notes*, 14 September 1912, unnumbered pages; Untitled letter, *Oriental Notes*, 31 January 1914, unnumbered pages.

99 Advertisement, *Chelsea Chronicle*, 12 October 1907, p. 3, and Advertisement, *Chelsea Chronicle*, 12 September 1908, p. 3.

100 See, for instance, *Woolwich Arsenal: Official Programme*, 23 October 1909, unnumbered pages.

101 Advertisement, *Tottenham Hotspur: Official Programme*, 26 November 1910, unnumbered pages, and Advertisement, *Tottenham Hotspur: Official Programme*, 27 December 1910, unnumbered pages.

102 Advertisement, *The Cottager's Journal*, 12 October 1912, p. 3.

103 George Robey, 'Football in the year 2000', *The Cottager's Journal*, 23 November 1912, pp. 12–13.

104 Advertisement, *Daily Mail*, 12 May 1911, p. 4, and Advertisement, *Daily Chronicle*, 3 June 1911, p. 7.

105 Catton, *Real Football*, p. 37.

106 'Music hall gossip', *The Era*, 26 January 1895, p. 19; 'Theatrical football', *The Era*, 25 January 1890, p. 10; 'Theatrical football', *The Era*, 15 February 1890, p. 9, and 'Variety gossip', *The Era*, 9 February 1907, p. 20; 'Theatrical football', *The Era*, 1 March 1890, p. 8, and 'Theatrical football', *The Era*, 22 March 1890, p. 14.

107 'Dramatic sports', *The Era*, 11 February 1893, p. 18; 'Pantomime football', *The Era*, 18 February 1893, p. 12; 'Theatrical football', *The Era*, 3 February 1894, p. 15; 'Theatrical football', *The Era*, 17 February 1894, p. 9; 'Theatrical football', *The Era*, 3 March 1894, p. 11, and 'Music hall gossip', *The Era,* 17 March 1894, p. 17; 'Theatrical football', *The Era*, 19 January 1895, p. 15; 'Music hall gossip', *The Era*, 2 March 1895, p. 16; 'Music hall gossip', *The Era*, 9 March 1895, p. 18; 'Theatrical football', *The Era*, 8 February 1896, p. 14; 'Music hall gossip', *The Era*, 15 February 1896, p. 19; Untitled, *The Era*, 22 February 1896, p. 9; Untitled, *The Era*, 18 April 1896, p. 11, and for the Liverpool match see 'Music hall gossip', *The Era*, 18 April 1896, p. 17; 'Music hall gossip', *The Era*, 18 September 1897, p. 19; 'Theatrical football', *The Era*, 10 December 1898, p. 8; 'Theatrical football', *The Era*, 21 January 1899, p. 9; Untitled, *The Era*, 15 April 1899, p. 18.

108 'Australian theatrical football', *The Era*, 1 September 1894, p. 13.

109 Leslie Henson, *My Laugh Story*, London, Hodder and Stoughton, 1926, pp. 126–127.

110 Albert Douglass, *Memories of Mummers and the Old Standard Theatre*, London, *The Era,* 1925, p. 118.

111 Billy Merson, *Fixing the Stoof Oop*, London, Hutchinson, 1926, p. 110.

112 Merson, *Fixing the Stoof*, pp. 110–111.

113 'Music hall gossip', *The Era*, 27 December 1902, p. 16, and George Robey, *Looking Back On Life,* London, Constable, 1933, p. 123.

114 Robey, *Looking Back*, p. 88.

115 Edward Robey, *The Jester and the Court*, London, Kimber, 1976, p. 19.

116 'Music hall gossip', *The Era*, 1 February 1902, p. 20.

117 Harding, *George Robey*, p. 66.

118 'Music hall gossip', *The Era*, 28 March 1903, p. 20, and for the quote see 'Music hall gossip', *The Era*, 7 November 1903, p. 20.

119 'Music hall gossip', *The Era*, 7 November 1903, p. 20.

120 'Music hall gossip', *The Era*, 15 October 1904, p. 20.

121 George Robey, *My Life Up Till Now*, London, Greening, 1908, p. 113.

122 'To-day's matches and teams', *Daily Chronicle*, 5 December 1904, p. 7, and 'The J. Jones benefit match', *Daily Express*, 6 December 1904, p. 6.

123 'For charity's sake', *Daily Mail*, 6 December 1904, p. 6.

124 'Music hall gossip', *The Era*, 16 December 1904, p. 22.

125 'Music hall gossip', *The Era*, 26 March 1904, p. 20.

126 'Music hall gossip', *The Era*, 2 January 1904, p. 26.

127 'Music hall gossip', *The Era*, 9 January 1904, p. 20.

128 'George Robey misses a penalty', *Daily Express*, 5 January 1909, p. 6.

129 'Music hall gossip', *The Era*, 21 January 1905, p. 20; 'Bravo, George Robey!', *Football Chat*, 14 February 1905, p. 1.

130 Robey, *My Life*, p. 104.

131 George Robey, 'My favourite dream', *George Robey's Christmas Annual, 1921*, p. 29.

132 Robey, *Looking Back*, p. 124.

133 'The variety stage', *Stage and Sport*, 19 May 1906, unnumbered pages.

134 E. H. D. Sewell, 'A sporting comedian', *C. B. Fry's Magazine*, 8 (1907–08), p. 416.

135 'The world of sport', *The Sketch*, 28 February 1906, p. 222.

136 Robey, *Life Up Till Now*, p. 104.

137 'George Robey's charity cup', *Football Chat*, 18 September 1906, p. 2.

138 'Music hall gossip', *The Era*, 14 March 1903, p. 22.

139 'Variety gossip', *The Era*, 16 February 1907, p. 20.

140 'Football and charity', *Football Chat*, 28 August 1905, p. 1.

141 'Variety gossip', *The Era*, 19 February 1910, p. 20.

142 Untitled, *The Era*, 26 February 1910, p. 18, and 'Variety gossip', *The Era*, 26 February 1910, p. 22.

143 'Variety gossip', *The Era*, 19 March 1910, p. 20.

144 'Variety gossip', *The Era*, 23 April 1910, p. 20.

145 'Variety gossip', *The Era*, 17 February 1906, p. 20.

146 'The world of sport', *The Sketch*, 28 February 1906, p. 222.

147 'Variety gossip', *The Era*, 3 March 1906, p. 22.

148 'Variety gossip', *The Era*, 25 May 1907, p. 20.

149 Full page front cover cartoon, *Chelsea Chronicle*, 6 April 1907, unnumbered pages.

150 'Variety gossip', *The Era*, 30 January 1909, p. 22.

151 'Variety gossip', *The Era*, 1 May 1909, p. 22.

152 'Variety gossip', *The Era*, 30 March 1912, p. 20.

153 'Variety gossip', *The Era*, 13 April 1912, p. 20.

154 W. R. Titterton, *From Theatre to Music Hall*, London, Stephen Swift, 1912, pp. 234–235.

155 J. P. Wearing, 'Edwardian London West End Christmas entertainments, 1900–1914', in Judith L. Fisher and Stephen Watt (eds), *When They Weren't Doing Shakespeare: Essays on Nineteenth Century British and American Theatre*, London, University of Georgia Press, 1989, pp. 232–233.

156 'Football; To-day's fixtures', *Daily Chronicle*, 30 April 1902, p. 5, and 'Millwall's carnival: "footer" serious and funny at North Greenwich', *Daily Express*, 1 May 1902, p. 8.

157 'The world of sport', *The Sketch*, 25 November 1903, p. 212.

158 'Comic football match', *The Fulham Observer*, 15 January 1909, p. 5, and for a photograph of the teams see Untitled, *The Era*, 16 January 1909, p. 17.

159 'Fulham team at the Lyric pantomime', *The Fulham Observer*, 15 January 1909, p. 5.

160 'Football pantomime', *The Cottager's Journal*, 16 January 1909, p. 8.

161 'Comic football match', *The Fulham Observer*, 15 January 1909, p. 5.

162 Untitled, *The Era*, 13 February 1909, p. 13, and Untitled, *The Era*, 20 February 1909, p. 21.

163 'Football panto', *The Cottager's Journal*, 11 December 1909, p. 3.

164 'Panto football charity match', *The Cottager's Journal*, 18 December 1909, p. 4.

165 'So gay', *The Cottager's Journal*, 15 January 1910, p. 5, and 'Football comedy', *The Fulham Observer*, 14 January 1910, p. 2.

166 'Funny football', *The Era*, 15 January 1910, p. 19, and 'Fulham footballers at the Lyric', *The Fulham Observer*, 14 January 1910, p. 2.

167 'Variety gossip', *The Era*, 11 February 1911, p. 22.

168 'Sir Aubrey Smith', *The Times*, 21 December 1948, p. 7, and 'Sir Charles Aubrey Smith', *Wisden Cricketers' Almanac 1949*, London, 1949, pp. 869–870.

169 Advertisement, *The Cottager's Journal*, 19 December 1910, p. 7.

170 'Clergymen defeat actor', *Daily News and Leader*, 20 December 1910, p. 8.

171 'V. J. W., A personal sketch of England's greatest amateur forward', *Pearson's Weekly*, 13 January 1910, p. 594; 'Church v. stage', *Daily Mail*, 17 December 1910, p. 9, and 'Churchmen beat actors', *Daily Express*, 20 December 1910, p. 6.

172 'Monday's big event', *The Cottager's Journal*, 9 December 1911, p. 3; Untitled cartoon, *The Cottager's Journal*, 9 December 1911, pp. 8–9; and 'Monday's match', 16 December 1911, p. 3. For the best photographs of the game see Untitled, *The Sketch*, 20 December 1911, p. 346.

173 'Jockeys at football', *Fulham Observer*, 15 December 1911, p. 2.

174 'Steeplechase riders versus flat-race riders at football', *The Sketch*, 14 February 1912, p. 190.

175 'Daisy cutters', *Chelsea Chronicle*, 8 December 1909, p. 1. 'Church v. Stage; next Monday's novel football match', *Daily Mail*, 9 December 1909, p. 9.

176 'Church v. Stage; next Monday's novel football match', *Daily Mail*, 9 December 1909, p. 9.

177 'Church v. Stage', *Daily Chronicle*, 14 December 1909, p. 9.

178 'Church v. Stage, actors decisively routed', *Daily Mail*, 14 December 1909, p. 9; 'Church not Stage, charity match at Stamford Bridge won by 7–1', *Daily Express*, 14 December 1909, p. 6.

179 'Variety gossip', *The Era*, 4 December 1909, p. 22.

180 'New Empire turns', *Daily Chronicle*, 14 December 1909, p. 8.

181 'Variety gossip', *The Era*, 24 December 1910, p. 20.

182 'Professional golfers as footballers', *The Sketch*, 3 February 1909, p. 128.

183 'Spurs v Music hall artistes', *The Era*, 1 March 1913, p. 22.

184 'Variety gossip', *The Era*, 1 February 1913, p. 20.

185 'Music hall world', *The Encore*, 30 January 1913, p. 14.

186 'Music hall world', *The Encore*, 6 February 1913, p. 6; 'Music hall world', *The Encore*, 13 February 1913, p. 18.

187 'Music hall world', *The Encore*, 20 February 1913, p. 6; 'Music hall world', *The Encore*, 27 February 1913, pp. 14–17, and the quote is found in Advertisement, *Tottenham Hotspur: Official Programme*, 6 March 1913, unnumbered pages.

188 'Spurs v. Music hall artistes', *The Era*, 1 March 1913, p. 22.

189 'Artistes at football', *The Era*, 8 March 1913, p. 25.

190 'Yesterday's charity match at Tottenham', *Tottenham and Edmonton Weekly Herald*, 7 March 1913, p. 3.

191 'Hotspurs v. variety artistes, a splendid success', *The Encore*, 13 March 1913, pp. 22–23.

192 'Music hall world', *The Encore*, 13 February 1913, p. 18.

193 'Tales of the cottagers', *The Cottager's Journal*, 6 December 1913, p. 3.

194 'Wells in a new role', *Daily Mail*, 12 December 1913, p. 9.

195 Eugene Corri, *Thirty Years a Boxing Referee*, London, Edward Arnold, 1915, p. 81.

196 The quote is taken from 'Actors beat golfers; semi-serious game for children's charity', *Daily Chronicle*, 12 December 1913, p. 8. The offer of a place in the Fulham line-up is found in 'Tales of the cottagers', *The Cottager's Journal*, 24 January 1914, p. 1.

197 'Bombardier Wells's brother', *The Cottager's Journal*, 21 February 1914, p. 3; 'Bandsman Blake's tuning-up', *Daily Express*, 16 February 1914, p. 9; and 'Bombardier Wells', *Cottager's Journal*, 28 February 1914, p. 1.

198 'Chelsea chatter', *Chelsea Chronicle*, 24 January 1914, p. 5, and 'Chelsea chatter', *Chelsea Chronicle*, 7 February 1914, p. 1.

199 Morgan D. Phillips, *Fulham We Love You: A Supporter's History of Fulham FC*, Bedford, The Author, 1976, p. 15.

200 'Bombardier Wells', *The Cottager's Journal*, 7 March 1914, p. 1.

201 'Variety gossip', *The Era*, 10 December 1913, p. 20.

202 'Music hall world', *The Encore*, 22 January 1914, p. 14; 'Music hall world', *The Encore*, 26 February 1914, p. 6.

203 'Variety gossip', *The Era*, 28 January 1914, p. 18; 'Variety gossip', *The Era*, 4 February 1914, p. 18.

204 'Sports Jottings: weather too bad for charity match', *Daily Chronicle*, 12 February 1914, p. 8.

205 'To-day's fun at Chelsea', *Daily Express*, 18 February 1914, p. 8.

206 'Referee joins the game: "fooling" at a charity football match', *Daily Express*, 19 February 1914, p. 8.

207 Reynard, 'All sorts of sport at Chelsea', *Daily Chronicle*, 19 February 1914, p. 8.

208 'Pro's gala day at Stamford Bridge', *The Encore*, 26 February 1914, p. 16.

209 'Referee joins the game: "fooling" at a charity football match', *Daily Express*, 19 February 1914, p. 8.

210 Reynard, 'All sorts of sport at Chelsea', *Daily Chronicle*, 19 February 1914, p. 8.

211 'Charity football', *Daily Mail*, 19 February 1914, p. 9.

212 'Variety gossip', *The Era*, 21 January 1914, p. 18; 'To-day's matches; jockeys and music hall artistes at Stamford Bridge', *Daily News and Leader*, 18 February 1914, p. 10. For Jones and the pantomime horse see Untitled, *Daily Express*, 19 February 1914, p. 8, and 'A "mount" for the King's jockey', *Daily Mail*, 19 February 1914, p. 9.

213 'Jockeys v artistes; fun on the football field at Stamford Bridge', *Daily News and Leader*, 19 February 1914, p. 8. For the quote see 'Variety gossip', *The Era*,

1 February 1914, p. 18, and the photographs are announced in 'Variety gossip', *The Era*, 6 May 1914, p. 18.

214 'Variety gossip', *The Era*, 25 March 1914, p. 18.

215 'Variety gossip', *The Era*, 25 March 1914, p. 18.

216 'Women footballers and tango training', *Daily Mail*, 5 March 1914, p. 5.

217 Untitled, *Tottenham Hotspur: Official Programme*, 5 March 1914, unnumbered pages.

218 'Variety gossip', *The Era*, 28 January 1914, p. 18.

219 '"Football" fun; large crowd at charity carnival at Tottenham', *Daily News and Leader*, 6 March 1914, p. 10.

220 'Music hall world', *The Encore*, 5 March 1914, p. 11.

221 'Music hall world', *The Encore*, 26 February 1914, p. 6;'Variety gossip', *The Era*, 4 March 1914, p. 18.

222 'The charity sports day at Tottenham', *The Encore*, 12 March 1914, p. 16.

223 'Variety gossip', *The Era*, 4 March 1914, p. 18.

224 'Beauties at football', *Daily Express*, 6 March 1914, p. 8, and for the quote see 'Fair footballers at Tottenham', *Daily Chronicle*, 6 March 1914, p. 8.

225 'Fun and frolic, a merry meeting at White Hart Lane', *Daily Chronicle*, 6 March 1914, p. 8.

12

The First World War

Britain reacted to the events of July and August 1914 with a mixture of puerile enthusiasm, patriotic bluster, despair, and splenetic disdain for Teutons and Junkers. Meanwhile, young men enlisted in the their thousands as the leaders of Ulster, Parliamentary Reform, Suffragetism and Labour, tensions which had threatened the Edwardian state, subordinated these causes to the new crusade. Because it was initially thought that Britain's contribution would be limited, few administrative reforms were implemented. Instead, the government announced that, despite the war, it was 'Business as Usual' for the country.[1] Lord Kitchener, Secretary of State for War, was charged with raising an army of volunteers. As a result, posters bearing Kitchener's stern gaze, accusatory finger and admonishment 'Your country needs you' chided young men to enlist. Recruitment perpetuated the image of the war as a schoolboy's lark, because friends were promised that they would serve together in so-called 'pals' battalions. Two million men, of whom a disproportionate number were Londoners, volunteered in the first six months.[2] Some, like the lance-corporal in the Fusiliers who christened his mate 'Harris' after the character in the comic novel *Three Men in a Boat,* saw the war as a jaunty adventure.[3] Such recruits anticipated a short, swiftly moving campaign in which men atop cavalry chargers and up-to-date inventions like bicycles, motor-cars, aeroplanes and railways would secure positions which had been 'softened' by long-range artillery. Climactic naval encounters between dreadnoughts would buttress these land battles, while zeppelin melodramas had proved that planes could protect the British Isles from invasion. In that August's vernacular, such an up-to-date war would surely be over by Christmas.

Though this is not a history of the war, some background is necessary. The war very nearly ended as quickly as anticipated. The momentum of the German armies charging through Belgium pushed the French and British forces back to the river Marne, outside Paris, in September 1914. However, the Germans were then driven back gradually throughout 1915, the year when substantial numbers of imperial troops entered the lines and a Ministry of Munitions was established under Lloyd-George. By 1916, this war of movement had ended, and two static lines of trenches had been dug from the North Sea to the Swiss Alps. The ensuing trench warfare was characterised by massive, futile battles. The British government had long since abandoned 'Business as Usual' and begun organising in earnest, and late in the year Lloyd-George became prime minister, as the country dedicated itself to total war. Conscription was introduced by Lord Derby under the Military Service Act, because protracted battles at Verdun, the Somme, Ypres and Passchendaele would cost millions of casualties without breaking the stalemate. And still the Germans came close to winning. After overthrowing the Tsar at the end of 1917, the Bolsheviks made peace with Germany, allowing Berlin to mass her armies for a great push towards Paris in the following spring. Initially, the Germans swept all before them, though by mid-summer momentum swung permanently to the allies, who pushed the enemy ever eastwards. The war was over in November.

For the greater part of the war, then, the Allied front in Flanders consisted of three parallel trenches. Firstly, the front, or fire trench. This was separated from the enemy lines by barbed wire, and the pitted, desolate swathe of No Man's Land which varied in breadth from a few dozen to several hundred yards. When ideally constructed, the fire trench was sufficiently deep to shield its occupants from rifle bullets, while safeguarding them from explosions by abrupt short kinks, called traverses, every ten or twenty feet.[4] A 'firing step' running along the trench's forward wall enabled men to see over the parapet, though only the foolish peered into No Man's Land during the day because of snipers and indiscriminate strafing by machine guns.

Immediate respite from this world was found in the underground dug-outs in which men sheltered and slept, and from which officers commanded their units. Attacks were feared constantly, forcing each side to watch the enemy as closely as possible. Short, shallow trenches called 'saps' projected into No Man's Land, where their solitary occupants listened for evidence of impending attack. Even on the most peaceful fronts, nervous troops 'stood-to' on the fire step with arms ready at dawn and dusk, the times that enemy raids were most feared. Despite the anticipation, pitched battles were not common. The battlefield was most active at night, as small parties of men crawled stealthily through No Man's Land reconnoitring and raiding enemy positions, succouring the wounded, collecting the dead and reinforcing defences.[5] In order to discourage these endeavours, machine guns swept No Man's Land throughout the night, while flares illumined the darkness. In this upside-down world men tried to sleep during the day, though each side fired an incessant, irregularly timed stream of shells, mortars, bombs and grenades into the opposing trenches.[6] Over time, men learned to judge the trajectory of slow-moving, whistling shells, while the delayed detonations of others allowed alert, nimble men to scramble for shelter. Swifter shells could not be heard and killed without warning.

Therefore, troops had to remain mentally alert, despite this constant physical discomfort. The front lines were claustrophobic. Men were unable to see the enemy, the battlefield, or more than a few feet to either side in a trench filled with mud, muck and scrofulous comrades. Safety could only be gained by burrowing further into the ground. While inhabiting these lines, men's bodies were assaulted by lice, bugs, nits, fleas, rats, contagious diseases, infections and 'trench foot', a severe swelling and blistering caused by constant immersion in the muddy water that collected at the bottom of the trenches. Such discomforts were not leavened by an unvarying diet of corned 'bully' beef, hard biscuits, tea and jam, which men ate amidst the stench of fetid water in summer, ice and sleet in winter, and putrefying unburied corpses. This unrelenting need for alertness exhausted men psychologically and 'shell shock', or battle fatigue, was gradually acknowledged to result from emotional deterioration due to stress.[7]

But there were releases from this terror. Only through being wounded, killed or deserting could one escape the constant carnage of the front line. However, every sixteen days, units were rotated between the front line and two rear, or support and reserve, trenches where 'the thin veil of a few miles' distance, a few weeks' respite, seem so heaven-sent', as troops allowed their taut nerves and emotions to unwind.[8] Men in the rear areas spent their days training, packing wagons, moving stores, and other labours. They also bathed, shaved, laundered, slept, lazed and exercised.[9] By combining mundane military duties with sport, rest areas addressed the deprivations of the front line directly. In the men's imagination these areas were 'Company drill and Cup-Ties'.[10]

The safety and comfort of 'Home' seemed physically remote, especially to imperial troops. However, in addition to regular rotations between the front lines and the rear areas where one was safe from all but the longest-range artillery, for every three months at the front a soldier received one week's leave, to be spent in France. An additional week of home leave – to be spent in the United Kingdom – was granted for every year in the trenches. Officers' leave was more liberal, giving them even greater access to Britain. Therefore, those who were not wounded or killed enjoyed regular, fairly frequent periods shielded from war's immediate dangers. The access to home which such leaves afforded men was increased by the constant stream of parcels and letters posted by families, friends, companies and benevolent associations. In addition, men returning from Britain were expected to bring books, newspapers, magazines, and recordings of the latest topical tunes for their mates. This connection to home heightened the role of up-to-date culture.

Up-to-date technology did not strip the war of its terror. However, popular culture was an important way in which troops understood and gave sense to this world, though not all aspects of troop culture were particular to the First World War. 1914's recruits were soon indoctrinated into the serving man's traditional pastimes: drinking, gambling and carousing.[11] Even when not in battle, military life was by turns violent, raucous, roistering and alcoholic.[12] In comparison, the front-line trenches, where a single tot of rum per day was issued to each man, were a relatively sober place. This meagre ration could, when out of the front lines, be topped up in canteens and the small bars called *estaminets* that were never far from military encampments.[13] Alcoholic binges blocked out the immediate horrors of the war, and so pervaded military life that some teetotallers forsook the pledge, while worried families like that of Arthur Lee needed to be reassured that 'we don't have them (binges) that often, and then usually only to celebrate something, like getting a Hun. Otherwise there's not a great deal of drinking'.[14]

Though important, drinking was only one part of First World War military culture. New recruits soon updated Edwardian music hall to make sense of the war. The prevalence of Londoners in the forces helped, but the city's role as a cultural capital meant that men hailing from opposite ends of the Empire, the country, or the social spectrum understood the same allusions. Firstly, these men created a new language. Nineteenth-century imperial expansion had compiled a military vocabulary punctuated by debased Hindi (for example, 'khaki', 'jodhpur' and 'dekko') and Afrikaans (like 'kop' and 'commando'). After 1914, bastardised French words, phrases and place names like 'Napoo' for 'Il n'y a plus' and 'Funky Villas' for Fonquevillers entered the military lexicon.[15] Even so, references to popular culture were far more common. The Army Service Corps, who were believed to serve in safe billets far away from the front lines, were derisively called 'Ally Sloper's Cavalry' after a famous music-hall character.[16] Both the Royal Naval Volunteer Reserve and the Dover Patrol were christened 'Harry Tate's Navy' because of their supposed ineptitude and lack of training, while the BEF, the first contingent sent to Europe in 1914, was labelled 'Harry Tate's Army' for the same reasons, and specific units were called

'Karno's Own'.[17] Men gloried in this last comparison, updating the first two lines of an army song that began:

> We are King George's Army,
> We are the ASC.[18]

To:

> We are Fred Karno's Army,
> The ragtime infantry:
> We cannot fight, we cannot shoot,
> What earthly use are we!
> And when we get to Berlin,
> The Kaiser he will say,
> 'Hoch! Hoch!' Mein Gott,
> What a bloody fine lot
> are the ragtime infantry! [19]

A song which the Northamptonshire Yeomanry further updated as:

> We are Fred Karno's Army
> We are the Yeomanry[20]

Similarly, various Scottish regiments were dubbed 'the Harry Lauders', while Scotland was called 'the land of Burns and Lauder'.[21] Other nicknames like 'the gas-pipe cavalry' for the Cyclists' Corps, or the Royal Naval Division referring to themselves as 'the Crystal Palace Army', invoked the spirit of music hall.[22]

More personally, those named Smith were called 'Gunboat', after the heavyweight boxer, while duck-footed men became 'Charlie Chaplins', for the Little Tramp's gait, and short soldiers might not 'come even as high as my Tich'.[23] Italians were 'Ice Creamos' evoking the itinerant vendors who had been so common in Edwardian London.[24] Alongside these, the enemy was deprived of full human attributes through such comic names as 'Fritz', 'Boche', 'Jerry' or 'Hun'.[25]

This topical argot extended to common events. The words 'ragtime' indicated any duty, event or activity, like Hendon stunt flying, which though hazardous, appeared comical or ludicrous.[26] Raids, attacks and battles were 'shows' or 'stunts', and soldiers on a spree were on the 'razzle'.[27] Men confronted the shells which maimed and killed them, by christening them variously, 'coal boxes', 'whizz-bangs', 'minnies', 'silent Suzies', or 'footballs', while anti-aircraft fire was alliteratively renamed 'Ack-Ack', 'Archibald', 'Archie', or 'Coughing Clara'.[28] 'Jack Johnsons' were high-velocity German shells which burst in clouds of black smoke, and exacted horrible casualties.[29] These last shells were incorporated into trench humour through such jokes as:

Literary Tommy (reading and resting in dug-out): O rare Ben Johnson – There's nothing like him for solace in the trenches.
Practical Tommy: Don't know much about Ben, but I'd like his brother Jack to be a bit more rare![30]

Meanwhile, much as during the 1911 boxing boom, the British countered these fearsome weapons with shells which often failed to detonate and could not penetrate strongly reinforced German defences. Such shells were known, appositely, as 'Billy Wells'.[31] Troops chalked words like 'Iron Ration' on other shells in reference to the trench diet of bully beef and hard tack.[32]

The discomfort and terror of the front lines was further mitigated by christening the trenches with names drawn from major landmarks, including London ones like The Strand, Picadilly Circus, Regent Street, Northumberland Avenue or facetious places like Lover's Walk, Centre Way, Munster Alley, Dead Mule Corner, Ten Tree Alley and Sausage Valley.[33] Such names persisted long after the landmarks they described had been obliterated by shells.[34]

This spoken lexicon was complemented by topical music. Indeed, Guards subaltern Harold MacMillan called this a 'singing war'.[35] 'Tipperary' an obscure music-hall number which was resurrected at the start of the war, was the first of these topical tunes, and was followed by 'Gilbert the filbert', 'If you were the only girl in the world', 'The galloping major' and many others.[36] In response to the troops' love of music, bellicose patriotic songs like 'Keep the home fires burning' and 'We don't want to lose you', were written to venerate the cause. These last songs were introduced typically in London revues, before being taken to the battlefront by the men.[37] Rather than reiterate the leaden propaganda of such tunes, men updated them to reflect their experiences of trench life. J. B. Priestley, who served several years in the ranks before being commissioned, divided war songs between the 'drivel' written for 'patriotic civilians' and those 'not composed and copyrighted by anybody, genuine folk song, for the sardonic front line troops'.[38] Patriotic songs were given 'the bird' in favour of those detailing what a man would do 'When I get my civvies on again' or 'If I had the wings of an Avro'.[39] Other songs dwelt wistfully on the joys of home.[40] Their crude lyrics mocked military discipline, anticipated the war's end and extolled the 'Blighty', a wound which did not maim, but was severe enough for its recipient to be sent home.[41] A typical example began:

Goin' back to Blighty,
Cross the sea to righty-tighty [42]

Wounded men were said to beam with the 'Blighty smile' when told they were being invalided to Britain.[43]

Desertion and dissent are military crimes, though such fatalistic up-to-date songs allowed ordinary soldiers to air their discontent. Unlike many officers, lieutenant John Glubb, scion of a distinguished military family, embraced patriotic airs, and questioned the effect on morale if men endlessly sang such things as

> I want to go home!
> I don't want to go to the trenches no more,
> Where the whizz-bangs and shrapnel they whistle and roar.
> Take me over the sea,
> Where the Allemans cannot catch me,
> Oh My! I don't want to die,
> I want to go home![44]

But other junior officers, like Priestley, and Robert Graves, who endeared himself to his troops in the Royal Welch Fusiliers by singing nonsense songs in the trenches, perceived that such tunes were wistful, harmless and a boost to morale.[45]

Up-to-date music was also performed at home. In September 1914 the War Office wrote to London variety theatres asking them to display recruiting posters and propaganda, and to present patriotic war tunes.[46] Business was difficult however, especially after the first zeppelin air raids on the capital, which forced performances to be scheduled for the afternoon and early evening, while restrictions on public travel and petrol curtailed provincial touring. Nevertheless, shows went on in the face of ongoing tension about whether to permit them as a means of boosting public morale and confidence, or whether to shut them down as out of character with the war. In the midst of this controversy, patriotic songs were updated by London artistes. The sharp-shooter Ada Vivian closed her act in late November 1915 by playing 'Tipperary' by firing at a series of bells with her pistols.[47] At the same time a 'celebrated music hall artiste' attempted to persuade the Prince of Wales, who was desperate for a useful part in the war, that the pair should be drawn in a cart through London's streets to Trafalgar Square, where the artiste would play patriotic airs on a piano, by hammering the keys with his nose.[48] Thankfully, the effect of such a display on Londoners' resolve was never discovered.

Military popular culture was so pervasive in part because actors, artistes, athletes and musicians joined up or were conscripted throughout the war. Amongst these were celebrated Hendon pilots like Henri Farman, Adolphe Pégoud and

B. C. Hucks.[49] Their performances at flying spectaculars had helped to romanticise aerial combat, leading men like Georges Carpentier, the actor Robert Loraine and Vernon Castle, who had introduced ballroom dancing to Edwardian London, to enlist as fighter pilots.[50] Loraine had an eventful war, winning the Military Cross, becoming a lieutenant-colonel and commanding a squadron, before receiving his 'Blighty' in August 1918.[51] Others, like Cecil Lewis, who as 'air-minded' youths had followed the careers of every celebrated pilot from Blériot and Cody onward, fought alongside their heroes in the air forces.[52] Such illustrious pilots only added to the élite image which the public had begun to attach to the RFC before the war.[53]

Celebrated performers also served on the ground. The actor George Grossmith was a member of the Royal Naval Volunteer Reserve, comedian Leslie Henson joined the Royal Flying Corps, Fred Evans, who as 'Pimple' was the most famous British cinema clown, served with the Surrey Rifles, and 46-year-old George Robey was a lieutenant in the London Motor Volunteers, a unit which permitted him to continue starring in *The Bing Boys* revue, and entertaining the wounded at the capital's hospitals, eventually raising more than £50,000 for war charities.[54] In an effort to induce young men to join up, photographs of prominent sportsmen and artistes in uniform were featured in newspapers and magazines, while some of these celebrities spoke at recruiting rallies.[55]

Talented performers and athletes served in all capacities and their endeavours provided a more structured framework within which popular culture flourished at the front. In the absence of official bodies, the responsibility for organising sports and concert parties fell to a mixture of professional artistes, athletes, amateur performers, officers and conscientious chaplains.[56] No single instinct motivated these organisers apart from an interest in maintaining 'morale' in its broadest sense; preventing boredom and disaffection by filling men's time with interesting activities.[57] Others were prompted by a sense of self-preservation, for subalterns like Guy Chapman had realised soon after joining up that 'during the days off we killed time as best we could, gaining our first experience of the greatest bane of the life of a soldier, boredom, *cafard*, or whatever you call it'.[58] In the hopes of staving off such feelings, men began organising sports and concert parties. By late 1914, professionals who had joined up had begun contacting their associates and acquaintances back home in order to request props, costumes, librettos, scores, and make-up for the Christmas concerts they intended to produce at camps, hospitals and aboard ships. Though the war did not end by Christmas 1914, the holidays saw celebrated pantomime characters like Widow Twankey, Aladdin and Dick Whittington appear among the troops. Fighting the war had taken men away from their jobs, families and mates, and deposited them in a world where frenetic ghastly duty was interspersed with periods of intense boredom and manual labour. In response, men recreated the pleasures of home at the fronts.

While these concerts began appearing on the battle fronts, other artistes turned their minds towards providing edifying, rational entertainment for the troops. In October 1914, Lena Ashwell, an actress who had trained with Henry Irving and Beerbohm Tree, asked the War Office to permit her theatrical troupe to tour the Western Front. When this official sanction was refused, the YMCA agreed to sponsor Ashwell because her dramas would complement that organisation's programme of providing tea, cocoa, cakes, lectures and seminars at dry canteens and huts, hospitals and training camps. That autumn was a frantic time for patriotic performers, for in the words of Ellaline Terriss, who began performing under Ashwell's aegis in France in December, 'there was hospital work, matinees to be got up, for the less seriously wounded and the convalescent. There were bazaars to organise, working parties to be arranged, recruiting songs to sing'.[59] Ashwell's first full-scale concert party, playing Shaw, Shakespeare and other works, reached France in February 1915.

By the end of the war Ashwell's initial endeavour had grown to at least twenty-five separate concert parties, composed of both salaried and unpaid actors, who toured the front, or performed at a Paris theatre. Ashwell raised the £100,000 required to run these parties through contributions, subscriptions and public concerts in West End music halls for which she enlisted the aid of professional colleagues like Ivor Novello and military bands. The appeal of these shows was twofold. Patriotism was played up to by the men in uniform; popular culture by the celebrities.[60] Ashwell's scheme was also benevolent in quite another way. Those of her performers who had been unable to earn a living because of the war received wages for touring the front.[61] In addition, Ashwell's companies encouraged men in uniform to assist with performances, in order to learn how to put on such entertainments themselves, though some troopers found it difficult to overcome their image of actors and artistes as disreputable.[62] Ashwell's work was mimicked by the Australians who, by March 1918, operated at least five field theatres staffed by professionals performing songs, skits, comedy and revues. These theatres were underwritten by the Australian War Comforts Fund, under whose aegis the *Anzac Coves*, a comedy troupe, played London variety theatres in the spring of 1918.[63]

Thanks to such efforts, concert parties were entrenched firmly in military life by Christmas 1915.[64] That year the holidays saw pantomimes which were as topical and up-to-date as any of Dan Leno and Herbert Campbell's. Pantomime, with its sly, fiendish villains and heroic everymen, was an apposite genre for men who were not fighting the glorious war they had expected. The enemy, profiteers and incompetent officers made convenient topical villains, who could be blamed for the misery of trench life. The schemes of these men were foiled by the heroic clear-headed rankers who stood in for gallant Dick Whittington. This tradition meant that pantomime allowed common soldiers to criticise allied leaders and comment on the predicament of unending war service in a manner that was usually forbidden to them by military law.

Two examples illustrate the nature of military pantomimes. Firstly, *Sandbag the Spader*, in which an Army Service Corps officer was the evil genie, was produced by the West Riding Field Ambulance at Christmas 1915.[65] Topical troop pantomime reached its apogee in 1916 when the Queen's Own Royal West Kent Regiment staged *Lance Corporal Aladdin*. The production summarised the regiment's war experience in 'two scenes (which) contained dialogue in a humorous strain showing the contrast in the men's outlook during the first and last times in the trenches'. In the first scene of this Faustian tale, a pair of 'rascally Jews', representing the international conspiracy which had started the war, stole an old lamp from 'Kaiser Bill' the wizard. Initially, the pair were munificent, ridding the regiment's camp of mud, the bane of existence on the Western Front. However, the two soon tired of garrison duties and so, in spite, caused the battalion to be sent to the Dardanelles. Here their attempt to marry a couple of wealthy maidens was foiled. In the finale, the entire cast forsook county jealousies in order to escape Gallipoli's horrors, singing wistfully 'We'd be far better off in the Buffs' – The Royal East Kent Regiment.[66]

In addition to these seasonal productions, permanent theatres began appearing in 1915, at hospitals and bases throughout France, some of which were staffed by permanent companies. These theatres recreated home life by imitating Edwardian pierrot, music-hall and theatrical companies.[67] Such an outfit was *The Follies* who in March 1915 played at a hall in which 'there was a stage, footlights, curtain and scenery. The party was got up just like the Follies, the stage was decorated with Chinese lanterns, and everything went without a hitch of any kind, for there was plenty of talent in the company' which played to officers and men from throughout the forces.[68] Meanwhile, at about the same time, Paul Jones, a subaltern with the Royal Army Service Corps, attended a 'remarkable concert' whose 'stage, paints, wigs, orchestra, curtains, scenery' all dazzled him.[69] By the end of the war's first year the press reported the success and growing number of these soldier-created concert parties.[70]

The initiative behind such concerts was found at many levels within the forces. Major Winston Churchill of the Royal Scots Fusiliers arranged a sports day and concert party which played music-hall tunes, almost as soon as he reached the front in early 1916.[71] That same year Lieutenant-colonel Ernest Swinton of the Royal Engineers argued that 'concerts, cinematograph shows, variety entertainments, boxing and football matches have been organised whenever circumstances have allowed' in order to alleviate the stresses of the front line.[72] Swinton's belief was echoed in the spring of 1918 when concert parties had 'become a recognised feature of our soldier life. They are something more than a luxury – they are a necessity. They provide mental recreation to keep the mind fit'.[73] Surviving programmes indicate that these concerts provided topical versions of current songs, and commentaries on the war, a kind of mockery that helped to keep soldiers' minds fit by acquainting men with their civilian lives continuously and concretely. War leaders were criticised in much the same way that miseries of civilian life had been mocked in the music halls. This effort was not directed by the government. It was an instinctual response by the men to safeguard their emotions using the methods they had learned before the war. The men who enlisted in 1914 had not bargained on a prolonged war of attrition, and those men conscripted under the Derby scheme were no more happy to fight. Topical culture allowed them to bemoan their fate.

An artiste who benefited undoubtedly from such patronage was Leslie Henson, one of the most famous pantomime actors of his generation. Henson joined the Royal Flying Corps in 1916 and was posted to Air Board Headquarters in the Strand, a billet which enabled him to continue appearing in a revue at the Prince of Wales Theatre. When his theatrical commitments had been fulfilled, Henson was transferred to Farnborough and Aldershot where he performed for the men in uniform. On reaching France, Henson was ordered by Sir Hubert Gough, who commanded the Fifth Army, to organise a concert party. Henson recruited artistes he knew who were in uniform for *The Gaieties*, a troupe of pierrots who performed music-hall standards. The Tank Corps built a portable theatre in which *The Gaieties* played all along the Western Front until the final push of 1918, when the troupe advanced behind the forces, playing in newly liberated cities and towns, commandeering such scenery, limelights and shelter as they could. Throughout their two-year career, *The Gaieties* performed topical music-hall skits and songs. This became overtly patriotic in the very last weeks of the war, when with morale running high, thanks to the whiff of final victory, *The Gaieties* staged an up-to-date revue in which Amazons, flag waving *poilus* and Tommies all sang *God Save the King*. This topical end-of-war show was attended by civilians, soldiers, the King, Prince of Wales and Duke of York and its profits were spent on civilian relief and footballs for the troops.[74] When Henson was ordered to produce a pantomime for Christmas 1918, he chose *Aladdin*. Though Henson's libretto has been lost, one can surmise that this production was the opposite of 1916's *Lance Corporal Aladdin* in that the genie granted every trooper's most desperately cherished wish, to return home. Given the success of these endeavours, the government called on Henson again in 1939 when the Entertainment National Service Association, or ENSA, was established to entertain the troops in the Second World War. The up-to-date militarism of Henson's final shows was reflected in London end-of-war pantomimes: at Christmas 1917 audiences at Drury Lane saw Dick Whittington dream of a procession of Allied troops, while in *Little Red Riding Hood* at the King's Theatre, Hammersmith, the wolf wore a German helmet, and the witch's castle was destroyed by a tank.[75]

Sport also carried over from civilian life into the trenches. Here too, the impetus and organisation was provided by professionals and amateurs. As they had with their theatrical props, artistes like Little Tich, Fred Karno and Leslie Henson publicly donated portions of their wages to be spent on footballs, cricket kits, boxing gloves and other sporting paraphernalia for the troops, while *Boxing* magazine collected money to send sports equipment to the front.[76] Many athletes also served in the forces. Footballers Steve Bloomer and Fred Pentland joined up and Prince Ranjitsinhji lead a troop of Indian cavalry. Sport required less formal apparatus and planning than concert parties and so it flourished wherever troops gathered. The popularity of many sports was restricted to particular units, reflecting their traditions and home bases, like the cavalry regiments who favoured polo, Anzac units who played the Australian rules of Gaelic football, and Rugby's popularity with Welsh troopers.[77]

Association football was the most popular sport in the military, a position which reflected its dominance in civilian life. Given that the country was carrying on with 'Business as Usual' the Football Association did not immediately suspend operations at the start of the war. However, as people realised that the war would not end by Christmas, and that only mass enlistment could meet the country's military obligations, they began castigating professional competitions for encouraging young men to shirk their duty. After consulting the War Office, the FA opened football grounds for military drill, teams declared that all ablebodied young men should enlist, and prominent sportsmen implored spectators to join up at match day recruiting rallies, at which funds were collected for

22   In the absence of professional football during the war, Londoners watched women's teams avidly.

war charities. Nevertheless, football continued to be criticised because none of these ventures touched off mass rushes to the recruiting stations. Attendances diminished steadily, though team owners were contractually bound to pay their players wages until the end of the season, and so the FA permitted fixtures and cup-ties to continue. Professional war-time football culminated on the 24th of April 1915, when Sheffield United met Chelsea at the patriotically named 'Khaki Final'. When Lord Derby, who would later introduce conscription, presented the winner's medals he admonished all present that it was now time to play 'a sterner game for England'.[78] This was an early sign that Business as Usual was an insufficient response to the war.

Though professional wartime football ended with the Khaki Final, the game continued to provide recreation at the front. Throughout the war music-hall carnival matches between military units, kicked off by soubrettes and assisted by comedians, took place all over the country.[79] At the same time teams of women munitions workers played in crowded stadiums throughout the country (Figure 22), whilst one-legged war veterans were encouraged to kick footballs at carnivals.[80] Other regional competitions saw ageing professional footballers play for the fans.[81]

Meanwhile, troops took the game to the front, where it was played in formal competitions, as a means of fighting boredom, and even in order to accustom men to wearing their gas masks (Figure 23).[82] The reasons for this popularity were the same as in peacetime; little proper equipment was needed and, because football's appeal crossed socio-economic boundaries, few men had never footed a ball before.[83] Nine days before the Khaki Final was played, ambulanceman

William Boyd visited an artillery battery whose members played football uninterruptedly because they were fleet enough to fire their weapons two and one half minutes after the receipt of an order.[84] Troops coming out of the front lines were desperate to know how their clubs fared, and positions in the rear were deserted when important football matches were played.[85]

The most important matches were the formal competitions held between rival divisions, brigades, regiments, units and companies.[86] Like concert parties, football matches were organised by enthusiastic officers and chaplains.[87] Even those who cared little for football, like lieutenant John Glubb, who had 'practically never played soccer in my life', encouraged the sport with his men in order to gain their trust and enjoy himself.[88] On the other hand, William Coxon, a Naval Reserve officer, wondered what the country would think of 'a certain commander in a patrol at Dover who keeps his men back on shore to play football'.[89] Some competitions were crowned with trophies, like that made out of shell casings and awarded by the Royal Sussex Regiment.[90] At times the passion for the game overrode caution, and pitches were strafed by enemy artillery while matches were in progress.[91]

Football provided one of the war's most poignant moments when at the battle of the Somme Captain Wilfred Nevill of the 8th East Surrey Regiment

Football proved an eye-catching if not effective way to train troops for gas warfare in 1917.   **23**

provided two balls, one inscribed 'The Great European Cup – The Final – East Surreys v Bavarians. Kick-off at Zero' and the other 'NO REFEREE' to his men.[92] Though Nevill had rarely played football himself, he updated the tradition of inscribing footballs to reflect the war. As with the balls which had been used at pre-war London charity matches, this would become a valued memento for the man who kicked it into the German trench. At the appointed hour the men went over the top, dribbling and passing the balls as they advanced, only to be killed well short of the enemy wire. R. Caton-Woodville, the most important British battle artist, drew the scene for *The Illustrated London News*, and the episode became proof of the British belief in war as a schoolboy's game. Though it has often been told, this was not an isolated incident. On another part of the front that July morning the Newcastle Commercials advanced across No Man's Land behind a well-known Geordie footballer who dribbled a ball.[93] A fortnight after these footballing incidents the men of the Gloucestershire Regiment, who had been physically shattered by this campaign, opted to play 'rag events' in their sports.[94] Footballs had a talismanic appeal to these troops. Though there was no real protection from bullets and bombs, by dribbling and passing balls during the advance the dangers of war were equated with football's hacking and tackling. In this sense, such expressions of senseless courage were not much different from naming shells after famous boxers.

Like football, the boxing boom continued unabated, with amateur, professional and carnival bouts being staged in London and at the front throughout the war. Many of the most renowned Edwardian fighters, who had learned to box in the military, re-enlisted after 1914, while others like Jimmy Wilde and Jim Driscoll, who had had no military experience, served in uniform.[95] Those boxers who returned to their units brought back with them a sport which had been transformed radically. Despite the importance of the sport to the Victorian and Edwardian armed services, boxing championships were suspended from 1914 until a celebratory tournament marked the end of the war. In the absence of a formal championship structure, music-hall boxing predominated.

Jack Johnson suffered during the war. In June 1913 Johnson had fled indictment on morals offences in the United States and settled in Paris, where he hoped to fight as often as possible. 'White hopes' queued for the opportunity. On 27 June 1914 he defeated Frank Moran in Paris, but the assassinations at Sarajevo the following day meant that he never collected his prize. Desperately

Boxer Pat O'Keefe does his bit for king and country in 1915 by showing off his skills.　　**24**

in debt, Johnson decamped for London where he demonstrated his physical strength in music halls by breaking chains, carrying men, and allowing horses to stand on his chest. In the first months of the war this act reminded Londoners vividly of Johnson's incomparable physical strength, leading one trench newspaper to publish a mock music-hall programme for the Cloth Hall, Ypres, that announced 'The Johnsons – a shout, a scream, a roar. This season the Johnsons have carried all before them'.[96] Johnson continued appearing in the British halls until the winter of 1915, when a championship fight in Havana, Cuba, was arranged with the American Jess Willard. Willard wrote the last chapter in the denouement of Johnson's fighting career by knocking him out in the twenty-sixth round, on 5 April 1916.[97]

Military boxing was resurgent. The first military boxer to come to public attention was the English middleweight champion Pat O'Keefe, who had been Tommy Burns's second at the Johnson bout and was a training partner of Billy Wells. O'Keefe was a popular London Irishman who, by the spring of 1915, was employed at Camberwell as a physical instructor for the 1st Surrey Rifles. Clad in his Lonsdale belt, he demonstrated boxing technique to the men while continuing to fight professional opponents like Bandsman Blake in London arenas (Figure 24).[98] Just as boxers had done on the eve of the war, O'Keefe balanced these serious professional endeavours by sparring with a military champion, at Stamford Bridge in August 1915.[99] Though uniformed, O'Keefe's life changed little during the war: he ran his south London pub, while boxing in both serious and carnival matches and training recruits.[100]

As in the boxing boom, professional bouts were balanced by boxing tournaments which were staged regularly throughout the services.[101] Boxing's popularity during the war caused *The Illustrated Sporting and Dramatic News* to comment in April 1918 that 'it has long been proved by experience that the troops in France cannot receive too many consignments of boxing gloves'.[102] Many of these competitions were seriously contested bouts between champions representing various units, while others reflected the Edwardian boxing boom's more comic aspects. One such tournament, hosted in October 1915 by the 7th Canadian Infantry Battalion, promised:

> 8th Battalion National Sporting Club, Madison Square and Wonderland in the front line trench.
> No Man's Land Boxiana
> Novices competition every Saturday night after the rum issue
> Ring side seats – 5.00 dollars
> Gallery seats on top of parapet – 2.00 dollars
> Safe seats on firing platform – two bits
> Periscopes for the Timid and for use of ladies 3d.
> Field glasses for use of staff officers on hire at reserve trench
> Batmen and children in arms admitted free on showing a copy of the *Listening Post*
> Results of each round sent to Head Quarters by our special pigonnier
> Moving picture rights reserved
> This celebrated club opened its second season with a ten round contest Between the machine Gun Kid and Cyclone Clark
> Unfortunately, the popular Referee Eugene Corri was unable to be present, as He is at the moment engaged in a scrap against Potsdam Willie.
> A popular preliminary was provided by 'Jack Johnstone'[sic] and 'One round Hogan'
> For the contest of the evening, the Medical detail of the 7th battalion lent their gramophone, to shout time at the necessary intervals. Owing to the barbed wire entanglements we could not get up to the ring-side, but from the fact the the Machine Gun Kid arrived at the dressing station and Cyclone Clark did not understand that the Lonsdale Belt went the latter.[103]

This long playbill juxtaposed the most prominent features of the ongoing boxing boom, from allusions to popular personalities, women, the NSC and films, with topical war references. Documents such as this prove how deeply music hall had changed boxing. Such contests were also staged in the capital. Six months after this tournament, Londoners saw Fred Evans perform an up-to-date boxing skit entitled 'Pimple versus the Kaiser' at a boxing festival at which Jimmy Wilde and boxing midgets, a staple of pre-war fighting, also appeared.[104] Other stars of the boxing boom were stationed at bases in France and Belgium as physical trainers. Part of their duties, like Pat O'Keefe's, were to entertain the men with sparring bouts. Some, like the three times bantamweight champion Digger Stanley, had long since passed the peak of their professional prowess, however their reputations made them coveted opponents at regimental boxing tournaments.[105]

Billy Wells had a more problematic, though lucrative, war. Despite the up-to-date boxing joke penned in early 1916 by a Yorkshire wag which ran:

Enthusiastic literary private. Isn't H. G. Wells just great?
Enthusiastic sporting ditto. Rather! Hasn't he a beautiful left?[106]

Wells did not re-enlist in August 1914, claiming that he supported his mother, wife, children and two teenaged brothers. Wells's position hardened after his brother, Alf, who had played football for Fulham, was killed in battle in September 1914. Instead of enlisting, Wells fought lucrative bouts: against Dan McGoldrick at Plymouth in February 1915, followed the same month by one in Belfast with Bandsman Rice, who was now serving with the Rifle Brigade. He then lost to Frank Moran at the London Opera House in March, and to Sergeant Smith at The Ring, Blackfriars. As was his custom Billy developed his stamina for these bouts by playing football. These fights paid well, though they did nothing to alleviate the criticism that Wells was avoiding his duty. Therefore Billy also sparred Pat O'Keefe in London halls to raise money for war charities. Nevertheless, the British press berated Wells until he relented and returned to the army, as a physical instructor, in May 1915. Even after enlisting, sergeant Wells was granted generous dispensations of leave to carry on his professional career. He met Bandsman Rice at Liverpool on Boxing Day 1915, and in 1916 he fought at Golders Green Hippodome on a card which also featured Pat O'Keefe, at Plymouth, Newcastle and the NSC.

Wells was posted to France in 1917, where he worked as a bayonet instructor, and toured the front, boxing before units who were in rest areas where 'his personality, position in the sporting world, and his knowledge of his work compel attention from these war-worn men'.[107] On one of these tours, in February 1917, Wells fought at the 2nd Division Boxing Tournament, where to private Donald Fraser he 'seemed a very skilful boxer, but he did not look rugged enough for world championship calibre'.[108] Given this meagre assessment of his skills by a front line soldier, it is little wonder why unreliable British shells were dubbed 'Billy Wells'.

Fraser's judgement of Wells's talent echoed what Jim Driscoll, who had held the world featherweight title in 1912 and 1913, had said about Wells during the lead-up to the Covent Garden match with Carpentier.[109] Though several years older than Wells, Driscoll's ring skills were sharper for, according to Guy Chapman at a regimental tournament:

> The great boxer [Driscoll] came, to my eyes an elderly man. But as soon as he stopped, we could see the lines of a master. Our hard-fighting boy, who had won the divisional welter-weights, melted to a child in his hands. Wherever he led, the older man was not. Amidst roars of applause and laughter, Driscoll danced and buffooned about the ring, swirling about the amateur, the peer of Nijinski.[110]

This performance was pure music hall. Driscoll was some twenty pounds lighter than his opponent: a disparity in size and skill he had playfully emphasised, to the crowd's amusement. The fight directly echoed his pre-war NSC music-hall bout against Carlton. In the mess after the bout, Driscoll complained that the famous athletes with whom he served as a physical trainer had at times been forced to carry rifles.[111] These men believed that their role was that of 'celebrity' trainers who helped recruit, fought for cash purses in professional bouts, and entertained war-weary troops behind the lines: they did not expect to fight. Hence the reluctance of Wells to join up. Jimmy Wilde refused to enlist voluntarily, continued to fight and unsuccessfully appealed his conscription notice in 1916, before relenting and joining up. Even then he was permitted to pursue his professional career, and, after Jack Johnson had left Britain, Wilde was asked to take over his part in the touring revue *Seconds Out*.[112]

One did not need a boxing celebrity to stage comic bouts. When the Gloucestershire regiment could not find a man big enough at their tournament to fight their champion Sergeant Boughton, 'he accordingly sparred a couple of rounds with a member of the audience in which both feet and hands were freely used'.[113] Boughton may not have been a professional boxer, but he was as canny a performer as Driscoll, Wilde and Carlton. Just as it had for artistes during the Edwardian boom, boxing provided fodder for concert parties, like the *Whizz-Bangs*, for whom 'Snowy Osborne' ('the White Hope') performed comedy bouts in 1918.[114] So important had celebrity boxers become by the last months of the war, that two of the most notable fighters at a tournament held at 'an aeronautical school near London' in June 1918 were 'Broadribb, the Englishman who once met Georges Carpentier' and a quondam sparring partner of Billy Wells.[115]

Londoners were more fortunate in September of that year, when Staff-Sergeant Jimmy Wilde returned to the city to fight J. Conn. With the end of the war in sight, this fight, won by Wilde in the twelfth round, reunited many features and faces of the Edwardian boxing boom: heavyweights Billy Wells and Frank Goddard, both in uniform, announced that they would meet in the ring; the actors Sam Mayo and George Graves were in the crowd, as was Eugene Corri, the referee who embodied the NSC ethos (Figure 25).[116]

Boxing prepares for peace as the main proponents of the pre-war boom reassemble in London in 1918.

Though the boxing boom had suffered very little interruption during the war, it must have been comforting to see how readily it was re-established.

The war saw London baseball appear for a third time thanks again to enthusiastic civilian expatriates, and Canadian and American troops. A baseball league existed amongst the Canadian troops in Flanders by the end of 1915, whose

26   With so many Canadian and American troops in London during the war, the city saw a third attempt at professional baseball.

regularly scheduled matches attracted thousands of spectators.[117] Baseball was just as frequently and eagerly played by North American men in rest areas as football was amongst the British.[118] Meanwhile, men on leave borrowed the baseball equipment that was freely available from clubs and refreshment huts which had been established throughout the city to entertain North American troops.[119]

From the autumn of 1916, these men formed the backbone of the huge crowds who watched baseball matches in London's biggest football stadiums. Professional football had been closed down, but baseball – which, like boxing, was easily identified as a means of boosting morale, without drawing men away from their duties – co-opted football stadiums. This was another means by which football clubs showed their support for the war effort. Originally, Canadian soldiers had played American expatriate workers and Oxbridge students, in these matches which were designed to appease the North American servicemen's appetite for the game (Figure 26).[120] The entry of the United States into the war in 1917 brought many more baseballers and fans of the game to England. In response a League was inaugurated in May 1918, when the American Army met their traditional sporting rivals, the Navy, at Highbury.[121]

The first season's highlight was a match played before the king and 40,000 fans on the fourth of July, American Independence Day, at Stamford Bridge.[122] But London's wartime craze for baseball was, as it had been before 1914, confined to North Americans, and the Anglo-American league folded at war's end.

Each aspect of First World War military culture discussed above demonstrated that there existed a constant, evolving, topical interaction between the battle-front and the homefront, which carried existing popular sensations over into the armed services. Another distinctive feature of First World War popular culture must be examined. Brief descriptions of several up-to-date wartime crazes will illustrate more concretely how these fronts interacted and how popular culture responded in a new way to the war.

Firstly, the sensation about the war itself began in August 1914, as newspapers, periodicals and cinema films all featured cheering crowds, men enlisting, troops marching, embarking and arriving in France. It is moot whether such images and stories reflected the public mood accurately.[123] It is enough to note that the public were fascinated by the war in these early weeks, before its gallant sheen had begun to tarnish. It is not surprising that topical military pantomimes spoofed a war that included such colossal heroes as Lords Roberts, Fisher and Kitchener, evil antagonists like the Kaiser, the enthusiastic leadership of Lloyd George and Winston Churchill, and the mythologised jocular heroism of the British Tommy, embodied in songs like 'Tipperary'. With an increasingly large audience, cinema became the cheapest, most accessible and most popular form of popular culture during the war years.[124]

In order to fulfil this widespread demand for war scenes, Geoffrey Malins, a film-maker who had worked in up-to-date Edwardian cinema, took his camera to the front in August 1914, believing that 'If the public wants those films … the public must have them'.[125] Initially, Malins followed the Belgian army, filming sensational scenes which encapsulated the public's understanding of modern warfare: machine guns in action, shells exploding and soldiers who 'could not resist looking round and laughing at the camera' as they awaited the order to attack.[126] Just as Edwardian film-makers had done with sensational movies of cup-ties and boxing bouts, Malins hurried home to London as soon as he had finished shooting these films, in order to edit and exhibit them as quickly as possible.[127] Malins returned to the front repeatedly, filming ever more sensational scenes for the London public. That first winter Malins updated the spirit of Christmas in wartime by filming the Prince of Wales attending holiday services in the Guards Brigade battlefield chapel.[128]

Such scenes satisfied the public, though Malins later distanced himself from these topical films, saying: 'time after time I crossed over to France and so into Belgium, and obtained a series of pictures that delighted my employers, and pleased the picture theatre public. But I wanted something more than snapshots of topical events'.[129] Malins disparaged these sensational films because in the spring of 1915 he was appointed an official War Office 'kinematographer', as military leaders tried to harness topical culture for propaganda.[130] The War Office was well served by Malins whose feeling for topical subjects never dulled; he scooped his rivals when at the battle of Saint Eloi in March 1916, he was the first man to film British troops in action. Later, searching for an even more up-to-date method of presenting the war, Malins flew above the front for two hours recording the immensity of the trench lines.[131] His camera lens was not sufficiently powerful to pick out individual soldiers, but the desire to present a view from above echoed Claude Grahame-White's flight over London on Alexandra Day in June 1912 and B. C. Huck's 1914 film of the Royal cruise to France.

Despite these continuous efforts to update the way the war was presented to audiences at home, Malins is best remembered today for one movie, *Battle of the Somme,* the most successful and controversial First World War film. With this film, which documented the opening salvoes of the massive battle designed to break through the enemy trenches, Malins had hoped he would be recording the end of the war. Such a film would be the most sensational ever made. As we know, the troops deployed on the Somme on 1 July 1916 failed to push through to Berlin, but the battle – whose prolonged artillery barrage was so fierce, almost three million shells were fired at the German lines, that it could be heard in south-eastern England – was sensational because of its immense carnage.[132] The British forces sustained over 400,000 casualties.[133] Once he had filmed at the front, Malins returned to London where Charles Urban, one of the most important Edwardian film-makers, who now oversaw the War Office film unit – run by a board called, significantly, the Topical Committee – helped edit the raw footage into a 75-minute film.[134]

Next, the government's publicity and propaganda resources ensured that *Battle of the Somme* was a sensational success when it was released in August 1916. Vigorous advance publicity included advertisements in newspapers, magazines, hoardings throughout London, and endorsements from Lloyd-George and the King. The film captured the public's craze for news of this great battle. As many as one million Londoners saw the film which played in thirty-four cinemas. Twenty million more people throughout the country saw the film in its first six weeks.[135] Just like the Johnson–Burns match eight years earlier,

Battle of the Somme's triumph was repeated throughout the Empire and the United States. The comparison to the earlier boxing film is apposite because, like *Battle of the Somme*, Edwardian topical sports films had allowed audiences to take part vicariously in these events. Reports of the battle had primed audiences' interest, and this, along with the unrelenting advertisements, made *Battle of the Somme* the greatest craze in British cinema history. Contemporary accounts reflected the public frenzy for the film, reporting that *Battle of the Somme* prompted unprecedented reactions from audiences who believed it to be the first 'true' representation of how their friends and relatives were fighting in France. In the way they had learned in music hall, cinema and pantomime, audiences expressed pity at the sight of Allied suffering and death, cheered British troops, and screamed abuse during scenes showing German prisoners. Audiences, therefore, responded to *Battle of the Somme* as they had to other topical films.[136]

Government propagandists failed to realise that *Battle of the Somme*'s popularity lay in the novel way it 'realistically' documented a topical public craze, and so the War Office tried to replicate the film's sensation again and again. The resulting year-long flurry of official war films drew steadily smaller audiences, as the craze for documentary battle scenes diminished.[137] But the flame was not extinguished quickly, for one year after the release it still played in small theatres and John Masefield still referred readers to the film as the most accurate depiction of the war.[138]

The *Battle of the Somme* craze lives on amongst historians though because the war's most famous and, to academics at least, controversial moving images were drawn from the film. This short sequence shows a squad of Tommies crouching in a muddy trench. Barbed wire stretches across the parapet, while smoke obscures the battlefield. At a signal, the men go 'over the top'. One man is hit as he leaves the trench and slides lifelessly into the dirt, while the others advance, disappearing into the smoke. Film historians assert that this scene was 'fake' because it showed soldiers in training. Much has been written to debate what contemporary commentators had already made known. On the heels of the film frenzy, the popular cartoonist W. Heath Robinson drew a series entitled *Wangling War Films: How to Make 'Em and Fake 'Em*. Drawings in this series, such as a 'U boat sinking a pleasure vessel off Brighton', and 'The fall of Przemysl' showed dramatic scenes being recreated by film-makers. Like *Battle of the Somme*, the movies in Robinson's cartoons are long, requiring winches, windlasses and barrels to collect the exposed film. Meanwhile, the proceedings are overseen by John Bulls, representing government propagandists.[139] Robinson's cartoons tacitly acknowledged that the public understood that some of what they saw was not real, while implying simultaneously that such scenes did not detract from the film's up-to-date interest. Malins echoed the message conveyed in Robinson's cartoons: that once the armies had bunkered down into trenches, fighting lost 'the traditional air of battle', and was difficult to convey sensationally on film.[140] Therefore, Malins had needed an up-to-date way of portraying the war as the civilian public wished to see it. Men clambering out of trenches in the face of enemy fire provided that sensation. If it was too dangerous, and very likely too ghastly, to film such scenes, then Malins would recreate them, while shielding audiences from war's real horrors. Such evidence counters historians' claim that *Battle of the Somme* was an instrument of hegemonic control to inculcate war fever, because the wider public were in the know about such scenes.[141]

Battle of the Somme's immense sensation spread from London throughout the world, giving civilians the vicarious, though sanitised, up-to-date thrill of the trenches. However, the various battlefronts also witnessed sensational crazes. The most important and enduring of these military sensations were those surrounding Charlie Chaplin, Harry Lauder and Harry Tate, each of whom came to personify certain aspects of the war experience. Like the ongoing military passions for sports and sensational war films, these crazes evolved through a dialogue between fighting men and the three protagonists. Similarly, their topicality set these sensations apart from Lena Ashwell's plays. Just like artistes had done during the Edwardian boxing boom and other pre-war crazes, these three canny artistes modified their performances in response to developments in the war. Even though home and the pleasures of two shows nightly at various Palaces, Alhambras and Empires was physically attenuated, the interaction between audiences and artistes that had been embodied in up-to-date culture remained vibrant in wartime on London stages and in concert parties. These three sensations (Chaplin, Lauder and Tate) were related integrally to the trench slang, music, sporting events and concert parties which had created a receptive atmosphere at the front for up-to-date culture. Malins' films had similarly primed London audiences for topical war performances. As a result, each of these sensations resonated simultaneously at the front and at home.

Charlie Chaplin was history's greatest physical comedian. The son of dissipated south London music-hall artistes, Chaplin had grown up on the stage, graduating in 1908 from West End boy parts to Fred Karno's troupe, in which he filled ever more prominent roles. Chaplin became one of Britain's most popular clowns after replacing Harry Weldon as 'Stiffy the Goalkeeper' in *The*

Football Match. Chaplin twice toured the United States with Karno, presenting scenes from the *Mumming Birds* and in late 1912, convinced that his future lay in cinema, Chaplin remained behind when Karno's troupe returned to London. Chaplin's American ascendancy was rapid. He signed a movie contract with Keystone, the country's top comedy studio, in late 1913, and filmed *Making a Living* before the year's end. The 'Little Tramp' character appeared the following February, when Chaplin first donned the greasepaint moustache, tiny frock coat and hat, and enormous trousers and boots. The Little Tramp was pure music hall. His penguin waddle was modelled on the gait of a character whom Chaplin recalled from the streets of Kennington, while the combination of big and small elements recalled Dan Leno and Herbert Campbell, music-hall cricket and boxing matches. Audiences loved the Little Tramp immediately, and so by April 1914 the character had starred in four more hit films. That June Chaplin's films reached Britain, where posters announcing his homecoming emphasised his innate Englishness and links to topical culture by asking 'Are you prepared for the Chaplin boom?', while reminding the public that they already knew 'the famous Karno comedian'.[142] By the first week of August 1914, twenty-two Chaplin films had been released in Britain.

The sensation these movies had caused on the eve of the war made references to Chaplin one of the most powerfully resonant elements of up-to-date troop culture. Chaplin's films were played for troops in rest areas and so it was commonly understood throughout the Allied armies why men sharing Chaplin's surname were called 'Charlie', duck-footed people were nicknamed 'Chaplin' and the terrified scrambling, reeling and tumbling to evade incoming shells was 'a bit of Charlie Chaplin'.[143] In at least one unit where the song rarely left the gramophone, such references might have been muttered to the strains of the 'Charlie Chaplin walk', 1916's 'Charlie Chaplin march grotesque', or any other of a myriad such up-to-date songs.[144] Meanwhile, the Little Tramp's example of shabby gentility, which troops recognised in their own decaying uniforms, enabled them to update at least one song, which now went:

Oh the Moon shines bright on Charlie Chaplin
His boots are crackin'
For want of blackin',
And his little baggy trousers they need mendin'
before we send him
to the Dardanelles.[145]

Similarly, references to Chaplin abounded in print because, like pantomimes and concert parties, trench newspapers updated the familiar pleasures of civilian life to suit the wartime setting. In January 1916, 'Some Chaplinisms' – a series of inane puns and jokes – appeared in *The Whizz-Bang*, the Durham Light Infantry's newspaper.[146] Sending up the advertisements for patent medicines and miracle inventions which had crowded the back pages of Edwardian tabloids and popular magazines, in December 1916 *The Wipers Times* asked its more hirsute readers, 'Why wear that Charlie Chaplin?' when one could cultivate an attractive new image with a patented moustache trainer.[147] Many Tommies sported facial hair, though few apparently heeded this advertisement, for in August 1917 the British High Command forbad Chaplin moustaches at the front, on the grounds that they were likely to provoke ridicule.[148] Many men grew moustaches at the front because of the lack of bathing facilities rather than out of a love of Chaplin. As a result, officers, whose access to shaving equipment was easier, wore the tidy 'Charlie Chaplin' moustaches, as opposed to the more fulsome 'toothbrush' variety which belonged to the ranks.[149]

In spite of this official reproach, troops continued to revere Chaplin. Chaplin's films were screened in rest areas, and imitators appeared frequently at concert parties, like the Canadian carnival in July 1917 which included the skit 'Charlie Chaplin and the Girl', or the RFC's 22nd squadron's 1917 Christmas revue in which a Chaplin imitator performed Karno's *Bloomsbury Burglars*.[150] In the spring of 1918 the Sentimental Blokes, an Australian concert party, included Private Anderson 'as Charlie Chaplin conducting the band' who, reviewers felt, 'threatens to outchaplin Chaplin'.[151]

Through such appropriations Chaplin had, unwittingly, become an allegory for military existence. Despite the affection with which he was held by the troops, Chaplin's personal relationship with the war was fraught. In the autumn of 1917 the Canadian trench newspaper *The Sling* published a fictitious note from Chaplin, giving reasons why he had not joined up. The text ran simply 'I wish I was there boys, but I hear they have Chaplains enough for the present'.[152] The humour was laced with meaning, for, unlike many of his contemporaries, Chaplin had not publicly endorsed the war. The reasons for Chaplin's silence are easy to deduce. Firstly, in August 1914 Chaplin had been in America for almost two years, during which time he had become one of the world's most recognisable and wealthiest celebrities. Subsequently, Chaplin chose to remain in California while his native country was at war, a decision for which he was consequently mauled by the British press.

However, in Hollywood, American neutrality insulated Chaplin, something the star took advantage of to continue making hit movies. But, as Chaplin's friend Alistair Cooke recalled somewhat apocryphally, Charlie was not immune to the war's reach. According to Cooke, Chaplin had been moved deeply when soldiers posted him a copy of the above-mentioned Dardanelles song. Cooke related that after informing himself about the Dardanelles, Chaplin agreed to sell war bonds and announced publicly on 4 August 1917, the day the High Command banned Chaplin moustaches, that he would obey his country's call to duty.[153] But this was no Damascene conversion. Rather, Chaplin had succumbed to the mounting pressure for him to endorse the war publicly. America's neutrality had shielded Chaplin from his British critics, but when his adoptive country went to war he was forced to respond. Even then, Chaplin's war work was carried out in America. He promoted Liberty Bonds in New York, Washington and the southern states in April 1918 at the insistence of his patriotic friends Douglas Fairbanks and Mary Pickford.[154] Chaplin's new-found relationship to the war went further: despite Cecil B. deMille's fears that audiences would react badly to a military spoof, *Shoulder Arms*, Chaplin's only war film, was released at the end of October and promoted in Britain with posters announcing that 'Charlie, in this picture, lies down his cane and picks up the sword to fight for democracy'.[155] *Shoulder Arms* revealed that the Little Tramp was equally plucky in uniform, passing through training to capture the Kaiser single-handedly.[156] Chaplin, who was by conviction a left-leaning pacifist, must have been appalled and offended by a war which consumed men by the tens of thousands. Liberty Bond tours were a way to rehabilitate his image and topically promote *Shoulder Arms*. This late conversion to war promotion was to cost Chaplin dearly, but the subject of the next craze was not so reticent about declaring his intense patriotic belief in the Allied cause.

Harry Lauder's enthusiasm for war work came closest to embodying the jolly jingoism and stoic forbearance captured in the films of August 1914. Forty-nine years old at the war's start, Lauder stood comfortably at the pinnacle of the professional music-hall ladder. Like Chaplin, Lauder had achieved unparalleled global celebrity before the war, though he had done so by touring the world constantly singing maudlin, sentimental, consoling songs to communities of expatriate Scots. So successful had he been as a performer that by 1915 Scotland had become 'the land of Burns and Harry Lauder', and, to at least some Americans, all Scotsmen had become imperfect representations of Lauder.[157]

Lauder was touring Australia, accompanied by his family, when the war began. On hearing the news John Lauder, who had only just graduated from Cambridge, hurried home to join up, while Harry, accompanied by his wife, fulfilled contracts in the United States before returning to London in the spring of 1915.[158] Lauder and Chaplin were the two greatest British celebrities in the United States. But, unlike Chaplin, Lauder had no scruples about exploiting his status to promote the Allied cause in North America. Therefore, after a brief stay in Britain, Lauder returned to America, for a further six-month tour, where in addition to his nightly performances, he 'did a lot of propaganda work' from the stage and at public meetings. Such patriotic undertakings were not always received kindly in a country which harboured much pro-German feeling, but Lauder's celebrity endowed him with the personal charisma with which to convince sceptics.[159]

Lauder returned to Britain in early 1916, and began touring the country, before making his first appearance in revue, in late autumn, in *Three Cheers* at the Shaftesbury Theatre. This salute to the troops culminated with Lauder singing 'The laddies that fought and won' backed by a chorus of Scots Guards wearing their dress uniforms.[160] Few scenes can have looked more powerfully patriotic during the war. Lauder's charisma amongst soldiers from throughout the Empire was immense. For years, the images of heathery glens, boozy nights and compliant lassies conveyed in his songs had conjured up romantic notions of home for Britons living on the Empire's peripheries. After 1914, such songs filled the same role for lonely troops as they listened to recordings of Lauder and other 'sentimental' singers, or sang along enthusiastically with the Lauder imitators and Scottish singers who appeared regularly in battlefront concert parties.[161] Serving-men's appetite for Lauder was insatiable; if a concert party lacked an adequate mimic, then a gramophone playing one of his records was placed on stage.[162]

During the First World War, Lauder's Scots songs were a universal expression of longing for home. His dour, pinch-penny persona was beloved by the Canadian troops, who mocked him in trench newspapers for breaking 'the law of treating'. This Canadian adoration was explained partly by the high number of Scots serving with the Dominion's forces, and the fact that Lauder had recruited men in Canada during his North American tours. That Lauder's songs had reminded troops wistfully of their various homes was indicated in the Canadian concert party of October 1917 whose penultimate turn was 'the inimitable Scot in Harry Lauder hits', which was followed by the entire company singing the sentiment 'Take me back to dear old Blighty'.[163] Though the arid outback bore little resemblance to the verdant Highlands, 'Roamin' in the gloamin''reminded Australians of home the following April when the *Coo-ees* concert troupe included a kilted Lauder impersonator carrying the trademark gnarled walking stick.[164]

Apart from such universal identification with the nostalgia of Lauder's lyrics, the prevalence of impersonators at concert parties also reflected Lauder's appearances at the battlefront. These concerts resulted from the letters Lauder received constantly from the troops. Initially, men thanked Harry for his overt support for the war, but correspondents later consoled him on the death in action of his only child. Lauder had learned of his son's death on the first of January 1917 while in his Shaftesbury Theatre dressing room. Despite the news, Lauder performed that night, and in the vernacular of a later day, channelled his grief into a re-invigorated dedication to the war effort. This stoic determination to carry on despite the death of his son became the basis for a deep emotional bond between Lauder, the troops and the public.[165] His songs already encapsulated the nostalgia for home, while John Lauder's death made Harry the personification of the grieving parent who remained convinced of the war's justness, and the need to carry it through determinedly.

Like any skilful topical artiste, Lauder capitalised on the sensation surrounding his son's death, albeit in aid of the war effort. In essence, this meant stepping up the pace of his earlier activities. During the remaining run of *Three Cheers* Lauder sang regularly in hospitals, and lectured throughout London about the need to conserve food. He also appeared alongside Arthur Balfour in a Drury Lane Theatre recruiting drive.[166] But staying in London was not sufficiently rewarding for Lauder who, in the months after his son's death, decided to lead a concert party to the trenches, in order to entertain the men, visit John's grave, and understand something of what his son had experienced. The War Office obliged Lauder, though military leaders were reluctant to let such a symbol of British steadfastness appear in the front-line trenches. War leaders could be assured of the patriotic intentions of this party, for the touring company reflected Lauder's earlier endeavours. Lauder, the only professional performer, was joined by Edinburgh MP James Hogge, who had championed benefits for widows and orphans, and George Adam, a Presbyterian curate from Montreal who worked for the Ministry of Munitions.[167] This triumvirate, who dubbed themselves the *Reverend Harry Lauder MP Tour* decided that at each concert Hogge would inform men of their pension rights, after which Adam would discuss the progress of the war, while Lauder would finish off the evening with songs.[168] This was a three-fold assault to convince the men of the justness of their cause, the successes of the allied armies and the material comforts which awaited them in peacetime. Before setting out, Lauder packed away one hundred pounds' worth of cigarettes to distribute at the front, and purchased a specially designed piano which fitted into his motor-car. An accompanist was chosen from amongst the troops in France. The tour first played Boulogne casino, which had been transformed into a military hospital, after which they performed at roadsides, hospitals, chateaux, shelters, shell holes and, in spite of War Office reticence, in the front-line trenches.[169]

When, during these performances, Lauder sang 'The laddies who fought and won' from *Three Cheers*, it was mainly officers and newly arrived men who recognised the song. This was likely because they had seen the show whilst on home leave. Indeed, military men on leave in London attended revues and music halls at such a manic pace that it was widely rumoured that in case of emergency theatres had been equipped to flash warnings on the screens telling them to return to their units.[170] Those who were not in the know about *Three Cheers* mistook it for a salutary, topical addition to the performance. One man who attended a concert at Limencourt believed that, like any up-to-date artiste, Lauder had added the song after being told, in secret, that the allies had won at Passchendaele. Lauder was unlikely to have omitted his latest hit from these concerts, but a suitable introduction from the singer, combined with the audience's understanding of topical performance techniques, made the song seem like an up-to-date Paschendaele tune, which was a:

> last-minute addition to his programme and provided the troops with an
> appropriately rousing Grand Finale.
>> When the fighting is over, and the war is won,
>> And the flags are waving free,
>> When the bells are ringing,
>> And the boys are singing
>> Songs of victory
>> When we all gather round the old fireside,
>> And the old mother kisses her son,
>> A' the lassies will be loving a' the laddies,
>> The laddies who fought and won.[171]

The belief that this was a topical song might have been strengthened by the way Lauder did update his performances in France, for example by débuting 'Australia is the land for me' when entertaining the Anzacs.[172] However, in the case of 'The laddies who fought and won', Lauder finished his performances with the same song he had recently used in Shaftesbury Theatre revue. Audiences assigned different meanings to the tune because, like his sentimental ballads, Lauder's war songs had been taken by the public as universal expressions of the war's spirit. The words encapsulated the spirit of Lauder's tour.

After returning to London, Lauder enlisted Lords Roseberry and Balfour to support his Million Pound Fund charity, and continued performing at music halls and hospitals.[173] Within a few months he was asked by the government to return to the United States and Canada in order to represent the British case in theatres, YMCAs, on Wall Street, before civic groups, and at training bases. Staying true to his music-hall roots, Lauder produced a topical song 'Marching with the president' to commemorate this tour.[174] The tour succeeded because Lauder was adopted by the Americans, who had now entered the war, as an example of unfettered patriotism. At the western extent of this tour, Lauder the great jingo met Chaplin the reluctant recruiter in Los Angeles in the spring of 1918. The pair starred in a 'British Wounded Soldiers Film' to raise money for the Red Cross Fund.[175] Like the Liberty Bond rallies he had begun attending that spring, the film was another way in which Chaplin could be seen to be doing his part for the war effort, in the company of a man with impeccable patriotic credentials.

Despite Lauder's popularity with troops from all nations, no performer resonated more powerfully with soldiers than Harry Tate, who had unwittingly secured this position by performing shambolic disasters for two decades in his skits *Motoring* and *Flying*. After 1914 these sketches became analogies for modern attrition warfare, during which few combatants had not seen comrades killed or maimed by misfiring guns and rifles, improperly primed shells, structural failure in aeroplanes and any manner of train, lorry or motor-car mishap. The relationship between these experiences and Tate's comedy was clear to troops. War is chaotic. Even the best disciplined troops, led by experienced officers, executing well-conceived plans encounter unforeseen obstacles. Men are killed and maimed quickly in such muddles.[176] In this sense the First World War was especially appalling because it was fought for the most part in a static troglodyte world of trenches, saps and night raids, which bore very little relation to the Victorian idyll of brightly plumed warriors charging valiantly. The randomness with which men died in mundane, apparently senseless, shelling, manoeuvres, equipment failures and tactical mistakes was grisly and horrifying. One result was that troops soon revered Tate's sketches, in which relatively simple undertakings went disastrously awry. Like Lauder's songs, Tate's sketches had universal appeal to troopers, in this instance because they rested on the unreliability of technology.

We have already seen how, from the start of the war, troops had evoked Tate's name to describe military ineptitude, or steadfastness in the face of mechanical failure. Tate also supported the war publicly from the beginning by appearing in numerous charity matinées in theatres and music halls throughout London.[177] Troops at the front first appropriated *Motoring* by updating it with an armoured anti-aircraft car for a 1915 Christmas revue.[178] The following spring Tate lent the automobile he had used on stage in Motoring, to a concert party from the battle-cruiser *Queen Mary*. Unfortunately, the car was lost when the ship was torpedoed in June.[179] Tate seems to have learned a lesson from this, for he lent only his support the following year to the Fifth Gloucestershire Regiment's concert party which ended with *Motoring*.[180]

In the autumn of 1916 Tate updated the *Motoring/Flying* sketch once again. The aeroplane and zeppelin sensations had abated by the beginning of the war. No subsequent invention was nearly as sensational until the autumn of 1916, when an addition to the battlefield captivated the public as both the war's funniest moment, and the instrument that could breach German trench lines at a stroke: tanks were the war's greatest sensation.[181] Because it rested on this hope of bringing a rapid end to the war, the tank sensation followed naturally from the craze for *Battle of the Somme*, which had gripped London only a few months earlier.

Tank technology was not completely novel in 1916. The public had seen agricultural vehicles sporting caterpillar tracks as far back as 1906, while H. G. Wells had predicted in the *Strand Magazine* in 1903 that 'land ironclads' would be used in twentieth-century warfare. In 1914 two syndicates began advocating the military uses of such machines to the government. Early the following year First Lord of the Admiralty Winston Churchill, who had already been influenced by Wells's writings and had been an early proponent of military aviation, allotted £70,000 to develop these 'mechanical elephants'.[182]

Despite residual doubt in the minds of senior commanders about the tactical utility of tanks, people were mesmerised almost immediately by them. As Lieutenant-colonel Edward Swinton, another admirer of Wells's writings who helped design the first tanks, recalled, the tank sensation began when the prototypes were tested on a secluded corner of Lord Iveagh's Suffolk estate. Absolute secrecy dictated that 'some non-committal word which would give no inkling of its nature to those not "in the know"' be used to refer to the invention.[183] At this stage, only those developing tanks had been captivated. The number of people 'in the know' about tanks expanded exponentially when the machines appeared for the first time in action on the Somme on 15 September 1916. Such was the sensation that men up and down the lines bragged about having been first to see the new contraption.[184] These cumbersome, lumbering, mechanically suspect, blisteringly hot, and decidedly ungallant, weapons enthralled people, for as corporal C. E. Jacomb recalled 'first impressions of a new thing are generally keener than those experienced on subsequent occasions when the novelty has worn off'.[185] These words summarised the tank craze appositely.

Unlike bicycles, motor-cars or aeroplanes, tanks were not handsome, fast or sleek. One tankie recalled that these 'huge, lumbering monsters … looked like nothing on earth', while a Canadian cavalry officer stared as tanks creaked by, only realising later that they made his role in war obsolete, and as though seeking some religious benediction, other men touched these wondrous new weapons which performed 'elephantine tricks' in battle.[186] Even if tanks had not yet proved their tactical worth, to an army still reeling from huge losses on the Somme:

> they supplied the touch of comic relief, and excited the mirth of the British soldier, always blessed with a keen sense of the ridiculous. They acted as an antidote to the effect of the Jack Johnsons, Weary Willies, Silent Susies, Whizz Bangs, Sausages, Rum Jars, Tear Shells, Gas Shells, and all the other frightfulness of the unspeakable Boche. They counteracted the weariness, the hunger and thirst, the dust, the mud, and all the squalor and filthy discomfort of war.[187]

Despite the lapidary prose, in this passage Swinton explained the tank sensation succinctly. These remarks were corroborated by Major H. F. Bidder, whose dispirited and drenched men were bogged down in the autumnal mud when:

> it was rumoured that the tank was around. In spite of all the gloom of failure and loss, nothing could make that tank anything but comic. We stood along the trench to watch it. First a humming sound, then the squat longish animal lurching along the Boche front line, every now and then firing a six pounder gun that stuck out the side. On it came, nosing along the trench; then, as if struck by a new idea, it turned off and went across to the Boche support line; and then went away, nosing along that. It produced for a time quite an air of cheeriness in our part of the world.[188]

Swinton further understood that their ability to sublimate horrors in men's minds endowed certain words with talismanic qualities. The name 'tank' – conveying no calibre, weight, range, speed or other intrinsically martial quality – fostered absurd, cosy and benign images which bolstered their supposed lugubrious, elephantine personalities. For civilians 'tanks' were cisterns which held water in loos, baths and municipal drains, not fighting men, while few words were more appealing to troops than 'tank': army slang for the wet canteen, where one 'got tanked'.[189] Swinton claimed the word had been chosen deliberately, and that:

the idea that this name would 'catch on' was justified beyond anticipation. Employed as a bluff during the stage of production and training, it stuck. It was adopted by the troops on the Western front and by the public at home, whose enthusiasm was aroused by the dramatic appearance and success of the new weapon, and whose fancy was tickled by its title. It thus obtained further sanction and was introduced to the whole world. In England the Tank became a popular gag in the revues, a subject for songs and the *motif* of dances. The word was, in fact, almost run to death.[190]

Only British machines had been so consecrated, for German ones were weighted down with elongated names that were unlikely 'to be used as the refrain of a topical song in vaudeville'.[191] Songs like 'The tank's saunter', 'The tank crawl', 'The tank ride', and 'Baby tank', celebrated the lugubrious qualities with which these weapons had been endowed in the public imagination and echoed the roles fat performers had played in Edwardian music hall and pantomime.[192] Tanks' absurdity was heightened by their classification as ships, which required them to possess names that were painted on their hulls. Most tanks were named for women, or the areas from which their crews had been recruited, though wits gave them names like *Autogophaster* and *Otasel*, or the titles of West End shows such as *Oh I Say*, *Look Who's Here*, *Watch Your Step*, *We're All in It*, *So Search Me* and *Keep Smiling*. However, in 1917, the High Command decreed they should bear more sober names like 'Apple' or 'Apricot'.[193]

Civilians learned about tanks from several sources. Reporters, who saw these machines creak into action for the first time, searched for ways to describe their comic and terrific aspects adequately, stumbling from 'Diplodocus Galumphant', 'Motor-monster', 'Jabberwock with eyes of flame', 'Land Dreadnought', 'Giant Toad' and 'Touring Fort'.[194] Each such description supported tanks' supposed slow-witted demeanour. Meanwhile, Whitehall had attempted to mould public understanding of the new weapon. The journalist Henry Wickham Steed visited the front with Lord Northcliffe during the summer of 1916: the pair had been told by Douglas Haig to have a look at the 'tanks', by which they thought the general was referring to water receptacles. Steed and Northcliffe both laughed when they saw the new weapons. Steed's laughter increased when the rotund Northcliffe, wanting to see the interior of the new weapon, became wedged in the hatchway.[195] Next, the government despatched Malins to the front with orders to film the 'Hush Hush'. Before his enigmatic subjects appeared, Malins was informed that they were called tanks, and that they were ' a sort of armoured car arrangement and shells literally glance off them'. Malins decided that, with the *Battle of the Somme* sensation over, tanks would provide the next up-to-date war scenes. Like his viewers would be, Malins was amazed by his first sight of the crawling, lumbering machines, saying 'I don't think I ever laughed so heartily at anything as I did on the first day that I saw the Tanks in action, and officers and men all agree that they never saw a funnier sight in their lives'.[196]

Just as they had during the *Battle of the Somme* sensation, London's illustrated magazines began simultaneously publishing eight tank cartoons drawn by W. Heath Robinson. Entitled 'For the war inventions board', these depicted fabulous new weapons, like the 'armoured corn crusher' which stamped on the enemy's sore feet, or the 'shell diverter for returning the enemy's fire', a device like an anemometer which spun the enemy's bullets back at them. Like tanks, Robinson's armour-plated contraptions were self-propelled and designed to defeat the enemy through mechanical ingenuity. Their ludicrous appearances and preposterous weaponry also related to the way in which tanks were seen by soldiers on the battlefield. A compendium of Robinson's cartoons, including the film and tank spoofs, was published with great success later in 1916 under the title *Hunlikely!*.[197]

By 1916 Harry Tate knew all about employing the products of 'mechanical ingenuity' as the basis for comedy. This excitement in the autumn of 1916 convinced Tate to update *Motoring* again, for the revue *Razzle Dazzle* at the Empire, Leicester Square. In this new skit Tate drove on to the stage in a cardboard tank, whose six guns pointed in all directions. As the machine lumbered into view, audiences saw a uniformed Tate grinning out of an open hatch. Tate cradled a rifle in his arms, a seeming bit of artistic fancy, that reflected how some officers at that time, unsure of how to deploy tanks most effectively, were assigning a sniper to every crew, though the practicality of a marksman in a sealed armoured box is questionable (Figure 27).[198]

Successive issues of *The Era* endorsed Tate's new sketch enthusiastically. On the eighteenth of October the newspaper articulated civilians' pragmatic, patriotic hopes by reporting 'some excellent fooling by Mr. Harry Tate round an impressionistic reproduction of the new land monsters which are striking such terror into the hearts of the Huns'.[199] The following week's notice encapsulated the impressions of tanks in battle, saying 'the comicality of the new tanks in the field has been the theme of amusing articles from several war correspondents, but for the most comical machine of the kind one must go to the Empire and see Harry Tate's formidable engine on the "razzle dazzle". It is a most worthy successor to his wonderful motor'.[200] In only a few months tanks had gone from the

     Harry Tate updates the tank sensation for the London stage in October 1916.

secrecy of a country estate to become the war's sensational stars. The comedic role given to tanks in the field, print, film and on stage suggests the latitude which government censors permitted in the depiction of the new weapon. In the trenches tanks articulated the men's fatalism, while to the larger public they embodied the jovial attitudes to death and sacrifice with which Tommies had been endowed by writers like Kipling, Newbolt and Henty, and early war films.

The tank sensation thrived at the front in the wake of Tate's sketch. In December 1916 a spoof playbill for the 'Guillemont Hippodrome' on the Somme, listing 'this week's revue' as *Hello Tanko*, an updated version of Tate's *Hello Tango*, which had been one of the most popular pre-war West End revues.[201] The sensation climaxed in January 1917 with the release of Malins' *The Advance of the Tanks*. Posters boomed the film, which opened simultaneously in over one hundred London cinemas, as 'your first opportunity of seeing the tanks as our brave soldiers saw them going into action against the enemy'. The War Office promoted this film as a sequel to *Battle of the Somme*; however, a more subtle reading of the film's advance publicity shows that it augured the end of the tank craze. Audiences were not beckoned to cinemas to witness how comic these up-to-date weapons were, but in order to see a film which 'had no fakes' while providing an uncensored view of the 'sea of mud which covers everything' on the battlefield.[202] Though this film, and a song that bore the same name, captured a sensation, audiences for topical war films dropped steadily throughout 1917 as people wearied of battle images.[203]

The abatement of the tank sensation mirrored the weapon's increased use on the battlefield.[204] In December 1916 the British possessed only sixteen serviceable machines in France.[205] However, as manpower shortages became acute the following year, the British High Command turned to tanks as labour-saving devices, which could, when deployed in large numbers, take the places of thousands of Tommies. The acceptance of such a policy came slowly. In May 1917 Douglas Haig ranked the importance of tanks to his forces below that of aircraft and railway locomotives. However, his views changed significantly by November, when he deployed tanks in significant numbers at the battle of Cambrai, their first effective use in the field.[206] Tanks had been funny, plodding and novel only so long as they had been deployed sparingly. By the autumn of 1917 tanks had become routine destructive weapons incapable of driving through to Berlin. Stripped of romantic and comic human characteristics, tanks ceased to be sensational.[207]

However, just as Tate's tank sketch began to run out of steam, *Flying* started to resonate with the Royal Flying Corps. In early 1917, the RE8, an artillery spotter and reconnaissance machine, was introduced. Said to have 'embodied practically every major body design fault which had already been identified and for which the cure was known' the RE8 was slow, difficult to manoeuvre, and exhibited a marked preponderance for spinning uncontrollably, flaws that made it an easy target for enemy gunners and pilots.[208] Because these attributes resembled the hazards and mishaps Tate had enacted in *Flying*, and the plane's name recalled Tate's 'T8' number plate, RFC personnel soon nicknamed the plane the 'Harry Tate', a pejorative designation it carried for the rest of the war.[209]

Flying was co-opted more sardonically by ground troops like the Anzac Concert Party, *The Sentimental Blokes*, who regularly performed 'Snail's Aeroplane Tour'. This updated version of Tate's sketch combined refined allusions to his comedy, Hendon flying carnivals, commentary on the war, the escapist fantasies that troops articulated in 'Blighty' songs and skits, and the resignation that leave would never arrive and the fighting would never end. For this sketch:

> A ragtime aeroplane is fitted up on the stage and the conductor (Pte Cerise) announces that he takes passengers for a trip around the world for thirty bob. 'The Blokes' all turn up one by one in various characters. The most original and humorous of these is Sergt. Goodall, as an aged, long-bearded Aussie. He asks for a ticket for a seat in the 'plane and explains that he wants to go back to his father's prickly pear farm in Australia. 'You're a very old man', says the conductor, as he hands him a ticket. 'Ah, yes' replies the ancient one in an age-shaken voice, 'I'm very

very old now – In fact I'm due for my first leave. I'm No. 9 – I've been through everything!' Later, the conductor announces that the 'plane is passing over Australia. 'I
want to get out here!' cries the old Aussie, excitedly. 'You can't get out it's deadly poi-
sonous!' 'Why?' 'One Drop will kill you!' Is that a shell hole down there? asks one of
'The Blokes' 'Oh no; that's "Our Harbour". The announcement 'We are now over
Footsoray' gets everybody busy. Old Aussie puts up a record getting into his gas mask
and the others do a humorous nose-pinching performance.[210]

Meanwhile, Tate's work continued to resonate in the front-line trenches as an
immediate solace for men who had seen routine chores upset by horrific
chaos. For example, subaltern Guy Chapman, after seeing the busy intersec-
tion of trenches named Leicester Square and Piccadilly Circus turned into a
charnel-house by a bomb, returned to his dug-out which now 'looked less
impervious, as we censored letters, played Canfield, and listened to Harry
Tate on soldiering'.[211] Despite this prosaic use of Tate's comedy, troops never
lost sight of the way his humour could be used as a commentary on situations
they faced at the front. At the start of the Germans' final offensive, in March
1918, the officers of an artillery battery that was about to be overrun decided
on an appropriate salute for the invaders. Before leaving the dug-out, a
recording of Harry Tate singing 'The watch on the Rhine' was placed on the
gramophone.[212] The Germans would not have realised the defiance embodied
in Tate's voice. This may not have been a conventional martial sentiment, but
to the troopers evacuating the position it indicated that though the war had
suddenly become terrifically chaotic, they, like Tate, would eventually
triumph.

A final, brilliant appropriation of Tate's comedy is worth noting. In the
summer of 1917 a Canadian horse carnival included 'a clever Harry Tate
inspired skit on local transportation (½ moke power)'.[213] This skit may have
been the one recalled by private Ernest Black who remembered a mule-driver,
called Happy, enlivening sports meetings in the summer of 1918 with a topical
version of *Motoring*. In this skit, Happy rode his mule about the crowded pitch,
until it stopped abruptly. He then dismounted and lay on his back beneath the
animal, mimicking the actions, 'then common with cranky motor cars', of
someone inspecting the engine and undercarriage. Once satisfied that he had
resolved the problem, Happy restarted the mule's engine by cranking its tail,
before riding away.[214] These two sketches had seized on Tate's habit of quoting
the power of the engines of his cars and planes in 'moke' or donkey power. Men
accustomed to driving temperamental mules, rather than automobiles, must
have appreciated this up-to-date sketch.

Once updated, Tate's rather simple sketches encompassed and articulated fighting men's experiences. Tanks broke down inopportunely, or were destroyed by shells. Driving them was sweltering, dangerous and about as enjoyable as the trip depicted in *Motoring*. Meanwhile, men who saw tanks endowed them with the dull qualities of large slow-moving land animals, or overweight music-hall and pantomime performers. Paradoxically, the RE8's inability to turn quickly made it an easy mark for artillery or enemy pilots, while its mechanical deficiencies made it deadly to fly. Mules are headstrong and difficult to control. Their drivers must have seen how like they were to early motor-cars.

The fates of these three men mirrored their wartime activities. Chaplin, the reluctant patriot, was banished from the United States in 1952 for his left-wing political views. He was not permitted to return until 1973. In his homeland, Chaplin was denied a knighthood until 1975. As a reward for his war work, Lauder was dubbed Sir Harry in 1919, proclaimed himself the 'first knight of music hall' and toured the world relentlessly playing his maudlin songs until his death in 1950. Tate continued to appear in music halls, revues and pantomimes. After seeing him in the revue *Box o' Tricks* at the Hippodrome in May 1918, Virginia Woolf wrote that Tate embodied English humour.[215] Despite such encomiums, Tate's was, increasingly, a nostalgia act, for *Motoring* could not be updated indefinitely. Nevertheless, Tate toured the skit relentlessly until he was killed, appositely, in an air raid in 1940.

First World War military recreation differed significantly from the brawling, violent alcoholic world of Victorian soldiers, who had garrisoned pestilential imperial outposts. Even though press gangs had disappeared, and the 21-year enlistment had been abolished by the end of the century, only the most desperate men joined up, because accepting such a post meant divorcing oneself permanently from normal, civilian life. Armies raised in war time are different, as a significant number of their members, from privates to generals are men without pronounced military ambition. Though they might never have contemplated military careers, men enlisted in 1914 for a definite purpose: to defeat the Germans quickly, before returning, heroically bemedalled, to homes, families and jobs. Each of these goals proved evanescent: the war dragged on past Christmas, medals were mired by the Flanders mud, and 'Blighty' seemed a distant place reached by none save the most gravely wounded.

Despite their reasons for joining, few of these men were as abstemious or as chaste as Robert Graves. Drinking, gambling and whoring were prevalent in the allied forces. However, they alone could not provide the recreation sought by a citizen army. None of these activities allowed troopers to connect with their homes and 'real' civilian existences, which seemed so distant.[216] It is far too reductionist to argue that men fought for Harry Tate or Harry Lauder, but the topical culture these men embodied consoled and comforted troopers, and thereby helped to make protracted trench fighting endurable. References to such men brought something of the homes troopers had left to the trenches. This widely diffused popular reaction to the war was in some places sanctioned directly by authorities, while in others, military leaders simply tolerated cultural activities.

The prevalence of music-hall allusions was novel, but sport had long been a part of military life. However, in the decades before 1914 sport had become 'entertainment'. Tottenham Hotspur had been the first southern professional side to win the FA Cup, just as the Boer War ended. From that point forward London and the provinces had regularly hosted comic football carnivals, which had included such 'professional' footballers as George Robey, Billy Wells and My Fancy. London had broadcast these links to the world. The links between serious Lonsdale boxing champions and music-hall boxing buffoonery had been closer still. First World War military sport, both in London and on the battle front, mirrored this relationship between serious competition and comedy, while wartime baseball, like its earlier incarnations, remained a sport for expatriate North Americans.

Notes

1 Jon Lawrence, 'The First World War and its aftermath', in Paul Johnson (ed.), *Twentieth Century Britain: Economic, Social and Cultural Change*, London, Longman, 1994, p. 151. For a personal reaction to the Kitchener posters see Harold Macmillan, *Winds of Change 1914–1939*, London, Macmillan, 1966, p. 60.

2 John Keegan, *The Face of Battle*, Harmondsworth, Penguin, 1983, p. 220, and Jay Winter and Jean-Louis Robert, *Capital Cities at War: Paris, London, Berlin, 1914–1919*, Cambridge, Cambridge University Press, 1997, p. 68.

3 C. E. Jacomb, *Torment*, London, Andrew Melrose, 1920, p. 76.

4 J. C. Manion, *A Surgeon in Arms*, New York, D. Appleton, 1918, p. 6.

5 Frederick Palmer, *My Year of the Great War*, Toronto, McClelland, 1916, pp. 304–305; John Masefield, *The Old Front Line*, Bourne End, Bucks, Spurbooks, 1972, p. 89; Macmillan, *Winds of Change*, pp. 83–84.

6 Eric Partridge, 'Frank Honywood, Private', in R. H. Mottram, John Easton and Eric Partridge *Three Personal Records of The War*, London, Scholartis Press, 1929, p. 327.

7   Richard Slobodin *W. H. R. Rivers*, Stroud, Sutton, 1997, *passim*.

8   R. H. Mottram, 'A Personal Record', in Mottram, Easton and Partridge, Three Personal Records, p. 102; for the rotation schedule see Keegan, *Face of Battle*, p. 212.

9   Palmer, *My Year*, pp. 224–225; R. A. L., *Letters of a Canadian Stretcher-Bearer*, Toronto, T. Allen, 1918, p. 214.

10 Ian Hay, *All In It: K(1) Carries On*, Toronto, W. Briggs, 1917, p. 73.

11 Desmond Morton, *When Your Number's Up*, Toronto, University of Toronto Press, 1993, pp. 3–21; John Rhode, *With the Guns By F.O.O.*, London, Eveleigh Nash, 1916, pp. 201–202.

12 Anonymous, *Death in the Air*, London, Greenhill, 1933, pp. 14–29, 39, 57, 79; John Dow, 48th Highlanders, Oral History Interview Transcript, Canadian Broadcasting Corporation fonds, National Archives of Canada, Tape 3, p. 18.

13 Anonymous, *Death in the Air*, pp. 64, 93, 119; Arthur Gould Lee, *No Parachute: A Fighter Pilot in World War I*, London, Arrow Books, 1968, pp. 17, 25.

14 For the quote see Lee, *No Parachute*, p. 59; John Glubb, *Into Battle: A Soldier's Diary of the Great War*, London, Cassell, 1978, p. 85; Anonymous, *Death in the Air*, p. 99; and Denis Winter, *First of the Few: Fighter Pilots of the First World War*, London, Allen Lane, 1983, pp. 174–191.

15 Manion, *Surgeon in Arms*, pp. 53–55. Also John Brophy and Eric Partridge, *Songs and Slang of the British Soldier: 1914–1918*, London, André Deutsch, 1930, pp. 105, 124, 126.

16 Brophy and Partridge, *Songs and Slang*, p. 93.

17 'Rumour has it', *The Gasper*, 15, 15 March 1916, unnumbered pages.

18 George Coppard, *With a Machine Gun to Cambrai*, London, Papermac, 1986, p. 55.

19 Brophy and Partridge, *Songs and Slang*, p. 26.

20 Arch Whitehouse, *The Fledgling: An Aerial Gunner in World War I – the Epic of a Volunteer Airman*, London, Nicholas Vane, 1965, pp. 52, 61, 65 and 70. Whitehouse had come from New Jersey to fight and was aware of who Karno was, because of the Mummers' American tours.

21 Harry Lauder, *A Minstrel in France*, London, Andrew Melrose, 1918, p. 226; The quote about Scotland comes from Paul Jones, *War Letters of a Public-School Boy*, London, Cassell, 1918, p. 47.

22 'Songs and their singers', *The Mudhook*, 1. 2, September 1917, unnumbered pages.

23 Guy Chapman, *A Passionate Prodigality*, London, Mayflower, 1967, p. 248.

24 Chapman, *Passionate Prodigality*, p. 210.

25 See for instance Stanley A. Rutledge, *Pen Pictures from the Trenches*, Toronto, W. Briggs, 1918, p. 66.

26 'Halte-la, The rag-time army', *The Jackass*, 5, October 1918, p. 11; 'He's a ragtime soldier', Brophy and Partridge, *Songs and Slang*, p. 65.

27 Brophy and Partridge, *Songs and Slang*, pp. 161, 154, 155.

28 Brophy and Partridge, *Songs and Slang*, p. 125; Hay, *All In It*, pp. 12 and 33.

29 For examples of the use of the words Jack Johnson, see Whitehouse, *Fledgling*, pp. 91, 225, and Palmer, *My Year*, p. 230; R. A. L., *Letters*, p. 262; 'Cricket! Eh What!',

The Listening Post, 6, 20 October 1915, unnumbered pages; F. McKelvey Bell, *The First Canadians in France*, Toronto, McClelland, Goodchild and Stewart, 1917, p. 287.

30 'A matter of taste', *The Gasper*, 14, 28 February 1916, unnumbered pages.

31 Eric Partridge, *A Dictionary of Slang and Unconventional English*, Vol. 1, London, Penguin, 1974, pp. 53, 362, 430.

32 Malcolm Brown, *Tommy Goes to War*, London, J. M. Dent, 1978, pp. 170–171; *The Year 1916 Illustrated*, London, no stated publisher, 1916, p. 119.

33 William Redmond, *Trench Pictures from France*, London, Andrew Melrose, 1917, pp. 35–38; Hay, *All In It*, pp. 41–43; Masefield, *Old Front Line*, pp. 75, 97; Peter Liddle, *Testimony of War 1914–1918*, Salisbury, Michael Russell, 1979, p. 54.

34 Keegan, *Face of Battle*, pp. 211–212.

35 Macmillan, *Winds of Change*, p. 94.

36 Lee, *No Parachute*, pp. 6, 25–26, 73, 75, 59, 140, 142; Glubb, *Into Battle*, pp. 36–41; for 'Tipperary' updated by a Canadian NCO to declare his desire to be at home on the prairie, see Anonymous, *Oh Canada, A Medley of Stories, Verse, Pictures and Music Contributed by Members of the Canadian Expeditionary Force*, London, Simpkin Marshall, 1917, pp. 73–74; Eric Scott (ed.), *Nobody Ever Wins a War: The World War I Diaries of Ella Mae Bongard, R.N.*, Ottawa, Janeric, 1998, p. 17; Patrick MacGill, *The Red Horizon*, London, Caliban, 1916, pp. 36, 40–55; C.M. Bowra, *Memories, 1898–1939*, London, Weidenfield and Nicolson, 1966, p. 82; Coppard, *Machine-gun*, p. 9; 'Entertainments', Cinque Ports Gazette, 1, May 1916, unnumbered pages; 'Nonsense parodies – with apologies to the filbert', *The Leadswinger*, 16 October 1915, p. 20.

37 Connigsby Dawson, *The Glory of the Trenches: An Interpretation*, Toronto, Gundy, 1918, p. 70.

38 J. B. Priestley, *Margin Released*, London, Heinemann, 1962, pp. 110–111.

39 Whitehouse, *The Fledgling*, pp. 166–167. Another mention of music-hall tunes is found in Edward D. Toland, *The Aftermath of Battle: With the Red Cross in France*, New York, Macmillan, 1916, pp. 8 and 14; and Martin Middlebrook, *The First Day on the Somme*, London, Allen Lane, 1971, pp. 105 and 238.

40 Anonymous, *Death in the Air*, p. 2.

41 Priestley, *Margin Released*, pp. 110–111, see also R. A. L., *Letters*, p. 4; 'A Christmas concert', *Hangar Happenings*, Christmas 1917, p. 9. For a non-musical evocation of the 'Blighty' see Bruce Bairnsfather, *Fragments from France*, London, Bystander, 1917, unnumbered pages.

42 *Oh Canada*, p. 27.

43 Dawson, *Glory*, p. 38.

44 Glubb, *Into Battle*, p. 36.

45 Robert Graves, *Goodbye to All That*, Harmondsworth, Penguin, 1976, pp. 89–90.

46 L.C. Collins, *Theatre at War, 1914–1918*, Basingstoke, Macmillan, 1998, pp. 22–23.

47 'Variety gossip', *The Era*, 3 November 1915, p. 10.

48 Philip Ziegler, *King Edward VIII*, London, Fontana, 1990, p. 52.

49 Claude Grahame-White and Harry Harper, *Aircraft in the Great War*, London, T. Fisher Unwin, 1915, pp. 60–673.

50 'Theatrical gossip', *The Era*, 6 October 1915, p. 10; and 'Theatrical gossip', *The Era*, 13 October 1915, p. 10. Winter, *First of the Few*, p. 35.

51 Winifred Loraine, *Robert Loraine: Soldier, Actor, Airman*, London, Collins, 1938, p. 210–245.

52 Cecil Lewis, *Sagittarius Rising*, London, Peter Davies, 1936, p. 7; Loraine, *Robert Loraine*, p. 179.

53 Matthew Paris, 'The rise of the airmen: the origins of Air Force elitism, c.1890–1918', *Journal of Contemporary History*, 28 (1993), pp. 123–141.

54 Coningsby Dawson, *Living Bayonets*, London, John Lane, 1919, pp. 69–70; '"The Prime Minister of Mirth" Mr. George Robey's war-time activities', *The Illustrated Sporting and Dramatic News*, 6 April 1918, p. 149; Collins, *Theatre*, p. 50; William Waldie Murray, *Five Nines and Whiz Bangs*, Ottawa, Legionary Library, 1937, p. 16; Sarah Street, *British National Cinema*, London, Routledge, 1997, p. 118.

55 See for instance 'Jessop still making hits! The famous cricketer appealing for recruits', *The Illustrated Sporting and Dramatic News*, 1 May 1915, p. 233.

56 Jones, *War Letters*, p. 51; 'Concerts', *The Fifth Glos'ter Gazette*, 22, March 1918, p. 8. Also, 'The third Canadian field ambulance minstrel troupe', *Now and Then*, 15 December 1915, p. 7; 'Patients enjoy concert', Scott, *Nobody Ever Wins a War*, p. 18.

57 Bell, *First Canadians*, p. 97.

58 Chapman, *Passionate Prodigality*, p. 25.

59 'Round the Theatres', *The Illustrated Sporting and Dramatic News*, 9 January 1915, p. 546; Collins, *Theatre*, pp. 44–45; For the quote see Ellaline Terriss, *By Herself and With Others*, London, Cassell, 1928, p. 212. See also Ellaline Terriss, 'The Fresh Air Fund – What it is and what it does', *The Dagger*, 2, February 1919, p. 11.

60 'Variety Gossip', *The Era*, 14 February 1917, p. 14.

61 *The Times Illustrated History of the War*, Vol. 4, London, Times Newspapers, 1920, pp. 49–56.

62 Lena Ashwell, *Myself a Player*, London, Michael Joseph, 1936, p. 194–208; Untitled, *The Era*, 23 August 1916, p. 12; Edwyn Campion Vaughan, *Some Desperate Glory: The Diary of a Young Officer, 1917*, London, Macmillan, 1981, p. 11.

63 'Aussie field theatres', *Aussie*, 5, June 1918, p. 16.

64 Rutledge, *Pen Pictures*, p. 100. See also Untitled, *The Dump*, 2, Christmas 1916, unnumbered pages; 'Pantomime', *The Standard of C Company*, July 1918, p. 7.

65 '"Sandbag the Spader" our topical pantomime', *The Leadswinger*, Christmas 1915, pp. 17–23.

66 'Theatrical notes', *Chronicles of the White Horse*, 2, April 1917, p. 10.

67 'Theatrical gossip', *The Era*, 17 November 1915, p. 10; Also Toland, *Aftermath of Battle*, pp. 161–162. *Cinque Ports Gazette*, 1 May 1916, unnumbered pages; 'The minstrel troupe', *Now and Then*, 1, 15 December 1915, p. 1. Also 'A Christmas concert', *Hangar Happenings*, Christmas 1917, p. 9; 'Variety gossip', *The Era*, 1

November 1916, p. 14; 'A Section notes', *The Iodine Chronicle,* 5, 20 January 1916, p. 2.

68 William Boyd, *With a Field Ambulance at Ypres*, New York, G. H. Doran, 1916, pp. 32-33. 'The soldiers' theatre in France', *The Illustrated Sporting and Dramatic News*, 11 September 1915, p. 38.

69 Jones, *War Letters*, p. 133.

70 'The soldiers' theatre in France', *The Illustrated Sporting and Dramatic News*, 11 September 1915, p. 38.

71 Martin Gilbert, *In Search of Churchill: A Historian's Journey*, London, Harper Collins, 1994 , pp. 94–95. See also 'A sector notes', *Iodine Chronicle*, 5, 20 January 1916, p. 2.

72 Ernest D. Swinton, *A Year Ago: An Eyewitness Narrative of the War from March 30th to July 18th 1915*, London, Edward Arnold, 1916, p. 44.

73 Untitled, *Aussie* 3, 8 March 1918, unnumbered pages.

74 Leslie Henson, *Yours Faithfully: an Autobiography*, London, John Long, 1947, pp. 59–71.

75 Lyn MacDonald, *To The Last Man: Spring 1918*, London, Viking, 1998, pp. 140–141.

76 'Variety gossip', *The Era*, 19 April 1916, p. 14; 'Variety gossip', *The Era,* 29 November 1916, p. 14. Stan Shipley, *Bombardier Billy Wells: The Life and Times of a Boxing Hero*, Whitley Bay, Berwick, 1993, pp. 131– 138; 'Liverpool Christmas', *Kamp Knews*, 22, 1917, p. 5; 'Football notes', *The Minden Magazine*, 1, November 1915, p. 4; 'Ranji out – at the front', *The Illustrated Sporting and Dramatic News*, 20 March 1915, p. 1; 'Sports gossip', *Dead Horse Corner Gazette*, 2, December 1915, p. 24; 'Sports gossip', *Dead Horse Corner Gazette*, 3, June 1916, p. 35.

77 Jones, *War Letters*, pp. 124, 136, 233; 'Sporting notes', *The Jackass*, June 1918, p. 15; 'Rugby', *The Fifth Glos'ter Gazette*, 15, October 1916, unnumbered pages; 'Football – Rugby', *The Fifth Glos'ter Gazette*, 16, December 1916, unnumbered pages. 'Football', *The Fifth Glos'ter Gazette*, 22, March 1918, p. 10; 'Sporting notes', *The Jackass*, June 1918, p. 15; Hay, *All In It*, pp. 81–83.

78 James Walvin, *The People's Game: The History of Football Revisited*, Edinburgh, Mainstream, 1994, pp. 92–95; Mason, *Association Football and English Society, 1863–1915,* Brighton, Harvester, 1980, pp. 251–255. The quote is from Mason, *Association Football*, p. 255; Michael MacDonagh, *In London During the Great War: The Diary of a Journalist*, London, Eyre and Spottiswoode, 1935, p. 44.

79 'Variety gossip', *The Era*, 20 September 1916, p. 14; 'Variety gossip', *The Era,* 4 October 1916, p. 14; 'An army team v. Essex soccer match at Leytonstone', *The Illustrated Sporting and Dramatic News*, 24 February 1917, p. 734; Glubb, *Into Battle*, pp. 160–163.

80 For the Worthington munition girl's football team see Liddle, *Testimony,* p. 71. See also 'A patriotic fete at Wembley to entertain wounded soldiers', *The Illustrated Sporting and Dramatic News*, 14 August 1915, p. 681; 'The fair sex at football at Portsmouth', *The Illustrated Sporting and Dramatic News*, 9 December 1916,

p. 425; 'A football team of women munition workers in the London district', *The Illustrated Sporting and Dramatic News*, 3 February 1917, p. 668; 'An unbeaten team of munition lady footballers', *The Illustrated Sporting and Dramatic News*, 16 February 1918, p. 734. Men wearing gas masks while they played football were found in 'Royal Engineers in training', *The Illustrated Sporting and Dramatic News*, 17 February 1917, p. 716; and 'Gas mask football', *The Illustrated Sporting and Dramatic News*, 30 March 1918, p. 117.

81 Percy M. Young, *A History of British Football*, London, Paul, 1969, p. 167.

82 Chapman, *Passionate Prodigality*, p. 274.

83 'Football notes', *Cinque Ports Gazette*, 1 May 1916, unnumbered pages Also Hay, *All In It*, p. 29; 'Football notes', *The Minden Magazine*, 2, October 1915, pp. 4–6; 'Football', *718*, 1, September 1916, p. 17; 'What we would like to know', *The Splint Record*, December 1915, p. 4; 'Football with the Lowland Sigs', *White and Blue*, 1.1, March 1918, p. 1.

84 Boyd, *Field Ambulance*, p. 56.

85 Whitehouse, *Fledgling*, pp. 42–43; Vaughan, *Desperate Glory*, p. 8; MacGill, *Red Horizon*, p. 65; James A. Kilpatrick, *Atkins at War, as Told in His Own Letters*, London, Herbert Jenkins, 1914, p. 35.

86 'Football notes', *The Leadswinger*, 16 October 1915, p. 7; 'Football', *The Gasper*, 17, 29 April 1916, unnumbered pages; 'Football notes', *Chronicles of the White Horse*, April 1917, p. 3.

87 William Duncan Geare, *Letters of an Army Chaplain*, London, Wells and Gardner, 1918, pp. 79.

88 Glubb, *Into Battle*, pp. 79 and 94.

89 Stanley W. Coxon, *Dover During the Dark Days*, London, John Lane, 1919, p. 140.

90 'Football notes', *Cinque Ports Gazette*, 1 May 1916, unnumbered pages.

91 'Sport gossip', *Dead Horse Corner Gazette*, 3, June 1916, p. 29.

92 Brown, *Tommy Goes to War*, pp. 170–171.

93 Keegan, *Face of Battle*, p. 250.

94 'Boxing sports', *The Fifth Glos'ter Gazette*, 13, July 1916, unnumbered pages.

95 Jimmy Wilde, *Fighting Was My Business*, London, Michael Joseph, 1938, pp. 141–145; 'Variety gossip', *The Era*, 23 August 1916, p. 12.

96 'Cloth Hall, Ypres', *The Wipers Times or Salient News*, 1.1, 12 February 1916, unnumbered pages.

97 Al-Tony Gilmore, *Bad Nigger!: The National Impact of Jack Johnson*, Port Washington, New York, Kennikat, 1975, pp. 133–135. Also Nat Fleischer, *Fifty Years at Ringside*, New York, Fleet, 1940, pp. 82–86.

98 'A first-class fighting man', *The Illustrated Sporting and Dramatic News*, 8 May 1915, p. 260; Shipley, *Billy Wells*, p. 81.

99 'The naval and military bank holiday carnival at Stamford Bridge', *The Illustrated Sporting and Dramatic News*, 7 August 1915, p. 644.

100 Shipley, *Billy Wells*, pp. 114–135.

101 Jones, *War Letters*, p. 178; R. A. L., *Letters*, p. 133; 'Sport in the British navy', *The Illustrated Sporting and Dramatic News*, 9 Oct 1915, p. 153; 'A boxing match

behind the lines', *The Illustrated Sporting and Dramatic News*, 11 November 1916, p. 287; 'Keeping fit on board a troopship', *The Illustrated Sporting and Dramatic News*, 18 November 1916, p. 317; 'Army Service Corps sports in Kent', *The Illustrated Sporting and Dramatic News*, 29 June 1918, p. 493.

102 'A London Scottish Battalion's boxing tournament on the British western front', *The Illustrated Sporting and Dramatic News*, 20 April 1918, p. 203.

103 '8th Battalion National Sporting Club', *The Listening Post*, 8, 25 October 1915, p. 32.

104 'Variety gossip', *The Era*, 31 May 1916, p. 18; 'Variety gossip', *The Era*, 24 May 1916, p. 14.

105 'Sports gossip', *Dead Horse Corner Gazette*, 2, December 1915, p. 15.

106 Untitled, *The Leadswinger*, 19 March 1916, p. 3.

107 Shipley, *Billy Wells*, p. 142.

108 Reginald H. Roy (ed.), *The Journal of Private Fraser, 1914–1918, Canadian Expeditionary Force*, Victoria, B.C., Sono Nis, 1985, p. 246.

109 Alexis Philotenko, *Histoire de la Boxe*, Paris, Critérion, 1991, p. 241.

110 Chapman, *Passionate Prodigality*, p. 253.

111 Chapman, *Passionate Prodigality*, p. 253.

112 Wilde, *Fighting*, p. 131.

113 'Battalion boxing tournament', *Fifth Glos'ter Gazette*, 23, July 1918, p. 18.

114 'The Whizz-Bangs', *The Jackass*, 5, October 1918, pp. 2–3.

115 'Open air boxing at an aeronautical school near London', *The Illustrated Sporting and Dramatic News*, 22 June 1918, p. 463.

116 'Wilde V. Conn – The victory of the "Mighty Atom"', *The Illustrated Sporting and Dramatic News*, 7 September 1918, p. 10.

117 Chapman, *Passionate Prodigality*, p. 258; R. A. L., *Letters*, p, 61; John Dow, 48th Highlanders, Oral History Interview Transcript, Canadian Broadcasting Corporation fonds, National Archives of Canada, Volume 21, tape 2, p. 11; 'Sports gossip', *Dead Horse Corner Gazette*, 2, December 1915, p. 15; 'Sports gossip', *Dead Horse Corner Gazette*, 3, June 1916, p. 29; Lester B. Pearson, *Mike: The Memoirs of the Right Honourable Lester B. Pearson*, Toronto, University of Toronto Press, 1972, p. 59.

118 Frederick Palmer, *My Second Year of the War*, Toronto, McClelland, 1917, p. 330.

119 'Baseball in the Strand', *The Illustrated Sporting and Dramatic News*, 23 March 1918, p. 102.

120 'Soldiers at play', *The Illustrated Sporting and Dramatic News*, 12 June 1915, p. 420; 'Baseball game at Queen's Club', *The Illustrated Sporting and Dramatic News*, 14 October 1916, p. 177; Tony Lewis, *Double Century: The Story of the MCC and Cricket*, London, Hodder and Stoughton, 1987, p. 190.

121 'The opening match of the Anglo-American baseball league at Highbury', *The Illustrated Sporting and Dramatic News*, 25 May 1918, p. 344.

122 'The Independence Day baseball match at Stamford Bridge', *The Illustrated Sporting and Dramatic News*, 13 July 1918, p. 557.

123 Niall Ferguson, *The Pity of War*, London, Allen Lane, 1999, pp. 174–212.

124 Andrew Davies, 'Cinema and broadcasting', in Paul Johnson (ed.), *Twentieth Century Britain: Economic, Social and Cultural Change*, London, Longman, 1994, p. 269. See also the early chapters of Jeffrey Richards, *The Age of the Dream Palace: Cinema and Society in Britain, 1930–1939*, London, Routledge, 1984.

125 Geoffrey Malins, *How I Filmed the War*, London, Herbert Jenkins, 1920, pp. 4, 40 and 44.

126 Malins, *How I Filmed*, pp. 10–12.

127 Malins, *How I Filmed*, pp. 14–15.

128 Malins, *How I Filmed*, pp. 61–64.

129 Malins, *How I Filmed*, p. 66.

130 Nicholas Reeves, 'Through the eye of the camera: contemporary cinema audiences and their 'experience' of war in the film *Battle of the Somme*', in Hugh Cecil and Peter Liddle (eds), *Facing Armageddon*, London, Leo Cooper, 1996, p. 781.

131 Malins, *How I Filmed*, pp. 91–92, 108.

132 Keegan, *Face of Battle*, p. 216.

133 Keegan, *Face of Battle*, p. 285.

134 Nicholas Reeves, 'Cinema, spectatorship and propaganda: Battle of the Somme (1916) and its contemporary audience', *Historical Journal of Film, Radio and Television*, 17.1 (March 1997), p. 13.

135 Hiley, as quoted in Reeves, 'Cinema, spectatorship', p. 8. Also S.D. Badsey, '*Battle of the Somme*: British war-propaganda', *Historical Journal of Film, Radio and Television*, 3.2 (1983), p. 99; also Reeves, 'Cinema spectatorship', pp. 14–15.

136 Reeves, 'Cinema spectatorship', p. 18.

137 Reeves, 'Through the eye of the camera', pp. 781–793.

138 Masefield, *Old Front Line*, p. 103.

139 W. Heath Robinson, *Hunlikely!*, London, Duckworth, 1916, pp. 42–53.

140 Malins, *How I Filmed*, p. 45.

141 See for instance see Advertisement, *The Era*, 27 October 1915, p. 2; also Modris Eksteins, *Rites of Spring: The Great War and the Birth of the Modern Age*, Toronto, Lester Orpen and Dennys 1989, pp. 95–131 and 208–227.

142 David Robinson, *Chaplin: His Life and Art*, London, Collins, 1985, p. 130.

143 For the first see Middlebrook, *First Day*, p 110; for the second see Glubb, *Into Battle*, p. 91; Roy, *Journal*, p. 240; Grace Keenan Prince (ed.), *John Patrick Teahan: Diary Kid*, Ottawa, Oberon, 1999, p. 169.

144 Glubb, *Into Battle*, p. 84; and the British Library Catalogue of Printed Music.

145 Alistair Cooke, *Six Men*, New York, Knopf, 1977, p. 29; another version of the song is found in Brophy and Partridge, *Songs and Slang*, p. 38.

146 'Some Chaplinisms', *The Whizz-Bang*, 1, January 1916, p. 7.

147 'Why wear that Charlie Chaplin?', *The B.E.F. Times, with which are Incorporated the Wipers Times or Salient News*, 1.1, 1 December 1916, unnumbered pages.

148 Robinson, *Chaplin*, p. 656.

149 Brophy and Partridge, *Songs and Slang*, p. 210.

150 'Athletics', *The Listening Post*, 20, 20 July 1917, p. 180; Whitehouse, *The Fledgling*, pp. 252–253.

151 'Aussie field theatres', *Aussie*, 1, 18 January 1918, p. 4.

152 'Appreciations of our first issue by noted celebrities (imaginary)', *The Sling*, 2, October 1917, p. 8; Cooke, *Six Men*, pp. 28–30.

153 Robinson, *Chaplin*, p. 656.

154 Robinson, *Chaplin*, p. 656. See also Charles Chaplin, *My Autobiography*, London, Bodley Head, 1964, p. 213.

155 Robinson, *Chaplin,* unnumbered photograph pages. See also Chaplin, *Autobiography*, p. 218.

156 Jay Winter and Blaine Baggett, *The Great War and the Shaping of the Twentieth Century*, London, Penguin Studio, 1996, pp. 142–143.

157 For the first quote see Jones, *War Letters*, p. 143; the second quote is found in Toland, *Aftermath*, p. 13; also Kilpatrick, *Atkins at War*, p. 32.

158 Harry Lauder, *Roamin' in the Gloamin'*, London, Hutchinson, 1928, p. 177.

159 Lauder, *Roamin'*, pp. 179–180.

160 Lauder, *Minstrel*, p. 65.

161 Chapman, *Passionate Prodigality*, p. 120; 'Songs and their singers', *The Listening Post*, 1, 10 August 1915, unnumbered pages; 'Concert notes', *Dead Horse Corner Gazette*, 1, October 1915, p. 8, 'A Company concert', *The Fifth Glos'ter Gazette*, 15, October 1916, unnumbered pages; Jones, *War Letters*, p. 133, Fraser, *Journal*, p. 74; 'Appreciations of our first issue by noted celebrities', *The Sling*, 2, October 1917, p. 8.

162 Glubb, *Into Battle*, p. 96.

163 'The battalion rumourists calendar', *The Listening Post*, 1, 10 August 1915, unnumbered pages; like the concert party song, that when published, was called 'Far frae hame', *Oh Canada*, p. 29; and 'Our entertainers', *The Sling*, 2, October 1917, p. 23; Lauder, *Minstrel*, p. 39.

164 'Australian field theatres', *Aussie*, 4, 4 April 1918, p. 5.

165 Lauder, *Roamin'*, p. 184; Lauder, *Minstrel*, pp. 82–83.

166 Lauder, *Roamin'*, pp. 186–187.

167 Lauder, *Minstrel*, p. 304, and Lauder, *Roamin'*, p. 189.

168 Lauder, *Minstrel*, p. 209.

169 Lauder, *Roamin'*, pp. 115, 189, 219.

170 Lauder, *Minstrel*, p. 266. For other examples of troopers play-going while on leave see, David Pierce Beatty (ed.), *Memories of a Forgotten War: The World War I Diary of Pte. V. E. Goodwin*, Port Elgin, New Brunswick, Baie Verte, 1988, pp. 264–276; R. A. L., *Letters*, pp. 218–220.

171 As quoted in Lyn MacDonald, *They Called it Passchendaele*, London, Joseph, 1978, pp. 56–57.

172 Lauder, *Minstrel*, p. 301.

173 Collins, *Theatre at War*, p. 50.

174 *The Times Illustrated History of the War*, 21, 1920, p. 104.

175 'Stars in Los Angeles', *The Illustrated Sporting and Dramatic News*, 16 March 1918, p. 74.

176 Hay, *All In It*, pp. 22–24.

177 Collins, *Theatre at War*, p. 16.

178 'The trouble of props', *Now and Then*, 1, 15 December 1915, p. 6.

179 'Variety Gossip', *The Era*, 14 June 1916, p. 14.

180 'The Curios', *The Fifth Glos'ter Gazette*, June 1917, unnumbered pages.

181 Palmer, *Second Year*, p. 336.

182 The amount of Churchill's naval commitment to tanks comes from Ernest D. Swinton, *Over My Shoulder*, Oxford, George Ronald, 1951, p. 154; Hubert C. Johnson, *Breakthrough: Tactics, Technology, and the Search for Victory on the Western Front in World War I*, Novato, California, Presidio, 1994, pp. 127–130; John Foley, *The Boilerplate War*, London, Frederick Muller, 1963, p. 7. For the quote see Martin Gilbert, *Winston S. Churchill, Volume III, 1914–1916*, London, Minerva, 1977, p. 538; T. H. E. Travers, 'Future warfare: H. G. Wells and British military theory, 1895–1916', in Brian Bond and Ian Roy (eds), *War and Society: A Yearbook of Military History*, New York, Croom Helm, 1975, pp. 69–73.

183 Ernest D. Swinton, *The Tanks*, London, L.U. Gill, 1916, p. 5. Also Travers, 'Future warfare', pp. 72–73. Like Wells's had been, Swinton's writings on tanks were published in *Strand Magazine*.

184 Jay M. Winter, *The Experience of World War One*, London, Macmillan, 1988, p. 100. For bragging see Palmer, *Second Year*, p. 339; also *The Year 1916 Illustrated*, pp. 167–168.

185 Jacomb, *Torment*, p. 118.

186 MacDonald, *Passchendaele*, p. 38. For the Canadian officer see W. H. F. Elkins, Oral History Interview Transcript, Canadian Broadcasting Corporation fonds, National Archives of Canada, volume 21, tape 1, p. 12. For touching tanks see Palmer, *Second Year*, pp. 340–346.

187 Swinton, *The Tanks*, p. 20.

188 Major H. F. Bidder, Royal Sussex Regiment, as quoted in Lyn MacDonald, *1914–1918: Voices and Images of the Great War*, London, Penguin, 1988, pp. 175–176.

189 Palmer, *Second Year*, pp. 339 and 354. For water tanks see Howard Green, 'The Battle of the Somme', introduction to Masefield, *Old Front Line*, p. 60; and Brophy and Partridge, *Songs and Slang*, p. 169. For 'getting tanked' see John Brophy and Eric Partridge, *The Long Trail: What the British Soldier Sang and Said in the Great War of 1914–1918*, London, André Deutsch, 1965, p. 190.

190 Swinton, *The Tanks*, p. 6.

191 Swinton, *The Tanks*, p. 6.

192 British Library Catalogue of Printed Music.

193 Foley, *Boilerplate War, passim*; and MacDonald, *Passchendaele*, p. 38; see also Fraser, *Journal*, p. 207.

194 Foley, *Boilerplate War*, p. 26.

195 Henry Wickham Steed, *Through Thirty Years*, London, Heinemann, 1924, p. 122.

196 Malins, *How I Filmed*, pp. 222 and 233.

197 Robinson, *Hunlikely!*, pp. 16–31.

198 Photograph, *The Illustrated Sporting and Dramatic News*, 21 October 1916; p. 213; Foley, *Boilerplate War*, p. 21.

199 'Variety Gossip', *The Era*, 18 October 1916, p. 14.

200 'Variety Gossip', *The Era*, 25 October 1916, p. 14.

201 'Guillemont Hippodrome', *The Wipers Times*, 11, 1 December 1916, unnumbered pages. Guillemont was a hill at the Somme which had been the scene of particularly heavy fighting; Martin Gilbert, *The First World War*, London, Weidenfield and Nicolson, 1984, pp. 271–272.

202 Advertisement, *Daily Mail*, 11 January 1917, as reproduced in E.S. Turner, *Dear Old Blighty*, London, Joseph, 1980, unnumbered pages.

203 Foley, 'Cinema spectatorship', p. 12; and British Library Catalogue of Printed Music.

204 Palmer, *Second Year*, pp. 358–359.

205 Foley, *Boilerplate War*, p. 36.

206 Johnson, *Breakthrough*, pp. 136–139.

207 R. A. L., *Letters*, p. 165.

208 E. H. Carroll, Oral History Interview Transcript, Canadian Broadcasting Corporation fonds, National Archives of Canada, volume 21, tape 1, page 7; Alan Clark, *Aces High: War in the Air Over the Western Front 1914–18*, London, Weidenfild and Nicolson, 1973, p. 123.

209 Bowyer, *Encyclopaedia*, p. 45. Until now the nickname has been attributed to rhyming slang: 'Harry Tate' = 'RE8'.

210 'Aussie field theatres', *Aussie*, 1, 18 January 1918, p. 4.

211 Chapman, *Passionate Prodigality*, p. 59.

212 MacDonald, *Last Man*, pp. 140–141.

213 'Athletics', *The Listening Post*, 20, 20 July 1917, p. 180.

214 Ernest G. Black, *I Want One Volunteer*, Toronto, Ryerson, 1965, pp. 41–42.

215 Anne Oliver Bell (ed.), *The Diary of Virginia Woolf: Vol. 1, 1915–1919*, London, Hogarth, 1977, p. 144.

216 Charles Douie, *The Weary Road: Recollections of a Subaltern of Infantry*, London, John Murray, 1929, p. 81.

13

Conclusion

When surveying London's popular culture from the final decades of Victoria's reign to the end of the First World War, one is struck by the continuity. No matter that in this period the world had evolved from the horse-drawn carriage and telegraph to the cinema, flight and the machine gun, or that leisure had become an industry, which advertised to an affluent middle-class. Sensation and public spectacle, which had driven 1860s music hall, were just as central to topical culture in 1918.

However, the paucity of fundamental change in music hall does not indicate stasis. London's popular culture was dynamic, malleable and voracious; it was updated time and time again to incorporate technological, sporting, criminal, political and all manner of other popular crazes. This rampant topicality, the outstanding feature of the popular culture of late-Victorian and Edwardian London, absorbed artistes and developments from throughout Britain and the world. Once incorporated, these elements were broadcast back across the globe thanks to London's position as an imperial and world cultural capital.

London popular culture was, therefore, to a very large degree derivative. Even though ubiquitous London costers like Gus Elen had supplanted swells at the end of the nineteenth century, topical artistes and managers continually incorporated both foreign, and especially American, developments like those introduced to London by Barnum, Sullivan, Cody and Corbett. Provincial sensations such as music-hall sports carnivals also migrated to London. The metropolis adapted itself readily to these new ways of performing, because for every London-bred artiste like Charlie Chaplin or Marie Lloyd many others like R. G. Knowles, George Robey or C. B. Cochran had settled in the city, bringing 'foreign' experiences with them. These new Londoners soon found that up-to-date culture was dynamic and transitory: when baseball failed, players like Eugene Stratton turned their attentions to cricket; when cricket died, George Robey turned to football. A typically London up-to-date culture emerged through this interaction. The evolution of London crazes is clear, though researchers must still illuminate exactly how music-hall sports began.

Though superficially it bore little physical resemblance to beer-soaked mid-Victorian music halls, Edwardian variety entertainment was a conservative institution. By 1914 the halls had been sanitised and professionalised, and yet syndicate directors had, for the most part, trained in music hall. Such men proclaimed their legitimacy with fetishistic links to the past: Oswald Stoll's mother collected tickets in his London halls, as she had done decades earlier in Liverpool; Sara Lane's late husband had opened the Britannia at mid-century; and the octogenarian Charles Morton managed the Palace Theatre in Shaftesbury Avenue. If performances were updated constantly, the structure of the industry in which they were presented had to proclaim its veneration of tradition. London audiences wanted favourite plots, gags and situations brought up-to-date. By and large they did not want anything new. Even though Isadora Duncan's barefoot dancing, Sarah Bernhardt's acting, opera, Diaghilev's Ballets Russes and other refined entertainments were staged in Edwardian London's West End variety theatres, these turns were book-ended by absurd up-to-date artistes.

London's West End halls may have been plush and ostentatious, but the rules by which artistes updated their performances had been laid down by P. T. Barnum and others in the middle of the nineteenth century. Simply, artistes had to link themselves to the latest public craze or sensation each time that they walked on stage. For this reason most celebrities enjoyed only very brief fame. Unicyclists, automatons and other sensational acts could only play for a limited time. Therefore, a history of up-to-date culture reads in part like a laundry list of people who emerged only very briefly to perform fairly unsophisticated acts, before retreating into obscurity. Having tasted success, some artistes tried again and again to secure it once more. J. W. Rowley had turned somersaults on stage in the 1870s, and forty years later, when he could hardly have presented a youthful image, he sang a football song in the halls. The ability to sing, swagger, tumble or tell a joke took many years to master, but topicality had to be studied, practised and perfected much more quickly. Preordaining some performers to obscurity does not negate their importance in the study of popular culture. There were simply dozens of aspirants for every Robey, Lauder or Chaplin. We may never have anything more than a crude understanding of their psychological motivations or personal histories, but this procession of obscure performers emphasises how important topicality is to understanding music hall.

Few artistes mastered up-to-dateness as completely as did Harry Tate or George Robey who reforged their public identities by shedding out-of-date performances. Robey was, at almost the same time, the automobile of comic singers, the football comedian, a Piltdown-inspired caveman, a music-hall boxer and a predictor of the future uses of aeroplanes. Harry Tate mastered celebrity better than any other performer thanks to a linear progression through successive technological changes from *Motoring*, to *Flying* and *Tank* sketches. *Motoring* was sustained by the public's unceasing love for the motor-car while as flying became safer and more common it became less sensational, and the terrible losses of 1916 soon robbed the tank of its comic qualities. Despite his remarkable ability to master up-to-dateness, Tate has been forgotten. Unlike almost all performers he left very few autobiographical clues, while his recordings and films are hard to find. After the war Tate performed his old routines in revue, film and pantomime.

This mastery of up-to-date culture was the basis of celebrity. However, topical performance demanded a balance of talent and humility, because the London public most often perceived that any attempt to master a second field of endeavour was done as a joke. Therefore, Robey and Colonel Cody were dismayed by their inability to convince the public about their talents in areas other than those which had made them famous. Billy Wells had no such reservations, happily alternating between title fights, carrying jockeys on his back, or boxing young Willy Sanders. Such good-humoured self-mockery is an uncommon trait. Though he was one of the most beloved performers of his day, Billy Wells's importance as a celebrity as opposed to a boxer has also been obscured. Wells continued fighting after the war, lost the British crown in 1919, tried his hand at sculling, sports journalism and played a boxer in *The Ring*, one of Alfred Hitchcock's earliest films. Eventually he retired to run a small hotel where legions of young London fighters like Henry Cooper came to pay their respects. If remembered at all today, Billy Wells is recalled as the man clad in a loincloth who rang the gong at the start of films made by the J. Arthur Rank studio.

Celebrity was always a personal characteristic of individual artistes, but it was supported by the emergence of the professional entertainment industry. Managers like Karno, Cochran and McIntosh were Barnum's true heirs in the way that they married topical sensations to the precepts of melodrama. Football, cycling, boxing and airship plays followed the same basic pantomime plot of good versus evil. Audiences must have known the parameters of these plots before the curtain rose, but this did not matter, because people had come to see sensational representations of the latest public crazes.

Modern celebrity emerged only after London entertainment had been professionalised and 'commodified'. Professional football clubs developed close relationships with the halls in Scotland and the midlands during the 1890s, and in London after the turn of the century. Because they relied on inchoate professional structures, neither baseball nor cricket was able to develop such a sustained relationship with the halls. When a sport ceased to be topical it was replaced. Yet the entertainment provided at these events changed very little. Harry Tate motored round the pitch at Leno's cricket matches, but flew his exploding plane at Hendon fifteen years later. The cycling, motoring and aeroplane industries were not set up for 'entertainment'. They, like so many briefly sensational performers saw association with the halls as an opportunity to expand business and profits. An exception to this rule was Grahame-White's London Aerodrome, which, with its refreshment rooms, ragtime flying, races, theme days and West End ticket office, resembled nothing so much as a music hall.

Therefore, like the Tottenham schoolboy John Bolitho who had felt surrounded by imperialism, so must many Londoners have felt enveloped by topical music hall. From the days of Tom Thumb, Leybourne, and Henry Mayhew's street singers, much up-to-date culture was public. Thanks to Barnum and Leybourne the streets were advertising venues in which music-hallers were to be seen constantly. At mid-century music hall had no rival as a popular entertainment industry, but as new types of venues, like football stadiums or the London Aerodrome, emerged they were co-opted into up-to-date public performance. Having insinuated itself into sport, technology, cinema and recorded music, up-to-date music-hall idioms pervaded the capital. During wars, diplomatic disputes or political crises these idioms might be belligerent and bellicose, however, such episodes were as brief as any up-to-date allusion.

Topicality made popular culture accessible to many of those who did not possess the price of admission to the halls. Seeing Marie Lloyd or Harry Tate on stage must have been a rare treat for many Londoners. However, one could watch any number of music-hall troupes parading the streets, hear the latest tunes played by organ grinders, or watch professional football teams practising in parks. If the most successful up-to-date artistes rarely played halls in London's poorest areas, their aspiring imitators included the latest sensations in topical performances throughout the capital. Celebrities must rarely have tread on people's toes in the streets, though they were not so physically distant that the majority of Londoners did not have some relationship with them.

Given their responsibilities for running the home, and unequal opportunities for paid employment, adult women may have had more restricted access to up-to-date culture. They would probably have been able to see this culture's public facets, but their access to professional entertainment would have been more limited. No matter their access, women were depicted most often in condescending roles. Either their sexuality was emphasised – as with women cyclists and footballers, La Belle Titcombe, or Marie Lloyd, who it was said could wring innuendo out of any lyric – or they were extolled as steadfast companions, as in songs such as 'My old Dutch'. Meanwhile, women's supposed illogical and impetuous nature commonly caused the hero's misfortunes and the country's peril in up-to-date melodramas. Female artistes could update their acts most easily through emphasising these bawdy characteristics. Even though female artistes earned as much as their male counterparts, up-to-date culture was not an avenue down which they would achieve social equality.

At times music hall provided a resounding voice for the ugliest intractable popular fears and aggression, but it was always, and in at least equal measure, mawkish, ridiculous and absurd. This latter feature of up-to-date culture cemented its position for the troops in the First World War. The metropolis proved to be amongst the most fertile British grounds for recruiting. The preponderance of Londoners in uniform meant that a good portion of the services possessed a lifetime's intimacy with the city's popular culture. In addition, the city's role as a national and imperial cultural capital made her popular culture a common language and means of expression for allied troops.

However, despite the evidence of diaries, memoirs, letters, newspapers, interviews, poetry and periodicals we do not yet fully understand trench culture. That it was sanctioned by military authorities and encouraged morale in the fighting lines has been proved conclusively.[1] This was not a culture which idolised heroism or jingoistic patriotism. Generally, overt expressions of such feelings were written by non-combatants and produced at home. Even then topical culture's more absurd elements were never removed from these jingoistic celebrations, whether it was Harry Tate's tank or Ada Vivian's sharp-shooting act. At the battle front, popular-cultural heroes, such as those depicted in the drawings of captain Bruce Bairnsfather, resembled Harry Tate or Charlie Chaplin.[2] They were ordinary men who persevered in a world that threatened them daily. Up-to-date idioms gloried in the ridiculous and absurd, and voiced the hope of a safe return. Because it was topical, First World War culture excluded some people, like the journalist Thomas Burke, who felt the demands made on artistes to appear in West End revues, recruiting drives and the time they spent 'cultivating allotments' detracted from their responsibility to cheer the public.[3] To those not in the know, revues like *Razzle Dazzle* showed artistes 'playing to an audience of overseas khaki and tired working-people, who applaud their most maladroit japes, [which] has had the effect of wearing them down. They no longer work. They take the easiest way, knowing that any remark about the Kaiser, Old Bill, meat-cards, or the Better 'Ole is sure of a laugh'.[4] Topical jokes derived from the war were not understood by such uninformed onlookers, while the war's up-to-date slang was 'modern Army rubbish, [which] besides being uncouth, is utterly meaningless, and might have been invented by some idiot schoolboy'.[5]

Because it was topical this culture enabled men to describe their world. The artillery bombardment and positioning of troops which preceded an attack was likened to the way the orchestra, chorus and supers announced the anticipated appearance on stage of Arthur Roberts in Edwardian revues. Roberts always took the stage in some sensational manner, like 'stepping out of a bathing-machine, or falling out of a hansom cab, or sliding down a chute on a toboggan'. The audience awaited his entrance with baited breath, just as men in the trenches did because it was impossible to predict how an attack, or 'show' would unfold before it had begun.[6] Similarly, up-to-date metaphors resonated at least as powerfully with the troops as the poetic stanzas which have come to symbolise the war. Troopers felt that terrified men scrambling for cover as shells descended, or frantically fitting their masks at the gas alarm, were performing 'a bit of Charlie Chaplin', where Wilfred Owen perceived 'an ecstasy of fumbling'.[7] Similarly, propagandists and poets described the war as a noble crusade, in which the 'dead' were revered as 'the fallen', while 'the army', was 'the host'.[8] But on a daily level, such references to sacrifice and veneration could not replace the fighting men's lexicon of bastardised foreign words and topical references, like that of the 5th Gloucestershire Regiment who described the war as a boxing bout between 'T. Atkins, the Hebuterne hope' and 'Fritz, the Bucquoy basher'. When this fight's scorecard was tallied in the summer of 1916, it read:

> Round 1 – (July 1915) – Very little happened
> Round 2 – (Feb 1916) – Fritz got some good hits
> Round 3 – (July 1916) – Both are strong
> 4th Round – unfinished [9]

Such allusions were not martial or sacrificial, but neither were the majority of the men serving with the colours. The patriotic motives which had prompted them to enlist had vanished with the experience of attrition warfare. Men wanted simply to survive the fighting and return home. Topical references and the continuation of up-to-date activities reminded men of their homes and the people they had once been, enabling them to communicate with others who were 'in-the-know', to express their anger, and, to a certain extent, create an illusion that civilian life had not been interrupted.[10] Though an apposite genre for the war, up-to-date culture mitigated but could not disguise its horrors, because events, the performers and subject matter used at one concert, pantomime or sports match might be dead or obliterated before the next.[11]

Between 1890 and 1918 topical culture was innovative but unoriginal. Thanks to a series of rules for up-to-dateness which had been established at mid-century, people, incidents and places were taken up, played for comedy, tragedy and the absurd, and then discarded. The sensational events changed, but the ways in which they were incorporated and represented on the halls altered little. Nevertheless, mastering up-to-dateness required a sophisticated understanding of just how to dazzle audiences with sensational performances. Though a steady stream of cyclists, boxers, footballers and pilots tried their skills on the halls, only the most tenacious performers remained in the public consciousness for long. Up-to-dateness and professionalisation in popular culture led to the emergence of modern celebrities who starred simultaneously in several different activities. This ability to transfer between different types of performance in turn reflected the way that popular sensations fuelled Londoners' appetites for up-to-date culture.

Notes

1 John F. G. Fuller, *Troop Morale and Popular Culture in the British and Dominion Armies, 1914–1918*, Oxford, Clarendon, 1990, *passim*.

2 Bruce Bairnsfather, *Fragments from France*, London, Bystander, 1917, *passim*.

3 Thomas Burke, *Out and About: A Note-book of London in War-time*, London, George Allen and Unwin, 1919, p. 68.

4 Burke, *Out and About*, p. 68.

5 Burke, *Out and About*, p. 12.

6 Ian Hay, *All In It: K(1) Carries On*, Toronto, W. Briggs, 1917, p. 64.

7 Reginald H. Roy (ed.), *The Journal of Private Fraser, 1914–1918, Canadian Expeditionary Force*, Victoria, B.C., Sono Nis Press, 1985, p. 240; 'Dulce et decorum est', in Edmund Blunden (ed.), *The Poems of Wilfred Owen*, London, Chatto and Windus, 1971, p. 66.

8 Paul Fussell, *The Great War and Modern Memory*, London, Oxford University Press, 1975, pp. 21–22.

9 'Boxing news', *The Fifth Glos'ter Gazette*, 13, July 1916, unnumbered pages.

10 F. McKelvey Bell, *The First Canadians in France*, Toronto, McClelland, Goodchild and Stewart, 1917, p. 99.

11 'Sport – base-ball', *Now and Then*, 15 December 1915, p. 3.

Bibliography

Archival material

John East oral history collection, Lambeth local history archives, London.
Tottenham oral history collection, Haringey local history archives, Bruce Castle, London.
Martha Vicinus oral history collection, National Sound Archives, London.
Jerry White oral history collection, Tower Hamlets local history archives, London.
'In Flanders fields', oral history interview transcripts, Canadian Broadcasting Corporation Fonds, National Archives of Canada.
British Library Catalogue of Printed Music.
British Theatre Museum, Covent Garden and Blythe House, London.
Viewing copy collection, British Film Institute, London.

Periodicals

The Aeroplane
The Amateur Stage
Anglo-American Times
Aussie: The Australian Soldiers' Magazine
The Autocar
Baily's Magazine of Sports and Pastimes
Bairns Gazette
The B.E.F. Times
The Bioscope
Boxing
Boxing World
C. B. Fry's Magazine
The Chelsea Football Club Chronicle, Official Programme of the Chelsea Football and Athletic Company Limited
Chronicles of the White Horse
Cinque Ports Gazette
Contemporary Review
The Cottager's Journal

Cycling
The Dagger
Daily Chronicle
Daily Express
Daily Mail
Daily News and Leader
Dan Leno's Comic Journal
Dead Horse Corner Gazette
The Dump
Edmonton and Tottenham Weekly Guardian
The Encore
The English Illustrated Magazine
The Era
The Fifth Glos'ter Gazette
Football Chat
Fortnightly Review
Fulham Observer
The Gasper – 18th, 19th and 21st (P.S.) Royal Fusiliers
George Robey's Christmas Annual
The Graphic
Hackney Express and Shoreditch Observer
The Hammers' Gazette: The Official Programme of the West Ham United Football Club
Hangar Happenings
The Illustrated London News
The Illustrated Sporting and Dramatic News
Invicta Times
The Iodine Chronicle
The Jackass
Kamp Knews
The Leadswinger: The Bivouac Journal of the 1/3 West Riding Field Ambulance
Licensed Victuallers' Gazette and Hotel Courier
The Listening Post
Living London
Lloyd's Sunday News
Lloyd's Weekly News
London American
Macmillan's Magazine
The Minden Magazine
The Mirror of Life
The Monthly Review
The Mudhook: With Which is Incorporated the Dardanelles Dug-Out Gossip
Music Hall and Theatre Review
Musical Opinion and Music Trade Review
New York Times

Nineteenth Century

Nineteenth Century and After

Now and Then

Oriental Notes: The Official Organ of the Clapton Orient Football Club (1906) Ltd

Outlook

Pearson's Magazine

Pearson's Weekly

Sandow's Magazine of Physical Culture

The Sketch

The Sling: A Little Journal Published by the Boys of a Canadian Field Ambulance on Active Service

The Splint Record

Stage and Sport

The Standard of C Company

Strand Magazine

The Sun

The Third Battalion Magazine

Thomson's Weekly News

Tichborne Gazette

Tichborne Times

The Times

Topical Times

The Tottenham and Edmonton Weekly Herald

Tottenham Hotspur Football and Athletic Company Limited, Official Programme and Record of the Club

The Umpire

White and Blue

The Whizz Bang

The Windsor Magazine

The Wipers Times or Salient News

Wisden Cricket Monthly

Wisden Cricketers' Almanac

Woolwich Arsenal Football and Athletic Company Limited, Official Programme and Record of the Club

The World's Work

The Wormlet

718 – The ACSMT 718 W. T. Company's Own Magazine

Primary sources

Abbott, John, *The Story of Francis Day and Hunter*, London, Francis Day and Hunter, 1952.

Adeler, Edwin and Con West, *Remember Fred Karno? The Life of a Great Showman*, London, John Long, 1939.

Allison, George F., *Allison Calling*, London, Staples Press, 1948.

Anonymous, *Death in the Air*, London, Greenhill, 1933.

Anonymous, *Narrow Waters*, London, W. Hodge, 1935.

Ashwell, Lena, *Myself a Player*, London, Michael Joseph, 1936.

Bairnsfather, Bruce, *Fragments from France*, London, Bystander, 1917.

Bamberger, Louis, *Bow Bell Memories*, London, Sampson Low, 1932.

Barnum, Phineas T., *The Life of P. T. Barnum, Written by Himself*, London, Sampson Low, 1855.

Barnum, Phineas T., *The Struggles and Triumphs of P. T. Barnum, Told by Himself*, London, MacGibbon and Kee, 1967.

Bayles, John, *Tichborne Correspondence*, Newcastle-Upon-Tyne, J. M. Carr, 1876.

Beatty, David Pearce (ed.), *Memories of a Forgotten War: The World War I Diary of Pte. V. E. Goodwin*, Port Elgin, New Brunswick, Baie Verte, 1988.

Bell, Anne Oliver (ed.), *The Diary of Virginia Woolf: Vol. I, 1915–1919*, London, Hogarth, 1977.

Bell, F. McKelvey, *The First Canadians in France*, Toronto, McClelland, Goodchild and Stewart, 1917.

Bettinson, A. F. and B. Bennison, *The Home of Boxing*, London, Odhams, 1922.

Black, Ernest G., *I Want One Volunteer*, Toronto, Ryerson, 1965.

Blacker, Harry, *Just Like it Was, Memoirs of the Mittel East*, London, Vallentine, Mitchell, 1974.

Blunden, Edmund (ed.), *The Poems of Wilfred Owen*, London, Chatto and Windus, 1971.

Boardman, W. H., *Vaudeville Days*, London, Jarrolds, 1935.

Booth, Charles, *Life and Labour of the People in London*, London, Williams and Norgate, 1892.

Bowra, C. M., *Memories, 1898–1939*, London, Wiedenfield and Nicolson, 1966.

Boyd, William, *With a Field Ambulance at Ypres*, New York, G. H. Doran, 1916.

Lord Brabazon of Tara, *The Brabazon Story*, London, Heinemann, 1956.

Brady, William A., *Showman*, New York, E. P. Dutton, 1937.

Buchan, Charles, *A Lifetime in Football*, London, Phoenix House, 1955.

Burke, Thomas, *London in My Time*, London, Rich and Cowan, 1934.

Burke, Thomas, *Out and About: A Note-book of London in War-time*, London, George Allen and Unwin, 1919.

Burke, Thomas, *Son of London*, London, Herbert Jenkins, 1946.

Burnham, Dorothy, *Through Dooms of Love*, London, Chatto and Windus, 1969.

Burns, Tommy, *Scientific Boxing and Self Defence*, London, Athletic Publications, 1908.

Busby, Matt, *My Story*, London, Souvenir Press, 1957.

Calthrop, Dion Clayton, *Music Hall Nights*, London, John Lane, 1926.

Carlton, *Twenty Years of Spoof and Bluff*, London, Herbert Jenkins, 1920.

Carpentier, Georges, *My Fighting Life*, London, Cassell, 1920.

Carter, Raich, *Footballer's Progress*, London, Sporting Handbooks, 1950.

Catton, James A. H., *The Real Football*, London, Sands and Co., 1900.

Chadwick, Henry (ed.), *Spalding's Official Baseball Guide*, London, no stated publisher, 1906.

Chaplin, Charles, *My Autobiography*, London, Bodley Head, 1964.

Chapman, Guy, *A Passionate Prodigality*, London, Mayflower, 1967.

Chapman, Herbert, *Herbert Chapman on Football*, London, 1934.

Chirgwin, George, *Chirgwin's Chirrup*, London, J. & J. Bennett, 1912.

Coborn, Charles, *The Man Who Broke the Bank*, London, Hutchinson, 1928.

Cochran, Charles B., *Cock-a-Doodle-Do*, London, J. M. Dent, 1941.

Cochran, Charles B., *I Had Almost Forgotten*, London, Hutchinson, 1932.

Cochran, Charles B., *The Secrets of a Showman*, London, Heinemann, 1925.

Cochran, Charles B., *Showman Looks On*, London, J. M. Dent, 1945.

Cockburn, Alexander, *Charge of the Lord Chief Justice of England*, London, William Ridgway, 1874.

Cooke, Alistair, *Six Men*, New York, Knopf, 1977.

Cooke, Conrad William, *Automata Old and New*, London, privately printed, 1893.

Coppard, George, *With a Machine Gun to Cambrai*, London, Papermac, 1986.

Corbett, James J., *The Roar of the Crowd*, London, G. P. Putnam, 1925.

Corri, Eugene, *Fifty Years in the Ring*, London, Hutchinson, 1933.

Corri, Eugene, *Gloves and the Man*, London, Hutchinson, 1927.

Corri, Eugene, *Refereeing 1000 Fights*, London, Edward Arnold, 1919.

Corri, Eugene, *Thirty Years a Boxing Referee*, London, Edward Arnold, 1915.

Coxon, Stanley W., *Dover During the Dark Days*, London, John Lane, 1919.

Crane, Newton, *Baseball*, London, G. Bell and Sons, 1891.

Datas, *Datas: The Memory Man, By Himself*, London, Wright and Brown, 1932.

Dawson, Coningsby, *The Glory of the Trenches: An Interpretation*, Toronto, Gundy, 1918.

Dawson, Coningsby, *Living Bayonets*, London, John Lane, 1919.

Desmond, Shaw, *London Nights of Long Ago*, London, Duckworth, 1927.

Devant, David, *My Magic Life*, London, Hutchinson, 1931.

Dewar, Thomas R., *A Ramble Round the Globe*, London, Chatto and Windus, 1894.

Douglas, James, *Adventures in London*, London, Cassell, 1935.

Douglas, Norman, *London Street Games*, London, St Catherine, 1917.

Douglass, Albert, *Memories of Mummers and the Old Standard Theatre*, London, The Era, 1925.

Douie, Charles, *The Weary Road: Recollections of a Subaltern of Infantry*, London, John Murray, 1929.

Dunville, T. E., *The Autobiography of an Eccentric Comedian*, London, Everett and Co., 1912.

Edge, Selwyn Francis, *My Motoring Reminiscences*, London, G. T. Foulis, 1934.

Finn, Ralph L., *No Tears in Aldgate*, London, Robert Hale, 1963.

Fitzgerald, Percy, *Music-hall Land*, London, Ward and Downey, 1891.

Fleischer, Nat, *Fifty Years at Ringside*, New York, Fleet, 1940.

The Football Who's Who, London, C. Arthur Pearson, 1906.

Foster, George, *The Spice of Life*, London, Hurst and Blackett, 1939.

Fry, Charles Burgess, *Real Diabolo*, London, George Newnes, 1908.

Furniss, Harry, *By Ways and Queer Ways of Boxing*, London, Harrison, 1920.

Geare, William Duncan, *Letters of an Army Chaplain*, London, Wells and Gardner, 1918.

Graham, Joe, *An Old Stock Actor's Memories*, London, John Murray, 1930.

Grahame-White, Claude and Harry Harper, *Aircraft in the Great War*, London, T. Fisher Unwin, 1915.

Grahame-White, Claude and Harry Harper, *With the Airmen*, London, Hodder and Stoughton, 1913.

Graves, Robert, *Goodbye to All That*, Harmondsworth, Penguin, 1976.

Gray, George, *Vagaries of a Vagabond*, London, Heath Cranton, 1930.

Gurnell, Robert, *Tichborne Almanack for 1877*, London, Co-operative Printing and Stationery Co., 1876.

Hapgood, Edris A., *Football Ambassador*, London, Sporting Handbooks, 1945.

Hay, Ian, *All In It: K(1) Carries On*, Toronto, W. Briggs, 1917.

Henning, Fred, *Fights for the Championship: The Men and Their Times*, London, Licensed Victualler's Gazette, 1902.

Henson, Leslie, *My Laugh Story*, London, Hodder and Stoughton, 1926.

Henson, Leslie, *Yours Faithfully: An Autobiography*, London, John Long, 1947.

Hepworth, Cecil, *Came the Dawn*, London, Phoenix House, 1951.

Hueffer, Ford Madox, *The Soul of London: A Survey of a Modern City*, London, J. M. Dent, 1911.

Hurdman-Lucas, F., *From Pit-boy to Champion Boxer: The Romance of Georges Carpentier*, London, Ewart Seymour, 1914.

Jackson, Nicholas L., *Association Football*, London, George Newnes, 1899.

Jackson, Nicholas L., *Sporting Days and Sporting Ways*, London, Hurst and Blackett, 1932.

Jacomb, C. E., *Torment*, London, Andrew Melrose, 1920.

Jasper, A. S., *A Hoxton Childhood*, London, Barrie and Rockliff, 1969.

Jennings, Henry J., *Chestnuts and Small Beer*, London, Chapman and Hall, 1920.

Jerome, Jerome K., *My Life and Times*, London, Hodder and Stoughton, 1926.

Jerome, Jerome K., *Three Men on the Bummel*, Bristol, J. W. Arrowsmith, 1900.

Jones, Paul, *War Letters of a Public-School Boy*, London, Cassell, 1918.

Kilpatrick, James A., *Atkins at War, as Told in His Own Letters*, London, Herbert Jenkins, 1914.

Knight, Albert, *The Complete Cricketer*, London, Methuen, 1906.

Knowles, Richard G., *A Modern Columbus*, London, T. Werner Laurie, 1916.

Knowles, Richard G. and Richard Morton, *Baseball*, London, London and Co., 1896.

Lauder, Harry, *A Minstrel in France*, London, Andrew Melrose, 1918.

Lauder, Harry, *Roamin' in the Gloamin'*, London, Hutchinson, 1928.

Leaska, Mitchell A. (ed.), *Virginia Woolf, a Passionate Apprentice: The Early Journals, 1897–1909*, London, Chatto and Windus, 1990.

Lee, Arthur Gould, *No Parachute: A Fighter Pilot in World War I*, London, Arrow Books, 1968.

Lewis, Cecil, *Sagittarius Rising*, London, Peter Davies, 1936.

Llewelyn Williams, Henry, *Buffalo Bill*, London, Routledge, 1887.

Loraine, Winifred, *Robert Loraine: Soldier, Actor, Airman*, London, Collins, 1938.

Lynch, John G. B., *Prominent Pugilists of To-day*, London, Max Goshen, 1914.

MacDonagh, Michael, *In London During the Great War: The Diary of a Journalist*, London, Eyre and Spottiswoode, 1935.

MacGill, Patrick, *The Red Horizon*, London, Caliban, 1916.

Macmillan, Harold, *Winds of Change 1914–1939*, London, Macmillan, 1966.

Malins, Geoffrey, *How I Filmed the War*, London, Herbert Jenkins, 1920.

Manion, J. C., *A Surgeon in Arms*, New York, D. Appleton, 1918.

Masefield, John, *The Old Front Line*, Bourne End, Bucks, Spurbooks, 1972.

Matthews, Stanley, *Feet First*, London, Ewen and Dale, 1949.

Mayhew, Henry, *London Labour and the London Poor*, London, London, 1861.

Merson, Billy, *Fixing the Stoof Oop*, London, Hutchinson, 1925.

Moir, Gunner, *The Complete Boxer*, London, Health and Strength, 1907.

Morton, W. H. and H. Chance Newton, *Sixty Years' Stage Service, Being a Record of the Life of Charles Morton, 'The Father of the Halls'*, London, Gale and Polden, 1905.

Morton, William, *I Remember: A Feat of Memory*, London, Goddard, Walker and Brown, 1934.

Mottram, R. H., John Easton and Eric Partridge, *Three Personal Records of The War*, London, Scholartis Press, 1929.

Mozart, George, *Limelight*, London, Hurst and Blackett, 1938.

Muller, Dan, *My Life with Buffalo Bill*, Chicago, Reilly and Lee, 1948.

Murray, William Waldie, *Five Nines and Whiz Bangs,* Ottawa, Legionary Library, 1937.

Newton, H. Chance, *Crime and the Drama*, London, Stanley Paul, 1927.

Newton, H. Chance, *Idols of the Halls*, London, Heath Cranton, 1928.

Oh Canada, A Medley of Stories, Verse, Pictures and Music Contributed by Members of the Canadian Expeditionary Force, London, Simpkin Marshall, 1917.

Onslow, Gilbert, *A Hundred Facts*, London, Englishman Office, c. 1875.

Ormiston Chant, Mrs, *Why We Attacked the Empire*, London, Marshall and Son, 1895.

Orton, Arthur, *Pictorial Souvenir*, London, no stated publisher, 1874.

Palmer, Frederick, *My Second Year of the War*, Toronto, McClelland, 1917.

Palmer, Frederick, *My Year of the Great War*, Toronto, McClelland, 1916.

Palmer, Joe, *Recollections of a Boxing Referee*, London, John Lane, 1927.

Pearson, George, *Flashback*, London, George Allen and Unwin, 1957.

Pearson, Lester B., *Mike: The Memoirs of the Right Honourable Lester B. Pearson*, Toronto, University of Toronto Press, 1972.

Pemberton, A. C., *The Complete Cyclist*, London, C. P. Sisley and G. Floyd, 1897.

Powell, Anthony, *Infants of the Spring*, London, Heinemann, 1976.

Priestley, J. B., *Margin Released*, London, Heinemann, 1962.

Prince, Grace Keenan (ed.), *John Patrick Teahan: Diary Kid*, Ottawa, Oberon, 1999.

R. A. L., *Letters of a Canadian Stretcher-Bearer*, Toronto, T. Allen, 1918.

Redmond, William, *Trench Pictures from France*, London, Andrew Melrose, 1917.

Reeve, Ada, *Take it for a Fact*, London, Heinemann, 1954.

Rhode, John, *With the Guns By F.O.O.*, London, Eveleigh Nash, 1916.

Roberts, Arthur, *The Adventures of Arthur Roberts by Rail, Road and River, Told By Himself and Chronicled by Richard Morton*, London, Bristol and Co., 1895.

Roberts, Arthur, *Fifty Years of Spoof*, London, John Lane, 1927.

Robey, Edward, *The Jester and the Court*, London, Kimber, 1976.

Robey, George, *Looking Back on Life*, London, Constable, 1933.

Robey, George, *My Life Up Till Now*, London, Greening, 1908.

Robinson, W. Heath, *Hunlikely!*, London, Duckworth, 1916.

Rolls, Charles S., *An Aeroplane Flight with Wilbur Wright*, Esher, Tabard, 1964.

Rose, Charlie, *Life's a Knock-out*, London, Hutchinson, 1953.

Rose, Clarkson, *Red Plush and Greasepaint*, London, Museum Press, 1964.

Roy, Reginald H. (ed.), *The Journal of Private Fraser, 1914–1918, Canadian Expeditionary Force*, Victoria, B. C., Sono Nis, 1985.

Rutledge, Stanley A., *Pen Pictures from the Trenches*, Toronto, W. Briggs, 1918.

Sala, George Augustus, *London Up To Date*, London, A. and C. Black, 1894.

Samuel, Raphael (ed.), *East End Underworld: Chapters in the Life of Arthur Harding*, London, Routledge and Kegan Paul, 1981.

Sanger, Lord George, *Seventy Years a Showman*, London, Pearson, 1910.

Scott, Eric (ed.), *Nobody Ever Wins a War: The World War I Diaries of Ella Mae Bongard, R. N.*, Ottawa, Generic Enterprises, 1998.

Seed, Jimmy, *The Jimmy Seed Story*, London, Phoenix, 1957.

Seely, John E. B., *Adventure*, London, Heinemann, 1930.

Sharpe, Ivan, *Forty Years in Football*, London, Hutchinson, 1952.

Smith, Albert, 'A go-a-head day with Barnum', *Bentley's Miscellany*, 21, (1847), pp. 522–527 and 623–628.

Smith, William, *Advertise, How? When? Where?*, London, Swan, 1863.

Steed, Henry Wickham, *Through Thirty Years*, London, Heinemann, 1924.

Strange, L. A., *Recollections of an Airman*, London, John Hamilton, 1933.

Stuart, Charles Douglas and A. J. Park, *The Variety Stage*, London, T. Fisher Unwin, 1895.

Swinton, Ernest D., *A Year Ago: An Eyewitness Narrative of the War from March 30th to July 18th 1915*, London, Edward Arnold, 1916.

Swinton, Ernest D., *Over My Shoulder*, Oxford, George Ronald, 1951.

Swinton, Ernest D., *The Tanks*, London, L. U. Gill, 1916.

Terriss, Ellaline, *By Herself and With Others*, London, Cassell, 1928.

The Times Illustrated History of the War, London, Times Newspapers, 1920.

Titterton, W. R., *From Theatre to Music Hall*, London, Stephen Swift, 1912.

Toland, Edward D., *The Aftermath of Battle: With the Red Cross in France*, New York, Macmillan, 1916.

Turner, C. C., *The Old Flying Days*, London, Sampson and Low, 1927.

Vaughan, Edwyn Campion, *Some Desperate Glory: The Diary of a Young Officer, 1917*, London, Macmillan, 1981.

Vee, Roger, *Flying Minnows: Memoirs of a World War One Fighter Pilot*, London, Arms and Armour, 1977.

Vincent, W. T., *Recollections of Fred Leslie*, London, Kegan Paul, 1894.

Wall, Sir Frederick, *Fifty Years of Football*, London, Cassell, 1935.

Walthall, Dorothy, *The A. B. C. of Diabolo*, Henry J. Drane, London, 1907.

Ward, David P., *Diabolo: The Game and its Tricks*, London, L. Upcott Gill, 1908.

Ward, Mrs Humphrey, *Manners for Women*, Whitstable, Pryor, 1993.

Wells, Bombardier, *Modern Boxing*, London, Ewart, Seymour, 1911.

Wells, H. G., *The Wheels of Chance*, London, J. M. Dent, 1896.

Wetmore, Helen Cody, *The Last of the Great Scouts*, London, Methuen, 1901.

Whitehouse, Arch, *The Fledgling: An Aerial Gunner in World War I – the Epic of a Volunteer Airman*, London, Nicholas Vane, 1965.

Wilde, Jimmy, *Fighting was My Business*, London, Michael Joseph, 1938.

Williams, Bransby, *An Actor's Story*, London, Chapman and Hall, 1909.

Willis, Frederick, *101 Jubilee Road: A Book of London Yesterdays*, London, Phoenix House, 1948.

Willis, Frederick, *London General*, London, Phoenix House, 1953.

Willis, Frederick, *Peace and Dripping Toast*, London, Phoenix House, 1950.

The Year 1916 Illustrated, London, no stated publisher, 1916.

Young, John, *Sir Roger Tichborne Up-To-Date – Or the Whirligig of Fate*, Cape Town, Bernard Quaritch, 1902.

Secondary sources

Alderson, Frederick, *Bicycling: A History*, Newton Abbot, David and Charles, 1972.

Allison, Lincoln, 'Batsman and bowler, the key relation in Victorian England', *Journal of Sport History*, 7.2 (1990), pp. 5–20.

Anthony, Barry, 'Earliest cricket on film', *Wisden Cricket Monthly*, December 1993, pp. 32–33.

Badsey, S. D., '*Battle of the Somme*', in Hugh Cecil and Peter Liddle (eds), *Facing Armageddon*, London, Leo Cooper, 1996, pp. 99–115.

Bailey, Peter, 'Champagne Charlie: performance and ideology in the music-hall swell song', in J. S. Bratton (ed.), *Music-Hall: Performance and Style*, Milton Keynes, Open University Press, 1986, pp. 49–69.

Bailey, Peter, 'A community of friends: business and good-fellowship in London music-hall management c. 1860–1885', in Peter Bailey (ed.), *Music-Hall: The Business of Pleasure*, Milton Keynes, Open University Press, 1986, pp. 33–52.

Bailey, Peter, 'Conspiracies of meaning: music-hall and the knowingness of popular culture', *Past and Present*, 144 (1994), pp. 138–170.

Bailey, Peter, 'Custom capital and culture in the Victorian music-hall', in Robert D. Storch (ed.), *Popular Culture and Custom in Nineteenth-Century England*, New York, Croom Helm, 1982, pp. 180–228.

Bailey, Peter, *Leisure and Class in Victorian England: Rational Recreation and the Contest for Control 1830– 1885*, London, Routledge and Kegan Paul, 1978.

Bailey, Peter, '"A mingled mass of perfectly legitimate pleasures": the Victorian middle-class and the problem of leisure', *Victorian Studies*, 21.1 (1977), pp. 7–28.

Bailey Peter, (ed.), *Music Hall: The Business of Pleasure*, Milton Keynes, Open University Press, 1986.

Bailey, Peter, '"Will the real Bill Banks please stand up?" towards a role analysis of mid-Victorian working-class respectability', *The Journal of Social History*, 12.3 (1979), pp. 336–353.

Baker, William J., 'The making of a working-class football culture in Victorian England', *The Journal of Social History*, 13.2 (1979), pp. 241–251.

Barker, Felix, *The House that Stoll Built: The Story of the Coliseum Theatre*, London, Frederick Muller, 1957.

Barker, T. C. and Michael Robbins, *A History of London Transport*, Vol. 2, London, George Allen and Unwin, 1974.

Baron, Wendy, *The Camden Town Group*, London, Scolar Press, 1979.

Baum, Jeffrey and Barbara, 'The Jews of Tottenham before the Great War', *Heritage #1*, Jewish Research Group of the Edmonton Hundred Historical Society, undated.

Bédarida, François, *A Social History of England, 1851–1990*, A. S. Foster and Jeffrey Hodgkinson (trans.), London, Routledge, 1990.

Bédarida, François, 'Urban growth and social structure in nineteenth century Poplar', *London Journal*, 1.2 (1975), pp. 159–188.

Beloff, Max, *Wars and Welfare: Britain 1914–1945*, London, Edward Arnold, 1984.

Bevan, Ian, *Top of the Bill: The Story of the London Palladium*, London, Frederick Muller, 1952.

Blake, Robert, *Disraeli*, London, Eyre and Spottiswoode, 1967.

Bottomore, Stephen, 'The coming of the cinema', *History Today*, March 1996, pp. 14–20.

Bowyer, Chaz, *The Encyclopaedia of British Military Aircraft*, London, Arms and Armour, 1982.

Bradley, James, 'The MCC, Society and Empire: a portrait of cricket's ruling body, 1860–1914', *The International Journal of the History of Sport*, 7.1 (1990), pp. 3–22.

Bramson, Alan, *Pure Luck: The Authorised Biography of Sir Thomas Sopwith, 1888–1989*, London, Stephens, 1990.

Brandreth, Gyles, *The Funniest Man on Earth, The Story of Dan Leno*, London, Hamilton, 1977.

Bratton, J. S. (ed.), *Music Hall: Performance and Style*, Milton Keynes, Open University Press, 1986.

Briggs, Asa, *The Age of Improvement*, London, Longman, 1959.

Broomfield, George A., *Pioneer of the Air: The Life and Times of Colonel S.F. Cody*, Aldershot, Gale and Polden, 1953.

Brophy, John and Eric Partridge, *The Long Trail: What the British Soldier Sang and Said in the Great War of 1914–1918*, London, André Deutsch, 1965.

Brophy, John and Eric Partridge, *Songs and Slang of the British Soldier: 1914–1918*, London, André Deutsch, 1930.

Brown, Malcolm, *Tommy Goes to War*, London, J. M. Dent, 1978.

Bruce, Frank, '"You had to be game to stay in yon business": a working life in variety theatre, 1920–1950', *Oral History*, Autumn 1996, pp. 67–74.

Bruce, Jack, 'The war in the air: the men and their machines', in Peter Liddle (ed.), *Facing Armageddon: The First World War Experience*, London, Leo Cooper, 1988, pp. 193–205.

Buford, Bill, *Among the Thugs*, London, Secker and Warburg, 1991.

Burnett, John, David Vincent and David Mayall, *The Autobiography of the Working-Class: An Annotated Critical Bibliography*, Brighton, Harvester, 1984.

Burton, Antoinette, 'Making a spectacle of Empire: Indian travellers in fin de siècle London', *History Workshop Journal*, 42 (1996), pp. 127–146.

Cannadine, David, *Aspects of Aristocracy*, London, Yale University Press, 1994.

Cannadine, David, 'The context, performance and meaning of ritual: the British monarchy and the invention of tradition, c. 1820–1977', in Terence Ranger and Eric Hobsbawm (eds), *The Invention of Tradition*, Cambridge, Cambridge University Press, 1983, pp. 101–164.

Cannadine, David and Elizabeth Hammerton, 'Conflict and concensus on a ceremonial occasion: the Diamond Jubilee in Cambridge in 1897', *The Historical Journal*, 24.1 (1981), pp. 111–146.

Chanan, Michael, *The Dream that Kicks*, London, Routledge and Kegan Paul, 1980.

Chapman, David L., *Sandow the Magnificent*, Urbana, Illinois, University of Illinois Press, 1994.

Chapman, Stanley D. (ed.), *The History of Working-Class Housing*, Newton Abbot, David and Charles, 1971.

Cheshire, Scott, *Chelsea: A Complete Record 1905–1991*, Derby, Breedon Books, 1991.

Chester, Charlie, *The Grand Order of Water Rats*, London, W. H. Allen, 1984.

Childs, Michael J., *Labour's Apprentices: Working-Class Lads in Late-Victorian and Edwardian England*, Montreal and Kingston, McGill-Queens, 1992.

Clark, Alan, *Aces High: War in the Air Over the Western Front 1914–18*, London, Weidenfeld and Nicolson, 1973.

Clarke, Peter, *Hope and Glory: Britain 1900–1990*, London, Allen Lane, 1996.

Collins, L. C., *Theatre at War, 1914–1918*, Basingstoke, Macmillan, 1998.

Coover, James, *Music Publishing, Copyright and Privacy in Victorian England*, London, Mansell, 1985.

Creek, F. N. S., *A History of the Corinthian Football Club*, London, Longmans Green, 1933.

Croft-Cooke, Rupert and W. S. Meadmore, *Buffalo Bill, the Legend, the Man of Action, the Showman*, London, Sidgwick and Jackson, 1952.

Crowhurst, A. J., 'The music-hall 1885–1922: the emergence of a national entertainment industry in Britain', unpublished Ph.D. dissertation, University of Cambridge, 1992.

Crowhurst, Andrew, 'London's "music hall war": trade unionism in an Edwardian service industry', *London Journal*, 21.2 (1996), pp. 149–163.

Dangerfield, George, *The Strange Death of Liberal England*, London, Constable, 1936.

Davies, Andrew, *Leisure, Gender and Poverty: Working-Class Culture in Salford and Manchester, 1900–1939*, Buckingham, Open University Press, 1992.

Davis, Jim and Tracy C. Davis, '"The people of the people's theatre": the social demography of the Britannia Theatre, (Hoxton)', *Theatre Survey*, 32.2 (1991), pp. 137–172.

Davis, John, *Reforming London: the London Government Problem, 1855–1900*, Oxford, Oxford University Press, 1988.

Davison, Peter, *Contemporary Drama and the Popular Dramatic Tradition in England*, London, Macmillan, 1982.

Davison, Peter, *Popular Appeal in English Drama to 1850*, London, Macmillan, 1982.

Deghy, Guy, *Noble and Manly: The History of the National Sporting Club*, London, Hutchinson, 1956.

The Dictionary of National Biography, (ed.), Sidney Lee, London, Smith Elder, 1894.

Disher, Maurice Willson, *The Greatest Show on Earth*, London, G. Bell, 1937.

Disher, Maurice Willson, *Winkles and Champagne*, London, B. T. Batsford, 1938.

Dunning, Eric, Patrick Murphy and John Williams, *The Roots of Football Hooliganism*, London, Routledge, 1990.

Dyos, H. J., 'The slums of Victorian London', *Victorian Studies*, 11.1 (1967), pp. 5–40.

Dyos, H. J. (ed.), *The Study of Urban History*, London, Edward Arnold, 1968.

Dyos, H. J., *Victorian Suburb A Study of the Growth of Camberwell*, Leicester, Leicester University Press, 1961.

Eksteins, Modris, *Rites of Spring: The Great War and the Birth of the Modern Age*, Toronto, Lester Orpen and Dennys, 1989.

Feldman, David, *Englishmen and Jews,* London, Yale University Press, 1994.

Feldman, David and Gareth Stedman Jones (eds), *Metropolis London: Histories and Representations Since 1800*, London, Routledge, 1989.

Ferguson, Niall, *The Pity of War*, London, Allen Lane, 1999.

Fielding, Raymond (ed.), *A Technological History of Motion Pictures and Television*, Berkeley, University of California Press, 1967.

Fishwick, Nicholas, *English Football and Society, 1910–1950*, Manchester, Manchester University Press, 1989.

Fleischer, Nat, *John L. Sullivan*, London, Robert Hale, 1952.

Foley, John, *The Boilerplate War*, London, Frederick Muller, 1963.

Francis, Lionel, *Seventy-Five Years of Southern League Football*, London, Pelham, 1969.

Fraser, Edward and John Gibbons, *Soldier and Sailor Words and Phrases*, London, Routledge, 1925.

Fuller, John F. G., *Troop Morale and Popular Culture in the British and Dominion Armies, 1914–1918*, Oxford, Clarendon, 1990.

Fussell, Paul, *The Great War and Modern Memory*, London, Oxford University Press, 1975.

Fyfe, Hamilton, *Northcliffe: An Intimate Biography*, London, G. Allen and Unwin, 1930.

Gallagher, J. P., *Fred Karno: Master of Mirth and Tears*, London, Hale, 1971.

Gardner, Charles (ed.), *Fifty Years of Brooklands*, London, Heinemann, 1956.

Gatrell, V. A. C., *The Hanging Tree: Execution and the English People, 1770–1868*, Oxford, Oxford University Press, 1994.

Gilbert, Martin, *Churchill: A Life*, London, Heinemann, 1991.

Gilbert, Martin, *The First World War*, London, Weidenfield and Nicolson, 1984.

Gilbert, Martin, *In Search of Churchill: A Historian's Journey*, London, Harper Collins, 1994.

Gilbert, Martin, *Winston S. Churchill, Volume III, 1914–1916*, London, Minerva, 1977.

Gillis, John R., *Youth and History*, New York, Academic Press, 1981.

Gilmore, Al-Tony, *Bad Nigger!: The National Impact of Jack Johnson*, Port Washington, New York, Kennikat, 1975.

Goodwin, Bob, *Spurs: A Complete Record 1882–1991*, Derby, Breedon Books, 1991.

Gore, Frederick and Richard Shone, *Spencer Frederick Gore*, London, Anthony d'Offay, 1983.

Greenwall, Harry J., *Northcliffe: Napoleon of Fleet Street*, London, Allan Wingate, 1957.

Greig, Murray, *Goring the Distance: Canada's Boxing Heritage*, Toronto, Macmillan, 1996.

Halévy, Elie, *The History of the English People in the Nineteenth Century*, London, T. Fisher Unwin, 1923.

Harding, James, *George Robey and the Music-Hall*, London, Hodder and Stoughton, 1990.

Harris, José, *Private Lives, Public Spirit, A Social History of Britain, 1870–1993*, Oxford, Oxford University Press, 1993.

Harrison, A. E., 'Joint-stock company flotation in the cycle, motor-vehicle and related industries, 1882–1914', *Business History*, 23 (1981), pp. 165–190.

Havighurst, Alfred, *Twentieth Century Britain*, New York, Row Petersen, 1962.

Hayter, Reginald J., *Official History of Queen's Park Rangers*, London, Newservice, 1950.

Heller, Peter, *In This Corner: Forty World Champions Tell Their Stories*, New York, Simon and Schuster, 1973.

Herbert, Stephen and Luke McKernan, *Who's Who of Victorian Cinema*, London, British Film Institute, 1996.

Hibbert, Christopher, *Edward VII: A Portrait*, Harmondsworth, Penguin, 1982.

Hibbert, Christopher, *London: Biography of a City*, London, Allen Lane, 1977.

Hinchcliffe, T. F. M., 'Highbury New Park, a nineteenth century middle-class suburb', *London Journal*, 7.1 (1981), pp. 29–44.

Hobsbawm, Eric, 'Mass-producing traditions: Europe, 1870–1914', in Terence Ranger and Eric Hobsbawm (eds), *The Invention of Tradition*, Cambridge, Cambridge University Press, 1983, pp. 263–307.

Hoggart, Richard, *The Uses of Literacy*, Harmondsworth, Penguin, 1958.

Holland, Julian, *Spurs: A History of Tottenham Hotspur Football Club*, London, Phoenix Books, 1956.

Holt, Richard, 'Cricket and Englishness: the batsman as hero', *The International Journal of the History of Sport*, 13.1 (1996), pp. 48–69.

Holt, Richard, 'Sport and history: the state of the subject in Britain', *Twentieth Century British History*, 7.2 (1996), pp. 231–252.

How Things Were, Growing up in Tottenham 1890–1920, London, no stated publisher, n.d.

Howard, Diana, *London Theatres and Music-Halls, 1850–1950*, London, Library Association, 1970.

Husbands, Christopher T., 'East End racism', *London Journal*, 8 (1982), pp. 3–26.

Hutchinson, John, *The Football Industry: The Early Years of the Professional Game*, Glasgow, 1982.

Isenberg, Michael T., *John L. Sullivan and His America*, Urbana Illinois, University of Illinois, 1988.

Jackson, Alan A., *Semi-detached London*, London, Allen and Unwin, 1973.

Johnson, Hubert C., *Breakthrough: Tactics, Technology, and the Search for Victory on the Western Front in World War I*, Novato, California, Presidio, 1994.

Johnson, Paul (ed.), *Twentieth Century Britain: Economic, Social and Cultural Change*, London, Longman, 1994.

Joy, Bernard, *Forward, Arsenal!*, London, Phoenix House, 1952.

Joyce, Patrick, *Visions of the People*, Cambridge, Cambridge University Press, 1991.

Kaufman, Neil and Alan Ravenhill, *Leyton Orient: A Complete Record 1881–1990*, Derby, Breedon Books, 1990.

Keegan, John, *The Face of Battle*, Harmondsworth, Penguin, 1983.

Kellett, John R., *The Impact of Railways on Victorian Cities*, London, Routledge and Kegan Paul, 1969.

Kerrigan, Colm, 'London schoolboys and professional football, 1899–1915', *The International Journal of the History of Sport*, 11.2 (1994), pp. 287–297.

Kift, Dagmar, *The Victorian Music Hall*, Cambridge, Cambridge University Press, 1996.

Kitson-Clark, G. S. R., *An Expanding Society: Britain 1830–1900*, Cambridge, Cambridge University Press, 1967.

Koritz, Amy, 'Moving violation: dance in the London music-hall, 1890–1910', *Theatre Journal*, 42.4 (1990), pp. 419–431.

Korr, Charles P., 'A different kind of success: West Ham United and the creation of tradition and community', in Richard Holt (ed.), *Sport and the Working Class in Modern Britain*, Manchester, Manchester University Press, 1990, pp. 142–158.

Korr, Charles, *West Ham United: the Making of a Football Club*, London, 1986.

Korr, Charles P. 'West Ham United Football Club and the beginnings of professional football in east London', *Journal of Contemporary History*, 13 (1978), pp. 211–232.

Kuhn, William M., 'Queen Victoria's Jubilees and the invention of tradition', *Victorian Poetry*, 25.3–4 (1987), pp. 107–114.

Laver, James, *Costume and Fashion: A Concise History*, London, Thames and Hudson, 1992.

Lawrence, Jon, 'The First World War and its aftermath', in Paul Johnson (ed.), *Twentieth Century Britain: Economic, Social and Cultural Change*, London, Longman, 1994.

Leavis, F. R. and Denys Thompson, *Culture and Environment*, London, Chatto and Windus, 1933.

Lee, Arthur Gould, *The Flying Cathedral*, London, Methuen, 1965.

Lees, Lynn Hollen, *Exiles of Erin: Irish Migrants in Victorian London*, Ithaca, Cornell University Press, 1979.

Leroy, George, *Music Hall Stars of the Nineties*, London, British Technical and General Press, 1952.

Lewis, Tony, *Double Century: The Story of the MCC and Cricket*, London, Hodder and Stoughton, 1987.

Liddle, Peter, *Testimony of War 1914–1918*, Salisbury, Michael Russell, 1979.

Lindsay, Richard, *Millwall: A Complete Record 1885–1991*, Derby, Breedon Books, 1992.

Low, Rachel and Roger Manville, *The History of the British Film, 1896–1906*, London, George Allen and Unwin, 1948.

Ludovici, L. J., *The Challenging Sky: The Life of Sir Alliott Verdon-Roe*, London, Herbert Jenkins, 1956.

MacDonald, Lyn, *They Called it Passchendaele*, London, Joseph, 1978.

MacDonald, Lyn, *To The Last Man, Spring 1918*, London, Viking, 1998.

MacDonald, Lyn, *1914–1918: Voices and Images of the Great War*, London, Penguin, 1988.

Macey, Gordon, *Queen's Park Rangers: A Complete Record*, Derby, Breedon Books, 1993.

MacInnes, Colin, *Sweet Saturday Night*, London, MacGibbon and Kee, 1967.

MacKenzie, John M., *Propaganda and Empire*, Manchester, Manchester University Press, 1984.

MacQueen-Pope, W., *The Melodies Linger On*, London, W. H. Allen, 1951.

Makin, W. J., *The Story of Twenty-five Years*, London, George Newnes, 1935.

Marwick, Arthur, *The Deluge*, London, Bodley Head, 1965.

Mason, Tony, *Association Football and English Society, 1863–1915*, Brighton, Harvester, 1980.

Mason, Tony, 'Football and the historians', *International Journal of the History of Sport*, 5.1 (1988), pp. 136–141.

Mason, Tony, (ed.), *Sport in Britain: A Social History*, Cambridge, Cambridge University Press, 1989.

Matthews, William, *British Autobiographies*, Berkeley, University of California Press, 1955.

McCord, Norman, *British History 1815–1906*, Oxford, Oxford University Press, 1991.

McCrone, Kathleen E., *Sport and the Physical Emancipation of English Women, 1870–1914*, London, Routledge, 1980.

McKibbin, Ross (ed.), *The Ideologies of Class*, Oxford, Oxford University Press, 1990.

McKibbin, Ross, 'Work and hobbies in Britain, 1880–1950', in Jay Winter (ed.), *The Working Class in Modern British History*, Cambridge, Cambridge University Press, 1983.

McWilliam, Rohan, 'The Tichborne case and the politics of "fair play", 1867–1886', in Eugenio F. Biagini and Alastair J. Reid (eds), *Currents of Radicalism*, Cambridge, Cambridge University Press, 1991, pp. 44– 64.

Meacham, Standish, *A Life Apart: The English Working-Class, 1890–1914*, London, Thames and Hudson, 1977.

Medhurst, Andy, 'Music-hall and British cinema', in Charles Barr (ed.), *All Our Yesterdays: 90 Years of British Cinema*, London, British Film Institute, 1986, pp. 168–188.

Melling, Althea, '"Ray of the Rovers": the working-class heroine in popular football fiction, 1915–1925', *The International Journal for the History of Sport*, 15.1 (1988), pp. 97–122.

Mellor, G. J., *The Northern Music Hall*, Newcastle Upon Tyne, Graham, 1970.

Mews, Stuart, 'Puritanicalism, sport and race: a symbolic crusade of 1911', in G. J. Cuming and Derek Baker (eds), *Studies in Church History*, 8 (1972), pp. 303–331.

Middlebrook, Martin, *The First Day on the Somme*, London, Allen Lane, 1971.

Morley, Sheridan, *A Talent to Amuse: A Biography of Noël Coward*, London, Heinemann, 1969.

Morton, Desmond, *When Your Number's Up*, Toronto, University of Toronto Press, 1993.

Moynihan, John, *The West Ham Story*, London, A. Barker, 1984.

Northcutt, John and Roy Shoesmith, *West Ham United: A Complete Record 1900–1987*, Derby, Breedon Books, 1987.

Ollier, Fred, *Arsenal: A Complete Record 1886–1992*, Derby, Breedon Books, 1992.

Olsen, Donald J., *The Growth of Victorian London*, London, Batsford, 1976.

Opie, Iona and Peter, *The Lore and Language of Schoolchildren*, Oxford, Oxford University Press, 1959.

Pardoe, Rex, *The Battle of London*, London, Tom Stacey, 1972.

Paris, Matthew, 'The rise of the airmen: the origins of Air Force elitism, c. 1890–1918', *Journal of Contemporary History*, 28 (1993), pp. 123–141.

Parratt, Catriona, 'Little means or time: working-class women and leisure in late Victorian and Edwardian England', *The International Journal of the History of Sport*, 15.2 (1988), pp. 22–53.

Partridge, Eric, *A Dictionary of Slang and Unconventional English*, London, Penguin, 1974.

Pearson, Geoffrey, *Hooligan: A History of Respectable Fears*, London, Macmillan, 1983.

Pemberton, Max, *Lord Northcliffe: A Memoir*, London, Hodder and Stoughton, 1922.

Perkin, Harold, *The Origins of Modern English Society, 1780–1880*, London, Routledge and Kegan Paul, 1969.

Phillips, Morgan D., *Fulham We Love You: A Supporter's History of Fulham FC*, Bedford, The Author, 1976.

Phillips, Murray G., 'Sport, war and gender images: The Australian sportmen's battalions and the First World War', *The International Journal of the History of Sport*, 14.1 (1997), pp. 78–96.

Philotenko, Alexis, *Histoire de la Boxe*, Paris, Critérion, 1991.

Porter, Roy, *London: A Social History*, London, Hamish Hamilton, 1994.

Price, Richard, *An Imperial War and the British Working-Class*, London, Routledge and Kegan Paul, 1972.

Priestley, J. B., *The Edwardians*, London, Heinemann, 1970.

Purkiss, Mike and Nigel Sands, *Crystal Palace: A Complete Record 1905–1989*, Derby, Breedon Books, 1990.

Reeder, D. A., 'A theatre of suburbs: some patterns in development in West London, 1801–1911', in H. J. Dyos (ed.), *The Study of Urban History*, London, Edward Arnold, 1968, pp. 253–271.

Reeves, Nicholas, 'Cinema, spectatorship and propaganda: Battle of the Somme (1916) and its contemporary audience', *Historical Journal of Film, Radio and Television*, 17.1 (March 1997), pp. 5–28.

Reeves, Nicholas, 'Through the eye of the camera: contemporary cinema audiences and their 'experience' of war in the film *Battle of the Somme*', in Hugh Cecil and Peter Liddle (eds), *Facing Armageddon*, London, Leo Cooper, 1996.

Richards, Jeffrey, *The Age of the Dream Palace: Cinema and Society in Britain, 1930–1939*, London, Routledge, 1984.

Richards, Thomas, *The Commodity Culture of Victorian England*, London, Verso, 1990.

Robinson, David, *Chaplin: His Life and Art*, London, Collins, 1985.

Roe, Michael, *Kenealy and the Tichborne Cause*, Melbourne, Melbourne University Press, 1974.

Rolt, Lionel T. C., *Horseless Carriage, The Motor Car in England*, London, Constable, 1950.

Rosa, Joseph G. and Robin May, *Buffalo Bill and his Wild West*, Lawrence, Kansas, University of Kansas Press, 1989.

Rossi, John P., 'A glorified form of rounders: baseball in Britain, February 1914', *Cooperstown Symposium on Baseball and the American Culture, (1990)*, Westport, Connecticut, Meckler, 1990, pp. 243–255.

Rowland, John, *The Rolls-Royce Men – The Story of Charles Rolls and Henry Royce*, London, Lutterworth, 1969.

Rubinstein, David, 'Cycling eighty years ago', *History Today*, (August 1978), pp. 544–547.

Russell, Dave, *Popular Music in England 1840–1914: A Social History*, Kingston and Montreal, McGill-Queens, 1987.

Sandiford, Keith A. P., 'Cricket and the Barbadian society', *Canadian Journal of History*, 221 (1986), pp. 353–370.

Saul, S. B., 'The motor industry in Britain to 1914', *Business History*, 5.1 (1962), pp. 22–44.

Senelick, Laurence, 'A brief life and times of the Victorian music hall', *Harvard Library Bulletin*, 19.4 (1971), 375–398.

Senelick, Laurence, *British Music-Hall 1840–1923: A Bibliography and Guide to Sources*, Hamden, Connecticut, Archon, 1981.

Senelick, Laurence, 'Politics as entertainment, Victorian music-hall songs', *Victorian Studies*, 19 (1975), pp. 149–180.

Shannon, Richard, *The Crisis of Imperialism, 1865–1915*, St Albans, Paladin, 1974.

Sheffield, Gary, 'Officer-man relations, discipline and morale in the British army of the Great War', in Hugh Cecil and Peter Liddle (eds), *Facing Armageddon: The First World War Experienced*, London, Leo Cooper, 1996.

Shipley, Stan, *Bombardier Billy Wells: The Life and Times of a Boxing Hero*, Whitley Bay, Berwick, 1993.

Shipley, Stan, 'Boxing', in Tony Mason (ed.), *Sport in Britain: A Social History*, Cambridge, Cambridge University Press, 1989, pp. 78–115.

Shipley, Stan, 'Tom Causer of Bermondsey: a boxer hero of the 1890s', *History Workshop Journal*, 15 (1983), pp. 28–53.

Signy, Dennis, *A History of Queen's Park Rangers Football Club*, London, Pelham, 1969.

Simon, André L., *History of the Champagne Trade in England*, London, Wyman and Sons, 1905.

Slobodin, Richard, *W. H. R. Rivers*, Stroud, Sutton, 1997.

Smith, Tori, '"Almost pathetic...but also very glorious": the consumer spectacle of the Diamond Jubilee', *Social History/Histoire Sociale*, 58 (1996), pp. 333–356.

Smyth, Ian, 'The development of baseball in northern England, 1935–1939', *The International Journal of the History of Sport*, 10.2 (1993), pp. 252–258.

Sorensen, Colin, *London on Film*, London, Museum of London, 1996.

Stansky, Peter, *On or About December 1910: Early Bloomsbury and its Intimate World*, London, Harvard University Press, 1997.

Stedman Jones, Gareth, *Outcast London*, Harmondsworth, Penguin, 1976.

Stedman Jones, Gareth, 'Working-class culture and working-class politics in London, 1870–1900: notes on the remaking of a working class', *Journal of Social History*, 7 (1974), pp. 460–509.

Street, Sarah, *British National Cinema*, London, Routledge, 1997.

Summerfield, Penelope, 'The Effingham Arms and the empire: deliberate selection in the evolution of music-hall in London', in Stephen and Eileen Yeo (eds), *Popular Culture and Class Conflict, 1590–1914*, Brighton, Harvester, 1981, pp. 209–240.

Summerfield, Penelope, 'Patriotism and Empire: music-hall entertainment, 1870–1914', in John M. MacKenzie (ed.), *Imperialism and Popular Culture*, Manchester, Manchester University Press, 1986.

Taylor, Rogan, *Football and its Fans*, London, Leicester University Press, 1992.

Taylor, Rogan and Andrew Ward, *Kicking and Screaming: An Oral History of Football in England*, London, Robson, 1995.

Thompson, Denys, *Discrimination and Popular Culture*, Harmondsworth, Penguin, 1964.

Thorne, Robert, 'The White Hart Lane Estate: an LCC venture in suburban development', *London Journal*, 12.1, (1986), pp. 80–88.

Tischler, Steven, *Footballers and Businessmen: The Origins of Professional Soccer in England*, New York, Holmes and Meier, 1981.

Travers, T. H. E., 'Future warfare: H. G. Wells and British military theory, 1895–1916', in Brian Bond and Ian Roy (eds), *War and Society: A Yearbook of Military History*, New York, Croom Helm, 1975.

Tritton, Paul, *John Montagu of Beaulieu, 1866–1929: Motoring Pioneer and Prophet*, London, Golden Eagle/George Hart, 1985.

Turner, Dennis and Alex White, *Fulham: A Complete Record 1879–1987*, Derby, Breedon Books, 1987.

Turner, E. S., *Dear Old Blighty*, London, Joseph, 1980.

Vamplew, Wray, *Pay Up and Play the Game: Professional Sport in Britain 1875–1914*, Cambridge, Cambridge University Press, 1988.

Vicinus, Martha, '"Happy times... if you can stand it", Women entertainers during the interwar years in England', *Theatre Journal*, 33.3 (1979), pp. 357–369.

Wagg, Stephen, *The Football World: A Contemporary Social History*, Brighton, Harvester, 1984.

Wallace, Graham, *Claude Grahame-White: A Biography*, London, Putnam, 1960.

Walvin, James, *The People's Game*, London, Allen Lane, 1975.

Walvin, James, *The People's Game: The History of Football Revisited*, Edinburgh, Mainstream, 1994.

Ward, Reginald A. J., *Clapton Football Club: Seventy Five Years of Football History 1878–1953*, London, C. E. Fisher, 1954.

Watt, Tom, *The End: Eighty Years of Life on Arsenal's North Bank*, Edinburgh, Mainstream, 1993.

Wearing, J. P., 'Edwardian London West End Christmas entertainments, 1900–1914', in Judith L. Fisher and Stephen Watt (eds), *When they Weren't Doing Shakespeare: Essays on Nineteenth Century British and American Theatre*, London, University of Georgia Press, 1989, pp. 230–240.

Weybright, Victor and Henry Sell, *Buffalo Bill and the Wild West*, London, 1956.

White, Jerry, *Rothschild Buildings*, London, Routledge and Kegan Paul, 1980.

White, Jerry, *The Worst Street in North London: Campbell Bunk, Islington*, London, Routledge and Kegan Paul, 1986.

Wiggins, David K., 'Peter Jackson and the elusive heavy-weight championship: a black athelete's struggle against the late nineteenth century color-line', *The Journal of Sport History*, 12.2 (summer 1985), pp. 143–168.

Wiggins, William H. Jr, 'Boxing's Sambo twins: racial stereotypes in Jack Johnson and Joe Louis cartoons, 1908–1938', *The Journal of Sport History*, 15.3 (1988), pp. 242–257.

Wild, Roland, *The Biography of Colonel His Highness Shri Sir Ranjitsinhji*, London, Rich and Cowan, 1934.

Winter, Denis, *First of the Few: Fighter Pilots of the First World War*, London, Allen Lane, 1983.

Winter, James, *London's Teeming Streets, 1830–1914*, London, Routledge, 1993.

Winter, Jay M., *The Experience of World War One*, London, Macmillan, 1988.

Winter, Jay, and Blaine Baggett, *The Great War and the Shaping of the Twentieth Century*, London, Penguin Studio, 1996.

Winter, Jay and Jean-Louis Robert, *Capital Cities at War: Paris, London, Berlin, 1914–1919*, Cambridge, Cambridge University Press, 1997.

Woodruff, Douglas, *The Tichborne Claimant*, London, Hollis and Carter, 1957.

Woods, Alan, 'James J. Corbett: theatrical star', *The Journal of Sport History*, 3.2 (summer 1976), pp. 162–175.

Young, Percy M., *A History of British Football*, London, Paul, 1969.

Ziegler, Philip, *King Edward VIII*, London, Fontana, 1990.

Index

Note: 'n.' after a page reference indicates the number of a note on that page.